THE NEW MEDIEVALISM

Indexed in

EGLI 1992

Parallax 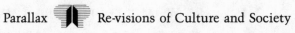 Re-visions of Culture and Society

Stephen G. Nichols, Gerald Prince, and Wendy Steiner, Series Editors

The New Medievalism

EDITED BY MARINA S. BROWNLEE,
KEVIN BROWNLEE, AND
STEPHEN G. NICHOLS

The Johns Hopkins University Press   Baltimore and London

The Johns Hopkins University Press
701 West 40th Street, Baltimore, Maryland 21211-2190
The Johns Hopkins Press Ltd., London

Chapters 1, 2, 4–10, and 12 originally appeared in *Romantic Review* 79, no. 1
(1988), © 1988 by The Trustees of Columbia University in the City of New
York. They appear here, in revised form, by permission.

∞ The paper used in this book meets the minimum requirements of
American National Standard for information Sciences—Permanence
of Paper for Printed Library Materials, ANSI Z39.48-1984.

LIBRARY OF CONGRESS CATALOGING-IN-PUBLICATION DATA
The New medievalism / edited by Kevin Brownlee, Marina Brownlee, and
  Stephen G. Nichols.
      p.   cm. — (Parallax)
  Includes bibliographical references and index.
  ISBN 0-8018-4171-2 (alk. paper). — ISBN 0-8018-4172-0 (pbk. : alk. paper)
    1. Literature, Medieval—History and criticism.   2. Criticism, Textual.
  3. Medievalism.   I. Brownlee, Kevin.   II. Brownlee, Marina Scordilis.
  III. Nichols, Stephen G.   IV. Series: Parallax (Baltimore, Md.)
  PN671.N48   1991
  809'.894'0902—dc20   91-2927

Contents

The New Medievalism: Tradition and Discontinuity in Medieval Culture

STEPHEN G. NICHOLS

This volume has two basic goals: first, to suggest that as a term "new medievalism" denotes a revisionist movement in Romance medieval studies that is resolutely eclectic yet relatively consistent in its concerns and presuppositions; second, to provide a coherent illustration, representative rather than exhaustive, of the work being done by new medievalists. Of recent currency, the term differs from a cognate rubric like the New Historicism in not predicating a specific methodology, designating instead a predisposition to interrogate and reformulate assumptions about the discipline of medieval studies broadly conceived.

By contrast, as Alan Liu has recently shown, the new Historicism focuses attention on paradigms of power in Renaissance literature, particularly the investment of power in a ruling subject, a monarch, viewed, like literature itself, as a self-fashioning cultural and political artifact.[1] The Renaissance preoccupation with representation, particularly in its theatrical manifestations, runs as a leitmotif through much New Historicist thought.

> [T]hese two interinvolved questions—what is the Subject? And what is the Action such Subject predicates?—bring New Historicism into the fold of the general structuralist and poststructuralist enterprise of rethinking mimesis. (Liu, 736)

New medievalism, on the other hand, may best be understood as arising initially from the need to interrogate the nature of medieval representation in its differences and continuities with classical and Renaissance mimesis. Poststructuralism freed medieval studies from the generic and linguistic taxonomies imposed by the invention of the discipline in the nineteenth century. It was no longer de rigueur to view literature as a more or less self-contained category of hierarchical genres with epic at the summit followed by lyric poetry and courtly romance. One did not necessarily need to see in the Chanson de Roland, as Gaston Paris parsed it in 1870, the highest expression of la nationalité française.[2] Nor did one have to take a genetic viewpoint à la Bédier— "au commencement furent les routes, les routes jalonnées de sanctuaires" (In the beginning were the pilgrimage routes blazed with sanctuaries). Largely formal and formulaic aspects of literary style in lyric, romance, and epic as set forth convincingly in the 1950s by Guiette, Vinaver, and the early studies of Roger Dragonetti, Jean Rychner, Paul Zumthor, no longer appeared sufficient unto themselves.

Instead, one was free to consider the nature of medieval discourse as a manifestation of a culture to be reconstructed afresh. A close look at the works and their manuscripts revealed the dynamics of cultural expression. We saw that the Middle Ages continually improvised new genres and modes of representation— manuscript illumination, lyric forms, polyphony, hagiography, to name but a few; it also revised and transformed classical modes. But rather than focusing on questions of representation tout court, the period appeared as preoccupied with the matter as with the method of representation. In the Middle Ages, one senses a fascination with the potential for representation, even more than with theories or modes of representation: something like an attempt to seek ways for extending the range of what was known of the material world and the world beyond matter through alchemy, through science, through physical and psychical voyages. Oneiric narratives—dream visions—can be seen from this viewpoint as an attempt to penetrate the boundaries of the known.[3]

So represented, the world could not be static or repetitious in the manner Liu ascribes to New Historicist studies of the Renaissance, for it was not primarily a mimetic world, a world created and self-fashioned for the purpose of fixing authority, that held the attention of medieval artists. Medieval representation was less an apanage of power than a means of affirming and describing—of reassuring—that there was a world of material reality whose boundaries (from our viewpoint) seem amazingly fluid. These boundaries may be spatial as in the cases of heroes of lay and romance who cross over from the real world to the *irréel* of the Celtic other world; they may be ontological boundaries like the polymorphous corporality of heroes of some of Marie de France's *Lais*, or the dual identity as alternately Christian and Saracen of certain characters in epic and romance; they may be social boundaries, boundaries of orthodoxy in matters of faith, or boundaries of gender, as chronicles, accounts of heresy trials, and legal documents reveal. All of these examples may be said to have historical correlates in the ever-changing political and religious boundaries that make medieval geopolitics so fascinating.[4]

The growing importance of boundaries of all kinds, coupled with scientific developments in optics gave rise to experiments with observing instruments like the astrolabe and armillary spheres. Fixed perspective had yet to be theorized in the manner of Alberti, but from the early Middle Ages, ways of viewing the world and the heavens by new modes of perception and optics fascinated avant garde medieval thinkers. Gerbert of Aurillac (Pope Sylvester II, 999–1003) studied mathematics and astronomy in Barcelona, point of contact for the Latin West of many Arabic innovations. Gerbert introduced Arabic numerals, used an abacus for teaching math, built armillary spheres for teaching astronomy, and constructed an astrolabe and polar sighting tubes. In a letter written from Rheims around 978, Gerbert explains how to make a hemisphere for observing the stars, then describes its use for fixing prominent boundaries of the world:

> Therefore, having placed the hemisphere in the aforementioned manner so that it is immovable, you will be able to determine the North Pole through the upper and lower first tube, the Arctic Circle through the second, the summer through the third, the equinoctial through the fourth, the winter through the fifth, the Antarctic [Circle] through the sixth. As for the south polestar, because it is under the land, no sky but earth appears to anyone trying to view it through both tubes.[5]

Towards the end of the Middle Ages, Chaucer produced a "Treatise on the Astrolabe" for his ten-year-old son Louis. He speaks of "so noble an instrument as is an Astrelabie,"[6] by which the boy will learn "conclusions" (propositions or theorems) about the world. The fascination with the astrolabe as a device for confirming the rational proportions of the universe is well documented in the treatises and descriptions of the instrument. Indeed, the "descripcioun of thin Astralabie" with which Chaucer begins his treatise suggests that the astrolabe was not only an observing instrument but also was crafted as an artwork reproducing the form of the universe that it was meant to observe. If we think of the "descripcioun" as essentially an ekphrasis of a work of art (the astrolabe) that is less a scientific instrument than a means of showing the earth and planets with their boundaries, we come close to the crux of perception as representation that sets the medieval world apart from the modern.

Chaucer tells us that the different parts of the instrument were coordinated with geographical and astronomical points, so that the astrolabe reproduced the world as a mathematically divided set of propositions suggestive of the teleology the astrolabe was meant to confirm. By showing the connection of the parts of the human body with the heavenly divisions or signs of the zodiac, it also reinforced the idea of a continuum between the individual human being and the visible world. The astronomical or upper world was a reciprocal of the lower world of humans and beasts, so that to perceive the universe scientifically was to know the boundaries of one's own being:

> Thy zodiak of thin Astrelabie is shapen as a compas which that contenith a large brede [breadth] as after the quantite of thyn Astrelabie, in ensample that the zodiak in hevene is yma-gyned to ben a superfice contenyng a latitude of 12 degrees, whereas alle the remenaunt of cercles in the hevene ben yma-gyned verrey lynes withoute eny latitude. Amiddes this celes-tial zodiak is ymagined a lyne which that is clepid the ecliptik lyne, under which lyne is evermo the wey of the sonne . . . And this forseide hevenysshe zodiak is clepid the cercle of the signes, or the cercle of the bestes, for 'zodia' in langage of Grek sowneth [means] 'bestes' in Latyn tunge. And in the zodiak ben the 12 signes that han names of bestes, or ellis for whan the sonne entrith in eny of tho signes he takith the propirte of suche bestes, or ellis for the sterres that ben ther fixed ben disposid in signes of bestes or shape like bestes, or elles whan the planetes ben under thilke signes thei cau-sen us by her influence operaciouns and effectes like to the operaciouns of bestes.
>
> And understond also that whan an hot planete cometh into an hot signe, than encrescith his hete; and yf a planete be cold, than amenusith [diminishes] his coldnesse by cause of the hoote sygne. And by thys conclusioun maist thou take ensample in alle the signes, be thi moist or drie, or moeble

or fixe, reknyng the qualite of the planete as I first seide. And everich of these 12 signes hath respect to a certeyn parcel of the body of a man, and hath it in governaunce; as Aries hath thin heved [head], and Taurus thy nekke and thy throte, Gemini thin armholes and thin armes, and so furth. (1.21, 668b)

Representation seems, then, to be governed by a principle of tautological perception that seeks to corroborate and convey known views. Science reveals the "nombres and proporciouns" that organize the world according to what Umberto Eco has called the "aesthetics of proportion."[7] We might not wish to go as far as Eco in saying that "the principle and criterion of symmetry, even in its most elementary forms, was rooted in the very instincts of the medieval soul" (40). And yet there is no doubt but that proportion enabled artistic forms to be generated, varied, and refined in ways that made them images of the ethical, ontological, and aesthetic structure of the world as perceived. Musical modes, poetic rhythms and meters, architecture, visual arts, all, from the early Middle Ages on, had been theorized as proportions or correspondences which allowed a particular symbolic form to analogize cosmic structures. With St. Thomas Aquinas these tendencies were homologized into a theological metaphysics for which Dante's *Commedia* offers the greatest vernacular example.

Proportion explained and governed change, but change did not necessarily imply a radical alteration of underlying qualities. By varying the proportions of a construct, one could produce a very different entity. In music, for example, as Eco reminds us, reversing the Lydian mode would produce the Dorian mode (42). This is not the same thing as Richard II's anamorphic response to Bolingbroke, "Ay, no; no, ay" (see note 1), that symbolizes for Liu "the theatricality of all culture [presupposed by] the bottomless spectatorship of New Historical consciousness [where] any cultural backdrop, at any time, can turn into its inversion . . . " (Liu, 724). For medieval culture, the problem was one of representing and explaining the violence of change and motion in the sublunary sphere, compared to the unchanging universe beyond; the focus in this ongoing debate might fall on the dynamics of change, on the unvarying elements, or the tension between them. As any reading of Dante or study of medieval cosmologies quickly shows, belief in a geocentric universe rendered these questions more urgent since earth was simultaneously the venue of change, the scene of all historical cataclysms, and the still point of a turning universe.

Dante offers a striking image of earth as oxymoron (changeless change) in *Inferno* 12, when Virgil guides Dante pilgrim over a landscape guarded by the Minotaur, representing in a moment fixed in time the overthrowing of the classical order by the Christian cataclysm here given literal shape:

> Così prendemmo via giù per lo scarco
>   di quelle pietre, che spesso moviensi
>   sotto i miei piedi per lo novo carco.
> Io gia pensando; e quei disse: "Tu pensi
>   forse a questa ruina, ch'è guardata
>   da quell' ira bestial ch'i' ora spensi.
> Or vo' che sappi che l'altra fïata
>   ch'i' discesi qua giù nel basso inferno,
>   questa roccia non era ancor cascata.
> Ma certo poco pria, sen ben discerno,
>   che venisse colui che la gran preda
>   levò a Dite del cerchio superno,
> da tutte parti l'alta valle feda
>   tremò sì, ch'i' pensai che l'universo
>   sentisse amor, per lo qual è chi creda
> più volte il mondo in caòsso converso;
>   e in quel punto questa vecchia roccia."
>
> (*Inf.* 12.28–44)[8]

(So we took our way down over that rocky debris, which often moved under my feet with the new weight. I was going along thinking, and he said, "Perhaps you are thinking on this ruin, guarded by that bestial wrath [of the Minotaur] which I quelled just now. Know then that the other time I came down here into the nether Hell this rock had not yet fallen. But certainly, if I reckon rightly, it was a little before He came who took from Dis the great spoil of the uppermost circle, that the deep foul valley trembled so on all sides that I thought the universe felt love, whereby, as some believe, the world has many times been turned to chaos; and at that moment this ancient rock, here and elsewhere, made such downfall.")

As Dante's narrative illustrates, variations in image, in material form, did not necessarily imply a disjunction in the essential properties of two dissimilar entities. Dante pilgrim moves the rocks of the classical debris as he walks over them by way of suggesting how the poem relies upon and reproportions classical myth and literature. The metaphysics of Virgil-Aeneas descending to Hell in *Aeneid* 6 are very different from Dante's. Yet he makes Virgil his guide in this poem to remind the reader that, despite the altered metaphysics that toppled the classical edifice, pilgrim and guide still traverse the *same* physical space and the rubble of the past retains the power to trip the traveler unwary enough not to recognize the multiple dimensions of this complex space.

Continuity across change was a crucial concept of the politics of proportion. This was true not only of the classical/Christian duality, but, in some thinkers, held true for one of that most vexed of dichotomies for medieval culture: the division of the sexes. In his philosophical anthropology, for example, Eriugena argued that what had been for Augustine a fundamental difference between humans, sexual differentiation, was historical, a consequence of the Fall, rather than the result of divine creation.[9] All humans possessed masculine and feminine qualities of intellect and sensual perception governing mind and body.

Marie de France illustrates Eriugena's concept when she devotes several of her lays to the proposition that a radical change in form or conditions of life does not necessarily betoken alteration of psychic qualities such as goodness. She uses narrative to focus on the obscure interstice between reality and superstition where the collective (folk) imagination adumbrates scenarios of transgression. She raises these scenarios from the level of received folklore, *aventures*, to make them instruments of cultural analysis by refusing the simple dichotomies of good and evil suggested by the Breton originals. In *Bisclavret* (Breton for 'werewolf'), for example, she argues the antiessentialist position that innate qualities exist independent of external form. *Bisclavret* initially records the cultural fears of the blurring of categories between humans and beasts that occurs in shapeshifting. But the lay quickly discards such a literal approach to show the levels of duplicity that exist between external appearance and inner qualities. Essence and appearance do not link unproblematically, either in the cosmos— as we shall see—or in human beings. Marie organizes her narrative around the dialectic between psyche and appearance: the innate goodness of her werewolf hero only becomes apparent when contrasted with the moral frailty of his beautiful wife when each has been fixed in dissimilarity: he trapped in his beast persona, she in her duplicitous liaison with a handsome nobleman. By overlaying the complex moral betrayals fostered by sophisticated courtly culture over the simple dichotomies of her folk informants, Marie adumbrates, like Dante, the paradox of a world at the center of the universe yet far removed from the model of perfection it is meant to emulate. In effect, she shows how discourse avoids the tautology of the observing instrument by revealing the dialectical underside of perception.

By affirming the oxymoronic status of change in medieval culture, the politics of perception undoes one of the most enduring myths medievalism has perpetrated on the Middle Ages: its putative modernity. Modernism sought to make the Middle Ages in its own image, as recent studies have argued. New medievalism has on the whole tried to avoid reading the Middle Ages onto the modern world except as a dialectical gesture of postmodernist inquiry in the manner of Umberto Eco's *Travels in Hyper Reality* and *The Name of the Rose*, Lee Patterson's *Negotiating the Past*, Brian Stock's *Listening for the Text: On the Uses of the Past*, or Brigitte Cazelles's and Charles Méla's *Modernité au moyen âge: le défi du passé*, to name but a few such studies.[10]

Instead, new medievalism tries to contextualize the concept of modernity as a process of cultural change, and thus to profit from the decline of modernism's hegemony both as the dominant period and the arbiter of methodological orthodoxy. In anxiously asserting its own legitimacy in its early phases, Modernity defined itself away from the Middle Ages. As Hans Blumenberg has argued, "[The Middle Ages] were lowered to the rank of a provisional phase of human self-realization, one that was bound to be left behind, and were finally disqualified as a mere interruption between antiquity and modern times, as a 'dark age.'"[11] Now at the other end of the process, Modernity has had to come to grips with its own historical identity. Its pastness is being surveyed, limits assigned.

The desire to draw the line more sharply between Modernity and its successor may explain the tendency to highlight, on the one end, the end of Modernity, while on the other pushing its origins back to the sixteenth century, as Stephen Toulmin has done in his recent book, *Cosmopolis: The Hidden Agenda of Modernity*:

> Today the program of Modernity—even the very *concept*—no longer carries anything like the same conviction. If an historical era is ending, it is the era of Modernity itself. Rather than our being free to assume that the tide of Modernity still flows strongly, and that its momentum will carry us into a new and better world, our present position is less comfortable. What looked in the 19th century like an irresistible river has disappeared in the sand, and we seem to have run aground. Far from extrapolating confidently into the social and cultural future, we are now stranded and uncertain of our location. The

very project of Modernity thus seems to have lost momentum, and we need to fashion a successor program.[12]

In a real sense, Modernity has become the "middle ages" of that successor program and we are free to pursue the historical identities of our own period, however we choose to identify the era from the fifth to the fifteenth century. We may, at last, leave the agenda of Modernity behind, reclaiming as we do the word itself, which, as many scholars have noted, first gained currency in the Middle Ages, by way of distinguishing its modes and methods (*moderni*) from those of classical precursors (*Antiqui*):

> The older Antiquity became, the more a word for "modern" was needed. But the word "modernus" was not yet available . . . Not until the sixth century does the new and happy formation *modernus* (related to *modo* "now," as *hodiernus* to *hodie*) appear and now Cassiodorus can celebrate an author in rolling rhyme as "antiquorum diligentissimus imitator, modernorum nobilissimus institutor" ("most diligent emulator of the ancients, most noble teacher of the moderns," *Variae*, IV, 51). The word "modern" (which has nothing to do with "mode") is one of the last legacies of late Latin to the modern world. In the ninth century, then, the new age of Charlemagne can be called "seculum modernum."[13]

Brian Stock shows exactly how modernity can be recontextualized in medieval culture as a vital part of the tension between new and old. He does so rather elegantly, in his article, "Tradition and Modernity: Models from the Past,"[14] by showing how post-Enlightenment thought invested the terms "tradition" and "modernity" with negative and positive social and cultural values, where "tradition" came to be associated with resistance to change and consequently was thought to oppose progress. By stripping these terms of their modernist ideological weighting, and questioning assumptions on which the ideological judgments were based (e.g., "But is tradition immobile?" [35]), he shows how they can be used as instruments of historical inquiry to track the cultural dynamics of the period that first put them into play.

He points out that the Enlightenment postulated a dichotomy between tradition and change in society, with tradition accorded a negative value, while change conveyed positive connotations. "The term normally applied to social, economic, or cultural transformations is 'modernity.' Most post-Enlightenment philosophies equate modernity and change" (33). With modernity bearing the positive implications of progress, tradition by association came to signify the past stage of society, either the Middle Ages, or, more recently, primitive, non-Western societies (34).

This dichotomy makes the assumption that tradition is static, the unchanging part of culture; that assumption is, in turn, a literal reception of tradition's own self-presentation. Traditions "are part of a narrative of social developments which begins in the past and leads to the present," and like all narrative, "they can be invented for economic or political motives." In fact, "traditions may not be very old"; it suffices that they be perceived to represent the past authoritatively. They do this by providing a cohesive sense of the unity of the past—another effect of good narrative (35). Tradition, then, is far from static, either in the Middle Ages or in any society that invests the "past" with a sense of authority.

Tradition, in fact, is very much a phenomenon of the present in medieval society, and, as such, is also an agent of cultural change. It was the necessity to isolate the change element within tradition that brought the term "modernus" into play (37). The terms really refer to two aspects of the same process of cultural movement: "Tradition and modernity are not mutually exclusive; they are mutually interdependent" (38).

In fact, Stock argues, modernity is a logical part of the cultural process of tradition. Medieval society as a whole tended to be traditional, in the sense of investing the past with a sense of authority and of providing the models on which to predicate social, economic, political, and intellectual structures. Innovation was vested with at least the semblance of guidelines from the past. This dynamic of continuity and change may be described as a positive interaction between traditional and traditionalistic action:

> Traditional action is substantive. It consists of the habitual pursuit of inherited forms of conduct, which are taken to be society's norm. Traditionalistic action, by contrast, is the self-conscious affirmation of traditional norms. It is the establishment of such norms as articulated models for current and future behavior. These guidelines imperfectly reflect the past, since at a given time individuals are only in contact with a part of their cultural heritage. Indeed, one of the features of traditionalistic action is that norms are consciously selected from the fund of traditional knowledge in order to serve present needs. (38)

Traditionalistic activity produced the reforms and renaissances that mark medieval history from late antiquity on. The reassessment of the Christian heritage in the eleventh and twelfth centuries offers a rich and complex example of traditionalistic activity (38–39). Modernity enters the scene as the last stage of the traditionalistic process, when the gap between the traditional and the traditionalistic becomes too great. Traditional activity continues past practices as unselfconscious habitual activity. It is practical, as opposed to the theoretical orientation of traditionalistic initiative that "predicates self-conscious innovation based on the recovery of an allegedly authentic tradition" (39). "Ratiocination applied to tradition," characterizes traditionalistic initiative.

> The past is thought about, codified, and, as an abstraction, made a guide for action. The models may be simple, and rest on nothing more than a reaffirmation of the *Rule;* or they may be full-scale utopian schemes like those of Joachim de Fiore. Viewed in the light of their common features, they constitute one of the period's strongest endogenous forces for change. For, as the distance widened between the contrasting notions of tradition, the acceptance of the past and the rethinking of the past parted ways. There were equally valid but incompatible interpretations of what tradition meant. Traditionalistic action became a statement of past norms of conduct, not as they were but as they were thought to be. And this restatement was considered by "reformers" to be more correct, truthful, and consistent than the welter of inherited customs which had been handed down from one generation to the next. The final stage of this evolution was the labelling of two types of tradition in ways that brought about the contrast. One remained known as tradition. The other emerged as modernity. (39–40)

This master paradigm for change within medieval culture is not meant to exclude examples of modernity which do not emerge from tradition but represent real discontinuity. Peter Abelard, certain church reformers, women like Heloise, Hildegard of Bingen, Marie de France, Christine de Pisan, the growing merchant class, Jewish bankers and physicians, all exemplify social phenomena that "are modern in a new sense" (40). Rather than seeing links with the past as providing social unity, they regard the internal coherence of the period as paramount. They sought recognition for contemporary achievements, like the new economic structures, professions, institutions, and other innovations such as the universities; all of these suggested discontinuities with the past in one way or another and could be labeled as modern.

In his elegant account of traditionalistic activity and discontinuity as agents of change, Brian Stock emphasizes an image of the Middle Ages in which change and innovation take pride of place. In short, he still appears to equate "modern" with change and progress. This works well for the cases Stock cites, but leaves out those instances of modern initiatives—some traditionalistic, others products of discontinuity—which, however innovative in their time, do not carry forward into subsequent periods. I am talking, of course, about the kind of initiative which left its mark on the period and yet scarcely figures in subsequent history. One thinks, for example, of a literary genre like *historia* that was fundamental both to traditional culture and traditionalistic initiatives, since it was the principal instrument for writing (and rewriting) history. Alchemy and the geocentric universe are two more quintessentially medieval phenomena whose significance has been obscured by prejudice arising from attitudes based on modern science rather than on study of their own methodological perspectives. These artifacts of modernity in the Middle Ages are essential for showing how the period really was unique, different from what went before and came after; in short, crucial for determining the hard-edged alterity of medieval thought.

Over twenty years ago, James Weisheipl argued that the Aristotelian principle, *omne quod movetur ab alio movetur* (Whatever is moved is moved by another) was erroneously believed to have been disproved by the inertia principle beginning in the seventeenth century.[15] The principle *omne quod movetur . . .* was basic to medieval physics: Aristotle had made it the proof of a First Mover in his *Physics* and *Metaphysics,* while St. Thomas Aquinas made it "his first proof for the existence of God in the *Summa theologiae, Summa contra gentiles,* and *Compendium theologiae.*"[16] Weisheipl notes that modernist refutations of the principle made several assumptions about the traditional nature of medieval physics, beginning with the univocality of medieval interpretations of Aristotle: that is, medieval tradition was static, hence one need not take great care to distinguish one medieval interpretation of *omne quod movetur ab alio movetur* from another.[17]

Motion was fundamental to natural philosophy in Aristotle's system, since it incorporated within each created thing "the reality of pure potentiality as a passive principle of change, a principle called 'first matter'" (35). This means that the ability to change was inherent in all created objects, requiring only an agent to initiate the movement. Through a closely argued analysis of Avicenna and, particularly, Averroës, Weisheipl shows that the version of Aristotle's principle discredited by modernism was not in fact Aristotle's own, nor Aquinas's, but Averroës's misinterpretation adopted by "Peter of Auvergne, Godfrey of Fontaines, Peter Olivi, Duns Scotus, and by the bulk of beginners' manuals popular in the fourteenth and fifteenth centuries" (38).

> The position of Averroës can be summed up as follows: every movement taking place in the universe, whether natural or violent or celestial, requires an accompanying mover, intrinsic in the case of natural and celestial motion, extrinsic in the case of projectiles. Thus everything moved [omne motum] requires an immediate mover. Thus omne motum is equivalent to omne in motu. Moreover every motion presupposes resistance either from the body itself or from some medium. Thus velocity is directly proportional to the moving force of weight, and inversely proportional to resistance; where there is no resistance, there can be no successive motion.
>   Clearly the position attributed by modern historians to Aristotle is, in fact, the position of Averroës. (37)

Now Aristotle's principle was much subtler than Averroës's version of it, and Aquinas was able to make it the basis for a fundamental reorientation of natural philosophy. Aquinas took the concept of nature as the basis for his explanation of Aristotle's principle, as Weisheipl notes. Building on Aristotle's insight that form and the potentiality for form were both *physis* (nature), so that form was the active principle of motion, and matter was the passive principle for receiving motion and form, Aquinas and other medieval scholastics developed the "twofold meaning of nature: 'form' as an active and formal principle [*principium activum*], 'matter' as a passive and potential principle" (38). Averroës had identified the active principle as a cause or a mover [*movens* or *motor conjunctus*], assuming that everything moved needs an attendant mover, a *motor conjunctus*. This version missed the point of Aristotle's two-fold construction of nature, which required only that a form be given a nudge, so to speak; once in motion it required no further agent, since its own inner potential for receiving motion and change could keep it in motion. "The word *principium*, St. Thomas insists, must be taken strictly; it is not a cause or a mover."[18]

Without engaging the details of a fascinating but complex debate, we need simply note here that, with the further refinement of the theory of impetus which Francesco Ross de Marchia and

Jean Buridan added to Aquinas's version of Aristotle's principle of motion, there is no reason to advance the modern theory of inertia to discredit the medieval reworking of Aristotle's principle.[19] "The principle *omne quod movetur ab alio movetur*, understood as Aquinas understood it, is still philosophically correct today" (45). The main difference between the medieval principle and inertia principle "is that inertia demands additional force to account for acceleration" (45). Nevertheless, even if modern dynamics do not contradict the Aristotelian theory as elaborated by Thomist scholasticism, neither do they have anything in common. Medieval physics, "the natural way," differs radically from "the mathematical way," to echo Newton's phrases; but we do need to bear in mind that modern conceptions represent another approach, not necessarily a change that invalidates the earlier philosophy.

We can appreciate the alterity of the natural way in medieval physics, and its influence on cultural forms by considering its geocentric view of the universe. Like Aquinas's interrogation of *omne quod movetur ab alio movetur*, medieval geocentrism formed a continuity with the ancient world, while occasioning what Stock would call a good deal of traditionalistic scientific inquiry.

Studies of the Copernican revolution, from Pierre Duhem on, have tended to stress the elements of this traditionalistic exploration of geocentrism that seemed to indicate a way out of the recursive loop of medieval thinking on the subject and to point towards the step that Copernicus finally took.[20] Jean Buridan, called "the most daring of the Parisian Nominalists in the fourteenth century," is a favorite in this respect for having raised the question "whether the daily rotation of the heaven of the fixed stars could not be explained by a corresponding axial rotation of the earth."[21] As we shall see, however, attempts to look for precocious signs of modern science fail to grasp the essence of the medieval project. It is far more interesting, and thus in keeping with the aims of new medievalism, to discover the symmetries and stresses in an alternative cosmological system. Viewed as a kind of science fiction in reverse, a historical predication of an alternate reality, medieval physics has much to tell us precisely because it affected forms of cultural thought and expression as much as it did science, which was not practiced as a discrete discipline, but as part of philosophy, mathematics, and logic. Any account of the medieval modernity of physics would certainly have to place issues associated with geocentrism close to the head of the list.

And rightly so. Geocentrism penetrated all aspects of the medieval world by providing the grounds for the tight coherence mapped

on it by theological and philosophical metaphysics. Spatially, physically, historically, everything that existed was perceived as
tightly linked in the present and through the past. The world, or
universe, really, fit together in a chain of causal relationships.
Physically, the universe consisted of concentric revolving spheres
with the earth more or less stationary at the center. Immediately
beyond earth was the lunary sphere, which formed the line of
demarcation between the heavens, composed of a nonmaterial
substance called ether, and the sublunary or material world. The
Prime Mover or God, who had set the world in motion, lay beyond
and outside the observable cosmos.

The Middle Ages did not forget for a moment the paradox of
this geocentric system. To be at the center of the universe meant
to be at the bottom of an ascending scale of quality at the furthest
remove from the unmoved center of perfection. Only in the sphere
of ether in the superlunary world did one begin to attain the regularity supposed by the symmetry of the plan; and that regularity
was expressed by the musical harmony thought to emanate from
the planetary spheres as they revolved. Farthest from the influence of the Prime Mover, earth did not share in the symmetry and
regularity of the heavens. As Hans Blumenberg observes: "The
cosmos of Scholasticism, moved and guided from without and
from above, had its weakest place—because it was most remote
from the divine origin of all causality—precisely in its center,
which was occupied by the inert mass of the Earth, exposed to
every kind of accident."[22]

As we saw above, motion was the concept on which the coherence of this system depended. We need to understand the force of
this principle in medieval culture since it illustrates how tradition and discontinuity merge to define a distinct profile for the
period, one whose philosophical and scientific predicates continue to instruct us in alternative intellectual processes. Since
motion provided intellectual and esthetic coherence for the most
diverse kinds of medieval activities, we need a comprehensive cultural artifact as a proof text. Dante's *Divine Comedy* offers the
synthesis of physics, philosophy, theology, history, and metaphysics that can illustrate the intellectual and spiritual force of this
concept.

We need only look at the noun and verb for motion in the *Divine
Comedy* to gain insight into the organizing power of Aristotelian
movement as refined by the Middle Ages. *Moto,* "motion," and
movere, "to move," figure programmatically in the three *cantiche.*
In fact, Dante uses these terms to mirror the decreasing potency

of efficient movement from the Empyrean to the world. Since earth receives the least of the ideal movement supplied by the primary sphere, and earth's center is the seat of Hell, *moto* does not occur at all in *Inferno*, while in *Purgatorio*, which reaches upwards to the heavens on top of the mountain of Purgatory, the word occurs four times in key passages associated with celestial, intellectual, or spiritual motion; *Paradiso*, appropriately (and revealingly) has nine occurrences.[23] Given Dante's penchant for linking key cantos across *cantiche*, it can hardly be accidental that of the four instances in *Purgatorio*, two occurrences (18.32 and 28.107) are echoed in corresponding stanzas in *Paradiso:* 18.114, 119 and 28.27.

Each of the instances in *Purgatorio* is important for the linking of physics and religion, a significance elaborated in the corresponding cantos in *Paradiso*. Let's look first at *Purgatorio* 18.32, which we will then compare to the two instances of *moto* in *Paradiso* 18.114 and 119. Each of the two cantos describes motion of the mind in a manner reflecting the motion of the universe described above. *Purgatorio* 18 deals with the human mind drawn upward toward the good by a *moto spiritale*, "a spiritual movement." *Paradiso* 18, in contrast, deals with the divine mind looking down towards a world besmirched with greed and a Church contaminated by politics. The two cantos thus reproduce the motion from above to below: *Purgatorio* 18 receiving it (an image repeated even more extensively in *Purgatorio* 28) and *Paradiso* 18 originating it.

The whole passage of *Purgatorio* 18.19–39 illustrates the interweaving of physics, theories of cognition, and metaphysics to make descriptions of the mind analogous with the movement of the highest sphere of the heavens: "which in its rotation lovingly imitated the reflexive circle, closed in on itself, of pure thought."[24] Similarly, the ascent of the mind is likened to another aspect of elemental physics, the movement of fire upward, described by Dante in terms of formal and efficient causation by way of illustrating how the mind also responds to the same causes:

"L'animo, ch'è creato ad amar presto
    ad ogne cosa è mobile che piace,
    tosto che dal piacere in atto è desto.
Vostra apprensiva da esser verace
    tragge intenzione, e dentro a voi la spiega,
    sì che l'animo ad essa volger face;
e se, rivolto, inver' di lei si piega,
    quel piegare è amor, quell' è natura

che per piacer di novo in voi si lega.
Poi, come 'l foco movesi in altura
    per la sua forma ch'è nata a salire
    là dove più in sua matera dura,
così l'animo preso entra in disire,
    ch'è moto spiritale, e mai non posa
    fin che la cosa amata il fa gioire."

(*Purg.* 18.19–33)[25]

("The mind, which is created quick to love, is responsive to everything that pleases, as soon as by pleasure it is roused to action. Your faculty of apprehension draws an image from a real existence and displays it within you, so that it makes the mind turn to it; and if, thus turned, the mind inclines toward it, that inclination is love, that inclination is nature which is bound in you anew by pleasure. Then even as fire moves upwards by reason of its form, being born to ascend thither where it lasts longest in its matter, so the captive mind enters into desire, which is a spiritual movement, and never rests until the thing loved makes it rejoice.")

Dante succinctly shows us in this passage how human existence functions very much as the world itself does, that is, as psychological and intellectual motion reciprocating forces from above and outside the individual. In accord with the principle of motion we saw earlier, the mind, once stimulated by the natural agent (in this case pleasure, ll. 19–21), functions on its own with no need for an external mover.

Through Virgil, the speaker of the passage, Dante invokes Aristotelian psychology of perception to explain the apparent paradox that humans are motivated to perceive and act upon impressions that come from without. St. Thomas Aquinas (the philosophical authority for much of the passage) explained this phenomenon by a theory of knowledge as apprehension that enables the human mind to imitate divine knowledge. Natural beings, he said, can only know themselves and their own forms. Superior beings define themselves by their ability to have knowledge of other things through the senses and intellect. The human psyche thus collects the impressions of all things sensible and intelligible "so that the soul of man is, in a way, all things by sense and intellect: and thereby, those things that have knowledge, in a way, approach to a likeness to God."[26]

The likeness to God comes about by the ability of humans to distinguish perception from understanding. Seeing, alone, as Aristotle pointed out in *De Anima*,[27] does not suffice for understanding. Only when the mind has turned and inclined towards the object of perception—the image "dragged" into the mind—can the work of understanding begin (ll. 22–24). Motivated by desire, the mind engages the image and the object itself [*da esser verace / tragge intenzione* (22–23)] in a quasi-physical participation. Discrimination as to nature, quality, and purpose of the perceived object separates thinking from perceiving, enabling people to analyze what they see. Desire involves the body and soul in perception, as Aristotle argues, and it is the imagination that enables the perceiving and thinking human to experience a subjective involvement with impressions originating from without.

> [T]hat which produces movement and is moved is the faculty of desire (for that which is moved is moved in so far as it desires, and desire as actual is a form of movement), while that which is moved is the animal; and the instrument by which desire produces movement is then something bodily. Hence it must be investigated among the functions common to body and soul . . . In general, therefore, as we have said, in so far as the animal is capable of desire so far is it capable of moving itself; and it is not capable of desire without imagination. And all imagination is either concerned with reasoning or perception. (*De Anima* 3.3 §433^b 13–21)

Perception and thought are thus far from tranquil activities. Virgil speaks Dante's conviction that perception must be accompanied by participatory reasoning when he concludes his lesson with an adaptation of the logic Aristotle used in *De Anima* against those who confused perception and thinking. "'Now it may be apparent to you how far the truth is hidden from the people who aver that every love is praiseworthy in itself, because perhaps its matter appears always to be good: but not every imprint is good, although the wax be good'" (*Purg.* 18.34–39).[28] Clearly, not every object of love is good, and precisely because love and other objects come from the outside, one must be capable of discrimination.

Reasoning and discrimination in thinking about and through images demands that the imagination and intellect move through the psychic landscape of the image as Dante pilgrim moves through Purgatory. The movement of narrator through the allegory becomes a figure for the engagement of the mind as described in *Purgatorio* 18.19–38. The passage not only provides a figure of the mind's ascent towards spiritual life, but shows to what extent the *Commedia* itself is a vast metaphor for the mind motion of the human striving to transform perception to thought and wisdom of a higher state.

Ed elli a me: "Quanto ragion qui vede,
dir ti poss'io; da indi in là t'aspetta
pur a Beatrice, ch'è opra di fede."

(*Purg.* 18.46–48)

(And he to me, "As far as reason sees here I can tell you; beyond that wait only for Beatrice, for it is a matter of faith.")

Paradiso 18 presents the reciprocal of the passage in *Purgatorio* 18 by invoking the divine mind's descent to contemplate the earth. Since the divine mind can only be postulated outside of and above the cosmos, there can be no analogizing of it to material or elemental physics. Instead, Dante resorts to a complex figure that conveys the sense of God as Mind. Dante pilgrim observes the souls of the just spelling out in fiery letters across the heavens: DIL-IGITE IUSTITIAM QUI IUDICATIS TERRAM (Love justice, you who judge the earth [18.91–93]). Then the admonition fades, leaving only the final "M" in TERRAM. The "M" transforms itself slowly into a schematic lily and then into a schematic eagle.[29] It is the schematic form of the eagle (which retains the "M" shape by simple elongation of the middle descender of the letter) that Dante pilgrim apostrophizes as *la mente*, The Mind, the beginning of divine motion and virtue:

O dolce stella, quali e quante gemme
mi dimostraro che nostra giustizia
effetto sia del ciel che tu ingemme!
Per ch'io prego la mente in che s'inizia
tuo moto e tua virtute, che rimiri
ond'esce il fummo che 'l tuo raggio vizia;
sì ch'un'altra fïata omai s'adiri
del comperare e vender dentro al templo
che si murò di segni e di martìri.

(*Par.* 18.115–123)[30]

(O sweet star, how many and how bright were the gems which made it plain to me that our justice is the effect of the heaven which you engem! Wherefore I pray the Mind, in which your motion and your virtue have their beginning, that It look on the place whence issues the smoke that dims your radiance, so that once again It may be wroth at the buying and the selling in the temple which made its walls of miracles and martyrdoms.)

Note how Dante incorporates motion as image in the rhetoric of this scene. He transforms the accusative object TERRAM into MENTE via the pivot point of the last letter, "M," which then becomes the first letter of *mente*. "Mind" connotes the opposite of "earth" on the cosmic map in which *terra* is the reciprocal (in the lowest possible position) of *mente*, the reflexive circle of pure thought beyond the *primum mobile* or outermost circle of the heavens. Dante reinforces this vertical reciprocal in a way that shows the spatio-temporal movement of language by citing *terra* in Latin, the paternal language of heaven (and the Church), while *mente* occurs in Italian: from the standpoint of heaven, earth is *terra*, while those attempting, like Dante (and his readers), to intuit the divine mind looking upwards speak Italian, the mother tongue of the earth.

This rhetorical pivoting also imitates the overall movement of the *cantiche* from *terra* towards the outermost sphere, as Dante himself describes in his famous *Letter to Can Grande*, using the language of Aristotelean physics (and theology), which he confidently and correctly expects his aristocratic patron to be conversant with:

> And having premised this truth, he goes on from it with a circumlocution for Paradise, and says that he "was in that heaven which receives most abundantly of the glory of the light of God"; wherefore you are to know that that heaven is the supreme heaven, containing all the bodies of the universe and contained by love, within which all bodies move (itself abiding in eternal rest), receiving its virtue from no corporeal substance. And it is called the *Empyrean*, which is the same as the heaven flaming with fire or heat, not because there is any material fire or heat in it, but spiritual, to wit holy love or charity.[31]

We find poetic versions of the same language used in *Purgatorio* 28.90–148, and *Paradiso* 28.22–45, where the narrator and Beatrice describe the role of motion in creating the characteristics of purgatory and paradise pertinent to those stages of the ascent.

Turning to the more extensively used verb form, the case of *movere* is even more complex than *moto. Movere*, in one conjugated form or another, appears forty-three times in *Inferno*, sixty-four times in *Purgatorio*, and sixty-seven in *Paradiso*. We have already seen one instance in *Inferno* 12.28–30, where the rocky debris from Christ's harrowing of Hell — a cataclysmic moving —

shifts under the weight of Dante pilgrim's feet, an apparently realistic detail which we now perceive to have a larger significance:
the moving of the old order *"per lo novo carco,"* by the new weight
of the new law that Dante illustrates. Since we cannot hope to
summarize adequately the 174 examples of *movere,* let it suffice
to show the self-consciousness of Dante's use of the term to recall
that the word appears in the last canto of each *cantica:* once in
Inferno 34.51, twice in *Purgatorio* 33.14, 134, and twice in *Paradiso*
33.144, 145. Dante begins and ends *Paradiso* with succinct affirmations of this principle:

La gloria di colui che tutto move
    per l'universo penetra, e risplende.

(*Par.* 1.1–2)

(The glory of the All-Mover penetrates through the universe
and reglows.)

A l'alta fantasia qui mancò possa;
ma già volgeva il mio disio e'l *velle,*
sì come rota ch'igualmente è mossa,
l'amor che move il sole e l'altre stelle.

(*Par.* 33.142–45)

(Here my power failed the lofty phantasy; but already my
desire and my will were revolved, like a wheel that is evenly
moved, by the Love which moves the sun and the other stars.)

Traditionalistic activity among the scholastics in the fourteenth
century modified the tight coherence of the geocentric system
Dante portrayed. Foremost among the scholastic revisionists were
men like William of Ockham (1285–1347), whose work on motion,
time, and place led to a revisionary view of nature, and Nicole
Oresme (c. 1320–82), who developed a concept of the relativity of
motion which allowed him, in contradiction of Aristotle, to posit
the possibility of a plurality of simultaneously existing worlds as
well as to argue that the diurnal rotation of the earth could explain
astronomical phenomena just as well as the geocentric rationale.
But Ockham still accepted the reality of natural causation, and
Oresme concluded that there was no scientific way of establishing
whether the geocentric explanation or that of the daily rotation of
the earth was the correct system for explaining observed astronomical phenomena. Thus, while modifying the understanding of
aspects of the system, Scholasticism kept intact the basic Aristotelian conception that motion came from above:

> In Scholasticism the orientation from outside to inside, from above to below, is at the same time the scale of value and dignity of physical reality. This orientation is governed by the Aristotelian principle that the causal direction of motion determines where "above" is: "Sursum unde est motus" (Above is where motion comes from).[32]

This is the lesson that Beatrice gives Dante pilgrim near the summit of the mountain of Purgatory at *Purgatorio* 28.22–45. It is also the principle that assured that traditionalistic scientific exploration in the Middle Ages, no matter how modern in respect to prior periods, could not have led inevitably out towards the Early Modern revolution of Copernicus and Kepler. Cosmic motions after Copernicus were the reverse of what the geocentric system conceived; "they were brought about not from outside to inside, from above to below but beginning from the system's interior, that is (in Aristotelian language), from below to above."[33] Copernicus thus became for the modern age "the most conspicuous turning point between itself and the Middle Ages and the clearest sign of its break with Scholasticism."[34]

For us, on the contrary, it should be a clear boundary assuring the integrity and intellectual and artistic vitality of the Middle Ages as an age capable of constructing an alternate view of reality in clear recognition of the uncertainties, undecidability, mutability and finiteness of the world. St. Thomas Aquinas illustrated the extent to which the philosophical system internalized undecidability (and tolerated contradiction) as regards "cosmological systematics in one sentence according to which the reverse of the accepted doctrine could also be accepted without danger to faith: 'Videtur tamen mihi contrarium posse tolerari absque fidei periculo.'"[35]

To return to the example with which we began, this viewpoint suggests that we view medieval observing instruments not as quaint precursors of early modern scientific tools, but as serving a quite different function. Rather than observing the world to confirm the already known—the concept of tautological perception advanced at the beginning of the paper—medieval observing instruments helped to situate the observer in a world characterized by continual motion that destabilized the symmetry and regularity found in the superlunary spheres, making it prey to cataclysm and change. The astrolabe, and other instruments for observing the heavens, really enabled humans to project grids of cognition on the natural world. They were a means for overlaying a complex and abstract order on a natural world known to resist such ordering.

In a world rationalized from appearance, the anxiety of the image was ever-present as a fear that observation would *not* confirm the calculation. This anxiety is implicit in the paragraph headings in Chaucer's paragraphs of instruction to his ten-year-old son in the *Treatise on the Astrolabe: to knowe the verrey degre of eny maner sterre . . . , to knowe the degrees of longitudes . . . , To knowe which degre of the zodiak . . . , To prove evidently the latitude of eny place in a regioun*, etc. Not to observe was thus not *to knowe*, not to have the knowledge Beatrice vouchsafes to Dante pilgrim and Chaucer to his son Louis. Not *to knowe* was to be lost, like Dante pilgrim in the *selva oscura* (dark wood) of *Inferno* I. The alternate reality of the Middle Ages was a slippery and dangerous world of motion. It is this world that new medievalism attempts to explore.

NOTES

1. "Charles [I] and Louis [XVI], illusion and disillusion: these two states and their actors, we realize, are finally indistinguishable in the analytic of theatricality as the two halves of the anamorphic answer Richard II returns Bolingbroke in Shakespeare's deposition scene: 'Ay, no; no, ay.' Once we premise the theatricality of all culture and enter the bottomless spectatorship of New Historical consciousness, we know that any cultural backdrop, at any time, can turn into its inversion . . . Every facade is merely the reversal or repetition of a previous facade." Alan Liu, "The Power of Formalism: The New Historicism," *ELH* 56 (1989): 724.
2. "La littérature est l'expression de la vie nationale: là où il n'y a pas de littérature nationale, il n'y a qu'une vie nationale imparfaite." Gaston Paris, "La Chanson de Roland et la nationalité française" (opening lecture at the Collège de France, December 8, 1870), *La Poésie du moyen âge: leçons et lectures*, 2d ed. (Paris: Hachette, 1887), 99.
3. Inventing new forms of representation did not seem to pose a problem requiring theoretical elaboration in the Middle Ages. Understanding the implications and significance of such initiatives did. Consequently, one finds treatises on reading, like Hugh of Saint Victor's *Didascalion* or Geoffrey of Vinsauf's *Poetria nova*. The *artes poeticae* of the Middle Ages, as well as prefaces to vernacular works, all stress the arduous task of reading as an almost mystical activity of penetrating veils.
4. For a suggestive view of how fluid were social and political boundaries when economic interests came into play, see David Aers, "Rewriting the Middle Ages: Some Suggestions," *Journal of Medieval and Renaissance Studies* 18 (1988): 221–40. Two other noteworthy examples of new medievalism in Middle English are: Lee Patterson, *Negotiating the Past: The Historical Understanding of Medieval Literature* (Madison: University of Wisconsin Press, 1987); and the seventeen essays in *Reconceiving Chaucer: Literary Theory and Historical Interpretation*, ed. Thomas Hahn, special issue of *Exemplaria* 2 (1990).

5. "Letter 2," *The Letters of Gerbert with his Papal Privileges as Sylvester II*, trans. Harriet Pratt Lattin (New York: Columbia University Press, 1961), 38.

6. *The Riverside Chaucer*, 3d ed., ed. Larry D. Benson (Boston: Houghton Mifflin, 1987), 662a.

7. Umberto Eco, *Art and Beauty in the Middle Ages*, trans. Hugh Bredin (New Haven: Yale University Press, 1986), chap. 3.

8. Dante Alighieri, *The Divine Comedy*, trans. Charles S. Singleton, *Inferno*, vol. 1 (Princeton: Princeton University Press, 1970), 120–21.

9. Eriugena, *De Divisione Naturae*, Book 4, Migne, *Patrologiae Cursus Completus, Series Latina* (Paris: J. P. Migne, 1853), 122:816D–817D.

10. Umberto Eco, *Semiotics and the Philosophy of Language* (Bloomington: Indiana University Press, 1984), and Eco, *Travels in Hyper Reality* (New York: Harcourt Brace Jovanovich, 1986); Patterson, *Negotiating the Past*; Brian Stock, *Listening for the Text: On the Uses of the Past* (Baltimore: Johns Hopkins University Press, 1990); Brigitte Cazelles and Charles Méla, *Modernité au moyen âge: le défi du passé*, Recherches et Rencontres 1 (Geneva: Librairie Droz, 1990).

11. Hans Blumenberg, *The Legitimacy of the Modern Age* (Cambridge: MIT Press, 1983), 77.

12. Stephen Toulmin, *Cosmopolis: The Hidden Agenda of Modernity* (New York: Macmillan, The Free Press, 1990), 3.

13. Ernst Robert Curtius, *European Literature and the Latin Middle Ages*, trans. Willard R. Trask (New York: Pantheon Books, 1953), 254.

14. Stock, *Listening for the Text*, 159–71; also in Cazelles and Méla, *Modernité au moyen âge*, 33–44.

15. James S. Weisheipl, "The Principle *Omne quod movetur ab alio movetur* in Medieval Physics," *Isis* 56 (1965): 26–45.

16. Ibid., 26.

17. "There were many interpretations of Aristotle in the Middle Ages. Not everyone who commented on works of Aristotle, nor everyone who quoted him enthusiastically, should be classified as an Aristotelian. It is well known that many did not fully appreciate what has been called Aristotle's fundamental discovery in natural philosophy, namely the reality of pure potentiality as a passive principle of change, a principle called [*prote hyle*] 'first matter.' Without this basic philosophical insight, the radical oneness of individuals is always in jeopardy. With this insight, however, there is no insolvable problem about the substantial unity of individuals, the unicity of substantial forms, the possibility of fundamental change, and a host of related questions disputed in the Middle Ages." Ibid., 35.

18. Ibid., 39. He continues, "A formal principle (*principium, arche*) is simply a spontaneous source of all that comes from it naturally, that is, all characteristic attributes and activities. Once it is brought into being it immediately (*statim*) and spontaneously manifests characteristic behavior, unless accidentally impeded from doing what comes naturally." See St. Thomas Aquinas, *In II Phys.*, lect. 1, n. 5: "Ponitur autem in definitione naturae *principium*, quasi genus, et non aliquid absolutum, quia nomen naturae importat habitudinem principii."

19. The points of commonality as enumerated by Weisheipl: "in the principle of inertia we admit that bodies 'are moved' and 'by another'"; "a body in natural motion does not need other forces to move it, since it already has everything it needs to move . . . [and] to accelerate naturally"; "neither the principle of inertia, nor the Aristotelian principle demands that there be movers to account for motion" (45).

20. Pierre Duhem (*Medieval Cosmology: Theories of Infinity, Place, Void, and the Plurality of Worlds,* ed. and trans. Roger Ariew [Chicago: University of Chicago Press, 1985]) repeatedly references medieval scientific developments in terms of modernist science. Copernicus is the historical divide for this kind of thinking in which any pre-Copernican developments that seem to point towards modernist science are viewed favorably. The following examples illustrate this thinking:

If Nichols of Cusa deserves to be numbered among the precursors of Copernicus, it is due more to his reflections on the plurality of worlds than his doctrine on the movement of the earth. (505)

[In the thirteenth century,] Campanus of Novara and Pierre d'Ailley put forth a position on the place of the universe identical to the position Copernicus accepted. (178)

By the condemnations that they brought forth in 1277, the theologians of the Sorbonne traced out a path to the system of Copernicus. (197)

When [Nicole Oresme] imagines an indefinite immobile space whose existence is real and independent from any body, when he keeps this space as the term of comparison to which one must relate all local movement in the final analysis, he formulates an opinion that was defended by the Stoics . . . but also one that became Newton's and Euler's. When he identifies this space with God's immensity, he may be submitting to the influence of Francis of Mayronnes, but surely he is preceding Clarke who later upheld the same doctrine against Leibniz, and he is preceding Spinoza who later formulated as an axiom that extension is an attribute of God . . . If Spinoza repeats what Nicole Oresme asserted, doubtless it is because Hesdui Creskas transmitted it to him. (266–67)

21. Hans Blumenberg, *The Genesis of the Copernican World* (Cambridge: MIT Press, 1987), 136.

22. Ibid., 138–39. The passage as a whole gives a succinct description of divine movement:

The unmoved mover God performed His causal function for the world only through His existence, not through His participation or His will, and indeed He exercised it only on the outermost and highest sphere of the heavens, which in its rotation lovingly imitated the reflexive circle, closed in on itself, of pure thought. The primary sphere moves all the other heavenly bodies and indirectly, through them, keeps all the processes of the world in motion. By way of the planets, the Sun, and the Moon, it reaches the region of the four elements in a diminished efficacy that is far removed from the purity and regularity of what it comes from, being, as it were, multiply refracted. The cosmos of Scholasticism . . . (138)

23. *Moto* appears in *Purgatorio* 4.79, 18.32, 28.107, 32.109, and in *Paradiso* 2.127, 7.141, 10.9, 12.6, 18.114, 18.119, 22.104, 27.115, 28.27.

24. Blumenberg, *Genesis*, 138.

25. Dante Alighieri, *The Divine Comedy*, trans. Charles S. Singleton, *Purgatorio*, vol. 1 (Princeton: Princeton University Press, 1973), 190–91.

26. "[S]icut sensus recipit species omnium sensibilium, et intellectus omnium intelligibilium. Et sic anima hominis fit omnia quodammodo secundum sensum et intellectum, in quo cognitionem habentia ad Dei similtudinem quodammodo appropinquant." (St. Thomas Aquinas, *Summa theologica*, I, q. 80, a.1, resp.), quoted by Singleton, *Purgatorio* 2: *Commentary*, 416.

27. *Aristotle's De Anima, Books II and III*, trans. D. W. Hamlyn (Oxford: Clarendon Press, 1974), III.3.427^{a}17.

28. "Or ti puote apparer quant' è nascosa
    la veritate a la gente ch'avvera
    ciascun amore in sé laudabil cosa;
    però che forse appar la sua matera
    sempre esser buona, ma non ciascun segno
    è buono, ancor che buona sia la cera."

29. The political identifications of these changes with the French monarchy (lily = fleur-de-lys) and Roman empire (eagle) need not concern us here except as an example of the economy of the geocentric system which permits such multiple typification of symbols. It is only natural within this analogy of the world as mind (and vice-versa) that political and metaphysical symbols could so readily intermingle.

30. Dante, *Paradiso*, vol. 1, 206–7.

31. "Et postquam premisit hanc veritatem, prosequitur ab ea circumloquens Paradisum; et dicit quod fuit in celo illo quod de gloria Dei, sive de luce, recipit affluentius. Propter quod sciendum quod illud celum est celum supremum, continens corpora universa et a nullo contentum, intra quod omnia corpora moventur, ipso in sempiterna quiete permanente***et a nulla corporali substantia virtutem recipiens. Et dicitur empyreum, quod est idem quod celum igne sui ardoris flagrans; non quod in eo sit ignis vel ardor materialis, sed spiritualis, quod est amor sanctus sive caritas." *Epistle* 13:66–68, quoted by Singleton, *Paradiso*, vol. 2, 7–8.

32. Blumenberg, *Genesis*, 139.

33. Ibid., 139. Blumenberg continues: "The motion—the revolution of the heaven of the fixed stars—that for reasons in reality was supposed to possess the most sublime regularity, because it represented the closest and most suitable effect of the mover God, was to turn out, in Copernicanism, to be a mere appearance that was caused by the rotation of the lowliest of all heavenly bodies. The unbearableness of such a reversal for Scholasticism and for its cosmological metaphysics is obvious" (139).

34. Ibid.

35. Quoted by Blumbenberg, *Genesis*, 143.

Theoretical Dimensions

The Mind's Eye: Memory and Textuality

MICHAEL RIFFATERRE

One of the most exciting controversies in today's literary theory concerns the shift from oral tradition to written literature, and its implications for the concept of text. This shift took place during the Middle Ages.

The majority of medievalists seek the consequences of orality on early texts. They try to define a medieval textuality that may differ from modern textuality because it still retains oral practices of composition and of style from which it was gradually emerging. I shall try, on the contrary, to focus on those aspects of orality that inhere in any literary text, indeed in the very concept of textuality, let alone of literariness. It is not just that I hope to show that orality endured long after textuality had conquered, although tracing orality in postmedieval texts might help our understanding of the medieval corpus. It is not just that we would better understand how modern texts differ from medieval if an influence of orality on text production were detected later than we tend to assume, in a corpus far removed from oral tradition, reflecting a long and firmly established written practice.

I would rather concentrate more on the similarity than on the difference between orality and textuality. In this respect it might be tempting to suggest that written texts resemble oral stereotypes and in general, formulaic style, which used to be the mnemotechnic grid that kept together long stretches of spoken narrative and protected the tradition (more specifically, the *traditio*) from a proliferation of *mouvance*. Despite the importance of these devices, I follow Dennis Tedlock in distinguishing memory from memorization, and making the former the major underpinning of orality. To quote Tedlock:

> The narrators in primary oral cultures . . . do not memorize stories, but *remember* them. They are not talking digital computers, programmed to retrieve stored formulas in the right order. The digital computer lacks what we call in English the *mind's eye:* a good narrator *sees* his story, and such ready-made phrases as he may use are not the substance of his thought, but an aid in the rapid verbal expression of that thought, not the internal equivalent of a written text but a bag of tricks.[1]

Turning Tedlock's illuminating remark inside out, I shall try to demonstrate that the written text is not the external equivalent of a remembered story, but a bag of tricks, a limited system of incomplete and deficient visual symbols that aid readers in the rapid recovery of vastly more extensive remembered representations. These symbols control their decoding and insure consistency from one reading performance to another, whether repeated readings by one reader or parallel ones by many, thus maintaining the identity of the work of art against the centrifugal tendencies of multiple interpretations. My point will be that the principal mechanism of the written text is memory, that reading the text is not a matter of decoding contiguous signs in linear sequence, but of matching those signs against simultaneous memories stacked in paradigms. Matching is done in two ways, by *referring* or by *repressing*. In the case of referring, the text makes sense only inasmuch as its signs (signifiers or representamens) stand for things, or rather, for other signs that we are trained to remember in connection with the signifiers. If repressing is at work, the text makes sense only because the signs are arranged so as to subvert their own referentiality, to displace their habitual referents with new ones that are complementary of, or contrary to, these habitual referents. In either case, memory is necessarily summoned up, since without it referring could not be verified, nor repressing detected.

By themselves the two signifying strategies I have outlined do not suffice to define textuality, or at any rate literary textuality, for they can also be observed in literary discourse, that is in fragmentary utterances that do exhibit literary features, but without the closure, repeatability, re-readability, and, therefore, without the formal permanence and hermeneutic stability that define the text proper, the self-contained and self-sufficient work of art.

Let us then combine formal resistance to change, interpretive imperviousness to the interpreters' variability, and the ability of signs to swing from referring to repressing, which should threaten the invariance common to the first two features. We can name three universals of literariness that correspond to these constants of the text: monumentality, catachresis, and artifice. All three are founded on memory.

Let us first tackle monumentality, the perception of the literary work as a shape that endures, that has authority, that cannot be touched without being changed altogether. Monumentality is based on the exemplarity, the illustrative, typical, or evident nature of whatever the text is about, and on overdetermination. It is obvious that exemplarity cannot be without reference to a type or class. The token of that type or class is written, whereas the type or class is elsewhere: in our past experience, in our linguistic competence or in the sociolect—in all three possibilities it is a matter of memory. Overdetermination can be both in the text (for instance, in multiple links between words, besides and on top of syntactic and semantic ones) and outside of it. If outside, whether fancied or found written elsewhere, overdetermining factors are *mnemonic*.

Take the simple case of hypogrammatic overdetermination, the perceived presence, parallel to the text and therefore outside of it, of a preexistent model. Such a model serves as authority for the text's form, and eventually makes up for its aberrance or just its singularity with respect to usage, or to grammaticality. The hypogram may or may not have any pertinence to the text; all that counts is that the text recalls it in some way. Anthony Trollope, for instance, in *Rachel Ray* (1863), describes a nephew as worthy of his uncle, a chip off the old block, we might say. Except that the uncle was a brewer, which authorizes Trollope to substitute wooden objects, more symbolic of the uncle's trade or second nature, for the all-purpose block and chip: hence the allusion to the nephew and successor to the uncle's business as *a stave out of one of Mr. Bungall's vats*. Even the family name of the brewer is emblematic, a pun on the *bunghole*, the hole in a keg to draw out the beer. The whole sentence is a pun, a lame joke perhaps— although I find it pretty good—but one that is the literariness factor itself: the joke is a parody, since that part of the novel is a mock epic about an internecine war, not before Troy, but between tradesmen. The joke is also an index of fictionality, representing as it does an authorial intrusion. The formula could be understood by analogy (the nephew is to the uncle what a stave is to a vat), but it would be merely gratuitous if it were not verified by our remembering the accepted proverbial phrase which it transforms.

The authority for the written text is thus *un*written, and the more original, or deviant, or fantastic a literary utterance, the more necessary it is for readers to look for, or to stumble upon, some comparable or opposable utterance in their mnemonic corpus. Putting the two together will then resolve the conundrum. For example, there is a poem by Rimbaud, "Enfance,"[2] which I analyse in a book of mine, where obscurity as a block vanishes and remains as a pleasurable hurdle once we get the hang of the overdetermining mechanisms. The poem is about memories of sweet childhood. The generating rule is simple enough: a matrix transforms *memory* into *childhood living yet dead*. From this matrix a derivation unfolds depicting a garden (as a commonplace of early years' remembrances) with characters—all relatives of the reminiscing adult—who are at once shown alive and yet said to be dead or absent: the *locus amoenus* is *amoenus* because it is floral, yet its occupants are but ghosts. Two sentences, however, had baffled me and I therefore forgot to comment upon them when I published the book. Only too late it occurred to me that they were capping off the paradigm of flower terminology.

In the first of the two sentences, the narrator's baby brother is depicted as if he were both there and yet long gone and far away. "Le petit frère (il est aux Indes) là, devant le couchant, sur le pré d'oeillets. [My little brother (he is in India) is standing right there before the sunset in the field of marigolds.]" The two locations are both acceptable taken separately. India is a satisfactory image of remoteness; the flowers are expected in context. But the fact remains that syntax here keeps together representations that are mutually exclusive. And yet together they are compatible and make the aptest reference to the fancied presence/actual absence, here/elsewhere dialectics of sentimental recollection, because the two words spread out and distribute along the line one single compound word: the *oeillet d'Inde,* literally India pink, a variety of marigold favored by knowledgeable gardeners. If this be a garden of gardens, then it must have *oeillets d'Inde;* and if the garden is the place where absent loved ones are remembered and scenes with them are reenacted in the mind, then the first part of the compound, *oeillet,* as well as the second, *Inde,* fit both functions, just as the compound nature of the word itself reflects the dual nature of the symbolic character. For only the baby brother's combined presence/absence makes him an index of childhood recollected.

As I pointed out before, there is no need for the hypogram to be topically or semantically related to the text. All that is required is a continuous sustained formal similarity and/or parallelism at any level (morphological, morphophonemic, syntactic) between text and hypogram. The text being difficult, hard to decode, or simply disconcerting or ungrammatical, makes readers slow down and wonder or ponder until they latch onto some dim memory of a verbal precedent that is no precedent except in the area or on a level which is irrelevant to the written text's significance. Irrelevant precedence becomes usable when a failure of communication in the text triggers a desperate search for validation.

Most of the time, however, textual overdetermination results from connecting the text with a remembered reference that *is* relevant. That is to say, the reference is intertextual, intertextuality being the key to the text's significance. The intertext may be as written as the text, but being elsewhere, outside the text, the relationship between the two is memorial, as if the intertext had lost its written materiality and survived only in memory, to be read solely through the mind's eye. The reason why the intertext is relevant is that it is selected by the text. There is around us, in our minds, a vast terra incognita of other texts and also, and perhaps above all, a terra incognita of mythologemes, ideologemes, descriptive systems and sememic structures that the sociolect feeds into texts, and which is the stuff, the precast, prefabricated stuff of literature. This universe of stories, whatever readers have garnered from the sociolect and their readings, lives a latent life and remains in a state of potential indeterminacy until it is activated, fired up, as it were, by what readers find in the text that is analogous and homologous to their stored-up possible worlds. The relevant area is literally selected, carved out from the rest by that analogy, homology, or plain identity if the text actually quotes from or alludes to the intertext. Carving out is but the first stage of the docking between the text we read and the intertext it brings before the mind's eye. *Docking,* a useful space-age metaphor, the process whereby two rockets from rival countries manage to link in orbit despite their technical differences, aptly describes the mutual adjustment that takes place between the text's idiolect and the intertext's sociolect as they meet. These two are indeed alien, yet related entities, for if intertextuality connects two verbal sequences, one written and idiolectic, and one unwritten segment of the sociolect, associable with the former, either they differ formally but share a structure, or they differ structurally while their forms are deceptively alike.

Since intertextuality is a dialectical, two-way relationship, the sociolectic fragment carved out or privileged by the text in turn valorizes or modifies the functions and especially the interpretation of that part of the text of which this fragment is now the mnemonic correlate. Thus is created within the text a new segmentation dictated by and pertinent only to the significance born of intertextuality. Instead of being perceived as a string of units already known from usage, of words or phrases embodying successive meanings based on referentiality—that is, the familiar memory of habitual relations between words and referents—the text is now perceived as a string of segments that had no existence before the text itself, that are not coterminal with words or phrases, and that posit new once-only relations between the segments' components and the intertext. We now have conflicting memories. On the one hand, there is familiarity with usage, namely linguistic competence. On the other hand, there is the memory of an intertext awakened by the pertinent segment for the very reason that the segment's grammatical or other features subvert, transform, even deny this intertext, or bend it to other ends at odds with usage. This intertext, an established narrative or diegesis, is remembered only to the extent needed for its manipulation or distortion to be noticed and for a new color to be put on everything it was about. The whole verbal sequence thus segmented points to the significance, the text's literary function, while the same sequence segmented as usage demands, points to the meanings, the text's linguistic function, now superseded by the literary.

The next stage of the docking process is twofold: first it consists in actualizing in the text only those components of the intertext that are derivative, secondary to its remembered meaning, and metonymic of its mimetic core; and second, it consists in suppressing that mimetic core, the original generator of the actualized (or rather textualized) derivatives, which determines the normal construction we put on meanings in common parlance. That core then is either rerouted to a new interpretation, figurative for instance, or cancelled out to make the text say something contrary to what we remember of the intertext.

The first alternative is at work in an elegiac sonnet from Ronsard's *Amours* (1552) in which a lover depicts himself nailed to the rock of his mistress's cruel indifference.[3] The torment of unrequited love is an eagle eating away at his heart. He would bear his passion patiently if he could only hope to be someday unshackled by her returning his love. Her longed-for favors are described as Hercules untying the captive's bonds. We instantly recognize in

these successive metaphors stereotypical metonyms for Prometheus in the descriptive system of that myth.

The fact that Prometheus is only implied does not prevent him
from becoming a metaphor for the lover. But by pushing the core
of the trope out of the written into the reader's mental lore, the
text does not simply combine metaphor and periphrasis. It makes
up for an absence on the page with a descriptive proliferation.
This lack is the key to its memorially present counterpart. Realism is born of the sequence of actualized metonyms. These metonyms are then valorized by having to stand for the image that in
the myth stands for all of them. And now that Prometheus is
replaced by his partial analog (the unjustly suffering lover), a paradoxical code is generated whereby in this text and only in this
text, rock, eagle, and Hercules are equivalent to the basic lexicon
of lovemaking. To put it briefly, the text in its most striking and
unique physical form would be ludicrous and unrealistic non-
sense, except for a convention and its arbitrary transformation
into a code at the level of the oral tradition, another name for collective memory. Thanks to that convention, text production has
taken place quite cogently; the literariness of the text literally
flows from orality.

Better still, this sets the stage for the segmentation that had just
issued from the intertext to be called into question again. Since
this segmentation is so peculiar and only for the nonce, it cannot
prevent readers from clutching at the sole segmentation they are
used to, namely words and phrases. A new set of memories is conjured up by that residual ghost of sociolectic normality.

As a result, the text produces a fine example of the second of
the three universals of literariness I was speaking about—*artifice*.
Its mechanism can be described as a conflict of memories. Hercules is metaphorized as the *Hercules of your good graces*
(*l'Hercule de ta grace*). Within the presupposition system set up
by the Promethean intertext, Hercules is to Prometheus what
love should be to the lover: freedom, surcease from pain, etc.
Within the convention, within the *as if* mode of allusion, this is
entirely true, in keeping with the inner logic of the system. But
there is no way readers can avoid being aroused by the phrase
itself, regardless of the ad hoc system that motivates it. From the
sociolectic vantage point, Hercules evokes only an image of beefy
strength. Statuary and painting offer quite a few young heroes
whose strength is also graceful, and who could be lady-killers as
well as monster-killers—Perseus and the Gorgon, sexy Theseus
and the Minotaur. Not so Hercules; he is a heavy. It thus matters

little that *grace* in the text has nothing to do with physical grace or feminine elegance, but with a kind heart and a loving, forgiving disposition. What surfaces here or takes over is the intertextual image of brawny, muscle-bound Hercules, and its opposite at the sememic level, the pliant willowy female. Hence there is a conflict between, on the one hand, the intertext specific to the phrase isolated by that idiolectically false but sociolectically accurate opposition, and, on the other hand, the intertext of convention. Therefore, we have an increased literariness, a conceit, a Baroque effect. This kind of stylistic device suggests that in the written text connotations, too, belong in the domain of memory.

In the case of the Prometheus of love, periphrasis is the means to put the burden of interpretation on what we know already, rather than on what the text tells us: the metonymic, or synecdochic and therefore repetitive, cumulative beating around the lexical bush is made easier to interpret by linguistic competence. Linguistic competence is not memory in the general sense, but memory focused on the verbal means of storing and retrieving information, a familiarity with sememes, descriptive systems, and associated sets. In short, it is memory focused on signs rather than experience.

The circular sequence works exactly like a dictionary, or better, like an encyclopedic definition. We decode it the way we solve a riddle, but with the difference that the riddle is being used to sketch a diegesis with a significant gap, and a narrative generated as much by the gap as by what is explicit. We have seen how the coexistence of components that fit the tale of the lover's predicament and of components that do not, give rise to a conceit which actualizes semantically the universal of catachresis (it says one thing and means another), and formally, that of artifice.

My examples so far have been short and, when narrative, mere sketches. Long narratives, specifically novels, those heirs to the epic of oral literature, give us convincing evidence that the unwritten is the most important part of the written. Fiction indeed is the genre that makes reader response not merely dependent on memory (every linguistic communication is dependent on memory), but *visibly* so, and in a way that becomes a generic marker of the novel.

This phenomenon could be a third category or class of textuality. If we distinguish between the text as a substitute for memory (the accepted explanation for the shift from oral to written literature), and the text as a presupposition of memory (for instance, an incomplete mimesis, or an analeptically determined prolepsis), we must also recognize the text as inscription of memory, as a sign system representing memory itself. The problem readers face in the case of novels is their length, which makes it harder for them not only to follow the thread of the plot as it unwinds half hidden through digressive subplots, not only to decode the multifarious signals of the diegesis and identify among those the truly symbolic, but above all to interpret the novel's symbols. The size of the novel makes it even harder for readers to proceed from the symbols to a perception of the unity of significance, the inner logic of the text's idiolect, without which there is no literary art.

One of the devices with which the novel palliates the confusing effect of length and complexity is the *subtext*. I define subtexts as follows. They are mini-stories or vignettes describing a scene or even a stylistic sequence that, like a sustained metaphor, develops into an idiolect separate from the overall idiolect of the narrative in order to illustrate a point or describe a situation and bring out its significance. The subtext is like a unit of reading, but it differs from Barthes's lexies in two respects. First, it does not depend on the reader's focus, but rather, it focuses the reader's attention. Second, it manifests itself repeatedly, its variants being more often than not spread at wide intervals throughout long narrative stretches, even overlapping other subtexts. It is not a theme or motif, for these are born before the text, and hence means to other ends now appropriated to the needs of the narrative that is borrowing them from elsewhere. It is not an episode, although it may comment on one, for an episode is a link in the chain of events, while a subtext can be excised without unravelling the fabric of the narrative. If you summarize a novel, you need never mention the subtexts. Finally, and most important, they actualize structures identical or related to the structures that inform the significance of the whole work, thus either mirroring the text they are embedded in or exemplifying one of the cardinal rules of this particular fiction's idiolect.

Now, in its development from one version to the next, the subtext requires memory, as any paradigm does. The most striking feature of its successive actualizations is also the one that points to memory gradually assuming dominance over the written text. The text seems to proclaim this by destroying its diegetic surface, leaving only fragmentary clues that may lead readers back to remembered symbols. It is as if the text were shutting itself to the reading eye and laying itself bare to the mind's eye.

Indeed, with each of its successive variants, the subtext becomes shorter, more fragmentary, less explanatory, less explicit.

It finally becomes so allusive that if readers do not remember the full-fledged initial version, they cannot decode the subtext in the degraded shadowy form that is now left of it. This gradual reduction or deterioration of the written verbal communication system puts the burden of recovering the message, by a process of filling in the gaps, entirely on memory.[4] And it is memory that insures that gaps are filled on the text's own terms and not in accordance with the reader's fancy.

Subtexts abound in Marcel Proust's multivolume novel, whose size and meandering progress, and involved thematic web, would make interpretation a daunting task if it were not for the clues they proffer. Most extensive among them is one I shall call the *underwater subtext*, which develops metaphorically the significance of snobbishness. Homosexuality, the staying of the course of Time, and snobbishness are the three main strands of the novel's fabric.

Social exclusion and the yearning to be admitted within circles from which one is kept out is not, of course, the forgotten concern of a long-vanished society, irrelevant to us, as critics have thought. Its relevance endures because it is a variant of an eternally valid structure of desire, transferred from the specifically sexual to the social libido. The dynamics of the structure are simple: an object is described as desirable, but the subject's reaching for it is frustrated by an obstacle. If fulfillment were possible, desire would cease to be, and the narrative would stop. Any representation of the object must therefore have as its corollary a representation of impediments interposed, a variant of interdiction.

The subtext's initial and fully developed version is found in a ten-page story of a benefit evening at the Opera. Subscribers' boxes have all been rented by the members of the Princesse de Guermantes's party, the most exclusive group in Paris. Less extraordinary spectators, who fill the orchestra seats, are more interested in watching the Guermantes crowd than in following the spectacle on stage. The barrier separating the two worlds is an invisible one that readers deduce from the description of the boxes as submarine caves, of the dimly lit house as the swimming chiaroscuro of the briny deep, of male spectators as Tritons and of their decolletéed ladies as half-naked sea nymphs. You can see this but you cannot touch, let alone enter, as if an aquarium's plate glass window separated the two worlds. This of course translates into mimetic terms the grammar of desire: craving for progress from one sensory perception to full sensual possession is frustrated. This imagery was developed long before aquarium or glass plate, with Latin poetry from Vergil to Catullus depicting sea goddesses in their sea caves, visible underwater, a temptation to the sentimental angler, but beyond the reach of mere mortals.

Thus, in the night at the Opera passage, the central image of another world seen through the transparency of water but unreachable by landbound creatures, is duplicated in the eyes of the ladies of that inaccessible society, as if these eyes were themselves parts of an aquarium's glass plate wall:

> Beyond began the orchestra stalls, abode of mortals forever separated from the sombre and transparent realm to which here and there, in their smooth liquid surface, the limpid, reflecting eyes of the water-goddesses served as frontier. For the folding seats on its shore and the forms of the monsters in the stalls were mirrored in those eyes in simple obedience to the laws of optics . . . as happens with those two sections of external reality to which, knowing that they do not possess any soul . . . analogous to our own, we should think ourselves insane to address a smile or a glance: namely, minerals and people to whom we have not been introduced. (1.36)[5]

Elsewhere one can see the monocle of an aristocrat, insignia of snobbery, from behind which a pleasant but condescending eye is looking: "his gaze" writes Proust, "[is] a disc of rock crystal."

In other variants absurdity stems from analogy. The derivative idiolect singles out and valorizes any barrier or limit that, like the glass plate, while physically flimsy, remains morally unbreakable: "while the rich young man's friends envied him because he had such a smartly dressed mistress, the latter's scarves hung before the little company a sort of fragrant, flowing veil, but one that kept it apart from the outer world" (1.733).

These images, whether or not authorized by figurative convention, are unacceptable and readers cannot, therefore, forget them. Since they keep exemplifying the libidinal dynamics, this coincidence makes the unacceptable a hyperbolic form of the illustrative.

Finally the semiosis incorporates representations incompatible with the given: a doormat at the door of a duke represents a border that excludes people one does not receive:

> the line of demarcation that separated me from the Faubourg Saint-Germain seemed to me all the more real because it was purely ideal; I sensed that it was already part of the Faubourg when I saw, spread out on the other side of that Equator, the Guermantes doormat of which my mother had ventured to

say, having like myself caught a glimpse of it one day when their door stood open, that it was in a shocking state.

And I must content myself with a shiver of excitement as I sighted from the open sea (and without the least hope of ever landing there), like a prominent minaret, like the first palm, like the first signs of some exotic industry or vegetation, the well-trodden doormat of its shore. (2.25–27)

Without the *Night at the Opera* version, we could not make sense of monocles described as fragments of the plate glass of an aquarium window, nor of eyes depicted as translucent barriers, nor could we understand Proust's partiality to glass enclosures through which the have-nots watch the haves. We would find it nonsensical that a doormat, the pedestrian symbol of acceptance, should give onto inaccessible luscious exoticism.

We have seen how the paradigms of repetition peter out as they unfold, losing more and more of their mimetic components, slowly reduced to allusions limited to one word only. An idiolect has thus been developed with rules that were given once in the subtext's first version, often at a great distance from the point readers have reached. This whole construction, its rules, its difference, its ability to do without the help of usage, or the sociolect, or its ability to do away with that sociolect, can now be evoked by one word, in which the subtext's features are concentrated. It is as if the text had returned from the written to the unwritten altogether. Its own interpretation, plus a collection of examples destined to prove the point, plus a system of signs meant to help readers perceive as a unified, harmonious whole a work of art—all this that gives the text its identity and its fullest artistic development is now as it were committed back to memory, as if the telos of the literary text were to spell out a story only as a rehearsal for an imaginary mnemonic possession of it. I am not just referring to our ability to remember a book we have read, which would amount to belaboring the obvious and would be nothing new. I am referring to the mechanism that has enabled the text to build within its fabric pockets of implicitly remembered, symbolic stories in which its essence is resumed and whose sole purpose is to store up indices of its significance, mementos of its important points, guidelines for easy control of the understanding of its fully developed complex. These traveller's aids all have their key, the word from which the subtext can be reconstructed whole (as the text can be inferred from the subtexts), and this key, this word itself is identifiable because it recalls the initial wording of the subtext's first instance. In other words, literariness of the written text is built on a circularity of memory.

But what about the beginnings of the subtexts, what about the beginnings of the texts? The answer is probably that memory, too, is responsible for the first valorization of a lexical or phrasal representation, making it capable of simultaneously carving out an intertext and generating a textual derivation as a consequence of the intertextual input. Since this memory is the original one, it is also an unconscious one, and you may well wonder how readers can have access to it and experience its motivational power, the ultimate authority for the text's truth. The answer, I think, may be in that symbol of the text's limits, the quotation, or the allusion, which is also, as the fragment that it is, *the* sign, whose special function is to stand for memory.

In my last example, the Proustian subtext, the unconscious memory that imparts to the subtext the full dynamics of the libido, by giving underwater imagery the primary role is, 18 pages into the 3,000-page novel, an apparently quite farfetched allusion to the story of Aristaeus in Vergil's *Georgics:* that mythological hero was the inventor of apiculture. Having problems raising his bees, he is said to have gone for advice into the underwater kingdom of his mother, the nymph Cyrene. Vergil shows him crying for help at the lip of the chasm opening onto the depths, heard by the nymph and her retinue of marine deities, and received, full of admiration for his mother's watery empire (*umida regna*). The whole story has furnished Proust with the setting for his subtext. The exclusion principle is repeatedly emphasized by the Latin source. As for Proust's motivation in making so much of the story, a revealing slip of the pen suggests what must have been. Proust substitutes a sea goddess much better known and often written about since Homer, for Vergil's nymph. Except that the Homeric goddess's name is Tethys, and Proust makes another mistake on top of the first, replacing her with Thetis, a lesser sea goddess, but the mother of Achilles. Twice shying before the name, this graphemic stuttering is readily spotted by readers of the post-Freudian era. I suspect that Thetis was mistakenly substituted for Cyrene, because Proust's problem was his fear of rejection by the mother. The first pages of *La Recherche* are about nothing else. The child's anxiety about not having his mother come to kiss him goodnight, the jealousy towards the father—all this is obvious and informs the whole novel. Vergil's text (a must at that time in Latin classes) must have riveted Proust's attention at school, because Aristaeus *is* anxious: when he asks for his mother's help, he is shut out of her intimate circle of attractive nymphs exactly as the narrator as a child will be from the family circle; and his anxiety manifests itself by a hint at family romance (was my father Apollo, as you claim?) and with his first question: *have you banished the love that you had for me?* Thetis was thus substituted for Cyrene because Thetis is a destructive mother. She meant to help her son Achilles, but she failed in protecting him. When she dipped her infant child in the waters of the Styx to make him immortal, she left him vulnerable at the heel where she was holding him, and that is where Achilles would one day receive a mortal wound. She failed him. One more reason for fusing Achilles and Aristaeus may have been that Aristaeus, pursuing Eurydice, Orpheus's wife, to rape her (this too is in Vergil) caused her to step on a snake, that bit her in the heel, and thus to die. Snake and arrow from Homer to Vergil to E. A. Poe perform the same way. The choice of the heel further suggests via fetishism that the wound suffered because of the mother's dereliction, inflicted by the mother, is a screen for castration. If so, then, the power of the mythological given is that it unites two symbolisms of rejection: maternal rejection and social rejection (furthermore, the ladies of society who will finally accept the narrator are clearly maternal figures). When Proust alludes to the myth, it is, revealingly, to say that Vergil shows Aristaeus received in the water underworld *à bras ouverts,* 'with open arms.' Vergil does not say that in fact Aristaeus is at first left out, but the phrase is a commonplace metaphor both for social acceptance and for a mother's embrace. I might add that the allusion to Aristaeus is as farfetched as can be, totally unmotivated within the narrative. It can therefore only be truth unwittingly surfacing from the depths. But all this is irrelevant to readers, for it plays no role in their grasping the import and the symbolism of the aquarium wall subtext. What does play a role in helping them uncover the hidden truth is the presence of ungrammaticalities in the mimesis, of unacceptable images, in short, of defects or rents in the fabric of verisimilitude.

In order for these ungrammaticalities to be properly understood and to work as cues to the interpretation of symbolic subtexts, they must affect the predication, the relationship that carries the symbolism. Alone, outside of such a sign-system, ungrammaticalities only point to the psychological unconscious and cannot guide anyone but an analyst. There is, for instance, a daydreaming sequence in which the narrator expresses his attraction to the Guermantes way, to the Guermantes name, and his sexual fixation on the Duchesse de Guermantes herself, as yet personally unknown to him. He does so by rationalizing: the country around the Guermantes *château* is pleasant to him because it is full of picturesque rivers. He even has a dream in which he is a guest of the Duchess and she teaches him the arcane art of trout fishing. This is crazy enough, but the telling detail is the use of the rarest of adjectives, *fluviatile*, to speak of a countryside that is full of mere streams and specifically not of large rivers for which *fluviatile* or more commonly *fluvial* would be suitable. The next time Proust uses *fluviatile*, it will be unaccountably to speak of places "*fluviatile* and poetic":

> [I] seemed to have before my eyes a fragment of that fluvial country which I had longed so much to see and know since coming upon a description of it by one of my favourite authors. And it was with that story-book land, with its imagined soil intersected by a hundred bubbling watercourses, that Guermantes, changing its aspect in my mind, became identified. (1.188)

"By one of my favourite authors" indeed! This is Vergil himself. *Fluviatile*, a hyperlatinate form, echoes and condenses the whole impact of Aristaeus's awe when, admitted to his mother's kingdom, he sees "all the big rivers flowing under the vast earth." The whole passage is a tremendous mimetic feat on Vergil's part, trying to cope with a description that has to transform a normal landscape into an imaginary netherworld. So much for proving that the Duchess is a mother image. And what should we think of the line: "the sad Aristaeus [with whom the narrator as child identifies] stands in tears on the bank of the waters of the river Peneus, the fatherly one"? In the Latin it reads *Penei genitoris ad undam*, where the name of the river Peneus in the genitive case (*Penei genitoris*) is nearly identical with the Latin for generating penis (*penis genitoris*).[6]

I have dwelt at length on this example because of *fluviatile* more than anything else. The rare form chosen by Proust is evidently like a signal that the Latin source is returning to the surface of the text, like a sign that stands for the whole intertext. If the written text functions like a screen (in the psychoanalytical sense of that word), it is to be expected that it will also, as in our dreams, contain an index pointing to where the anamnesis begins.

This is of course an isolated case. You may have noticed in my examples the recurrence of syllepsis (*bunghole, Inde, grace*). This double-headed sign may actually create two simultaneous and yet incompatible representations, or it may only propose a surface meaning and invite at the same time reader response to a hypothetical, or fancied representation. In either case, it points to the text's faculty of signifying along two parallel tracks: the written high road and the implicit memory-lane low road.

Looking back at the facts I have just described, the conclusion is inescapable that the text's unwritten component is vastly more developed than the written. For the same reason that a sememe is a text while the sign that embodies it is only a word, the intertext dwarfs the text. And no matter how many texts form the intertext, they are all elsewhere, present only through the reader's remembering of them. Better still, the important gearwork in the semiotic mechanism of the text, structures, hermeneutic guidelines, attention-controlling gaps, etc., are all on the unwritten side, a fact that extends to the dynamics of genre. It is not by chance that prolepsis, among the most essential cogs and wheels of the narrative, should be a mnemonic process. Finally, the very interpretive rules and devices applicable to the written are themselves mnemonic, since even the segmentation defining units of reading is based on the unwritten intertext.

I would venture to say that the text is never a substitute for memory, aside from the historical fact (historical and therefore irrelevant to the timelessness of the work of art) that, at the beginning of texts, when they took over from orality, writing was a help to memorization. Memory is the essence of textuality. If there is a difference in the degree to which this essence shapes textual functions, it is the difference between forms like the syllepsis or the *as if* mode that are presuppositions of memory, and forms like the deterioration of the subtext that are an inscription of memory.

To be sure, memory is the domain of psychology, but it is essentially language, the repository of knowledge. It is thus possible to state that when the linguistic practice of memory becomes conscious, we are witnessing the birth of literariness.

NOTES

1. Dennis Tedlock, "Toward an Oral Poetics," *New Literary History* 8 (1977): 507.

2. Arthur Rimbaud, "Enfance," *Illuminations*, in *Oeuvres complètes* (Paris: Garnier Frères, 1960), 255. I analyzed the poem in my *Semiotics of Poetry* (Bloomington: Indiana University Press, 1978), 120–21, but I was then unable to see the hypogram.

3. Pierre de Ronsard, *Les Amours de 1552*, (in *Oeuvres complètes*, ed. Paul Laumonier [Paris: Hachette, 1924]: 4.17), Sonnet 13:

Pour estre en vain tes beaulx soleilz aymant,
   Non pour ravir leur divine estincelle,
   Contre le roc de ta rigueur cruelle
   Amour m'atache à mille cloux d'aymant.
En lieu d'un Aigle, un soing horriblement
   Claquant du bec, & siflant de son aille,
   Ronge goulu ma poictrine immortelle,
   Par un desire qui naist journellement.
Mais de cent maulx, & de cent que j'endure,
   Fiché, cloué, dessus ta rigueur dure,
   Le plus cruel me seroit le plus doulx,
Si j'esperoys, apres un long espace,
   Venir vers moy l'Hercule de ta grace,
   Pour delacer le moindre de mes nouds.

It is only because I love in vain your sun-like eyes,
   not because I have stolen a divine spark from them,
   that Love has fastened me with a thousand magnetic nails
   to the rock of your cruel harshness.
Instead of an eagle, a cruel torment, a desire born anew
   each day, with noisy beak and whistling wing
   avidly comes to eat away at my undying heart.
But of these ills and all that I suffer,
   fastened and nailed as I am onto your cruel hardness,
   the harshest would seem the sweetest,
   if only I could, at long last, hope that the Hercules
   of your good graces would come to me and untie
   the least of these bonds.
                (my translation, practical if perhaps unpoetic)

4. Notice that the progressive deterioration of the subtext ends in a kind of tachygraphy or shorthand that results from pushing the mimesis back into the mind, and that is identical with the use of mythology in Ronsard's lyric. Ronsard summarizes a myth and implicates its descriptive background through mere name-dropping.

5. For a detailed analysis of the first instance of the subtext, see my paper "Descriptive Imagery," *Yale French Studies* 61 (1981): 107–25, esp. 119–25. The subsequent quotations from Proust refer to C. K. Scott-Moncrieff and Terence Kilmartin's translation, *Remembrance of Things Past*, 3 vols. (New York: Random House, 1981).

6. Vergil, *Georgics*, trans. H. Rushton Fairclough, Loeb Classical Library (Cambridge: Harvard University Press, 1974), 4.317–558; see esp. 4.355.

Antiquity and the New Arts in Petrarch

GIUSEPPE MAZZOTTA

The convention of partitioning history according to distinguishable and discrete intellectual periods has not gone unchallenged in recent times.[1] Historiographic categories such as "Renaissance," "Modernity," and "Middle Ages" continue to retain at least a nominal validity as terms of chronological demarcation (certainly useful for primers of literary history), but the historical specificity of each epoch, which in the nineteenth century could be defined with ease, is now hard to pinpoint. In 1870 Francesco De Sanctis published his *Storia della letteratura italiana,* which is shaped by the Hegelian belief in the organic, teleological process of history. The security of the Hegelian historiographic model, wherein contradictory individual phenomena can be manipulated into an overarching totality or significant unity, is in question from a variety of perspectives. Paradoxically, two radically contrasting premises about history usually end up agreeing in their dismissal of historical boundaries. These boundaries are arbitrary, it is said, because "human nature tends to remain much the same in all times." The judgment is underwritten by those who believe in the irreducible individuality of each spiritual and artistic experience.[2] But the major doubts about the legitimacy of traditional historical periodizations occur to scholars who, engaged as they are in interpretive practices, inevitably come to discover that data cannot be rigidly classified or epistemological breaks identified, and how crude is the notion of originality and foundation in literary history. They discover, in short, that textual details do not always fit the generality of formulas established a priori and that canons of a culture repress or exclude what may contradict the myths of that culture.

These doubts need not be thought of merely as the domain of Deconstruction. Renaissance scholars, for instance, have long been aware of how blurred the dividing line between "medieval" and "Renaissance" culture is. They have wondered whether the concept "Renaissance" is, in the words of Erwin Panofsky, an accurate "self-definition" or a mere "self-deception," and they have probed the degree to which the Italian Renaissance extends the Carolingian revival and the Ottonian resurgence of the tenth century.[3]

The notion of "modernity" is certainly no less problematical. In an important study written some twenty years ago, *The Legitimacy of the Modern Age*, Hans Blumenberg argues that modernity, a period that broadly stretches from the 1600s to the present, is a legitimate category of history in that it inaugurates a new configuration in the field of knowledge. The "epochal threshold" or reversal of direction from the core of theological dogmatics that characterizes the historical process until the 1600s is not embodied by Nicholas Cusanus, as Gadamer maintains, but by Giordano Bruno's "heretical" casting of the plurality of worlds in an infinite cosmology.[4] Blumenberg never stops to consider "modernity" as a theoretical, persistently present construct that posits a break from tradition, only to discover that modernity is forever inscribed in the archives of the past. Nor does he probe the self-evident aporia of any historicist philosophy which affirms the ceaseless mobility of the historical process and yet must arrest history's flow in order to impart a new direction to it. His aim, rather, is to counter Löwith's assertion that the discourse of modernity is a secular retrieval of medieval themes. The legitimacy of the modern age, stated simply, resides in the scientific subversion of the authority of the canon as well as the paradigms of knowledge rampant in the theological, medieval models of the economy of creation.

Medieval and Renaissance scholars could easily criticize Blumenberg's concept of a prolonged, unified "Middle Ages," as well as his version of an unscientific Middle Ages, as the last in an endless series of myths modernity keeps forging about the past in order to justify itself. Looking at the recent issue of *New Literary History* devoted to the "Alterity of the Middle Ages," one can perceive the fallacy of, say, Henry O. Taylor's *The Mediaeval Mind*, with its overt claim of the Middle Ages as a time of spiritual homogeneity.[5] One can also see the yawning gulf between the present state of medieval studies and the nineteenth century, when Gaston Paris at the Collège de France, Francisque Michel at Bordeaux, Léon Gautier, and, eventually, Bédier made the knowledge of the Middle Ages (in the double value of the genitive case) central to the curriculum. These *savants* could even object to the distortions as to what the Middle Ages were (and the list of perpetrators goes from Rabelais to Voltaire to Chateaubriand to Hugo), without themselves escaping other distortions they inevitably committed in the name of paleography, philology, and archeological research.

The old myths about the Middle Ages linger tenaciously in new guises. Because the encyclopaedia of Vincent of Beauvais, written toward the middle of the thirteenth century, in many ways derives from Isidore's *Etymologies,* written some seven centuries earlier, it is still assumed by medievalists that the inventory of knowledge remains unchanged.[6] That Vincent makes available to the general public the new Aristotle, Arabic writings on the sciences, and the Chartrians is not deemed sufficient to dispel the notion that knowledge in the Middle Ages is a perpetual anachronism, an immutable, closed-off space of superstitious beliefs. The impression of an immobile universe of knowledge is reinforced by the practice of Biblical exegesis (notoriously conservative) which, in its quasimechanical repetitiveness, seeks to shelter the sovereignty of the Biblical text from subversive encroachments. The infinitely selfsame message of Biblical exegesis, of the Neoplatonic structures, and of forever-fixed scholastic arrangements of the totality of creation unavoidably project the Middle Ages as the parable of an untroubled utopia of the soul, of an otherness no longer accessible to us, of an "alterity" (the word, of course, is the matrix of allegory), which is both an alibi and a scandal to current intellectual concerns.

This powerful and alluring vision of an ordered world is a repression of history, of the contradictory voices punctuating the philosophical debates, the spiritual lacerations, and the political struggles of the thirteenth and fourteenth centuries. One would only have to mention the impact of Aristotle's *De Anima* and its commentary by Averroës at the universities of Oxford and Paris in the thirteenth century; Marsilius's doctrine of law as coercive power [*potentia coactiva*], and his determination of the ground of authority and popular sovereignty; or the crisis of Biblical exegesis, which was the genuine bone of contention between St. Bernard of Clairvaux and Abelard.[7] And finally, one would have to mention the consciousness of poets such as Jean de Meun, Dante, and Chaucer of the crisis investing the various forms of knowledge. Because of the steady interrogation of their own values and epistemological premises, these poets and philosophers question us the moment we recognize the problematic status of the Middle Ages as a category of cognition.

I have no wish to cut through this swath of problems in an abstract manner. I shall focus on Petrarch, instead, because he consistently reflects, both in his prose meditations and his poetry, on his own radical difference from the world of the past as well as his apartness from his own times. This private experience of apartness is the basis for the articulation of a larger historical rupture. It is Petrarch, as a matter of fact, who posits a clear-cut division between the Middle Ages and modernity as the historical time that supersedes and alters the achievements of what has come to be known as the "Dark Ages."[8] The phrase, which reappears in D'Alembert as "la nuit médiévale" to be opposed to "l'époque de lumière," had circulated even before Petrarch.[9] For Petrarch it designates limits of vision—the limits of a culture which ignores the values of the classical world and which spans the time between the birth of Christ and his own age. In truth, Petrarch will also say that the advent of Christ marks "the end of the darkness and the night of error . . . the dawn of the true light." Yet, the decline of Rome and the concomitant eclipse of classical antiquity has cast a thick shadow on man's earthly life.[10]

In and of itself, the desire to promote the rebirth of classical antiquity and its rich spiritual deposit cannot be said to start with Petrarch. The twelfth century revival of classicism simply belies such a hypothetical claim. In Italy, on the other hand, the likes of Albertino Mussato, Lovato Lovati, Geremia da Montagnone, and Giovanni del Virgilio were involved in the early fourteenth century in salvaging what seemed to be the hopelessly defaced documents and texts of the pagan past. And few poets understood as well as Dante the radical modernity of Vergil. Modernity, as a matter of fact, is a thematic strain in Dante's poetic thought. Guinizelli is acknowledged as the ranking poet in the "uso moderno"— a phrase that makes modernity another term for the ephemeral, for the predicament of temporality in which each experience will be unavoidably transcended by a succeeding one.[11] But Vergil's modernity is asserted as his power to enter and affect the concerns of the present. More generally, a mere listing of well-known titles, *Poetria Nova, Logica nova, Vita nuova,* or of the awareness of a new poetic style, the *stil nuovo,* shows that there is a rhetoric of the "new" that is systematically invoked for the accretion of knowledge or for stressing departures, whether real or not, from established practices.

We must, however, distinguish between the new as a fact and the new as an idea or way of thinking. New facts and experiences are indisputable throughout the medieval centuries. The idea of the new, paradoxically, was introduced by Christianity's subversion of the most cherished myths of Classicism, by the insertion, that is, into history of the story of redemption that was bound to perplex the exacting rigor of the natural philosophers. The paradox consists in the fact that the renewal of man's spiritual history entails the closure of history. The laicization of culture that Petrarch calls for is an imaginative extension of the "dawn of light" ushered in by the Incarnation.

If there is any radicality in Petrarch's epistemological break from the Dark Ages, it will be found in the retrieval of antiquity not as an episodic, contingent event, but as a systematic undertaking, as a total personal enterprise that involves him in a fundamental rethinking of the whole canon. Even after making allowances for the genuine affection Boccaccio felt for Petrarch, one is struck by how deeply Boccaccio grasped the significance of Petrarch's role when he acknowledged that Petrarch, alone among the figures of his times, had reinstated "Apollo in his ancient sanctuary"; that he had "reinvested the muses, soiled by rusticity, with their ancient beauty"; and, finally, that he "had rededicated to the Romans the Capitol."[12]

Contemporary critics of Petrarch, Petrarch's own claims notwithstanding, continue to consider him as a belated poet, painfully aware of the long shadow Dante casts on him; as a self-absorbed, narcissistic figure forever moaning over impermanence in the world of time. This common perception of Petrarch's pathos superimposes on Petrarch the fads of later Petrarchism and mistakes the pose of later poets for Petrarch himself, as if he were unaware that the ruptured sense he has of himself turns into the imaginary space where larger concerns are tested. But how exactly does Petrarch's insight into his own self affect his impulse to forge a new culture? In what ways is this culture new?

There are many texts one could study to explore how the figuration of a broken self issues into a sustained intellectual project. I shall look at a well-known letter on familiar matters Petrarch wrote as a response to Giovanni Colonna, who bid him to write down the conversation they held one day while wandering through the ruins of Rome.[13] I should remark on how essential conversations, letters, and polemics (his hatreds are famous) are to Petrarch's style of thought. It is a style that needs the support of objective evidence, of different minds *turning together*, in conversation, as if the discovery of truth were inseparable from the ability to communicate. But Petrarch will never lapse into the illusions of what in modern times has come to be known as objectivist literature.

He begins his letter by evoking wistfully their wandering— "deambulabamus Rome soli"—until the two of them sit among the Baths of Diocletian. The chief rhetorical move of the latter is to insist that he is unable to duplicate the intensity of the pathos felt that day: "Redde michi illum locum, illud otium, illam diem, illam attentionem tuam, illam ingenii mei venam . . . Sed mutata sunt omnia; locus abest, dies abiit, otium periit, pro facie tua mutas literas aspicio." The anaphoric sequence, "illum . . . illud . . . illam," which makes poignant the impossibility of regaining the multifaceted moods of that day, stresses from the start the awareness of the gaps of time, the sense of disjunction between proximate temporal experiences, or, to put it simply, the perpetual fragmentation in the ordinary texture of life.

The rhetorical structure of this paragraph aims at providing the revelation of time's fleeting essence: it introduces time as the principle of difference and as a devastation which leaves nothing untouched. But the metaphor of "wandering" [*deambulabamus*] which opens the text forces us to considerations of the complementary problem of space. Wandering is a favorite metaphor with Petrarch, for it brings to one focus the movement of the Augustinian unquiet heart and pure drifting. Many of Petrarch's texts present images of such ambivalent motion. The ascent of Mount Ventoux is the record of a quest and a gratuitous mountain climbing. *On His Ignorance* is written during a ride on the Po river, as if the tortuous flow of the river were a metaphor for the rambling of the mind. "Wandering," properly speaking, is neither a journey with a destination, nor is it quite an exile, for "home"—whether Platonic or Biblical, a place of departure and arrival one longs for— is not the issue. To wander is a pure adventure in pursuit of the ghostly traces of time, a moving about which allows a worldview to emerge. This worldview combines the aimlessness, the utter dislocation of the sightseer as he confronts alien objects, which are themselves dislocated out of any intelligible framework, with the muteness of the ruins. The ruins, in turn, recall something else, but what is conjured up does not appear as it once was. Because ruins suspend the principle of identity and show that the past is out of reach, they are the material signs of time as it effaces all signs, emblems of a difference made materially immanent. The shifting viewpoints in the two friends' perambulation, finally, yield the figuration of a noncommunicating world which stands in stark contrast to the conversational mood enveloping them.

This figuration puts Petrarch, as well as us, in the path of a revelation: the revelation of both time and space as ruptured both in themselves and from each other. But the fragmentariness of viewpoints, time, space, and objects also reveals the power of local, partial shapes. The principle of localization, I submit, is central to Petrarch's imagination: the source of the Sorgue river, the grass of Vaucluse, the Capitol, in Rome and not Paris, as the place where the crowning of the poet must occur, Avignon, the Roman forum, etc., are privileged spots which show that for Petrarch there is a truth of the moment as well as the truth of a place. The irreducible *genius loci* lays a trap, ensnares the poet and forces him to extract its secret essence.[14]

The thematic burden of the letter is the record of the (un)recognizable spots of Roman myth. Petrarch and Giovanni Colonna see, the letter says, where Evander's residence stood; they point out the cave of Cacus and the she-wolf that nursed Romulus and Remus. They remember the duel of the Horatii and Curiatii, the Tarpeian Rock, and the place of Caesar's triumph and death. They wander from the column of Trajan to Hadrian's tomb, to the palace of Nero and that of Augustus. Giovanni Colonna, for his part, takes special note of the Christianized pagan ruins—Trajan's bridge, which has taken the name of St. Peter; he points out the place where St. Peter was crucified, St. Lawrence grilled, and Constantine healed of his leprosy.

The dual perspective on history, pagan and Christian, shows that history is not a homogeneous totality or a monolith. There are in the same theatre of history divergent lines, diversified chronologies, and residual layers buried under or scattered over the ground: "As we walked over the shattered city, with the fragments of the ruins under our eyes, we talked about history, which we appeared to have divided between us in such a fashion that in modern history [*historiae novae*] you, and in ancient history [*historiae antiquae*] I, seemed to be more expert; and ancient were called those events which took place before the name of Christ was celebrated in Rome and adored by the Roman emperors, modern, however, the events from that time to the present."[15] In this penumbral world of graves and of time's dominion, history is an archeological palimpsest whereby time turns into laminations of space. In a primary way, however, history is memory, the poetic recollection of the legends and the realities of Rome, whose ground is hallowed by its antiquities.

Petrarch's synoptic sketch of Rome is a profound alteration of medieval historiography of Rome.[16] The fall of Rome in A.D. 410 was more than the collapse of a city, for what had been shattered with that fall was the Vergilian myth of the eternity of Rome. The Fathers of the Church, from St. Jerome to St. Augustine, responded with shock at the news of the havoc wrought in the city of Rome. Vergil's prophecy in the *Aeneid*, "I give them (the Romans) dominion without end," had deluded men into believing in the stability of the earthly city. The fall of Rome, which exposes the fallacy of the Vergilian prediction, elicited contrasting assessments.[17]

In a way, the early Church apologists longed for the fall of the Empire. The Book of Revelation, after all, had identified Rome with Babylon, while the Roman persecution of the Christians, it was felt, justified the Christians' harsh judgment of the Empire. Irenaeus eagerly waits for the fall, as does Tertullian.[18] But for Lactantius the fall of Rome, which had inevitably to take place, was identified with the imminent fall of the world: "The fall and ruin of the world will shortly take place, although it seems that nothing of that kind is to be feared as long as the city of Rome stands intact. But when the capital of the world has fallen . . . who can doubt that the end will have arrived for the affairs of men and the whole world? It is that city which sustains all things. And the God of Heaven is to be entreated and implored—if indeed his laws and decrees can be delayed—lest sooner than we think that detestable tyrant should come who will undertake so great a deed and tear out that eye by the destruction of which the world itself is about to fall." Such apocalyptic ruminations are echoed by St. Augustine in his *Sermon on the Ruin of the City* and by the Pseudo-Bede who writes the famous lines, "Quamdiu stabit Coliseus stabit et Roma; quando cadet Coliseus, cadet et Roma; quando cadet Roma, cadet et mundus."[19]

That Petrarch is aware of this apocalyptic strain deduced from the fall of Rome is beyond question. The *canzone* on Rome, "Spirto gentil . . ." recalls the sepulchres of the ancient Romans who will be remembered, "se l'universo pria non si dissolve." But in the letter to Giovanni Colonna, Petrarch puts himself at the end, at the point where history is already over, and he is bewildered by the incommensurability of the fragments and their death-like fixity. The pathos of his prose initially reminds the reader of St. Jerome's reaction on hearing, while in Bethlehem, the news of Rome's fall: "When the brightest light on the whole earth was extinguished, when the Roman empire was deprived of its head and when, to speak more correctly, the whole world perished in one city, then I was dumb with silence, I held my peace ... and my sorrow was stirred."[20] The initial response in Petrarch, who is not in the place of a new birth as Jerome is, can be called an *aesthetics* of ruins, for they are adumbrations of his own mortality. The time of reflection, which is the recollection of the promenade among the ruins, swerves from the apocalyptic visions of an Irenaeus, a Lactantius or a Pseudo-Bede. He perceives discontinuities at the heart of the tradition that someone like Dante would still view as a uniform reality; he recognizes the pastness of the past in the sense that the monuments of the past appear to him as taciturn shadows of a shattered historical discourse, obscure signs of the withdrawal of what men have made into the opaque surface of the ground. The archeological findings, finally, excite the writer's imagination. By the imagination, which has the power to unify and totalize the parts of the broken world, the past takes shape in the mind of Petrarch. From the gloom of piled up ruins, distinct shapes emerge; buildings are resurrected from the dust in which they lie and are rearranged in the rigorous topography of the eternal city.

This is not to say that Petrarch's reconstruction happens simply in his mind, as if the mind were a theatre of chimeras and private phantasms. The ruins, which are narratives of lost realities, are not lifeless relics: rather, they are inexhaustible coils of memory, tumultuous signs rising up from the dark depths of time. Because in the very effacement of the columns the legend of time is indelibly inscribed, the relics draw him within their ghostly boundaries. Objects become subjects capable of summoning us into the enigma of their presence, prodigious points of force from which memories endlessly radiate. To miss the power of what amounts to Petrarch's poetics of objects and places would mean missing the sensuous signs of his desire.

In this authentic place of desolation and imaginative excitement the *commonplaces* of Roman history arise. But there is more to it. Petrarch does not surrender to the forebodings of a general apocalypse nor does he get absorbed in thoughts of personal annihilation. The text tells us that after discussing history, Petrarch and Giovanni Colonna turn their attention to problems of moral philosophy, the arts, their authors and practitioners. He even writes that a book is needed in order to go over the origin of the figurative arts.[21] In *De Remediis utriusque fortunae* (chapters 34 to 41), Petrarch discusses the origin of the liberal arts and of painting and sculpture. In the letter he seems to announce a speculative work on painting, sculpture, and architecture.

Here lies the novelty of Petrarch's cultural project. This awareness of death, which he experiences in a variety of ways and from which he never quite frees himself, triggers a rethinking of the sense of tradition. He discovers that the canon of knowledge, like the plot of history, is not a sacrosanct, untouchable concept, but a historical construction liable to change and subject to manipulations. The circle of knowledge he proposes excludes current scientific fashions; he jettisons the metaphysical baggage of the scholastics; he dismisses physics and dialectics, and circumscribes the status of medicine. At the same time, he responds to the new musical theories and experiments of the fourteenth century, and he gives pride of place to rhetoric, historiography, and the figurative arts. In theology he replaces Aquinas's abstractions with the detailed, steady self-analysis of St. Augustine's *Confessions* and the meditative strains of St. Bonaventure's *Itinerarium Mentis in Deum*. And in his poetics he contrives to place his voice in the interval between the real world and the elusive now of his consciousness. The real world remains, in all its obduracy, outside, but the poet carries within himself an internal world etched with discontinuous moments, varied places, sounds, memories, footprints, wanderings, murmurings, flights and halts — the ephemeral profiles of his exorbitant experience.

What binds together the different aspects of this massive cultural shift is the conviction that history is, above all, the work of man's language and the construction of his imagination. Dante wrote with the knowledge, however ironic, that the poet could impart a moral direction to history: history, for him, has an objective, recognizable reality which his vision would shape. Petrarch, on the contrary, installs the intellectual as the agent of history, as the hero in the empire of culture. The dense tangle of ruins comes alive only in the mind of the intellectual, who is a rhetorician, poet, and moral philosopher, by virtue of his power to evoke history's sedimented memories, echo its myths, and wrest its voice from its sepulchral silence.

From this perspective it is clear why Petrarch, hemmed in by the crumbling images of history, internalizes the outside world. Philology and antiquarianism are his tools for retrieving and safeguarding the relics of the past, but the empire of knowledge is under the sovereignty of the imagination. As a book collector, antiquarian and philologist, Petrarch is the custodian of memories. To internalize this world means that nothing is blotted out, because nothing can be blotted out except at the risk of self-annihilation. In this internalization, finally, the self is not an isolated figure: Petrarch implicates, rather, the ghosts of the past and present in his consciousness, where there occur perpetual encounters with other minds—incongruous encounters, across epochs—with St. Augustine, Seneca, Cicero, and numberless other figures of his displacement of self.

A question, however, forces itself on us. Is there ever a principle of transcendent order, an objective norm by which the world of history is imaginatively re-formed? Or does a political act, such as the making of the self as a public *persona*, depend purely on the subjective taste, the whim and self-interest of the individual? To answer this crucial question I shall look at the role the city of Avignon plays in Petrarch's discourse as it is registered in his *Sine nomine* and in two sonnets from his *Rerum vulgarium fragmenta*.

Petrarch's political judgement of Avignon's usurpation of what properly belongs to the history of the city of Rome is well-known.[22] As the illegitimate see of the popes, Avignon is variously the "golden labyrinth," "Babylon on the Rhone," a "den of thieves," the "woman clothed in scarlet" from Apocalypse 17. And the crimes Petrarch witnesses elicit from him a sinister catalogue of unnatural acts perpetrated by the likes of Pasiphaë, Semiramis, Nero, Domitian, and Nimrod. Playing, as he consistently does, with the Latin etymology of Avignon (*Avinio*), this is the city of drunken frenzy where the authority of God's laws and the laws of nature are perverted.[23]

The exposure of the curia's moral transgressions recalls the language of the Franciscan Spirituals (e.g., Ubertino da Casale's description of the church as "ecclesia carnalis"), Dante's arguments in *Monarchia* and political letters, and Catherine of Siena's appeal to the Popes to return the church to its proper place.[24] But Petrarch's sense of Avignon's political illegitimacy surfaces in the effort and subsequent failure of Cola di Rienzo's attempt to restore the Roman republic against the tyranny of the barons. In the crisis, Petrarch argues, the authority of the church is weakened by its illegal practices, which are a flaunting mockery of the principles of Roman justice. When the tribune Cola di Rienzo is imprisoned, Petrarch writes: "Like a thief of the night or a traitor to his country, he pleads his cause from chains. And, what is never even denied to a sacrilegious person, he is deprived of the right to defend himself before the judges of the world and the magistrates of justice . . . But Rome does not merit this, for in times past her citizens were untouchable and exempt from punishment by law."[25]

Both in *Sine nomine* 4 and in the invective *Contra eum qui maledixit Italiae* Petrarch maintains the impossibility of a *translatio* from Rome to Avignon. The legitimacy of Rome is grounded in the divine plan, for the Incarnation took place, he says, echoing *Monarchia,* when Rome had established peace and justice on earth.[26] Emperors may wander, but the empire is "fixed and stable." The perpetuity of the Empire, secondly, is guaranteed by Vergil's divine prophecy of a dominion without end granted to the Romans. Aware of St. Augustine's disapproval of this prophecy, Petrarch takes him to task, much as Dante had obliquely done.[27] Thirdly, in *Contra eum* Avignon is deemed illegitimate because the eternal city has not completely fallen: its walls and buildings are crumbling, but "gloria nominis immortalis est." The statement, which finds its extension in a rhetorical question such as "what else, then, is all history if not the praise of Rome?"[28] draws history within the orbit of rhetoric, and Clio or Fama is its muse. In sum, Rome is the literal ground of any legitimacy. The claim rests on a theological rationale as well as on a rhetorical understanding of names as forces and topics of discourse. The resistance to the political *translatio* from Rome to Avignon effaces the basis of metaphor, which is the Greek term for *translatio* and which is a trope, as Quintilian writes, whereby "a noun or a verb is transferred from the place to which it properly belongs to another where there is either no literal term or the transferred is better than the literal."[29] The implicit contradiction between a political conviction and poetic metaphor casts poetry into an area of illegitimacy.

There is no palpable causality between the empirical experience of lawlessness in Avignon and Petrarch's rearrangement of the cultural paradigms of his times. Positive philological proofs are unavailable, yet it is of interest to note that exactly in Avignon Marsilius and Ockham elaborate heterodox doctrines on authority. Petrarch, a onetime student of law at Montpellier and Bologna, may have known all along what jurisprudence states, that laws are nothing but legal fictions. At any rate, over and against his harsh judgment of Papal Avignon, it is clear that Avignon, which had become a cosmopolitan intellectual crossroads, was a major catalyst in Petrarch's thought. In Avignon were to be found Nicholas Trivet, Marsilius of Padua, Pierre Bersuire, Ludwig van Kempen, Luca delle Penne, Ockham, Jean de Jandun, Convenevole da Prato, Philippe de Vitry and Richard de Bury. More important in Avignon Petrarch came to know the painter Simone Martini.[30] Painting was a truly novel art form in his time, an art which the Dark Ages had forgotten and modernity had brought back to light. What exactly is painting for Petrarch? And how does he stage a confrontation between painting and poetry in some of his texts?

The kinship between the two "sister arts," as they are so often called, is a cliché of literary history. From Plato's statement that "the poet is like a painter," to Horace's notion of poetry's pictorialism, contained in the dictum "Ut pictura poesis erit. Non erit dissimilis poetica ars picturae," to Leonardo's assertion of the superiority of the graphic over verbal expression, the focus falls on the insight that painting is mute poetry and poetry is a speaking picture.[31] Poets, in turn, have always deployed pictorial or figurative devices: Vergil's *ecphrasis* of Aeneas's shield, Guillaume de Lorris's sculptures in the garden of the *Roman de la Rose*, Boccaccio's *Amorosa Visione*, Chaucer's *House of Fame*, and many other texts exemplify the persistence of the technique. In the lyrical tradition of Provence and Sicily one consistently finds the *topos* of the painted image of the beloved the lover carries within his heart.

These poets entertain no suspicion about the illusionism of painting, embodied in the Platonic repudiation of painting as sheer deception and as a mimetic art listed among activities such as weaving and interior decoration. This suspicion of painting is voiced in the Middle Ages by Isidore of Seville, who in his *Etymologies* states that "*Pictura* is the representation expressing the appearance of anything, which when it is beheld, makes the mind remember. *Pictura* is, moreover, pronounced almost *fictura*. For it is a feigned representation, not the truth. Hence it is also counterfeited, that is, it is smeared over with a fabricated color and possesses nothing of credibility or truth."[32]

What to Isidore is a counterfeit (color, he believes, is a sign of painting's unreality) is greeted by Dante and Boccaccio as the art of the new age.[33] Petrarch's involvement with painting goes beyond their excitement at the discovery of this visual art by Giotto. Petrarch owned a painting by Giotto, which he bequeaths to Francesco da Carrara; in the *Familiarum rerum libri* he links Giotto and Simone Martini with Apelles and Phidias; and he alludes to paintings by Giotto and Simone he had seen in Naples. Of the two he favors Simone, whom he had met in Italy and saw again in Avignon during the years 1339–44 when painters such as Matteo Giovannetti, and Thomas Daristot, and Hugh Wilfred from England were brought in to work at the Palais des Papes.[34] But Petrarch's preference for Simone is also intellectual, for he belongs to the tradition of Duccio and Byzantine miniaturists, a tradition that opposes the mimetic representation of reality that Giotto embodies. Boccaccio, writing of Giotto's aesthetics, praises the powerful illusion of reality he achieves, though he also understands how inscrutable appearances in Giotto's realism are. Simon Martini's painting, on the other hand, places natural objects and the phenomenal world out of their ordinary context in a transfigured space. This is, at least, what one can infer from the two sonnets Petrarch writes on Simone Martini's now lost portrait of Laura.

Per mirar Policleto a prova fiso
con gli altri ch'ebber fama di quell'arte,
mill'anni, non vedrian la minor parte
de la beltà che m'ave il cor conquiso.

Ma certo il mio Simon fu in paradiso
(onde questa gentil donna si parte),
ivi la vide, et la ritrasse in carte
per far fede qua giú del suo bel viso.

L'opra fu ben di quelle che nel cielo
si ponno imaginar, non qui tra noi,
ove le membra fanno a l'alma velo.

Cortesia fe'; né la potea far poi
che fu disceso a provar caldo et gielo,
et del mortal sentiron gli occhi suoi.

(Sonnet 77)

(Even though Polycletus should for a thousand years compete in looking with all the others who were famous in that art, they would never see the smallest part of the beauty that has conquered my heart. But certainly my Simone was in Paradise, whence comes his noble lady; there he saw her and portrayed her on paper, to attest down here to her lovely face. The work is one of those which can be imagined only in Heaven, not here among us, where the body is a veil to the soul; it was a gracious act, nor could he have done it after he came down to feel heat and cold and his eyes took on mortality.)

Quando giunse a Simon l'alto concetto
ch'a mio nome gli pose in man lo stile,
s'avesse dato a l'opera gentile
colla figura voce ed intellecto,

di sospir' molti mi sgombrava il petto,
che ciò ch'altri à piú caro, a me fan vile:
però che 'n vista ella si mostra humile
promettendomi pace ne l'aspetto.

Ma poi ch'i' vengo a ragionar co·llei,
benignamente assai par che m'ascolte,
se risponder savesse a' detti miei.

Pigmalïon, quanto lodar ti dêi
de l'imagine tua, se mille volte
n'avesti quel ch'i' sol una vorrei.

(Sonnet 78)

(When Simon received the high idea which, for my sake, put his hand on his stylus, if he had given to his noble work voice and intellect along with form, he would have lightened my breast of many sighs that make what others prize most vile to me. For in appearance she seems humble, and her expression promises peace; then, when I come to speak to her, she seems to listen most kindly: if she could only reply to my words! Pygmalion, how glad you should be of your statue, since you received a thousand times what I yearn to have just once.)[35]

That the two sonnets are meant to be read together is made clear by their common argument: Laura's painting by Simone Martini. Textual details, such as "mill'anni" in sonnet 77 and "mille volte" in sonnet 78, as well as the two symmetrical references to the sculptors Polycletus and Pygmalion, respectively in sonnets 77 and 78, certainly mark them apart from the poetic sequence. On the face of it, there is even a thematic progression in the two sonnets, which is also suggested by the mythic resonances of the two sculptors. In sonnet 77 the focus is on the artistic process: Simone Martini is said to have been in Paradise to be able to produce this portrait of Laura. The conceit behind the encomium of Simone is the praise of the incomparable beauty of the model. In sonnet 78 the lover is not simply engaged in an aesthetic contemplation of the icon, for a disruptive tension is introduced by the lover's will to animate the figure and possess her. If Polycletus is the emblem of a most excellent sculptor who has been surpassed by Simone, Pygmalion is the sculptor who, according to Ovid's *Metamorphoses* and Jean de Meun's *Roman de la Rose*, carved an ivory statue of an unresponsive maid and is seized by a love-sickness for it until Venus transforms the statue into a living woman.[36] A mythographer such as Arnulf d'Orleans interprets the Ovidian fable as the allegory of idolatry, as the narrative of the artist who loves the work of his own hands as though it were a true woman.[37] The import of such an allegorization is not immediately clear in the two Petrarchan sonnets. At an explicit, literal level, the similes of the mythic sculptors break down in the unfolding of the poetic argument: Polycletus, the text says, could not find an adequate beauty for his art, as Simone did: Petrarch can never embrace, as Pygmalion did a thousand times, Laura's living body.

This collapse of the analogies the poet institutes is meant to suggest, first of all, the otherworldly uniqueness of Laura's beauty and, second, the anguish of the forever unrequited lover. It also suggests, more generally, Petrarch's disjunctive consciousness dramatized over the two sonnets. Thus, in sonnet 77 the painting transposes Laura into an enigmatic, spatial dimension where an otherwordly vision is available. The distinction between the ordinary perception of reality and its aesthetic transfiguration is stressed by the repeated juxtaposition of terms of place: "ivi" (7) is balanced by "qua giú" (8); "nel cielo" (9) by "qui tra noi" (10). The spatial contrast crystallizes the sense of Simone's representation as a supreme visionary experience. The language of vision punctuates the movement of the sonnet: the word "mirar" (1)—literally a gazing—introduces Polycletus's hypothetical contest; we are told that Polycletus and the other painters would never be able to see a portion of Laura's beauty (3); the work of art could only have been imagined in Paradise and not by mortal eyes (9–11). The icon, in its visionariness, opens our eyes to the knowledge that images force us to look within them. If for Dante and the mystics a visionary experience comes forth as a real event, in sonnet 77 vision is an aesthetic construction, the effect of art. This aesthetic vision is suspended between two contradictory experiences of vision: beauty (4) and faith (8). A standard definition of beauty holds that beauty, which is a principle of form, is that which, being seen, pleases. The term "fede," on the other hand, suggests that this painting is not a counterfeit or a *falsigraphia*, but it is a "simia veri," a faithful reproduction of Laura's beauty. Faith, however, is also the evidence of things unseen.[38] This buried resonance of the term questions the referentiality of the model and stresses the iconic value of the portrait.

Sonnet 78 undoes the pattern of signification of sonnet 77. The timeless, transfigured spatiality which painting simulates turns out in sonnet 78 to be illusory. The image of painting is mute and unresponsive to the lover's entreaties (9–11). The muteness of the image is the counterpart of its deceptive surface: Laura in appearance seems humble (7); her expression promises peace (8); she seems to listen most kindly (10). Painting, in short, falls short of the expectations it stirs: its elision of voice and the immobility of the image reveal the portrait to be the mask of death: to look at it is to be caught in the contemplation of death. But we are not to see here a version of the traditional rivalry between painting and poetry. Unlike painting, poetry speaks, but because it speaks it is under the sway of time. By the end of the two sonnets, then, an aporia sets in: painting and poetry are provisionally brought together, only to return, like noncommunicating vessels, to their originary disjunction.

In this contemplation of death emerging from the work of art, the poet, who is unlike Pygmalion, turns out to be like Narcissus. In the *Romance of the Rose*, when Pygmalion discovers his own passion for the image he had carved, he compares his insane love to that of Narcissus, who loved "sa propre figure." Whereas he can touch and kiss his statue, Narcissus is more of a fool because he only has a shadow in the fountain as the object of his desire. Later in the narrative, when the statue turns into living flesh, Pygmalion does not know whether or not what he beholds is a sorcery, a "fantosme ou anemis." The maid, who earlier had been unresponsive to either his speech or prayer (a motif which Petrarch explicitly picks up in sonnet 78), answers that she is no demon and no phantom shape.[39] By his question, however, Pygmalion uncovers the narcissistic quality of his fixation: like Narcissus, who is suspended in a self-fascination in the mirror of the water, Pygmalion is in pursuit of an *eidolon*, which is a Greek term for image or phantom of his own mind.

To claim that Petrarch is like Narcissus entails some notable consequences. Like Narcissus, who gazes at his reflected image and discovers himself, discovers, that is, that he, too, is a shadow, Petrarch looks at Simone's painting of Laura and "sees" in it his own mute reflection. The painted image's fixity, one may add, seduces the lover into its boundaries of beauty, which, ironically, has the fixity of death. Second, to claim that Petrarch is like Narcissus, the figure who never coincides with itself and who mistakes the self for another, implies that desire has an imaginary structure in that it is forever a desire for a figure or a shadow that cannot be reached. That figure can be oneself, another being, or a phantasmatic self-image, which, in the labyrinthine articulation of the imagination, are never identical with and never wholly different from each other. It is of interest, finally, that Petrarch can voice these insights about the self through the new art form of his own times, painting. Just as the figuration of Narcissus shows, there are no clear-cut boundaries between the self and the other, the outside and the inside, the old and the new. The boundaries Petrarch steadily posits between Avignon and Rome (or barbarians and Italians), which are emblems of his vision of political order, are blurred by his poetic practice.

From this standpoint Petrarch can be viewed as "epochal," but on condition that the term be taken in its etymological sense, from the Greek "epoché," which means a halt and a suspension. Petrarch is "epochal" in the sense that his poetry marks a pause and occupies the interval where cognition and judgment hang, and events that are separated from each other in actuality are gathered in thought. What is truly epochal, then, is thinking, which is a fairly common word in Petrarch's diction and which designates the rambling of the mind or the pause of reflection. The essence of thinking for Petrarch, as his *canzone* "Di pensier in pensier" shows, can (and must) be divined from the etymological resonance of "pensier"—from the Latin *pendere*, which means to hang or to suspend. Thought is a suspension, the insertion of a break in the flow of history, the effort to arrest the unseizable flight of time.

This in-between time, which historically we call *medium aevum*, is the unavoidable, forever-recurring time of audacious thought—which is what poetry is. In this in-between time the poet retrieves images of the past and discovers that the achievements of modernity are always inscribed in the past; that the figures of the past have the power to unsettle the complacencies of the present. This in-between time, finally, is the time of contradiction, in which an ideology of power (Rome over Avignon) is reasserted, and in which the imaginative, noncanonical, transgressive experience of Avignon turns out to be the beginning of a new poetic canon, which was to be known as Petrarchism.

NOTES

1. The bibliography on the question of historical periodization is obviously vast. I shall list here some of the items I have found particularly valuable: G. Falco, *La polemica sul Medio Evo* (Turin: Falco, 1933), vol. 1; L. Thorndike, "Renaissance or Prenaissance," *Journal of the History of Ideas* 4 (1943): 65–74; the same issue of this journal is devoted to papers on tradition and innovation in fifteenth-century Italy and contains important contributions by H. Baron, E. Cassirer, P. O. Kristeller, etc., which are pertinent to the questions at hand. Cf. also G. Boas, "Historical Periods," *Journal of Aesthetics and Art Criticism* 11 (1953): 248–54; cf. also "The Prob-

lem of Periodization," in *The Late Italian Renaissance,* ed. Eric Cochrane (New York: Harper and Row, 1970), 23–73, which contains an English version of B. Croce, "La crisi italiana del Cinquecento e il legame del Rinascimento col Risorgimento," *La critica: Rivista di letteratura, storia e filosofia* 37 (1939): 401–11.

2. These viewpoints are sketched by Erwin Panofsky, *Renaissance and Renascences in Western Art* (New York: Harper and Row, 1960), 1–35, which are devoted to "'Renaissance'—Self-definition or Self-deception?" See also E. Garin, "Interpretazioni del Rinascimento," in *Medioevo e Rinascimento* (Bari: Laterza, 1976), 85–100.

3. The notion that there is no dividing line between the culture of the Middle Ages and that of the Renaissance is upheld by L. Thorndike, "Renaissance or Prenaissance," esp. p. 70. The uniqueness of the Italian Renaissance is debated by Charles H. Haskins, *The Renaissance of the Twelfth Century* (Cambridge: Harvard University Press, 1927); cf. also the remarks by J. Boulenger, "Le vrai Siècle de la Renaissance," in *Humanisme et Renaissance* 1 (1934), esp. pp. 9–12, which are in the same spirit as Haskins's assumptions. Of interest may also be the following statement by Etienne Gilson: "La différence entre la Renaissance et le moyen âge n'est pas une différence par excès, mais par défaut. La Renaissance, telle qu'on nous la décrit, n'est pas le moyen âge plus l'homme, mais le moyen âge moins Dieu, et la tragédie, c'est qu'en perdant Dieu la Renaissance allait perdre l'homme lui-même." *Les idées et les lettres* (Paris: J. Vrin, 1932), 192. For a different sense of continuity, cf. P. Renucci, *L'Aventure de l'humanisme européen au Moyen-Age* (IVe–XIVe siècle) (Clermont-Ferrand: Bussac, 1953).

4. Hans Blumenberg, "Aspects of the Epochal Threshold: The Cusan and the Nolan," in *The Legitimacy of the Modern Age,* trans. Robert M. Wallace (Cambridge: MIT Press, 1983), 457–596. The main impulse behind Blumenberg's polemics is the desire to offset the opinions by Karl Löwith, *Meaning in History. The Theological Presuppositions of the Philosophy of History* (Chicago: University of Chicago Press, 1949). The opinions by Hans Georg Gadamer are debated by Blumenberg, 476ff.

5. Henry Osborn Taylor, *The Mediaeval Mind* (London: Macmillan and Co., 1938), vol. 2. For the issue on the "Alterity of the Middle Ages," see *New Literary History* 10 (1979).

6. This sense of the past as not entirely past is best conveyed by a famous image which John of Salisbury in the twelfth century attributes to Bernard of Chartres (eleventh century) and which Alexander Neckham picks up in the thirteenth century: "We are dwarfs on the shoulders of giants: thanks to them, we see better and farther away than they did."

7. Gordon Leff, *Paris and Oxford Universities in the Thirteenth and Fourteenth Centuries. An Institutional and Intellectual History* (New York: John Wiley and Son, 1968). Cf. also *Chartularium Universitatis Parisiensis,* ed. H. Denifle and E. Chatelain, 4 vols. (Paris: Delalain, 1889–97); P. Mandonnet, *Siger de Brabant et l'Averroïsme latin au XIIIe siècle,* 2 vols. (Louvain: Institut supérieur de philosophie de l'université, 1908–11); D. A. Callus, "The Introduction of Aristotelean Learning to Oxford," *Proceedings of the British Academy* 29 (1943): 229–81; more generally see

C. H. Haskins, *The Rise of the Universities* (Ithaca: Cornell University Press, 1957). For Marsilius see his *The Defender of Peace,* trans. Alan Gewirth (New York: Columbia University Press, 1956). See also Alan Gewirth, "John of Jandun and the *Defensor Pacis,* " *Speculum* 23 (1948): 267–72; G. Post, *"Plena Potestas* and Consent in Medieval Assemblies," *Traditio* 1 (1943): 355–408. On Biblical exegesis see Henri de Lubac, *Exégèse médiévale. Les quatre sens de l'Écriture* (Paris: Aubier, 1959–64).

8. On this see the still classic article by Theodor E. Mommsen, "Petrarch's Conception of the 'Dark Ages,'" *Speculum* 17 (1942): 226–42, reprinted in *Medieval and Renaissance Studies,* ed. E. F. Rice, Jr. (Ithaca: Cornell University Press, 1959), 106–29. See also F. Simone, "La coscienza della Rinascita negli Umanisti," *La Rinascita* 2 (1939): 838–71, and 3 (1940): 163–86; W. K. Ferguson, "Humanist Views of the Renaissance," *American Historical Review* 45 (1939): 1–28. G. S. Gordon, *Medium Aevum and the Middle Ages* (Society for Pure English, Tract. No. 19) (Oxford: Oxford University Press, 1925), studies the early occurrences of terms such as *media tempora, media aetas,* and *medium aevum.*

9. The history of the attitudes toward the Middle Ages has been studied by Lucie Varga, *Das Schlagwort vom "finsteren Mittelalter"* (Baden: R. M. Rohrer, 1932).

10. The quotation is from *De sui ipsius et multorum ignorantia,* from F. Petrarca, *Opere Latine,* ed. A. Bufano (Turin: UTET, 1975), 1070. In *De Africa* (9. 453ff.) Petrarch envisions a better future time when "Letheas . . . sopor" will cease and the pure radiance of the past will be regained: "Poterunt discussis forte tenebris / Ad purum priscumque iubar remeare nepotes."

11. The phrase "uso moderno" occurs in *Purgatorio* 26.113. The "new" or modernity is not necessarily a term for progress in the *Divine Comedy.* There is a ceaseless pattern of alternation between times of artistic achievements and ages of barbarism—and never simple progress—in Dante's imagination. Cf 11.91–102: "Oh vana gloria de l'umane posse! / com' poco verde in su la cima dura, / se non è giunta da l'etati grosse. / Credette Cimabue ne la pittura / tener lo campo, e ora ha Giotto il grido, / sì che la fama di colui è scura. / Così ha tolto l'uno a l'altro Guido / la gloria de la lingua; e forse è nato / chi l'uno e l'altro caccerà del nido. / Non è il mondan romore altro ch'un fiato / di vento, ch'or vien quinci e or vien quindi, / e muta nome perchè muta lato."

12. G. Boccaccio, *Lettere edite ed inedite,* ed. F. Corazzini (Florence: Sansoni, 1877), 189ff.

13. F. Petrarch, *Le familiari,* ed. Vittorio Rossi and Umberto Bosco, 4 vols. (Florence: Sansoni, 1933–42), 2.6.2, 55–60. For the date of the letter see F. E. H. Wilkins, *A Tentative Chronology of Petrarch's Prose Letters* (Chicago: University of Chicago Press, 1929). On the letter see the excellent remarks by Thomas M. Greene, *The Light in Troy. Imitation and Discovery in Renaissance Poetry* (New Haven: Yale University Press, 1982), 88–93. Greene brings to bear both the *Mirabilia Urbis* and book 8 of the *Aeneid* on Petrarch's imaginative reconstruction of Rome. Of interest are also the remarks by Mommsen in "Petrarch's Conception of the 'Dark

Ages,'" 114–18. On the motif of Roman ruins cf. W. Rehm, *Der Untergang Roms in abendländischen Denken* (Leipzig: Dieterich, 1930).

14. The sense of place—which is central to Petrarch's imagination—can best be illustrated by this memory of Vaucluse: "There, I remember happily, I began my *Africa* . . . There I wrote a large share of my letters in prose and verse, and I composed almost all of my *Bucolicum Carmen* . . . No locality ever gave me more leisure or a keener stimulus" (*Fam.* 2.8.3, 160). The translation is taken from *Letters from Petrarch*, trans. Morris Bishop (Bloomington: Indiana University Press, 1966), 69ff.

15. The translation is from Mommsen, "Petrarch's Conception of the 'Dark Ages,'" 115.

16. For this question of Rome in the Middle Ages (which includes St. Augustine's *City of God* as well as Dante's *Monarchia* and the *Divine Comedy*) see C. N. Cochrane, *Christianity and Classical Culture: A Study of Thought and Action from Augustus to Augustine* (Oxford: Oxford University Press, 1968); Charles T. Davis, *Dante and the Idea of Rome* (Oxford: Clarendon Press, 1957); Giuseppe Mazzotta, *Dante, Poet of the Desert. History and Allegory in the Divine Comedy* (Princeton: Princeton University Press, 1979).

17. The fall of Rome had been predicted, according to Biblical exegetes, by Nebuchadnezzar's dream of the statue as told by Daniel 2, 31ff. Cf. the gloss on this by Philip of Harvengt, "De somnio regis Nabuchodonosor," *Patrologia Latina* 203, col. 586. See on this J. W. Swain, "The Theory of the Four Monarchies: Opposition History under the Roman Empire," *Classical Philology* 35 (1940): 1–21. Vergil's prophecy is from *Aeneid* 1.278ff. It was the event of the fall of Rome, furthermore, that lay behind St. Augustine's decision to write *The City of God*, in which the eternity of the earthly city is a counterfeit of the real eternity in the Heavenly City. On this see Mazzotta, *Dante, Poet of the Desert*, 170–75. For the reaction of St. Jerome see below, note 20.

18. Irenaeus, *Contre les hérésies* (Paris: Editions du Cerf, 1952), 2.5.26; Tertullian, *De resurrectione carnis*, PL 2, cols. 791–836.

19. Lactantius, "De postremis temporibus ac de urbe Roma," in *De divinis institutionibus*, 7.25, PL 6, col. 811. For an excellent treatment of St. Augustine's reflections on the city in ruin see Theodor E. Mommsen, "St. Augustine and the Christian Idea of Progress: The Background of *The City of God*," *Journal of the History of Ideas* 12 (1951): 346–74, reprinted in *Medieval and Renaissance Studies*, 265–98. My indebtedness to this excellent article is great. The lines by the Pseudo-Bede are from *Flores ex diversis, quaestiones et parabola*, PL 94, col. 543.

20. St. Jerome is quoting Psalm 39.2. The passage, here given in the translation by Mommsen, "St. Augustine and the Christian Idea of Progress," 266, comes from his *Commentaries on Ezekiel*, PL 25, cols. 15–16. The remark is an introduction to the exegesis of the first book.

21. "Itaque die quodam, dum in eam mentionem incidessemus, flagitasti ut dicerem explicite unde putarem liberales et unde mechanicas initium habuisse, quod carptim ex me audieras . . . Accipe igitur quod tunc dixi, verbis forte aliis sed eadem profecto sententia. Verum quid agimus? nam et non parva res est et epystola hec abunde crevit . . .

differamus que restant in proximum diem ... Sed quid rursum cogito, quid ve polliceor tibi diem proximum epystolamque alteram? nec diei unius opus est nec epystolare negotium; *librum exigit*, quem non prius aggrediar — si tamen curis maioribus non retrahor atque disturbor — quam in solitudinem meam me fortuna revexerit." *Fam.* 2.6.2, 58–59 (my emphasis). Cf. also the speculations by L. Venturi, "La critica d'arte e Francesco Petrarca," *L'Arte* 25 (1922): 238–44.

22. F. Petrarca, *Sine nomine*, in *Lettere polemiche e politiche*, ed. Ugo Dotti (Bari: Laterza, 1974). See especially Letter 10, to Francesco Nelli, where Avignon is called Babylon, golden labyrinth, etc.

23. *Sine nomine*, Letter 2, to Cola di Rienzo, has the following: "O Avinio, cuius vinea, si quid coniectoribus fidei est, botros amarissimas et cruentam proferet vindemiam" (20). The pun is operative in sonnet 137: "L'avara Babilonia à colmo il sacco / D'ira di Dio e di vitij empij e rei / Tanto che scoppia, ed à fatti suoi dei / Non Giove et Palla, ma Venere e *Bacco*" (my emphasis).

24. See *Babylon on the Rhone. A Translation of Letters by Dante, Petrarch, and Catherine of Siena on the Avignon Papacy,* trans. Robert Coogan, *Studia Humanitatis* (Madrid: J. P. Turanzas, 1983) for the various spiritual perspectives on Avignon.

25. The translation is taken from *Babylon on the Rhone,* Letter 4, 54.

26. "When was there ever such a peace, such tranquillity, such justice, such esteem for virtue, such reward for goodness, such punishments for the wicked, and such sound judgement in the affairs of state as when the world had one head and that head was Rome? Was it not in that epoch when the most powerful lover of peace and justice chose to be born of a virgin and to visit the earth?" Ibid., Letter 4. Cf. the corresponding notions in Dante's *Monarchia* 1.16.1–3, and 2.10.4; 2.11–12.

27. "'Imperium sine fine dedi.' Here Augustine reasonably comments: 'For how shall he give an empire without end who never gave nor was ever able to give anything except that which a sinful and mortal man can give? ...' I will not treat this matter of who passed down the Roman Empire, for it is certain that none but the omnipotent God gave it ... Augustine asks where this kingdom might be: 'Is it on earth or in heaven? Certainly it is on earth ... If those things that God himself has made shall pass away, how much more swiftly will pass that which Romulus founded!' In these things Augustine reproaches Vergil ... And so in this instance, Augustine, employing different words, accuses and excuses Vergil as I understand it." Ibid., letter 4, 57–59. For Dante's oblique polemic with St. Augustine over the vale of Rome, see Mazzotta, *Dante, Poet of the Desert,* 180–88.

28. *Contra eum qui maledixit Italiae* in F. Petrarca, *Opere Latine,* ed. A. Bufano (Turin: UTET, 1975), 1164. The statement is the radical reversal of St. Augustine's conviction that Rome is one of the series of earthly cities. Cf. *The City of God,* 15.5.

29. *Institutio Oratoria,* ed. Jean Cousin (Paris: Société d'édition "Les Belles Lettres," 1975–80), 8.6.4.

30. Useful information on the city of Avignon at the time of the popes is available in Robert Brun, *Avignon au temps des papes* (Paris: Librairie A.

Colin, 1928); E. Castelnuovo, *Un pittore italiano alla corte di Avignone* (Turin: Einaudi, 1962); see also Beryl Smalley, *English Friars and Antiquity* (New York: Barnes and Noble, 1960), esp. 240–307. Of great interest, although tangentially relevant to the present argument, is Eugenio Garin, "La cultura fiorentina nella seconda metà del trecento e i 'barbari britanni,'" *La Rassegna della letteratura italiana* 62 (1960): 181–95.

31. Jean H. Hagstrum, *The Sister Arts* (Chicago: University of Chicago Press, 1958); R. Lee, *Ut Pictura Poesis* (New York: Norton, 1967); Mario Praz, *Mnemosyne* (Princeton: Princeton University Press, 1970); E. Panofsky, *Studies in Iconology* (New York: Icon Books, 1972); cf. Horace's *Ars Poetica*, 361–65. Cf. also Plato's *Republic*, 10.605A; and Aristotle's *Poetics*, 1448a.5.

32. Isidore of Seville, *Etymologiarum sive Originum Libri XX*, ed. W. M. Lindsay (Oxford: Clarendon Press, 1966), 19.16.1–2: "Pictura autem est imago exprimens speciem rei alicuius, quae dum visa fuerit ad recordationem mentem reducit. Pictura autem dicta quasi fictura; est enim imago ficta, non veritas. Hinc et fucata, id est ficto quodam colore inlita, nihil fidei et veritatis habentia. Unde et sunt quaedam picturae quae corpora veritatis studio coloris excedunt et fidem, dum augere contendunt, ad mendacium provehunt."

33. Cf. Adolfo Venturi, "Le arti figurative al tempo di Dante," *L'Arte* 24 (1921): 230–40; see also the excellent articles by Creighton Gilbert, "Cecco d'Ascoli e la pittura di Giotto," *Commentari* 24 (Jan.–June 1973): 19–25; "The Fresco by Giotto in Milan," *Arte Lombarda*, n.s., 47–48 (1977): 31–72. Cf. *Purgatorio*, 11.91–99. The praise of Giotto, however, is placed within the context of punished pride—a strategy by which Dante undercuts the belief in the permanence of artistic achievements. Boccaccio's praise of Giotto is in *Decameron* 6.5: "E per ció, avendo egli quella arte ritornata in luce, che molti secoli sotto gli error d'alcuni ... era stata sepulta ..." Boccaccio's metaphor of light, to describe Giotto's exhuming the buried art, reverses the image of eclipse ("sì che la fama di colui oscura") in *Purgatorio* 11.96. For Petrarch's involvement with painting see also his *Testament*, trans. and ed. T. E. Mommsen (Ithaca: Cornell University Press, 1957). See also M. Meiss, *Painting in Florence and Siena after the Black Death* (Princeton: Princeton University Press, 1951). Cf. Petrarch's *De remediis*, ed. R. Schottlaender (München: W. Fink, 1975), 1.40; *Fam.* 5.17, 23.19; *Seniles* (Basil: Petri, 1554), 2.3.

34. Castelnuovo, *Un pittore italiano alla corte di Avignone*, 15ff.: Valerio Mariani, *Simone Martini e il suo tempo* (Naples: L.G.E., 1968). For the pictoral descriptions of allegorical moralizations (figures, images, pictures, etc.) see B. Smalley, "Commentators and Preachers in France," in *English Friars and Antiquity in the Early Fourteenth Century* (Oxford: Blackwell, 1960), 240–64.

35. The Italian text is from *Canzoniere*, ed. G. Contini (Turin: Einaudi, 1964). I rely heavily on the comments in *Le rime*, eds. G. Carducci and S. Ferrari (Florence: Sansoni, 1960). The English translation is taken from *Petrarch's Lyric Poems*, trans. and ed. Robert M. Durling (Cambridge: Harvard University Press, 1976).

36. *Metamorphoses*, 10.243ff; Jean de Meun, *Le Roman de la Rose*, ed. E. Langlois (Paris: E. Champion, 1924), 5.20817ff.

37. Arnulf of Orleans, *Arnolfo d'Orléans, un cultore di Ovidio nel secolo XII*, ed. Fausto Ghisalberti, *Memorie del Reale Istituto Lombardo di Scienze e Lettere di Milano* 24 (1932): 223.

38. Epistle to the Hebrews 11, 1, for the standard definition of faith. Cf. also *Paradiso* 24.64–66. For a definition of beauty in terms of vision see *Summa Theologica*, 1.5, ad. 1. Cf. also note 32, above, for Isidore's sense of the links between "fides" and "painting."

39. *Roman de la Rose*, 21154.

An Intellectual Anthropology of Marriage in the Middle Ages

STEPHEN G. NICHOLS

We don't marry for ourselves, whatever people say; we marry as much or even more for posterity, for our family. The customs and concerns of marriage affect our race well beyond ourselves.

MONTAIGNE

Medieval Marriage and the Marginality of Women

Marriage and literature had a great deal to do with the cultural status of women in medieval Europe. In both instances, women occupied a paradoxical role: their participation was crucial, but their power and autonomy were marginalized. At the same time, particularly in literature, they managed repeatedly to bring about fundamental changes in cultural perceptions, and in the nature of the phenomenon for which their participation was requisite, but their power strictly limited.

Marriage, like literature, was mimetic, a symbolic representation of the political order. As Georges Duby says: "Marriage, which is necessarily overt, public, ceremonious, *surrounded by special words and deeds*, is at the center of any system of values, at the junction between the material and the spiritual. It regulates the transmission of wealth from one generation to another, and so underlies and cannot be dissociated from a society's 'infrastructures.'"[1]

Just as medieval literature participated in the dual codes of the patristic tradition in religion and the profane tradition of Latin and the vernacular, so, as Duby again points out, "The codes by which marriage is governed belong to two orders: the profane and what we may call the religious."[2]

The two systems of marriage and literature tended to reinforce one another in the early Christian era. They did so in a way that relied on religion to marginalize women in terms of authority and power. Four precepts, drawn from the Old Testament, reinforced by the teachings of Christ on marriage, assured the primacy of the masculine:

1. "It is not good that man should be alone." God decreed that the human race should be of two sexes, and that there should be a union between them.
2. But he created the sexes unequal: "I will make him an help [adjutorium] meet for him [similem sui]." Man came first, and kept that precedence. He was made in the image of God, while woman came second, a reflection of his image. Eve's body was flesh of Adam's flesh, made from one of his ribs, and thus inferior.
3. The two bodies were designed to merge into one: "A man shall leave his father and mother, and shall cleave unto his wife: and they shall be one flesh." Marriage led to unity.
4. But marriage did not do away with inequality. Woman was inferior, weak; it was because of her that man fell and was driven out of Paradise. Henceforth, husband and wife were doomed to imperfect couplings, to love that must be mingled with shame. The woman was awarded an additional share of punishment, having to suffer the domination of the man and the pains of childbirth.[3]

Genesis 2 and the Feminine Anthropology of the Church Fathers

Duby does not point out the link between the disenfranchisement of women in this religio-political system of marriage and the fundamental assumption of the illegitimacy of female discourse. Yet, both in the original texts of Genesis 2 and in Patristic literature, we find a direct link between the marginalization of woman and hostility towards her speech. Patristic exegesis, from Augustine on, took Genesis 2–3 as a basic text for construing the Christian philosophical anthropology—the nature of humans in the divine order of things—so important for the medieval construction of social and political systems.

Since it concerned the creation of man and woman, and recounted the Fall, as the primordial event determining the historical shape of the postlapsarian world, Genesis 2–3 played a significant role for the Latin West in shaping notions of marriage and the relative status of the sexes. The two chapters were also perceived as a drama of discourse and interpretation. Genesis 2 established the principle of direct communication between humanity and the divine creator, while Gen. 3:14–19 detailed the destruction of the "harmony of Adam and Eve's relationship with the rest of the created world and with God himself."[4] As G. R. Evans recently observed: "The most important effect, in the eyes of a number of early christian writers, was the breakdown of communication between man and God . . . It is upon this supposition, that man, through his own fault, is no longer able to understand what God says to him except dimly and imperfectly, that the whole of medieval exegesis is founded."[5]

In extensive commentaries on Gen. 1:26–7 and 2–3, two basic trends emerged in the late classical and early medieval period: one shaped by the Latin Fathers, particularly Saint Augustine, the other coming from the Greek Fathers under the influence of Origen (c. 185–c. 254) and Plotinus (204 or 205–270). The Latin movement interpreted the Creation and Fall as history conceived as a mimetic model for personal conversion and salvation.[6] The Greek view, particularly in the work of Gregory of Nazianzus (c. 330–389/90) and Gregory of Nyssa (c. 335–c. 394) treated the Creation allegorically.[7]

In the opinion of the Latin Fathers, Creation was an event in real (historical) time which viewed gender differentiation and hierarchy as part of the divine model for humans. In this view, sexual differentiation at the time of creation showed God's wisdom in creating a weak, inferior being, woman, as the instrument of the Fall which, although not preordained, was anticipated. Woman's sexual differentiation emphasized the body, the seat of sensuality and irrationality, which qualities were said to characterize feminine discourse. For the Latin Fathers, this "historical" view amply justified the subordination of women in marriage.

The Greek allegorical interpretation, however, took a different turn. Historical time did not begin until after the Fall, and sexual differentiation was a consequence and mark of the postlapsarian world. Prior to the Fall, humans were not sexually divided. Not Genesis 2–3, but Gen. 1:26 and 1:27 serve as the text for this perspective:

Let us make man [*adam*, "mankind"] in our image, in the likeness of ourselves, and let *them* be masters . . .

God created man in the image of himself, in the image of God he created him, male and female he created them.

This text authorized a double model of the creation: one into divine image without sexual division, the other, foreseen by God, but not intentionally part of the divine model, according to sexual differentiation.[8]

The Fall could not then be taken as confirmation of a divine intention to differentiate the sexes by gender and hierarchy, nor used as proof of woman's inherent inferiority. We will return to these issues when we consider the Latin philosopher, Johannes Scotus Eriugena, who translated—and transformed in no small measure—the Greek model into Latin in the ninth century. It is through the kind of nuancing of mainstream patristic thought represented by Eriugena's philosophical anthropology, especially as it influenced the schools in the eleventh and twelfth centuries, that a few women writers were able to provide a new and controversial view of female sexuality and marriage as social institution and literary thematic.

Genesis 2–3 and Augustine

Genesis 2 establishes dual orders of discourse. The first represents the language of order and authority, the sheer power of creation by divine command [*dixit Dominus Deus*]. Second comes the sorting and ordering process by which the created beings (and objects) are categorized. That is the act that God authorizes Adam to undertake. Adam's discourse figures, in the Vulgate, as a kind of test, an experiment to define the potential powers of language in laying down categorical boundaries that also work as descriptors of the world as it emerges from chaos into meaning. But Adam's language is also an experiment in delegating authority: "The Lord God . . . brought these [beasts] to Adam to see what he might call them" [*adduxit ea ad Adam ut videret quid vocaret ea* (2:19)]. Gen. 2:19–20 set forth both the limits of legitimation for the authoritative human discourse—it may name, but not create—while showing the collaborative relationship between God's creative *dixit* and the man's ordering *vocavit:*

[O]mne enim quod vocavit Adam animae viventis ipsum est nomen eius (19) appellavitque Adam nominibus suis cuncta animantia / et universa volatilia caeli et omnes bestias terrae / Adam vero non inveniebatur adiutor similis eius. (20)

(For what Adam called all living souls that is its name. [19]
And Adam called by names all animals, and all birds of the
heavens, and all wild beasts of the land but Adam did not find
a helpmate like himself. [20])

It is in this context that we find the creation of woman and the definition of marriage. Gen. 2:22–23 recount the dream God sends to
Adam and the consequent creation of Eve from his rib. This material creation from the flesh — prefiguring postlapsarian childbirth —
contrasts directly with Adam's own earlier creation, where God
literally breathes life into him [*et inspiravit in faciem eius spira-
culum vitae* (2:7)]. Moreover, in the case of Adam's creation, the
word *caro* (flesh) does not occur, whereas it figures prominently
in Eve's.

It occurs descriptively in 2:21: *tulit unam de costis eius et re-
plevit carnem pro ea* ([God] drew forth one of [Adam's] ribs and covered it with flesh). More significantly, Adam uses *caro* twice in
the first instance of direct discourse ascribed to him (2:23). The
gnomic quality of this speech gives it an epigrammatic force that
suggests the mnemonics of folk law.

[D]ixitque Adam / hoc nunc os ex ossibus meis et caro de
carne mea / haec vocabitur virago quoniam de viro sumpta est.

(And Adam said: This now is bone from my bone and flesh
from my flesh; this will be called woman for it was taken
from man.)

Two important movements take place in this and the verse that
follows. First, if God provides the living being in Adam's image
[*adiutor similis eius*], Adam determines its gender by his naming.
The transformation from neuter *hoc* to feminine *haec*, and then
to subspecies, *virago*, takes place in a rhetorically overdetermined
insistence on Eve's metonymic relationship to Adam: *os ex ossibus meis et caro de carne mea*, etc.

Second, the law of marriage follows the linguistic gender determination, again as a metonymic hierarchizing legal formulation
in Gen. 2:24.

[Q]uam ob rem relinquet homo patrem suum et matrem / et
adherebit uxori suae et erunt duo in carne una.

(Thus on account of this event, a man will leave his father
and mother and join himself to his wife and they will be two
in one flesh.)

Note the simultaneous introduction of a new set of gender terms: *uxor* (wife), *pater*, and *mater*. Missing, of course, is the term *maritus* (husband). Instead, we have the generic *homo* (man). Finally, marriage restores the original unity of male flesh by the marital union of "two in one flesh."

Adam's authoritative discourse distinguishes the woman only as type, not as individual. The pair are called *Adam et uxor eius* (2:25), and throughout the narrative of the Fall, she appears as *mulier* when cited alone, or *uxor eius* when they're together. Only after the Fall does Adam name Eve [3:20]. From the viewpoint of the dominant discourse on marriage, the feminine remains stereotyped and undifferentiated: the inchoate Other identified by role and general characteristics. Deuteronomy 21, 22, and 24 continue this tendency, even though the marriage laws define some rights for the wife.

It is in this identification of woman by characteristic behavior that we find the second order of discourse laid down in Genesis. If Genesis 2 offers the paradigm of legitimation for human speech, Genesis 3 characterizes feminine discourse, by negative example, as dangerous, not through intentionality, but through its power to translate the unconscious. Female discourse is the unmediated representation of the libido, or fleshly desire.

The term for woman, *virago*, suggests the ambiguous resemblance to man, *vir*, as a kind of gender code-switching implicit in the classical term, which meant "man-like woman."[9] In the same way, the woman's discourse, and its context in Genesis 3 parodically resembles the man's, but with a difference. Adam has God as an interlocutor; the woman has the serpent, described as "shrewder than all other beasts made by God." God makes affirmative or imperative propositions to the man, who simply carries them out. There is neither dialogue nor interrogation.

But Genesis 3 initiates the first dialogue between created beings, and that dialogue questions the legitimation process of divine authority. Satan's first word is *cur* (why), introducing the question: "Why did God order you not to eat . . . " The question introduces a scene that is predicated on an assumption of ego gratification as a stereotypical feminine behavior. The woman is perceived as the sum of actions responsive to external stimuli. The larger philosophical or metaphysical issue of divine authority has been submerged under the more immediate one of deferred pleasure. The woman's part, even in this starring role, is limited to responding to Satan and acting upon his insinuations. The woman's actions (3:6) mirror the serpent's discourse (3:5) by way of illustrating the danger of language's mimetic power in the absence of a controlling *mens*. The consequence of this parodic dialogue lies in the demonstration of the woman's ability to effect a radical change (for the worse) in her husband's condition. It offers explicit justification for limiting her autonomy, and her power in marriage, while graphically illustrating the principle that the human capacity for libidinal behavior, while present in both sexes, may be found in its purest form in the female. This assumption became a cornerstone for misogynistic marriage laws.

In commenting on this passage, Saint Augustine explicitly connects serpentine discourse and female language, thus realizing the metonymy that Genesis 3 suggests. In Book 14, Chapter 11 of *The City of God*, Augustine analyzes Lucifer's choice of the serpent as the instrument for "work[ing] his way into the heart of man."

> This slippery animal, of course, which moves in twisting coils, was a suitable tool for his work . . . [A]nd misusing it as his instrument, he conversed deceitfully with the woman. In so doing, he no doubt began with the lower member of that human couple in order to arrive gradually at the whole. Presumably he did not think that the man was readily gullible or that he could be snared by his own mistake, but only if he gave way to the mistake of another.[10]

The serpent and the woman occupy the same metaphorical space here as "instruments misused" by Lucifer. The not-so-subtle connecting thread of speech from Lucifer to the serpent to Eve determines this metaphoric resemblance. Eve's role, like that of the serpent, determines her ethical or metaphysical status. She does not simply and unwittingly transmit a message from Lucifer to her husband. In effect, there is no message to transmit, but rather a set of variable emotions—beginning with Lucifer's rage and envy—that motivate each speaker in turn: first the serpent, then Eve. Eve's seduction by the serpent and then her seduction of Adam turn out to be discursive reenactments of her creation in Genesis 2. The seductions demonstrate her status as *caro* (flesh), the material antiphrasis to the spiritual *caritas* (*carus*, "valued, esteemed") that will ultimately redeem the Fall in this typological struggle between flesh and spirit.

In Eve's narrative syntax, perception and gesture follow rapidly as direct object to verb:

[V]idit igitur mulier quod bonum esset lignum ad vescendum / et pulchrum oculis aspectuque delectabile / et tulit de fructu illius et comedit deditque viro suo. (3:6)

(The woman saw then that the wood was good to eat and beautiful to the eyes and of delightful form and she plucked some of its fruit and ate it and gave it to her husband.)

Augustine saw this passage as describing the genesis of transgressive lust, relating it to Christ's stricture in Matt. 5:28: "If anyone looks at a woman lustfully, he has already committed adultery with her in his heart" (*The City of God* [14:10]).[11] By conflating the two passages, Augustine equates Eve's primordial desire for the tree in Gen. 3:6 with the carnal lust of Matt. 5:28; in one movement, he thus makes Eve's desire the model for masculine (adulterous) concupiscence. In other words, Augustine sees carnality as mimetic gender switching: men may lust, but in so doing they cast themselves in a feminine image. Adam, Aaron, and Solomon (exemplary sinners cited by Augustine) did not sin because they were deceived, as Eve was deceived by the serpent, but through imitative solidarity with their female companions: "nor is it credible that Solomon mistakenly thought he should serve idols; he was driven to such acts of irreligion by the blandishments of women."

> Similarly, when we consider the situation of that first man and his woman, two fellow human beings all alone and married to each other, we must suppose that he was not led astray to transgress the law of God because he believed that she spoke the truth, but because he was brought to obey her by the close bond of their alliance.[12]

The Fall is thus a negative recreation. Made from male flesh in Genesis 2, Eve remakes Adam in the image of *her* flesh in Genesis 3, thereby imprinting him with the ineradicable image of her own deception. Even before the Fall, Eve embodies, *in potentia*, the imperfect language of the fallen state. She seduces Adam into speaking the carnal vernacular introduced by Satan rather than the spiritual and hierarchical language authorized by God. If Adam demonstrated the political status of institutional language in Genesis 2—where we saw this, literally, to be the language of identity, of naming—Eve demonstrates its vulnerability.

In Genesis 3, she reveals the dualism exacted on the subject by the masculine language of identity. In social terms, the dualism lies between the hieratic language of law [writing] versus the demotic folk culture associated with orality. Augustine under-lines the dualism by linking two other archetypal transgressions against the law in the Old Testament—by Aaron and Solomon—with Adam's: both the priest, Aaron, and the ruler, Solomon, aban-don orthodox, that is, rule-governed, law in favor of and in response to the demotic. What's more, the demotic and the femi-nine appear interchangeable: the "mistaken multitude" [erranti populo] in Aaron's case, and the "blandishments of women" [blan-ditiis femineis] in Solomon's.[13]

In short, such interpretations cast Genesis 2–3 in what we rec-ognize as an opposition between socio-political, cultural, and lin-guistic forces: literally, the canonical versus the noncanonical. Latin *canon*, derived from Greek *kanon* = *regula*, bore a range of connotations linking literary and linguistic rule governance to religio-political orthodoxy. "Canon" connoted "grammatical rule; metrical scheme or type; annual payment to Rome from the prov-inces; other forms of scheduled payments." In the early Christian community, it came to designate "lists of Biblical books or tables of rituals; rules (statute, canon) of the Christian life (especially such as are settled by a church synod or council as binding, partic-ularly on the secular clergy, or—later—on monks); the canon of the Mass."[14]

The canonical defines the expressive forms of high culture; these, in turn, encode the orthodox concepts of human behavior consonant with the philosophical anthropology espoused by the church Fathers. For Augustine this meant attacking directly the *motus animae* or vital force of individual self-expression, which he identified, on the strength of Gen. 3:6, with the erotic. For Augustine, sex is the idiom of the carnal vernacular, and the libido the moving force of the uncanonical demotic. Through the woman, he says, the man was confirmed in his fleshliness: "Man, who would have been spiritual even in flesh [*carne spiritalis*] if he had observed the rule, became carnal in mind [*mente carnalis*] as well."[15]

He uses spatializing metaphors to define the tension between the spiritual and the material, mind and body, with the feminine serving as the vehicle for the eroticized space. "Pleasure [*volup-tas*], however, is preceded by a certain craving that is felt in the flesh as its own desire [*cupiditas*] such as hunger, thirst, and the desire that is most commonly called lust [*libido*] when it affects the sex organs, though this is a general term applicable to any kind of desire."[16]

Marriage for Augustine and the Latin Fathers was problematic

precisely because, in authorizing sexuality, it seemed to authorize the body as eroticized space, where the sex act ritually
repeated Eve's remaking of Adam in her fleshly image. In this economy, such motivations as *libido, voluptas,* and *cupiditas* reify the
flesh and threaten both the mind-body distinction and the primacy of mind over body on which patristic anthropology set such a
high premium:

> [T]his lust asserts its power not only over the entire body, nor
> only externally, but also from within. It convulses all of a
> man when the emotion in his mind combines and mingles
> with the carnal drive to produce a pleasure unsurpassed
> among those of the body. The effect of this is that at the very
> moment of its climax there is an almost total eclipse of acu-
> men and, as it were, sentinel alertness. But surely any friend
> of wisdom and holy joys, who lives in wedlock but knows, as
> the Apostle admonished, "how to possess his bodily vessel in
> holiness and honour, not in the disease of lust like the gen-
> tiles who do not know God" (Thess. 4.4), would prefer, if he
> could, to beget children without this kind of lust. For he
> would want his mind to be served, even in this function of
> engendering offspring, by the parts created for this kind of
> work, just as it is served by the other members, each assigned
> to its own kind of work. They would be set in motion when
> the will urged, not stirred to action when hot lust surged.[17]

If Augustine articulated the concept of the feminine as the eroticized space, the demotic idiom of postlapsarian marriage, he was
not alone among the church Fathers in viewing libido as central
to the problem. As a matter of fact, he was far more positive
toward marriage than either Jerome or Gregory the Great, both
more strident than Augustine in seeing marriage and women as
constant threats to "the holiness of the Christian (male) vessel."[18]
Duby points out that by the Carolingian era a more positive attitude toward marriage developed. One sign of the attempt to
improve the moral standing of marriage was the Council of Paris
in 829, presided over by Charlemagne's son Louis the Pious. The
council affirmed eight main propositions, of which the first reasserted that God instituted marriage and that the link between religion and marriage was to be found in Genesis. Libido was con-
demned, but men were to "cherish their wives in chastity and
honor them as they would any weaker being."[19]

Eriugena and Sensual Perception

The Council of Paris may have been conservative in affirming what was essentially Augustine's position. But the Carolingian court in the ninth century was the scene of a much more radical development.[20] It was there that one of Charles the Bald's philosophers, Eriugena [c. 810–c. 877], a translator and admirer of Greek Christian Platonism, reconceived the Genesis narrative as allegory, rather than as history, thus opening possibilities for new conceptualizations of women.

Eriugena could not abolish the negative image of Eve promulgated by mainstream patristics, but he was one of the first to enable a revisionist approach to female anthropology, however tentative. And he did so by espousing what was in the ninth century itself a marginal discourse: the neo-Platonism of the Greek Fathers. Marginal, that is, until Eriugena's translations and the synthesis of their thought he provides in his monumental and dense *Periphyseon* (*On the Division of Nature*) shifted this important philosophical discourse to the center of Carolingian consciousness.[21]

Eriugena followed Gregory of Nyssa in arguing that, were it not for the Fall, humans "would have multiplied in the manner of the angels, spiritually and without sexual intercourse. Adam's fall was from unity into diversity, from a sexless state into a state of division into male and female."[22] Sexuality, for Eriugena, is not evil in itself. Once humans had taken on carnal form, God provided that they procreate in the manner of the animals. On the other hand, sexuality is a consequence of the Fall, and it was foreordained by God in Eve's creation. Eve was created as she was, Eriugena says, because God knew Adam would sin.[23] But she was not created as the expressive form for that sin.

Eriugena's approach allows for a human anthropology where gender is an accidental rather than an essential category of human existence. In the original divine model, humans were not spatial, but spiritual, and thus whole rather than divided into two sexes. Eriugena's innovation[24] was to argue that the inner human being consisted of a trinity of creative faculties: intellect [*nous*], reason [*logos*], and sense [*dianoia*]. Corresponding to these inner qualities were, Eriugena postulated, a pair of external cognate faculties, *nous* and *aisthesis*,[25] seen as masculine and feminine on the basis of their grammatical genders in Greek. All humans possess this configuration of faculties and thus contain within themselves, as part of their essential makeup, the "masculine" and the "feminine" qualities of sense and intellect.

Furthermore, it is the so-called feminine quality of the senses, *aisthesis*, that integrates the outer being to the inner as a kind of messenger shuttling back and forth between them.[26] Eriugena shows sensuality to be crucial in mediating between the outer world and the inner, while images of sensual things, fantasies [*phantasiae*] play an equally crucial role in the human economy, linking sense and intellect.[27] Masculine and feminine, in this conception, play equal roles in constituting the human as a creating, thinking being. Eve is not the instrument of Adam's fall, but a necessary component, of which Adam is another (see note 26). Sexuality becomes more interesting, because more nuanced, in Eriugena.

The erotic, in this perspective, was not necessarily a space where a predetermined narrative of the Fall would be perpetually replayed, as Jerome held, and Augustine seemed to concur. Eriugena conceives of humans, in their dual nature, as poietic, that is, beings whom one could view not as products of the already said, but as potential and unresolved narrative. For Eriugena, the Fall had revealed the human as a dynamic site of languages, of narrative. Thanks to the Fall, humans contained within themselves conflicting language models: the postlapsarian language of division, and the prelapsarian language of unification.[28] The drama, as Eriugena recognized, lay in superposing the two models of identity and difference in the same person.

Humans thus constitute language models capable of expressing a full range of discourses simultaneously. Whatever the narrative or issues, in Eriugena's system, discourse has the potential of representing the dynamic division and reunification of nature itself. To the extent that the markers of division — sexual identity, class, and the other accidents of form and matter — predominate, discourse uses the spatialized lapsarian idiom to represent the material world and historical human as they actually exist in the world. This idiom does not seek to balance the masculine and the feminine categories of cognition (*nous* and *aisthesis*), but rather deploys them asymmetrically, with one or the other predominating.

There is, however, another model, a discourse based upon *phantasiae* (images of the senses), which posits a double representation of the world: the simultaneous representation of the external world as it appears, coupled with an ideal representation, based on the cognitive reprocessing of external sense data, to produce a new image.[29] In short, this discourse represents the world as a tension between the historical and material, on the one hand, and the lost ideals of the reunification theory on the other. By overlaying a fantasized ideal image on the material, or fallen state, Eriugena shows the subsistence of the original concept in the historical individual. Genesis ceases to be simply an historical exemplum, a cautionary tale from the beginning of history.[30] Instead, it becomes a model of human nature, showing how individuals necessarily incorporate multiple discourses within themselves.

Two aspects of Eriugena's ideas contribute to the revision of the canonical marriage model emerging from Genesis. The first, clearly, lies with the substitution of gender equivalence for gender hierarchy. The second, even more significant, lies with the "logic of the senses" Eriugena derives from his narrative. Adam and Eve become types of human nature, and figures of the sensual and intellectual cognitive faculties working together. As complementary universals of human nature, "Adam" and "Eve" function in each individual to form a balanced cognitive economy.[31] Adam equates with *nous* or intellect, which protects the senses from deception, which leads to transgression. Deception does arise through and with the senses, identified with Eve, but Eriugena's break with tradition here consists in the major role he accords to *aisthesis*, the senses as a vital life force, equated with Paradise itself.[32]

> There was a fount to irrigate Paradise. What is this fount? Our Lord Jesus Christ, the Fount of Eternal Life, and His Father too. For it is written: Seeing that you have in you fount of life ... This fount, then, as you have read, is in Paradise. For it is written that the fount proceeds out of Eden. That is to say, the fount is in your life force [*in anima tua*][33] ... This is the fount which proceeds from that well-tilled and pleasureful soul [*ex illa exercitata et plena voluptatis anima*]; and this fount, which irrigates Paradise, is the power (or moral perfection) of the life force [*virtus est animae*] which bursts forth from the highest fount.[34]

Let us not ignore the dramatic opposition in Eriugena's equation of intellect and sense, mind and body, as balancing life forces, equally necessary to each human. That opposition lies not between sensual pleasure and intellect, per se, but in the moral intentionality, the *virtus*, of sensuality. Sensuality by itself, *voluptas*, constitutes a vital life force, the *anima*. Only when the senses set out to deceive the intellect does *voluptas* shade over into delectation, which from the Fathers on had the connotation of deception, temptation [In specie serpentis figuram accipiens delectationis].[35] None of these aspects is new by itself, as the quotation from Ambrose (embedded in Eriugena's passage) shows.

What is new is Eriugena's combination of the diverse elements in an allegorizing context in which intellect and sensuality, *nous* and *aisthesis*, link simultaneously to Adam and Eve, hence the creation, but in a way which makes gender hierarchy an historical phenomenon rather than essential, an element of divine intention manifested in the creation. The difference is not trivial, since, as an historical accident, gender hierarchy was a human problem that could be overcome in seeking to return to prelapsarian unity. Adam and Eve, as joint principles of inner being, symbolize the true marriage of being, predicated on the balancing of intellect and sensuality.

The role of fantasy and the senses in elaborating this conception suggests its simultaneous potential as a narrative model for showing marriage as the image of *adunatio*, or unification. The unification of natures will begin from man—as the division ended with the splitting of humans into male and female.[36] The conjoining of the male and female in a harmonious discursive state thus becomes a first, crucial step. Eriugena takes that step by conceding a major role in human cognition to the "feminine" concept of *aisthesis*—sensual perception. The masculine and feminine principles of intellect and compassion, mind and body, thus work together to achieve "the perfect unification with the proper reason through which one subsists."[37]

The model of marriage here proposed is one destined to change the vernacular literary horizon in the twelfth century. For we can see in this narrative model that Eriugena managed, unwittingly, to lay the foundations for a discourse that perpetually activates the tension between *voluptas* and delectation: which is another way of describing romance.

Eros in the Cloister: Aisthesis and the Language of the Body

But the evolution from theology to romance did not happen all at once, although the impetus did come from within the cloister walls. In a first movement, we find literary examples of a surprising eroticism in such epistolary exchanges as those from the late eleventh century between an older monk and a young nun, Baudri of Bourgueil and Constance, a nun at the convent of Le Ronceray (Angers). Baudri, evoking the erotic tension between reading and sexuality that Dante will later condemn in *Inferno* 5, had written to Constance: "Your naked hand will touch my naked page . . . / You can safely lay it in your lap."[38] Constance renders the eroticism of Baudri's equation of page and caress fully explicit in terms of her own erogenous zones, thereby making the page a metaphor for the body, and reading a kind of intercourse:

> Night hateful of my study, envious of her who reads . . .
> I put my letter under my left breast—
>   they say that's nearest to the heart . . .
> At last, weary, I tried to get to sleep,
>   but love that has been wakened knows no night . . .
> I lay asleep—no, sleepless—because the page you wrote,
>   though lying on my breast, had set my womb on fire.[39]

Since both Baudri and Constance take care to stress the chaste nature of their relationship, the erotic badinage has been put down to a kind of intellectual game in the Ovidian style. Dronke quite rightly senses something more materially erotic, "flirtatious" in Constance's poem,[40] and she does indeed represent her body as an expressive space eroticized by the mutual interaction of reading and writing, "With my hand I have touched your naked songs."[41]

Our enjoyment of the open sensuality of Constance's poem should not obscure the deft containment of that sensuality by the intellectual play of rhetoric. The sensuality itself, uncanonical though it be—Dronke found nothing comparable prior to Constance—seems less startling than its juxtaposition with affirmations of chastity: "I am chaste, I am chaste in manner, I wish to live chaste, O if only I might live as the bride of God!"[42] Clearly, Constance sees no difficulty in reconciling the erotic and the sacred: "Jus et lex nostrum semper tueatur amorem, / Commendet nostros vita pudica jocos."[43] (Custom and law guard our love, / A chaste life justifies our games.)

Constance's rhetoric deploys two languages in tense balance: the erotic and the spiritual. The focus on the erotic tension, rather than the spiritual resolution, gives dramatic impact to Constance's verse—and makes Baudri's pallid by contrast. That tension, in turn, comes from the graphic presence of the body conjoined to the life force (anima) daringly construed as voluptas. In short, Constance provides a graphic example of the aisthesis coefficient, illustrating the equivalence of the poetic text and the female body as expressive spaces of sensuality. In a second movement, we see the repeated conjoining of bodies and minds, Baudri's and her own, in the text of her lyric ode (carminis oda). Her body, like her ode, has become a representative space for both of them: "Hoc jacet in gremio dilecti schedula nostri, / Ecce locata meis subjacet uberibus."[44] (Here lies on my breast the record of our desire / There placed lying under my breasts.)

Aisthesis authorizes sensuality as a common trait, a trait that bonds male and female in a mutual experience of the body as an instrument of emotional cognition—an authentic instrument for discovering the other. *Aisthesis* constitutes the principal ingredient for romantic love as mutual affection, since it guarantees the quality of being (*virtus*) in love, by making *voluptas* a shared discourse of desire. The insistence in Baudri and Constance's letters on reading and the physicality of the equation body/text, text/body, suggests that we may see here a witty reference to Augustine's *Confessions*. The key passage in the story of Augustine's conversion is the mystical experience in Book 8, where, alone in a garden, he hears a voice like a child crying *tolle lege, tolle lege* (Take and read, take and read). What Augustine took up and read, of course, was a page from Saint Paul warning against worldliness and the pleasures of the body.[45]

For Baudri and Constance, the reversion to God must begin with a reading of the *carta*, the letter or page of the body. They offer an example of union of male and female based on the conjoining of *nous* and *aisthesis*, but, in keeping with Eriugena's concept of Eden, their union precludes physical love. For Constance, nun and *sponsa dei* (bride of God), writes their desire on a surrogate body, her wax tablet, because wax does not know shame: *aggrediar ceram quia nescit cera pudorem.*[46] So long as the tablet stands between the body and the experience of physical love, *aisthesis* remains theoretical, and the myth of the abolition of sexual difference secure.

Heloise, the protagonist in one of the great legends of romantic love, and a nun against her will, was the first medieval (woman) writer to recount her experiences with physical love. She did so a generation after Constance, around 1135, in three letters in which the aisthetic principle assumes dialectical dimensions. For the first time, *aisthesis* and eros confront each other in the experience of an articulate woman. Heloise shows how eros bares the fault lines between male identity and female alterity, the abyss which *aisthesis* must somehow bridge in order to maintain the ideal of transcendent unification of the sexes.

Since Heloise writes these incomparably dialectical letters to her husband and former lover, Peter Abelard, they bear directly on the nature and roles of the woman in marriage, as well as dealing explicitly with sexuality and religion. Peter Dronke has shown Heloise's "profound originality" in arguing that "in marriage . . .

love must play precisely the rôle that friendship can in other relationships. Marriage for anything less than pure love is prostitution. Each partner must value the other, and cherish him or her, as the best on earth."[47]

Heloise pithily expressed this ideal in a proposition whose fame extended to the thirteenth century, when Jean de Meun reported it in the *Roman de la Rose:*

Ele meïsmes le raconte
et escrit, et n'en a pas honte,
a son ami, que tant amoit
que pere et seigneur le clamoit,
une merveilleuse parole . . .
qu'il est escrit en ses espitres . . .
"Se li empereres de Rome,
souz cui doivent estre tuit home,
me daignet volair prendre a fame
et fere moi du monde dame,
si vodroie je mieuz, fet ele,
et Dieu a tesmoign en apele,
estre ta putain apelee,
que empereriz coronee."

(She herself unabashedly says something wonderful in a letter to her lover whom she loved so much that she called him father and lord . . . and it's written in her letters . . . "If the emperor of Rome, to whom all men should be subject, deigned to wish to take me as his wife and make me mistress of the world, I would prefer," she said, "and I call God as my witness, to be called your whore, than to be crowned empress."[48])

Heloise's attitude toward marriage is part and parcel of her general feelings about the relation of the personal to the institutional. Whether it be marriage or the religious life, she objects to imposed constraints which do not accommodate the legitimate needs of the body on an equal basis with those of the mind. She and her sisters, she argues in her third letter, are expected to submit to *regulae,* canons of monastic behavior, wearing clothes and observing rituals designed for men, without concern for the canons, the *regulae* of their own bodies. The point, yet again, is the ultimate illegitimacy, the hypocrisy of institutions which cannot accommodate "the logic of the senses." For Heloise, this means always linking the inner spirit [*animus*] to the body [*corpus*], as a human, not a gender principle: "immediately at your bidding I changed my clothing along with my mind, in order to prove you the sole possessor of my body and my will alike."[49] "For your manhood was adorned by every grace of mind [animi] and body [corporis]."[50]

The link between spirit (animus) and body (corpus) as a human bond rather than a principle of gender encouraging subjugation allows Heloise to construct a social model for lovers that remains constant across the whole range of interactions from the most intimate to the most public. Heloise will voluntarily associate herself with Abelard's will, on condition that their bond be one of mind and body joined. That is her definition of love [amor] and the social bond [amicitia] predicated on it. "My heart [animus] was not in me, but with you; and now, even more, if it is not with you, it is nowhere: truly without you it cannot exist."[51] Heloise is not being abject here, for she holds Abelard to the same standards as herself. Reciprocity, the ideal of mind and body (Adam and Eve) joined by voluptas, the principle of aisthesis, motivates her letter. Her suffering and fidelity to their bond have proved that "while I enjoyed with you the pleasures of the flesh [tecum carnali fruerer voluptate],"[52] those pleasures were in fact amor and not simply libido.

Now, however, Abelard must prove the same thing, that he was motivated by amor—that is, amor and amicitia conjoined as aisthesis and nous—and not simply concupiscence. She levels the accusation, on the lips of all, as she says, that "concupiscence more than true friendship [amicitia] joined [sociavit] you to me, sexual passion [ardor libidinis] more than love [amor]." Heloise challenges Abelard to renew their bond through the act of writing, as she has done. Writing will be to their present state what the caress was earlier, an act of contact: "While I am denied your presence, give me at least through your words—of which you have enough and to spare—some sweet semblance of yourself."[53]

There has been a tendency to see Heloise's words simply as reproaches or accusations leveled at Abelard. In fact, they are carefully constructed rhetorical propositions adumbrating a definition of their personal compact and what he needs to do to maintain his part of it. To call them accusations obscures their positive dialectical status. It risks overlooking the analytical force by which Heloise lays out the basis for a union which, like Constance's and Baudri's, but for different reasons, will no longer be based on physical love, although it certainly will not be devoid of physical desire, as her second letter vividly recounts. That union must be predicated on their willingness—particularly Abelard's—

to see her as she is in body and spirit, a spirit continually dialogized by the body: "Now particularly you should fear, now when I no longer have in you an outlet for my incontinence."[54]

Heloise's real contribution to the rewriting of marriage lay in her ability to transform her body into a polemical space in which sensual perception [aisthesis] motivates logic [nous] in ways never intended by Eriugena, to create a literature of institutional reform. If Heloise creates a model for reform, it is another woman writer, Marie de France, who, in the mid-twelfth century, creates a new poetic genre for the purpose of joining fantasy and sensuality, to rewrite the marriage canon. In Marie's lays — short verse romances — we see how the female anthropology of aisthesis enters the mainstream of European literature to create a new expressive space for the marginalized other.[55] Her lays take poetic techniques and oral themes (particularly the fantasies of marriage that combined sensual gratification with fulfilling companionship) drawn from folk culture and join them to high cultural elements from the Latin tradition. With this combination of marginal and mainstream culture, Marie innovated a new literary space that appealed to a new aristocratic audience of whom women formed a significant part.

Marie draws upon folk repertories, such as the so-called spinning songs women were said to have sung to each other while engaged in domestic activities, to elaborate archetypes like the mal mariée, the unhappily married woman. Using the poietic anthropology set forth by Eriugena, coupled with the insistence on speaking through the body formulated by writers like Constance and Heloise, Marie makes romance a reforming discourse that challenges the canon of patristic authority from the margins of the feminine erotic. The discursive space we have defined as aisthesis, to suggest its philosophical dimensions, was seen more simply by Marie as a language of compassionate sensuality:

Cil que ceste aventure oïrent
Lunc tens aprés un lai en firent,
De la pité, de la dolur
Que cil suffrirent pur amur.[56]

(Those who heard of this adventure
Made a lay out of it long afterwards,
About the trials and pain
That these two suffered for love.)

Marie de France, like Constance and Heloïse before her, uses the resources of language, the marginal vernaculars like Breton and

English, juxtaposed with the canonical (and legal) Latin, in a code-switching pattern intended to illustrate the possibility of integrating different attitudes towards love and marriage from those officially sanctioned. Her linguistic code-switching—she may give equivalences for key words in three languages (Anglo-Norman, Breton, or English), and Latin is constantly in her subtexts—liberates narrative voices to recount parallel versions of love and marriage. So we find in her poems accounts of official and socially sanctioned marriages between old, jealous, and often lubricious men and young, unhappy women juxtaposed with a competing "voice-over" fantasy of a world where women are free to engage a partner of their choice; in short, sexuality without violence.

Those competing fantasies take the form of "fairy tale" narratives where charming, wealthy knights contrive ways of reaching the young women incarcerated by jealous husbands. Not infrequently, the women, whose official marriages have been barren, become fertile and give birth to children with their fairy-tale lover; indeed, the lay may bear the child's name, as in *Yonec*, where we know neither the name of the mother nor of her lover. The utopia of the fantastic appears normal within her narratives, as women bear children to men who love them, and whom *they* love in return. In contrast, the socially sanctioned marriage practices of the period appear barbarous.[57]

Marie's lays do not portray a romantic myth of love as union that abolishes difference. On the contrary, she emphasizes the alterity of her heroines by their powerlessness and marginality, by the domestic realism in the lays—including details on childbirth and child care. Her view of marriage is not that of a union where two become one, but rather a marriage of true reciprocity, beginning with the equitable—as opposed to the equal—apportionment of pleasure and pain, choice and attraction. Just as Constance makes a text of her body for writing her oxymoronic chaste sexuality, or Heloise, more insistent, demands that the canon of the female body be incorporated in the canons of monastic rule, so Marie continues the tradition of joining reason and sensual perception, *nous* and *aisthesis*, in creating a new genre, the narrative lay, that she fashions into a powerful critique of traditional marriage practices. By seeking her material, as she tells us, from the linguistic and social margins represented by Breton folklore, Marie de France moves the intellectual anthropology of marriage into the mainstream of vernacular culture in the twelfth century—by naturalizing the fantastic in her *Lais* as a transgressive appropriation of the extraordinary by the commonplace.

NOTES

Epigraph: On ne se marie pas pour soy, quoi qu'on die; on se marie autant ou plus pour sa posterité, pour sa famille. L'usage et interest du mariage touche nostre race bien loing par delà nous (Montaigne, "Sur des vers de Virgile," *Essais,* 3.5, in *Oeuvres complètes,* textes établis par Albert Thibaudet et Maurice Rat, Bibliothèque de la Pléiade [Bruges: Éditions Gallimard, 1962], 827).

1. George Duby, *The Knight, The Lady, and the Priest: The Making of Modern Marriage in Medieval France,* trans. Barbara Bray (New York: Pantheon Books, 1983), 19.

2. Ibid.

3. Ibid., 24.

4. G. R. Evans, *The Language and Logic of the Bible: The Earlier Middle Ages* (Cambridge: Cambridge University Press, 1984), 1.

5. Ibid.

6. Karl F. Morrison, *The Mimetic Tradition of Reform in the West* (Princeton: Princeton University Press, 1982), 52ff.

7. Allegorical interpretation of the creation could overlay historical understanding in the Latin Fathers without affecting, as Augustine said, the "veritate narrationis historicae de corporali loco" (veracity of the historical narrative of [paradise's] existence in the material world) (Saint Augustine of Hippo, *The City of God Against the Pagans,* vol. 4, trans. Philip Levine, Loeb Classical Library, 414 [Cambridge: Harvard University Press, 1966], 13.21, 216–17). In the same chapter, he also observes, "Nemo itaque prohibet intelligere paradisum vitam beatorum, quattuor eius flumina quattuor virtutes" (No one therefore prevents us from understanding paradise allegorically as the life of blessed men, its four streams as the four virtues). This is quite different from Johannes Eriugena who takes his cue from Gregory of Nyssa to view the creation story itself allegorically.

8. Edouard Jeauneau, "La division des sexes chez Grégoire de Nysse et chez Jean Scot Erigène," *Eriugena: Studien zu seinen Quellen,* ed. Werner Beierwaltes (Heidelberg: Carl Winter, Universitätsverlag, 1980), 38ff.

9. Ovid uses the term "metuenda virago" (frightening Amazon) to describe Minerva transformed by rage in *Metamorphoses* 2.765. The later connotation of virago, thoroughly pejorative, comes from the implication of ill-temper, shrewishness, and above all a disagreeable tongue.

10. [A]nimal scilicet lubricum et tortuosis anfractibus mobile, operi suo congruum, per quem loqueretur elegit . . . et tamquam instrumento abutens fallacia sermocinatus est feminae, a parte scilicet inferiore illius humanae copulae incipiens ut gradatim perveniret ad totum, non existimans virum facile credulum nec errando posse decipi, sed dum alieno cedit errori (*City of God* 14.11, 328–31).

11. Augustine casts the equation in rhetorically negative language: "Absit ut hoc existimemus fuisse ubi nullum erat omnino peccatum . . . Absit, inquam, ut ante omne peccatum iam ibi fuerit tale peccatum ut hoc de ligno admitterent quod de muliere Dominus ait: *Sit quis viderit mulierem ad concupiscendum eam, iam moechatus est eam in corde*

suo" (Heaven forbid that we should suppose it to have been so where no sin at all existed! . . . Heaven forbid, I say, that we should think that before all sin there already existed in paradise such sin as to cause them to commit in regard to the tree the very offence of which the Lord says, referring to a woman: "If anyone looks at a woman lustfully, he has already committed adultery with her in his heart" [*City of God* 14.10, 320–23]). Theological accuracy demands the disclaimer. Nonetheless, it does not mitigate the force of Augustine's equation of the tree as an object of desire with the woman as an object of lust ("such sin as to cause them to commit in regard to the tree [de ligno] the very offence of which the Lord says, referring to a woman [de muliere] . . . ").

12. *City of God* 14.11, 330–31.

13. Ibid.

14. Alexander Souter, *A Glossary of Later Latin to 600 A.D.* (Oxford: Clarendon Press, 1949).

15. *City of God* 14.15, 346–47.

16. Ibid., 350–51.

17. Ibid., 14.16, 352–55.

18. Duby, 27–28.

19. Ibid., 30.

20. Eriugena seemed to have recognized the radical nature of the doctrines he proposed. At one point in the Socratic dialogue between *magister* and *alumnus,* the student observes to the master: "Ut non dicam, quantum haec doctrina omnium aut paene omnium latialis linguae sanctorum magistrorum autoritati resistat, qui unanimiter post resurrectionem omnium utriusque sexus integritatem futuram esse asserunt, ita ut vir in formam viri, femina in formam feminae" (To say nothing of how much this doctrine conflicts with the authority of all or almost all the holy masters of the Latin tongue, who unanimously declare that after the resurrection of all things each sex will have its integrity, so that man returns into the form of a man, woman into the form of a woman) (J. P. Migne, *Patrologiae Cursus Completus,* Series Latina [Paris: J. P. Migne, 1853] 122:543B [hereafter cited as "*PL* 122"]; Iohannis Scotti Erivgenae [Johannes Scotus Eriugena], *Periphyseon: de diuisione naturae,* ed. and trans. I. P. Sheldon-Williams, Scriptores Latini Hiberniae [Dublin: The Dublin Institute for Advanced Studies, 1968–81], 2:42–43 [hereafter cited as "*DDN* S-W"]).

21. "[T]he study of the early tradition of the *Periphyseon* suggests that the work was far more widely and variously read than has been imagined." (John Marenbon, *From the Circle of Alcuin to the School of Auxerre: Logic, Theology, and Philosophy in the Early Middle Ages* [Cambridge: Cambridge University Press, 1981], 104).

22. Johannes Scotus Eriugena, *Periphyseon: On the Division of Nature,* ed. and trans. Myra L. Uhlfelder, summaries by Jean A. Potter (Indianapolis: Bobbs-Merrill, 1976), 262.

23. *PL* 122:533A–533B; *DDN* S-W 2:20–22. See also *PL* 122:793B–800; Johannes Scotus Eriugena, *Periphyseon (The Division of Nature),* trans. I. P. Sheldon-Williams, rev. John J. O'Meara (Washington, D.C.: Dumbarton Oaks, 1987), 443–52 [hereafter cited as "*DDN* O'Meara"]).

24. "Cette donnée de la tradition va prendre des contours nouveaux dans le cadre de la conception érigénienne tripartite de l'homme intérieur (*nous, logos, dianoia*), articulée selon la dynamique des trois mouvements universels de l'âme. Le processus se déploie ici sur la base de la métaphore traditionnelle du sapiens artifex et de sa triple activité psychologique, consilium, conceptum, operatio" (Guy H. Allard, "Vocabulaire érigénien relatif à la représentation de l'écriture," in *Eriugena: Studien zu seinen Quellen*, ed. Werner Beierwaltes, [Heidelberg: Carl Winter, Universitätsverlag, 1980], 20).

25. "Videsne, quantum aperte denuntiat, hominem ad imaginem et similitudinem Dei conditum sexus differentia omnino caruisse, et adhuc, quantum in eo imago et similitudo conditoris permanet, carere, ipsamque divisionem propter peccatum secundum corpus solummodo accidisse. Quamquam enim in anima spiritales sexus intelligantur, νοῦς siquidem intellectus veluti quidam masculus in anima est, αἴσθησις vero, id est sensus, veluti quaedam femina, non tamen ibi cognoscimus naturae divortium" (Do you see how openly he declares that man created in the image and likeness of God was entirely without difference of sex, *and is still without it* to the extent that the image and likeness of the Creator persists in him, and that that division was an accident affecting only his body, as a consequence of sin? For although spiritual sexes are understood to exist in the soul—for νοῦς, that is, intellect, is a kind of male in the soul, while αἴσθησις, that is, sense, is a kind of female—yet we do not recognize there any deviation from nature) (*PL* 122:541A; *DDN* S-W 2:38–39). See also: *PL* 122:815C–D: "[I]n specie serpentis figuram accipiens delectationis, in figura mulieris sensum, in animi mentisque typo virum constituens; quem, sensum videlicet, αἴσθησιν vocant Graeci . . . Recte igitur in Graeco νοῦς in figura viri accipitur, αἴσθησις vero in figura mulieris" (he took the form of a serpent to represent pleasure, and the form of the woman to represent sense, and saw a representation of man in the mind and the intellect. Now the Greeks call sense αισθησις . . . It is appropriate then that in Greek νοῦς has a masculine form and αισθησις a feminine [*DDN* O'Meara 470]).

26. *PL* 122:569C–D; *DDN* S-W 2:98.

27. *PL* 122:576C–577A; *DDN* S-W 2:114–5.

28. "Omnis siquidem corporalis sensibilisque creatura ex materia et forma constituitur . . . accedente vero forma visibilis dicitur et composita, solidaque atque perfecta, naturae suae certis finibus circumscripta. Invisibilis vero creatura, id est intellectualis et rationalis, informis dicitur, priusquam ad formam suam, Creatorem videlicet suum, convertatur. Non enim ei sufficit ad perfectionem ex essentia essentialique differentia subsistere, his enim duobus omnis intellectualis creatura componitur, nisi ad Verbum unigenitum, Dei Filium dico, qui est forma omnis intellectualis vitae" (For every corporeal and sensible creature [corporalis sensibilisque creatura] is composed of matter and form . . . [and] when it receives form it is said to be visible and composite and solid and perfect, being circumscribed within the certain limits of its proper nature; but the invisible creature, that is, the intelligible and rational, is called formless before it turns towards its proper Form, that is to say, towards its Creator.

For to achieve perfection it is not enough for it to have subsistence from essence and essential difference—for every intellectual creature is composed of these two—, without the perfection of being turned towards the only begotten Word, I mean the Son of God, Who is the Form of all intelligible life) (*PL* 122:548B; *DDN* S-W 2:54–55).

29. "Tertius motus est compositus, per quem, quae extra sunt, anima tangens, veluti ex quibusdam signis apud seipsam visibilium rationes reformat . . . Primo siquidem phantasias ipsarum rerum per exteriorem sensum quinquepertitum . . . accipiens, easque secum colligens, dividens, ordinans disponit; deinde per ipsas ad rationes earum, quarum phantasiae sunt, perveniens, intra seipsam eas, rationes dico, tractat atque conformat" (The third motion is composite, [and is that] by which the soul comes into contact with that which is outside her as though by certain signs and reforms within herself the reasons of visible things . . . [F]irst the soul receives the fantasies of things themselves through the exterior sense, which is fivefold . . . and by gathering them to itself and sorting them out it sets them in order; then getting through them to the reasons of the things by which they are the fantasies, she moulds them, I mean the reasons, and shapes them into conformity with herself) (*PL* 122:573A–B; *DDN* S-W 2:107–109). See the rest of the passage for Eriugena's discussion of the two fantasies, the one attached to the body, the other to the soul.

30. "Videsne, quemadmodum spiritualiter intelligit paradisum?" (See in what a spiritual [i.e., allegorical] way he interprets Paradise?) (*PL* 122:816B; *DDN* O'Meara 470).

31. *PL* 122:815C–D; *DDN* O'Meara 470.

32. Even though Eriugena draws heavily on Saint Ambrose's commentary in *De Paradiso* 1.5.8–11 (*Corpus Scriptorum Ecclesiasticorum Latinorum*, ed. Carolvs Schenkl [1896] 32:1, 267) in this section of *DDN* 4, the context and conclusions differ markedly from Ambrose, precisely because of Eriugena's position on the division of the sexes. See Jeauneau, 49–50.

33. "Anima" denotes the animal principle of life as distinct from "animus," the spiritual, reasoning and willing principle (*A New Latin Dictionary*, ed. C. T. Lewis and Charles Short [New York: American Book Co., 1907], 280).

34. *DDN* O'Meara 470. [Erat fons, qui irrigaret paradisum. Quis fons? Dominus Jesus Christus, fons vitae aeternae, sicut et Pater; quia scriptum est, quoniam apud te fons vitae . . . Hic ergo fons, sicut legisti, in paradiso est. Fons enim procedit, inquit, ex Eden, id est, in anima tua fons est . . . Hic est fons, qui procedit ex illa exercitata et plena voluptatis anima; hic fons, qui irrigat paradisum, virtus est animae eminentissimo fonte pullulans" (*PL* 122:815D–816A)].

35. *PL* 122:815C. ([H]e took the form of a serpent to represent pleasure [*DDN* O'Meara 470]).

36. *PL* 122:532A; *DDN* S-W 2:20.

37. *DDN* S-W 2:20. [P]erfectam adunationem ad propriam rationem, per quam subsistit (*PL* 122:532C).

38. Peter Dronke, *Woman Writers of the Middle Ages: A Critical Study*

of Texts from Perpetua to Marguerite Porete (Cambridge: Cambridge University Press, 1984), 86. For Latin, see Baudri's poem (hereafter cited as "Baudri 238"), in Baudri de Bourgueil, *Les Oeuvres poétiques*, Édition critique publiée d'après le manuscrit du Vatican par Phyllis Abrahams (Paris: Librairie Ancienne Honoré Champion, 1926), 338 (hereafter cited as "Abrahams"):

Dum tanget nudam nuda manus folium.
. . . .
Inque tuo gremio ponere tuta potes.

(ll. 12–14)

39. Dronke, 88. For Latin, see Constance's poem (hereafter cited as Constance 239") in Abrahams, 345:

Nox studiis odiosa meis, invisa legenti,
    Me cessare meo compulit a studio.
Composui gremio posuique sub ubere laevo
    Schedam, quod cordi junctius esse ferunt
. . . .
Tandem fessa dedi nocturno membra sopori,
    Sed nescit noctem sollicitatus amor
. . . .
Insomnis, insomnis eram, quia pagina vestra
    Scilicet in gremio viscera torruerat.

(ll. 7–18)

40. Dronke, 86.
41. Ibid., 88. "Et tetigi nuda carmina vestra manu" (Constance 239.2 [Abrahams, 344]). *Carta, nuda carmina, pagina, scheda, liber,* and *volumen* are terms for the expressive space of writing used by Constance in the first eighteen lines of her poem; these are juxtaposed with terms for the body (*gremium, uber, membra, viscera*) and for sensual emotion (pleasure, dislike, fatigue, arousal). See Constance 239.1–18 (Abrahams, 344–45).
42. Constance 239.114–15 (Abrahams, 347).
43. Constance 239.122–23 (Abrahams, 347).
44. Constance 239.68–69 (Abrahams, 346).
45. Baudri's poem begins with a series of imperatives: "Perlege . . . Perlege . . . Perlege" (Read . . . Read . . . Read) (Baudri 238.1–4 [Abrahams, 338]); Constance begins her letter: "Perlegi" (I read) (Constance 239.1 [Abrahams, 344]).
46. Constance 239.104 (Abrahams, 347).
47. Dronke, 117.
48. Guillaume de Lorris et Jean de Meun, *Le Roman de la rose,* publié par Félix Lecoy, Les Classiques français du moyen âge, 95 (Paris: Librairie Ancienne Honoré Champion, 1966), 2:8777–8794. Heloise's statement comes from her first letter to Abelard: "Et si uxoris nomen sanctius ac validius videretur, dulcius mihi semper extitit amice vocabulum aut, si non indigneris, concubine vel scorti; ut quo me videlicet pro te amplius humiliarem, ampliorem apud te consequerer gratiam, et sic etiam excellentie tue gloriam minus lederem" (The name of wife may seem more sacred or more binding, but sweeter for me will always be the word mistress, or, if you will permit me, that of concubine or whore. I believed that the more I humbled myself on your account, the more gratitude I should

win from you, and also the less damage I should do to the brightness of your reputation) (Peter Abelard, *Historia calamitatum*, publié par J. Monfrin, Bibliothèque des textes philosophiques [Paris: Librairie Philosophique J. Vrin, 1978], 114: 147–51 [Hereafter cited as "Monfrin"]; *The Letters of Abelard and Heloise*, ed. and trans. Betty Radice [New York: Penguin, 1974], 113 [hereafter cited as "Radice"]).

49. [A]d tuam statim iussionem tam habitum ipsa quam animum immutarem, ut te tam corporis mei quam animi unicum possessorem ostenderem (Radice, 113; Monfrin, 114 [141–43]).

50. Quod enim bonum animi vel corporis tuam non exornabat adholescentiam? (Radice, 115; Monfrin, 115 [207–8]).

51. Non enim mecum animus meus, sed tecum erat; sed et nunc maxime, si tecum non est, nusquam est: esse vero sine te nequaquam potest (Radice, 117; Monfrin, 116 [248–51]).

52. Radice, 117; Monfrin, 117 (258).

53. Dum tui presentia fraudor, verborum saltem votis, quorum tibi copia est, tue mihi imaginis presenta dulcedinem (Radice, 116; Monfrin, 116 [232–34]). See also: Monfrin, 117 (266–69): "[T]e obsecro ut quo modo potes tuam mihi presentiam reddas, consolationem videlicet mihi aliquam rescribendo." (I beg you to restore your presence to me in the way you can—by writing me some word of comfort) (Radice, 177).

54. Nunc vero precipue timendum est, ubi nullum incontinentie mee superest in te remedium (Radice, 135; Monfrin, 124 [280–81]). Heloise's frank analyses uncover a fundamental truth about love and its relationship to the feminine that Levinas has expressed as follows: "la différence de sexes n'est pas . . . la dualité de deux termes complémentaires, car deux termes complémentaires supposent un tout préexistant [as Eriugena showed]. Or, dire que la dualité sexuelle suppose un tout, c'est d'avance poser l'amour comme fusion. Le pathétique de l'amour consiste dans une dualité insurmontable des êtres. C'est une relation avec ce qui dérobe à jamais. La relation ne neutralise pas *ipso facto* l'altérité, mais la conserve. Le pathétique de la volupté est dans le fait d'être deux" (Emmanuel Levinas, *Le temps et l'autre*, Presses Universitaires de France, 2d ed. [Paris: Quadrige, 1985], 78).

55. I have developed these concepts in respect to vernacular women writers in an article entitled, "Medieval Women Writers: *Aisthesis* and the Powers of Marginality," in *The Politics of Tradition; Placing Women in French Literature*, ed. Joan DeJean and Nancy K. Miller, *Yale French Studies* 75 (1988): 77–94.

56. Marie de France, *Yonec*, in *Lais*, ed. Alfred Ewert, Blackwell's French Texts (Oxford: Blackwell's, 1944), 551–54.

57. See my article, "Marie de France's Common Places: Classical Rhetoric and Medieval Style," in *Art and Literature in the Middle Ages*, ed. Daniel Poirion and Nancy Regalado, special issue of *Yale French Studies* (Fall 1990).

The New Philology

The Medieval Text—"Guigemar"—As a Provocation to the Discipline of Medieval Studies

R. HOWARD BLOCH

Let us begin somewhat perversely, as I have done in a recent article in the *Romanic Review*,[1] with a quotation by that famous anti-medievalist Ferdinand Brunetière:

> Si l'on commence par poser résolument en principe ou en fait que notre littérature du moyen âge, nos *Chansons de geste* elles-mêmes, nos *Fabliaux* (ou *Fableaux*), nos *Mystères* aussi n'ont aucune valeur littéraire, alors, mais seulement alors, il devient aisé de s'entendre;—et peut-être y a-t-il moyen d'en dire des choses assez intéressantes.[2]

While the phrase "aucune valeur littéraire" may seem to contradict the "possibility of saying interesting things," it represents for Brunetière the only possibility of interest, since the lack of literary value serves as the guarantor of literature's historicity, its status as cultural index. Literature whose interest is historical, literature as history—this is the sentence under which medievalism has labored, still labors, and indeed to which it willingly submits. The view of Gaston Paris, institutional organizer of the discipline in France and certainly no enemy of the Middle Ages, is essentially the same as that of Brunetière: "Notre vieille littérature . . . est une mine inépuisable de renseignements sur les moeurs, les usages, les costumes, toute la vie privée de l'ancienne France."[3]

The medieval text's historical status as the literary form of everyday life or of social history has, on the one hand, worked to deny the importance of theory for its interpretation, while, on the other hand, it has (unwittingly?) contributed to the theory of the "natural text," the work of art which, in the words of J. Rychner, "is more engaged in the social, . . . less gratuitous, and less playful," or, to quote Ph. Ménard, "the work which speaks for itself."[4] Historically, medieval literature has offered the fantasy of a language of beginnings, a poetic vehicle that remains to its object invisible and, therefore, innocent, pristine, unencumbered by artifice, unmannered, and unrepressed—the transcription of "a direct observation of men," in G. Paris's terms, a "sketch from nature" in the phrase of E. Faral, literature "devoid of all literary pretension" according to J. Bédier's slogan that has become a commonplace of Old French studies.[5]

Until relatively recently, the only critical gesture before such a conception of the text as a poor poetic cousin whose ancestry predates "the imposition of style" (Brunetière) has been a philological one—that is, geographical, dialectical, or chronological identification; location within the context of an external historical referent or within the family of variant manuscripts; recreation of a manuscript stemma; description of the particularities of an individual scribe's orthography or lexicon; establishment either through etymology or situation in a semantic field of the original meaning of individual words; and, by way of corollary, the reconstitution of something on the order of an authorial intention (which is not without a certain nonsensical ring in an age in which most works were anonymous).

Despite its obvious success, in inverse proportion to the limits of its ambitions, the philological enterprise not only remains incapable of producing a reading, an interpretation of the text that would account for its specificity as literature, but entails several tautologies that characterize more generally the discipline of Old French studies. The first lies in the tendency to read the poetic work against the background of history that is itself based to some degree upon literary sources. This trend is particularly marked in an age in which written traces in the vernacular, the *via regia* to so-called everyday life, were, with the exception of literary examples, still relatively rare. The second resides in the temptation to read Old French against the defining context of the dictionary; for not only are dictionaries themselves predicated upon the very texts they are summoned to interpret, but the signs of the dictionary, as Umberto Eco has shown in a recent book entitled *Semiotics and the Philosophy of Language*, assume meaning to be the equivalent of synonymy. The dictionary is a signifying tautology.

It is my purpose to show the extent to which the poetic text resists any such effort to reduce it to dictionary definitions. For the pretension of philology is to the literal; and the reaction to anything but the pretense at reconstitution of a fantasized original meaning or intention supposedly to be found in the codifying equivalences of the dictionary is that it is not rooted in the text. "You do not know how to read" is the tiresome recrimination of those for whom the assumption of the transparency of the literary work without literature eliminates the question of what reading is or means. "You don't know how to translate" usually follows and, taking for granted the possibility of lexical univocity, usually means "Your reading is not the same as mine" or "I can't find it in my dictionary." Worse still, "How dare you show the impertinence to read medieval literature as if it were just like any other," since to do so is to disobey one of the unspoken taboos of an interpretative community, which from the beginning has confused an invaluable technical tool with the production of sense.

Far from working to insure the accessibility of Old French texts, philology as a discipline, pressured from above by the explosion of theoretical linguistics and from below by a certain exhaustion of its own projects, has only conspired to prevent any possibility of dialogue between the guild of medievalists and the intelligent general reader. With the predictable result of a disappearance of Old French studies at many major university centers. But what, it may be asked, is the risk in guarding the medieval text as if it were an alchemical secret, what is at stake in reading it like any other? What would happen if we were to take literally the possibility of reading *à la lettre*, or according to interpretative criteria suggested by the text itself?

Let us begin again, then, with a passage from the *Lais* of Marie de France. But first, let us open the OF dictionary to see what the word *lai* can itself mean, for no single syllable casts greater doubt upon the imagined possibility of reading OF literature based on the certainty of dictionary definitions. The word *lai* is, of course, taken to refer to "song," though the etymology (i.e., whether from the German *lied* or the Old Irish *laid* or *loíd*) is hotly debated. On p. 694, vol. IV, of Godefroy we find that the word *lai*, and its variants *lay, laye, laie, laiz, laes, lais*, can be used as an adjective to connote the secular realm and as a substantive to designate a lay person. By extension, it can refer to anyone not belonging to the university community, or, as a corollary, to someone considered ignorant.[6] The word *lai* and its homonyms *laid* and *lait* are used variously as a synonym for the word "staddle" (MF *baliveau*), for that which is ugly, or, as in the *Miracles de Notre Dame,* as the word for another Marie's milk. The adjectival homonyms *lé, ley, lay, let, lait, leit, laé, le* summon the idea of lightness, happiness, joy (Lat. *laetus*), just as *las, lax, lais* are used to connote sadness, misery, misfortune (Lat. *lassus*). Where the syllable *lai* becomes more interesting, however, is in its power to signify that which is left, an excess, or testament *(legs)*, which not only suggests a connection between the notion of residue, mark, or trace and the *Lais,* as the written traces of the preexisting Breton *lai,* but a place or *locus* from which to speak, or from which poetry becomes possible. "*La, lai, lay,* adv. se dit d'un lieu qu'on désigne d'une manière précise," specifies Godefroy on p. 685 of the same volume. Nor, in the same vein, would it be an exaggeration to link the *Lais* with the principle of poetic construction or binding subsumed under the rubric of the *laisse* and elaborated in Old Provençal as the process of linking verses *(lassar)*. As a link or leash, the homonym *laz* is to be found alongside the other traps used to capture the nightingale in "Le Laüstic."[7] Finally, the word *lai* is used in its OF forms *loi, lei, ley, lo, lays* to designate custom, usage, justice, or the law.

The "Prologue" to the *Lais* of Marie de France defines perhaps better than any other passage in Old French the extent to which medieval writers in the vernacular conceived of their own task in philological terms. Thus we pass from glossary to gloss:

> Custume fu as ancïens,
> Ceo testimoine Precïens,
> Es livres ke jadis feseient,
> Assez oscurement diseient
> Pur ceus ki a venir esteient
> E ki aprendre le deveient,
> K'i peüssent gloser la lettre
> E de lur sen le surplus mettre . . .
> Pur ceo començai a penser
> D'aukune bone estoire faire
> E de latin en romaunz traire.
>
> ("Prologue," 9ff.)

(As Priscian bears witness, it was the custom of the Ancients to speak obscurely enough in their books so that those who came afterward and would be obliged to teach [or learn] them would be able to gloss the letter and with their sense [meaning] fill in the rest . . . For this reason I began to think of making a few good stories and of translating them from Latin into Romance.)

The historical distance between letter and sense cannot be dissociated from a relation of desire cast, in Marie's "Prologue" as in
Augustinian theology as well as the "etymological grammar" of
the early Middle Ages, in terms of memory:[8]

Des lais pensai, k'oïz aveie.
Ne dutai pas, bien le saveie,
Ke pur remambrance les firent
Des aventures k'il oïrent
Cil ki primes les comencierent
E ki avant les enveierent.
Plusurs en ai oï conter,
Nes voil laissier ne oblier.

("Prologue," 33ff.)

(I thought of the lais that I had heard. I did not doubt but
knew well that those who first began them and first sent
them forth did so for the sake of remembrance of the adven-
tures that they had heard. I have heard several told and would
not want to leave them off or forget.)

Just as there can be no direct access to the past, there is no unmediated access to the text, any text, which, because of the degraded
nature of verbal signs, requires interpretation or gloss. Marie's
"Prologue" contains a virtual programme for the writing and reading of medieval literature. France's first woman writer, at over six
centuries remove from Priscian, places herself in the same position as the author of the *Institutiones Grammaticae* in relation
to the Ancients; and indeed in a position analogous to our relation to her.[9] So, too, Marie poses more generally the problem of
the reader before any text; for the project in which she is engaged
is not so much a philological as an epistemological undertaking,
one that collapses the distinction between historical otherness
and the otherness of writing, reading, and interpreting. "Gloser la
lettre," means, of course, "to gloss" or "to interpret," which in
medieval poetics is also always eroticized. "To gloss the letter" is
"to desire" or "golozer" (Latin *glutio*) the letter, as in the Patristic
association of letters with the corporeal. Then, too, the "surplus
of sense" that gloss produces, and which is assimilable to a certain textual *legs*, sustains such a gloss on gloss. For *sens* can mean
in Old French "sign," "sense," but also "seed" or "semen" (Latin
semino); and the word "surplus" as "excess" and a spilling of seed,
equivalent to the much-abused French "jouissance," is regularly
used in Old French to indicate the sexual act, pleasure which

exceeds language. ("Ensemble gisent e parolent / E sovent baisent e acolent. / Bien lur covienge del surplus, / De ceo que li autre unt en us!" ["Guigemar," 531ff.]).

That which is desired, through gloss, is something like a proper signification or the full word, a place (*locus* or *lai*) from which to speak that is conceived to be ontologically grounded. "Locus," says Varro, in discussing the first element of speech, "is where something can be *locatum*, 'placed,' . . . where anything comes to a standstill is a *locus*, 'place.'"[10] The reader or interpreter desires access to the zone where, within such a verbal epistemology of return, all movement toward a source halts, where meaning is imagined to come to rest and to be immutable.

Words, figured to be ontologically grounded, become the objects of desire because they are imagined to be rooted, full, autonomous. Like Aquinas's proofs of God as the One who moves but is not moved, the One on whom others depend but who depends on nothing, the hypothetical full word is also without origin and contains its own value. Where poetry is concerned, it is the creator, the one who introduces obscurities, gaps, or holes in language (the trouvère) and who is most capable of attaining to the full word, who himself becomes the object of desire; and of jealousy, since "goloser" also means "to rival" or "to be jealous of":

Ki de bone mateire traite,
Mult li peise si bien n'est faite.
Oëz, seignurs, ke dit Marie,
Ki en sun tens pas ne s'oblie.
Celui deivent la gent loër
Ki en bien fait de sei parler.
Mais quant i ad en un païs
Hummë u femme de grant pris,
Cil ki de sun bien unt envie
Sovent en dïent vileinie:
Sun pris li volent abeissier;
Pur ceo comencent le mestier
Del malveis chien coart, felun,
Ki mort la gent par traïsun.
Nel voil mie pur ceo leissier,
Si gangleür u losengier
Le me volent a mal turner:
Ceo est lur dreit de mesparler!

("Guigemar," 1ff.)

(He who fashions [draws, treats] good material is very pained if it is not well done. Listen, lords, to what Marie says, she who in her time does not forget her duty. People should praise the one who has a good reputation; but when there is a man or a woman of great worth, those who are envious of his or her good fortune often say villainous things. They want to lower his or her standing. In this way they are like the evil, mad, cowardly dog that bites people treacherously. I do not want to leave off writing for this reason. If badmouthers and liars want to distort things, it is their right to speak ill.)

Thus begins the *lai* of "Guigemar," the story of an uninitiated knight's ill-fated hunt, journey to the Other World where he meets the imprisoned wife of a jealous old man, loves her for a year before being discovered, then returns—via a mysterious boat that seems always to be waiting—to his original point of departure. The unhappily married woman eventually escapes to join him and undoes the knot she has placed in his shirt as the sign of recognition.

Like the poet capable of the full word, Guigemar is at the outset an autonomous being—the one who, unspoiled, remains sexually undefined, foreign to desire: "De tant i out mespris Nature / Ke unc de nule amur n'out cure" (57f.) ("He had so scorned nature that he had no use for love"). And yet, he is at the same time, and precisely because of such a lack of definition, the object of universal desire:

> Suz ciel n'out dame ne pucele
> Ki tant par fust noble ne bele,
> Se il d'amer la requeïst,
> Ke volentiers nel retenist.
> Plusurs l'en requistrent suvent,
> Mais il n'aveit de ceo talent.
>
> (59ff.)

(In the whole world there was not a lady or maid no matter how noble or beautiful who, if he were to request her love, would not willingly give it. Many asked him for it often, but he had no desire for such things.)

The hero participates in the fantasy of self-sufficiency, a being dependent on no other, Being itself. Until, of course, he meets the same—the doe that is also "hors de série," unique because of its whiteness, but also because this doe with antlers is as sexually undetermined as Guigemar:

En l'espeise d'un grant buissun
Vit une bise od un foün.
Tute fu blaunche cele beste,
Perches de cerf out en la teste.

(89 ff.)

(In the thick of a great wood he saw a doe with her fawn. The beast was completely white and had a stag's antlers on its head.)

And until he shoots the arrow that signals directionality, the entrance of becoming upon the represented scene of Being, the contingent upon the necessary, history, time, and narrational kinesis upon the hypostatized fantasy of plenitude: "Il tent sun arc, si trait a li! / En l'esclot la feri devaunt" (94f.). ("He holds his bow, he draws it to him; he struck the doe in the front hoof [or breastbone]"). The shooting of the arrow that is drawn to him—"trait a li"—is, in short, an inscription on the level of theme of what narrative elaboration is all about and remains indistinguishable from Marie's drawing of her own project: "Ki de bone mateire traite, / Mult li peise si bien n'est faite."

The semantic range of "traire" is rich indeed and presents another challenge to the premise that reading Classical or medieval texts is merely a matter of dictionary definitions. For "traire" (MF *tirer*) means "to shoot"; but it also means "to draw out," or simply, "to draw," as suggested by the "traits" of the portrait of Venus painted on the wall of the lady's prison tower:

La chaumbre ert peinte tut entur;
Venus, la deuesse d'amur,
Fu tres bien mise en la peinture:
Les traiz mustrout e la nature . . .

(233ff.)

(The room was painted all around. Venus, the goddess of love, was well represented in the painting, which showed her nature and her traits.)

Then, too, "traire" also signifies "to translate," "to transmit," or "to transform" and is the term for that which any author does in extruding or drawing one text from another: "D'aukune bone estoire faire / E de latin en romaunz traire." As translation, "traire" implies the transformation of the same into the other; and if it means "to shoot," "to distance," or "to introduce difference," it is because such terms of alienation are the homonym of "to deceive." Indeed, given the fact that Old French, even though written, was intended for the ear (either to be recited or read aloud), there can be no difference between the words "traire" and "trahir." "To draw or shoot" and "to betray" stand as proof of the treacherousness of a homophonic lack of difference in the sound of a word that can also mean "to differ."

The arrow that is drawn also betrays, returns to the self that shoots, is deflected, wounding the archer in exactly the same place as the impotent Fisher King of Grail tradition:

> La seete resort ariere,
> Guigemar fiert en tel maniere,
> En la quisse desk'al cheval
> Ke tost l'estuet descendre aval.

(97ff.)

(The arrow returned in the direction from which it came and struck Guigemar in the thigh up to the horse in such a way that he had to dismount.)

Guigemar's wound, the "plaie en la quisse," is a dismemberment, a gap or "faille" in the body, which, in seeking to be filled, provokes the quest for health that is a thematic version of the narrative quest for meaning: "Chaut le senti e le quor sein" (300): "He feels it hot, and his body bleeds," or "signifies." "En la quisse m'ad si nafré, / Jamés ne quid estre sané" (319f.): "I am so wounded in the thigh that I despair of ever being healed," or "I despair of ever being signified (sané)." For the homophonic pair "sené" / "sané" can mean "sign," "sense," and "health," as in the common designation of the "forcené" as the one who is both "outside of signs" and "out of his mind [senses]" or "unhealthy."

Such an assertion suggests that the hero's wanderings and attempt to overcome or reverse his own dismemberment are, on the level of plot, assimilable to the trouvère's avowed project of memory or "remembrement" to use the Old French word; neither of which can be detached from the lacks—the trous—of the letter seeking a surplus of sense. Guigemar's displacements—to the Other World and back—represent an attempt to heal the wound opened by the deflected arrow: "Començat sei a purpenser / En quel tere purrat aler / Pur sa plaie faire guarir" (125f.) ("He began to wonder in what land he could go to have his wound healed"). Displacements, of course, without consciousness that the desire for bodily wholeness cannot be detached from the desire for plenitude of meaning, and that this desire—the one thing that Guigemar lacks—is, ultimately, the desire for desire (as well as the desire for gloss). For the boat in which the knight drifts carries him to the land of jealousy and desire with the understanding that it is in the wound that desire originates and that desire is a wound: "Amur est plaie dedenz cors" (483).[11]

Marie, and she is not alone, makes a persuasive case for the analogy between sexual jealousy and the desire for the word. Thus, the husband's dread of losing his young wife—"Gelus esteit a desmesure" (213)—is analogous to Marie's own anxiety at the thought of misappropriation, as the fear of having one's wife turned away from prison becomes equivalent to the fear of misprision: "Si gangleür u losengier / Le me volent a mal turner: / Ceo est lur dreit de mesparler!" Nor should it be thought that desire originates in anything like nature, the body, or a naturalism of the body that is so often mistakenly associated with medieval literature as preliterary or natural. On the contrary, the walled tower that is supposed to contain the woman and constrain her desire is lined with pictures and a book:

> La chaumbre ert peinte tut entur;
> Venus, la deuesse d'amur,
> Fu tres bien mise en la peinture;
> Les traiz mustrout e la nature
> Cument hom deit amur tenir
> Et lealment e bien servir.
> Le livre Ovide, ou il enseine
> Comment chascuns s'amur estreine,
> En un fu ardant le gettout,
> Et tuz iceus escumengout
> Ki jamais cel livre lirreient
> Ne sun enseignement fereient.
> La fu la dame enclose e mise.
>
> (233ff.)

(The room was painted all around. Venus, the goddess of love, was well represented in the painting which showed her nature and her traits and how a man should nurture love and loyally and faithfully serve. The book of Ovid in which he teaches how one can hold love in check she [Venus] threw into a burning fire, and excommunicated all who would read this book or follow its teaching. It was there the lady had been put and kept.)

Guigemar's voyage, in other words, takes him to the Other World, but the Other World is a book, or the very letters and pictures that are the source of desire envisaged, as in the Paolo and Francesca episode of the *Inferno*, as an infinite regression toward other books, the works from which the present catalyst to sexual longing has been drawn or "trahi." A book, furthermore, that contains its own formula of mandatory misreading in the promise to excommunicate all who read and follow its command. The book is the very embodiment of the paradoxical law—or *lei*—which prescribes its own transgression.

All of which poses the questions: To what does the letter, do letters, refer? Does the letter bear us to a sense outside of the text? To an Other World? Or does it refer, as the example suggests, only to other letters? Does the letter take us back to a place in the Varronian sense? To a nature? Toward the body? What is the relation of the letter to Guigemar's trajectory? What determines his course? Why is he necessarily drawn to the place of desire? Why does he return to the original point of departure? Are the voyages of the mysterious boat without pilot in some sense programmed or prescribed (see 629, 678)? Is the question of the boat, finally, the same as whether or not the letter hits the mark, as whether or not sense returns to a place? If so, is there then a place, a code, a set of criteria, or a doctrine outside the text from which to interpret its perambulations? Does the letter hit the mark or, like Guigemar's arrow, only ricochet back to open a difference within the body, a difference from itself?

A reading of misreading that would return the letter to itself, turn it upon itself, is also implicit in Guigemar's wound; for the "plaie" which bleeds and signifies, is also a "plait," or plea, the equivalent of speech itself. "Bele dame, finum cest plait! (526), says the frustrated lover, urging that they pass from speech to the lovemaking that Marie situates as a surplus beyond letters. Nor can the attentive reader avoid the identity of the wound that is a plea with the pleat or knot which, according to the traditional love ordeal, Guigemar and his lady alone can untie as the guarantee of reading each other. The shirttail which in the beginning staunches the wound ("De sa chemise estreitement / Sa plaie bende fermement" [139f.] [With his shirttail he binds his wound tightly]) is also a tangle of meaning, an undoable surplus of sense. The "plait" that is a pleat or a fold serves, in other words, and this according to Marie's own thesis concerning obscurity, as a reminder not only that the letter remains closed ("Unc ne la purent despleier" [654]), but, once again, that desire is a function of the pleat's closedness: "Amur est plaie dedenz cors." Which comes to be read, finally, as "desire is a wound, knot, pleat, or plea in the body, or in the (textual) corpus." Rather, since the reader remains incapable of positing priority for a reading that would privilege either "pleat" or "plea," desire can be identified with the folds of a text, its pleats, its pleas, its resisting obscurities that form the undoable knot of fiction. For the undoing of the shirttail—thematized at the end of "Guigemar" as an untying without cutting—merely gives way to the unfolding of another tale:

> A ses costez li met ses meins,
> Si ad trovee la ceinture.
> "Bele, fet il, queil aventure
> Que jo vus ai issi trovee!
> Ki vus ad ici amenee?"
> Ele li cunte la dolur,
> Les peines granz e la tristur,
> De la prisun u ele fu,
> E coment li est avenu.
> Coment ele s'en eschapa.
> Neier se volt, la neif trova.
>
> (820ff.)

(He put his hands on her hips and found the belt. "Sweet friend, he said, what a lucky adventure that I've found you like this! Who brought you here?" She recounted the pain and the great hardships and the sadness of the prison where she was, and all that had happened to her—how she escaped, how she wanted to drown herself but found the boat instead.)

Guigemar's circuit—from home to the fantasy-filled world of the book and back—is, at bottom, the closed cycle of fiction. This is where the discovery of the lovers, a supposed laying of hands upon the body and capture of the truth of adultery in *flagrante delicto*, comes into central focus: "Cel jur furent aparceü, / Descovert, trové, e veü (577f.). ("That day they were perceived, discovered, found, and seen.") It is the fact of being found—"trahit," compromised, and invented, "trové"—that sends Guigemar home and leaves the reader with the understanding that to find, invent, or compose (contract, negotiate) represents a despoiling, uncovering, unfolding of the pleat that betrays. Herein lies the text's link to the ideology of so-called courtly or secret adulterous love. For the poet, in composing, does to the lovers exactly what the jealous husband does to his wife and her lover: she betrays by revealing, and thus destroys at the very moment she creates. Such a premise justifies, I think, a reading at the level of the letter—"sulunc la lettre e l'escriture" (23)—which also pleases. It is, according to Marie, a pleasure to deplete the tale of sense: "Mult est bele, ki la depleie" (160).

NOTES

1. R. Howard Bloch, "Naturalism, Nationalism, Medievalism," *Romanic Review* 76 (1986): 341–60.

2. F. Brunetière, "Les Fabliaux du moyen âge et l'origine des contes," *Revue des Deux Mondes* 119 (1893): 189.

3. Gaston Paris, "Préface" to L. Petit de Julleville, *Histoire de la langue et de la littérature françaises* (Paris: Armand Colin, 1910), p. n.

4. J. Rychner, "Les Fabliaux. Genre, Styles, Publics" in *La Littérature narrative du moyen âge* (Paris: Presses Universitaires de France, 1961), 51; Ph. Ménard, *Les fabliaux: contes à rire du moyen âge* (Paris: Presses Universitaires de France, 1983), 13.

5. Bloch, *Scandal of the Fabliaux* (Chicago: University of Chicago Press, 1986), chap. 1.

6. "Un gros exemple em porroit metre / As genz *laiz* qui n'entendent lettre." Jean de Meun, *Le Roman de la Rose*, ed. D. Poirion (Paris: Flammarion, 1974), 17393.

7. "Il n'ot vallet en sa meisun / Ne face engin, reis u laçun, / Puis les mettent par le vergier. / N'i ot codre ne chastainier / U il ne mettent laz u glu, / Tant que pris l'unt e retenu" ("Le Laüstic," 95ff. in Marie de France, *Lais*, ed. J. Rychner [Paris: Champion, 1983]).

8. Bloch, *Etymologies and Genealogies* (Chicago: University of Chicago Press, 1983), chap. 1.

9. The best treatment of the "Prologue" that I know is that of M. J. Donovan, *The Breton Lay: A Guide to Varieties* (Notre Dame, Ind.: Notre Dame Press, 1969), 15–24. See also: K. Brightenback, "Remarks on the Prologue to Marie de France's Lais," *Romance Philology* 30 (1977): 168–77; R. Dragonetti, "Le Lai narratif de Marie de France," in *La Musique et les lettres* (Geneva: Droz, 1986): 31–53; P. Gallais, "Recherche sur la mentalité des romanciers français du moyen âge," *Cahiers de Civilisation Médiévale* 7 (1964): 479–92; T. Hunt, "Glossing Marie de France," *Romanische Forschungen* 86 (1974): 396–418; Ph. Ménard, *Les Lais de Marie de France* (Paris: Presses Universitaires de France, 1984), 17; L. Spitzer, "The Prologue to the *Lais* of Marie de France and Medieval Poetics," *Modern Philology* 41 (1943): 96–102.

10. Varro, *De Lingua Latina*, ed. R. Kent (Cambridge: Harvard University Press, 1951), 1:14.

11. Though E. Sienaert is conscious of wordplay in this passage of "Guigemar," he hardly capitalizes upon its full potential: "Tout le vocabulaire de la scène de la chasse et celui de la souffrance physique est transposé maintenant dans le domaine moral: *féru, nafré, anguisus, guarir*, et jusqu'au parallèle de la peur de mourir par la blessure à la cuisse (v. 128), qui devient ici la certitude de mourir par un refus d'amour (vv. 396–98). Ces glissements sémantiques, jeu conscient et élaboré dans le goût nou-

veau mis à la mode par l'*Enéas,* culminent dans cette réflexion d'auteur: 'Amur est plaie dedenz cors.'" (E. Sienaert, *Les Lais de Marie de France. Du conte merveilleux à la nouvelle psychologique* [Paris: Champion, 1978], 56.)

Reading It Right: The Ideology of Text Editing

D A V I D   F .   H U L T

Textual criticism as a specialized discipline within the larger framework of literary studies occupies a curious, in-between position, to the extent that by its very nature as mediation between disparate textual artifacts and a modern public it constantly vacillates between the treatment of individual cases and the consideration of broader ideological or methodological stances. The frequency with which general statements of principle give way to specific examples (or counter-examples), and conversely, the overarching tendency for these examples to engender certain methodological generalizations suggests that, in this very special involvement between reader and text, praxis can never be cleanly divorced from theory. It is perhaps with this inevitability in mind that I begin, not with my own statement of principles, but rather with three anecdotal examples, each of a different nature, that are evocative of some of the concerns that have led me to write about text editing and its relation to literary theory.

The first is a story that could happen to any one of us. Whether it is real or fictional is not of any particular significance. Assume that you are the personal friend of a moderately successful novelist, whom we will refer to as the Author. The Author has just finished writing his third novel and sent you a photocopy of the page proofs since he knows you are a fan of his work. In reading the proofs, you notice an obvious inconsistency: in a dialogue between the novel's two protagonists, reported in direct discourse, one of them clearly mixes up the name of his own daughter and that of his interlocutor's daughter. The inconsistency can be considered obvious since the context makes no doubt about the referent of the name in question. Upon some reflection, it occurs to you that the "confusion" might have been intentional. In a subtle way, the authority of the printed page, be it in the form of page proofs or a bound volume, here manifests itself: instead of assuming a natural or verisimilar logic of characterization that dictates one and only one possibility, you wonder whether the switch in names might not play a role in what would then be an unorthodox novelistic characterization. Not unreasonably, you might be moved to telephone your friend, the Author, and mention your query by way of alerting him to the mistake or, alternately, discovering his true intention. The Author, seemingly unaware of any such complication, checks his typescript and finds that he had genuinely confused the two names when he wrote down that passage. He then proceeds to call his editor and find out whether, at that late stage, the error can be corrected.

This story is totally unremarkable and therein lies its significance. Anyone who has ever known an author and observed his writing practices (or paid any attention to his own) knows that authors make mistakes and that they also on occasion forget the detail of what they have written. Suppose the error was not brought to the printer's attention in time to be corrected. We might at the very least expect the correction to occur in the second edition; but what if the novel did not sell enough copies to reach a second edition? Will the future reader detect the error and attribute it merely to the printer? Will he assume the possibility that the mix-up of names was intended? Let us imagine a further possibility: namely, that the author so appreciated the inadvertent appropriateness of his own mistake that he decided to retain it. In this case, the text—itself unchanged—reflects two different intentions from two different moments of the author's awareness of his own work. Is it possible or desirable for us to register this difference at the level of the text itself?

I do not wish to belabor this example, except to point out the problematical nature of the concept of intention when it is applied to the interpretation of literary works. To be more specific, intention of action or of word is a real human phenomenon, but its nature in the realm of human action is not the same as in that of writing. When we speak of intention in or of a text, we are transferring our detection of meaning within the readerly transaction to its presumed human source, which can no longer explain what it meant. An author's expressed or unexpressed intention can change through time, but a text made public does not change along with it.

My second example is also a modern one, but one that actually took place and for which we have an enormous quantity of documentation. In the first edition of *Du côté de chez Swann*, published by Bernard Grasset in 1913, the publisher included, by way of advertisement, an outline of the two succeeding volumes that were intended to complete the protracted work. The first of these was announced for the following year.[1] All three volumes, taken together, comprised Proust's vision at that time of his monumental *À la recherche du temps perdu*. This had already marked an expansion (or at least a reapportionment) of what had been Proust's expressed intention in a letter of 1912, where he foresaw two volumes, *Le temps perdu* and *Le temps retrouvé*.[2] It is well known that one of the great flukes of publication history was that the outbreak of the Great War in Europe in 1914 stopped short the printing of Proust's second volume while it was still in galleys. Proust would spend the war years revising and interpolating, and the project would grow to five volumes in 1919, when the second volume, *À l'ombre des jeunes filles en fleurs*, appeared, this time at the Nouvelle Revue Française. The final state of the work at Proust's death in 1922 would be five volumes in print, one volume in galleys (in the process of being corrected), and two volumes in a rather disordered manuscript form.

This brief sketch can only begin to give an idea of one of the most astounding panoramas of authorial creation and its development that remains documented for us. Even the most stable parts of the text, the opening lines of *Combray*, for instance, have been shown to conceal an astonishingly complex, and not necessarily regular, development through a series of *avant-textes*, or pre-texts, no fewer than twelve extending from first drafts written in 1908 to the last set of page proofs corrected late in 1913.[3] What are we to make of the clearly marked intention governing the artistic totality as conceived in 1913? Is this less of an authorial intention than that of 1922? What do we make of such details as textual partitioning that, we know from Proust's letters, did not go according to his wishes but rather according to the desires of the printer? We are accustomed to speak of the moment when a text leaves an author's hands, or the author's last wish as the ultimate mark of authority, perhaps comparable to a last will and testament. But how can we apply this to a text that never really left its author's hands, to an aesthetic that could not abide by a final form except insofar as an accident such as death severed text from author? What status, indeed, can we confer on a will that remains unsigned, caught in a limbo between legal authority and personal wishes?

I do not wish to suggest by these two examples anything other than the possibly too obvious fact that most practical experience we have with authors shows that the work of writing is not divorced from the material and social aspects of this activity. Authors write for a public, and frequently modify their production to conform to the physical and economic aspects of book publication. Indeed, it has recently been argued for the body of modern texts that the textual editor must take account of a work's social production, the "collaboration" between artist and institution.[4] This does not of course keep us from imagining or idealizing an artistic intention behind poems or novels — such a gesture on our part is perhaps a necessity of any interpretive approach to literature. We must nonetheless keep in mind the sharp distinction between the idealized mask of the author-and-his-intention *as a function of reading*, and the human face behind the mask that is to be discovered in the material genesis of any human artifact.

Let me now turn to a third example, which will bring me to the main focus of this chapter, the ideology of textual criticism. What I would like to relate is an exchange between two editors that occurred at an international conference some ten to fifteen years ago.[5] The first editor, whom I will call Editor A, explained his choice of one reading over another in a particular poem of Marcabru, stating, "There I believe that one is authorized to make a choice and, if one does not choose, one is providing the average reader with a faulty working instrument (*instrument de travail*) . . . One must eliminate a certain noise (*bruit*), this noise is constituted by the word *planissa*, which is banal and commonly used, whereas the word *calmissa*, which would have been understood with difficulty by an Italian scribe, is a localized, technical term . . . If we give the average reader a text with *planissa*, we are giving him a more banal idea of Marcabru's text, which we can in fact recover through reasoning and interpretation."[6] Evoking a previous edition of the poem by the turn-of-the-century German scholar Karl Appel which used the same methodology but incorporated the common reading, Editor B replied, "the method you chose did not lead you to this reading, it was your own personal taste."[7] Reiterating that it was not his taste but rather his reasoning, Editor A added, "A critical edition is always perfectible, it is always an open-ended work . . . Karl Appel did not sufficiently exercise his faculty of interpretation. And I insist that interpretation is essential for a critical edition . . . and I believe that Appel himself, if he were here today, would recognize the correctness of my reasoning and of my choice."[8] Editor B retorted, "Nothing proves that the technical word is not a correction made by a reader well-versed in Old Provençal. You cannot prove it. You can incorporate it because it seems better to you, and you have every right to do so. But nothing proves that it is more authentic."[9] Editor A restated his argument as follows: "An Italian scribe could not substitute a technical and local Provençal term for a word that he would have understood readily, such as *planissa*. So, if his text contains this word, that means that it must have been the text that transmitted it to him."[10] Editor B: "It is not impossible that your Italian scribe had a Provençal speaker next to him who provided him with the word."[11] And so the argument goes.

We can detect in this brief exchange a number of important moves related to textual criticism, not the least of which is the striking fictionalization of the scribal moment, useful for the purposes of eliminating any stroke that can be attributed to that moment. Did the scribe know enough Provençal to have included that word or not? Whatever the answer, we are always safe in ascribing ignorance to the scribe. But it should be stressed that once the methodological argument turns to material contingency, the least common denominator of chance will take over, and no clear-cut solution is possible. What is even more significant is the enlisting of Karl Appel (bringing him back from the dead, as Editor B will remark nastily) to support an editorial choice. Appel did not push his interpretive faculties far enough to make this choice, says Editor A, in effect, but I could convince him with my reasoning. He of course stops short of making the logical yet unmentionable further claim, that his reasoning could probably also convince the author, "if he were here today."

Before I comment any further, I would like to say a few words about these two eminent philologists, whose real names are Aurelio Roncaglia and Félix Lecoy, and the two methodological tendencies they have so conveniently been chosen to represent under the guise of anonymity. They are reprising a debate that has polarized the field of textual criticism for at least the past fifty years: namely, the debate between the Lachmann method of text editing and the method attributed to the great French scholar Joseph Bédier. Most succinctly, the method credited to Lachmann advocates the reconstruction of an author's original text as based upon the genealogical classification of manuscript exemplars into groupings known as families.[12] Ideally, the resultant genealogical tree will provide a mechanical (i.e., objective) means of eliminating those readings erroneously introduced into the author's text and reconstructing the lost original. The Bédier method involves the detection of a single "best" manuscript from among those transmitting a given text and printing that single exemplar with as little editorial intervention as possible. Since Bédier's strongly polemical, definitive statement refuting textual reconstruction was published in 1928 (this was a reworking and elaboration of more schematic remarks made in his 1913 edition of the *Lai de l'ombre*), all textual editors have had to deal at least implicitly with one or the other of these positions.[13]

I have recalled this debate not so much in order to reenact it in all of its excruciating details, which are all too familiar to practicing textual editors, but to bring out the exemplary nature of the debate as well as its implications for those of us who are more oriented to the practice of interpretation than textual criticism. The two positions I have outlined have become much more important for what they represent as attitudes toward the medieval text than for the achievements or even the precise statements of the two scholars in the debate. Indeed, few of us have read Lachmann's statements of editorial policy, and even Bédier's view of Lachmann was based largely upon Gaston Paris's particular interpretation and importation of the stemmatic approach to textual criticism.[14] Since that time, Lachmann has become for us, via Bédier, the representative of German idealism in scholarship, a mechanistic, scientistic approach to method that is governed, ultimately, by a deceptive measure of subjectivity. Bédier, on the other hand, is read by his detractors as a blind advocate for scholarly laziness or uncritical methodology, in the form of an editorial method that chooses the easy way out. Some critics dismiss this approach summarily: to print the version of one manuscript, even a "best" manuscript, is quite simply, they feel, not to edit at all.[15]

In the broadest sense, Lachmann and Bédier have taken their places as symbolic signposts along the narrow path tread by text editors, representing two contrary dispositions characteristic of medievalists in general, which I will call the interpretive and the historical, respectively. The interpretive disposition is the one most characteristic of literary scholars in all fields, who accept the literary object as a given, the unmediated communication between an authorial figure and the present-day reader.[16] Implicit assumptions accompanying this view of the text include the precedence accorded to authorial intentionality (or in its stead, to a more vague notion of textual expression), textual closure, and originality. The Lachmannian editor's goal is to present the text to the modern reader by means of an editorial method that neatly balances reconstructed archetype and authorial original. The author is the unabashed hero and the scribe responsible for defacing original textual readings is the villain in the picture. The scribe stands for the historical contingency to which the transcendent literary object is submitted in the transmission of its manuscript. This vision of the field also posits a practicable division between subjective and objective faculties in the establishment of the text. In the well-chosen words of Lee Patterson, according to this ideal "the edition . . . is a calculation of the laws of genius."[17]

The historicizing trend represented by the Bédier side of the polarity sees the medieval text for all its materiality, and, as is characteristic of a twentieth-century archeological view, the "best manuscript" editor is willing to dust off the artifact but most hesitant to alter its material form. It has been pointed out that the archeological analogy is largely a specious one. To compare the reconstruction of a *Lai de l'ombre* with, say, a medieval city such as Carcassonne quite possibly involves two very different undertakings, just as the restoration of a fresco or of a statue might well affect its aesthetic impact without altering its semiotic status. But the real problem is that the medieval literary text genuinely partakes of both of these domains: it is simultaneously a cultural communication that should be able to transcend material corruption, and an artifact, irremediably bound up in the fact of its transmission and resultant corruption.

I have always found it striking that whereas in literary criticism various movements or fashions come and go, the field of textual criticism seems to continue to define itself in terms of this polarity, even when editors are situated somewhere in between, which is increasingly the case. My suspicion is that the reason for this state of affairs is related to the possibility that the editorial debate evokes something basic to our perception of the literary work, some potential that is all too often left aside or simply taken for granted in theoretical discussions. I have already alluded to the dual nature of the literary text, its ideal form in contrast with its material creation, making reference to a couple of modern examples. However much the genesis of a text might be affected by unforeseen events—what we might call historical accidents, containing elements outside the author's intention—once we as readers have the text before us, we shift ground and the conventions of readership take over. In this situation comparable to conventions of theater-going, the author automatically assumes his mask, we lend credence to the mask, and the concretely mortal or fallible nature of the author/actor slips behind it. The two sides of the editorial debate dig even deeper, however, for they directly beg the question of whether, for any writer, unformulated intention and linguistic expression can truly coincide. The balance could swing in either direction depending upon whether we believe in the transendence of thought and inspiration or are caught up in the opaque materiality of language. The debate is, of course, endless, for literary language partakes of both the material and the transcendent.

It can be useful to set the emblematic polarity I have just described in the field of textual criticism against the backdrop of the *langue/parole* distinction articulated by Ferdinand de Saussure at the turn of the century. This has become one of the founding notions of modern structural linguistics.[18] Whatever knowledge we might possess in the present-day of Old French language, vocabulary, and syntax, it must be kept in mind that this knowledge is the result of encounters with texts, a transactional relation that operates in the absence of normative grammars or dictionaries. In this way, like the linguist doing fieldwork, the reader of Old French must constantly form abstractions out of the material data and, in circular fashion, test these hypotheses against still more individual manifestations of the language. The parallel with Saussure's bipartition of language study should be fairly straightforward. For Saussure, *langue* is a "social product"; it is, he tells us, "the social side of speech, outside the individual, who can never create nor modify it by himself; it exists only by virtue of a sort of contract signed by members of a community."[19] *Parole,* usually referred to as "speech" in English, is an individual act that combines a competence in the essential matters of a given language with the "accessory and more or less accidental" attributes of the individual speaker. Now, at first glance it would appear that the Lachmannian editor is simply trying to distinguish *parole* from *langue* when he reconstructs the authorial text from a morass of manuscript variants. But to leave it at that would overlook a glaring dilemma. To reconstruct an Old French text we must first understand the language as a system, the "community standard" that makes the language comprehensible in the first place. However, as Saussure has said, "although dead languages are no longer spoken, we can easily assimilate their linguistic organisms. We can dispense with the other elements of speech; indeed, the science of language is possible only if the other elements are excluded."[20] Our understanding of the Old French language comes from an analysis lying outside of speech, one that factors out any individual aberrations. But then where is the authorial text to be found? How do we go about "calculating the laws of genius"? As a matter of fact, the gesture of the Lachmannian editor consists in the establishment of a new *langue/parole* dichotomy within the restricted corpus of a particular manuscript tradition. The "community of speakers" is redefined as the group of manuscript exemplars of a given text. The new, considerably more specified *langue* translates as the general law that can be established from that group, and the *parole* is the individual, aberrant manuscript reading. Thus, seen from the point of view of the entire Old French corpus, the reconstructed text of an author such as Chrétien de Troyes represents the voice of an individual speaker. But from the point of view of the manuscripts, it involves the studied elimination of all that is individual, accessory, and accidental from what is supposed to be a unique authorial voice.

The dilemma to which I referred above is apparent in one of the most automatic of the editor's choices, the attribution of authenticity to the *lectio difficilior*. What this means is that if a particular reading is "more difficult," which is to say less banal or commonly acceptable, it is more likely to be the author's text — the logic being that scribes are only capable of trivializing a text they are copying. We saw a clear example of this in Roncaglia's defense of the Lachmannian edition. However, it cannot be too difficult, for then it would turn back into an undesirable reading. This is the complementary, though nearly contradictory, editorial concept known as the *usus scribendi*, which counterbalances the difficult reading by the habits of the author as well as of the scribe.[21] Isolating the exceptional reading from the common one always involves measuring the limits of what must still be considered the possibilities of culturally acceptable speech. And since we have no native speakers left to test new possibilities on, we must rely on the corpus as it has already been established. By eliminating all excesses and preserving a modicum of individuality, the Lachmannian edition finds as its goal the positing of a language replete with laws and regularities within a larger language consisting of all the extant possibilities in Old French. The latent irony in all of this is that Old French texts are by their nature less respectful of grammaticality than editors would like them to be, and thus the push toward regulation of the text and its language is a denaturing of it. The situation is equivalent to a linguist recording the American language who would correct the pronunciation and grammar of his native informants, say a random group of individuals from Brooklyn, and use the corrected version as the data for his study.

It is perhaps at the point of intersection between a normative, socially determined linguistic code and individual performance that the strongest objections can be raised to the Lachmannian reconstruction. Saussure has himself been criticized on the grounds that he was not able to theorize the relation between the store of linguistic rules and individual sentence formation that is not, strictly speaking, a part of language.[22] This amounts to the difference between linguistic competence and linguistic performance. We can all read, understand, and appreciate a Shakespearian play, but it has yet to be proven that any of us could write one. To formulate the stylistic norms of a given author or a given literary work is something that all literary critics do in one way or another, but to make use of these norms for the purpose of generating text, to turn from description to prescription, is equivalent to turning from literature to pastiche, from the accident of individual creation to the predictability of normative laws.

We could say that the Lachmannian ideal has respected one of Saussure's criteria for analyzing the individual act of speech, namely "the combinations by which the speaker uses the language code for expressing his own thought." But there is a second characteristic of *parole* that has in the process been left to the side: "the psychophysical mechanism that allows him to exteriorize those combinations" (Saussure). It is precisely this factor—the text's materiality—that the Lachmannian editor wishes did not exist, but that the Bédier editor attempts to recover in his edition. For the latter, the materiality of the manuscript text becomes a part of the individual act of speech, our closest equivalent to the phonic resonances of voice within a literature whose spoken aspects are integral to it and yet all but lost to us. This is perhaps why recent theoretical developments in the area of oral literature have had such an impact on editorial policy in the past ten or so years, as filtered primarily through Paul Zumthor's notion of *mouvance*. Even when, or I might say especially when, these theories are not directly applied to works whose production was heavily influenced by oral performance, such as the *Chanson de Roland* or much of the lyric corpus.[23] The notion of oral composition functions emblematically as a reassertion of contingency and individual difference within the broader perception of the text as a transcendent creative gesture. The scribal individuality of a given manuscript retains its status as an act or a performance of the authorial text, and is thus admissible for what it attests to as far as the manipulation of the Old French language is concerned, its practice. If the Lachmannian hypostatizing of the author figure amounts to a submission of individual *parole* to an ordered discourse ruled by specifiable laws, the Bédier approach (perhaps, when carried to its extreme, somewhat grotesquely) accentuates the accidental and the accessory, precisely what Saussure found to be characteristic of speech, understood as the actualized counterpart of the abstract construct known as human language.

Not surprisingly, perhaps, discussions of specific text-editing problems frequently turn to debates concerning the relative virtues and crimes attributed to the scribe. It is, after all, a matter of exercising authority, and the scribe who defaces the author's text has clearly misused the authority delegated to him. As Saussure states with regard to the nature of *parole*, "execution is never carried out by the collectivity. Execution is always individual, and the individual is always its master."[24] Indeed, the problem of text-editing, the problem of literary creation, is one of mastery—the imposition of individual marks upon a collective edifice. Or, as d'Arco Silvio Avalle has put it so eloquently, a matter of devotion to a lost original: "The critical edition . . . should be understood as a last homage paid to the hidden truth, to the autograph manuscript that has since disappeared."[25] But however much an editor might liken his situation to that of the medieval scribe in his attempt to preserve and transmit the author's text, his own need for authority in a modern economy of collegial scrutiny leads him to accentuate his own individuality—in method, in technique, and in authority. In objecting to the frequent predilection of early philologists for the oldest manuscript, Giorgio Pasquali words his question in a way that should remind us of the continuity of method from scribes to editors: "And our own critical editions, are they not, in the last analysis, based on our copies and collations, that is upon manuscript witnesses of the twentieth century?"

The scribal/editorial affinity does indeed appear to generate a psychological density that materializes in the editorial gesture itself. To the extent that he attempts to embody the authorial ideal, the Lachmannian editor's similarity to the scribe turns into a relation of mimetic rivalry, where all the scribe's best impulses to make the text understandable are considered vices (although these often constitute the editor's favored *modus operandi*) and the cardinal virtue to be sought after—a judgment voiced by innumerable editors—is mechanical stupidity. The scribe is the necessary scapegoat. This complex psychological scenario also explains the occasional appearance of phantom authorities, such as the ghost of Karl Appel, that in their absence sanction the editor's choices. It is precisely this facet of the editorial process that

Bédier undoubtedly meant to evoke when he wrote his critique of a certain stance of editorial objectivity that denies the continuity between medieval writers and scribes, on the one hand, and modern editors and critics, on the other. By treating editors and author figures as potential figments of our own imagination, by suggesting the uncertain border between medieval scribes and authors, by referring to "legions of scribes, redactors and philologists who, by distraction or ignorance, by fantasy or pedantry, have over the course of centuries altered literary works," Bédier was pointing to the fictional quality and participation inherent in our own serious, objective undertaking.[26]

To come back to our discussion of literary theory and its relation to text-editing methodology, should it appear that Bédier comes out ahead, that was not my intention. That his approach to text editing is more appealing to modern literary fashions is unquestionable, with its emphasis on discontinuities, fragmentation, and questioning of authorial intentionality. And whereas the two poles I have described constitute different, but not necessarily better or worse, methods for the practical production of a textual edition, they also stand for two theoretical positions, one of which is largely discredited in current literary discussions. The scientificity attributed to Lachmann suggests the possibility of a neat division between objective and subjective faculties, of a domain of textual criticism separate from theory or interpretation. The methodological skepticism attributed to Bédier stems from a theoretical skepticism that does not take its own vocabulary or metaphors for granted. Bédier was bold enough to say that he could not affirm the difference between an intelligent or gifted scribe and an author. Furthermore, in the midst of his technical discussions in La Tradition manuscrite, Bédier found clever rhetorical ways to deflate (might I say deflower) some of the most powerful metaphors of textual criticism. As when, in the following quote, he mocks reviewers who sketch out elaborate genealogical trees, but never press them into service in order to produce an edition: "Let us indeed stop concentrating our attention on these [genealogical] trees that have never borne any fruit, the beautiful fruits of a 'critical text': these are desiccated and sterile fig trees."[27] The perversion of the natural metaphor justifying stemmatics has already been perverted in its results, leading to family complications involving, possibly, inversion or illegitimacy: "The reasoning is founded on this solitary principle: two brothers must normally resemble each other more than they resemble one of their cousins. And this principle is just. But what if one of the two brothers were to put on makeup and women's clothes?"[28] To end his discussion, Bédier will tacitly alter the metaphor from a natural to a man-made creation: "If we consider that mass of constructions that are called *stemmata codicum* ... the principal groupings of manuscripts, the ones that are aligned up at the bottom of the table, appear to be determined in a very correct fashion: the construction's base, the ground floor, is solid. But it is another matter when we consider the upper parts."[29] In transforming the stemmatic tree into a building, Bédier literally turns the metaphor upside down, showing that the "natural" growth of the tree is really backward, logically and methodologically.

I have gone on at some length about the motives and presuppositions of editorial approaches, but would like to mention a concern of a slightly different nature: not the constitution of an edition, but its afterlife. The neo-Lachmannian school of text editors in Italy, represented by scholars such as Avalle and Segre, has vigorously and persuasively defended reconstructed textual editions in terms of their constituting a "working hypothesis" subject to revision.[30] This defense is somewhat disingenuous, inasmuch as once an edition—any edition—reaches the status of a published work, it attains an authority which is commonly unquestioned, occasionally because it is the only edition we have. In this, the editor's results are quite distinct from those of the literary critic. I may write an article on the style of Chrétien de Troyes that no one will read or lend any credence to, but if I edit one of his romances, using my ideas as a basis for choosing among manuscript readings, my edition, once published, will assume a tacit authority and possibly, with time, become *our* Chrétien de Troyes. And in this, as far as the concrete result is concerned, there is little difference between a Lachmannian or Bédierist edition. For all of its backward concentration, the critical edition is a modern literary act pointed toward a future readership and thus takes its place within a present-day economy of literary production.

In this regard, the question of audience, or reception, is one that deserves some rethinking. The model for what an editor is supposed to be doing has remained largely what it was in the nineteenth century, when medieval studies were first being formed, and yet the field has changed considerably since then. At the time of Gaston Paris, an entire literary canon was being salvaged, if not created outright, along with a battery of texts illustrative of the history of the French language as much as of the culture of a specific period. It is clear from Paris's preliminary remarks in his landmark edition of the *Saint Alexis* that paying homage to the author was only part of his goal. As Hans Ulrich Gumbrecht has recently documented, Paris wanted the new science of text editing, as he observed its practice in Germany, to help realign and strengthen university education in France.[31] Accordingly, Bédier's later reaction against his master's method, overlaid with his anti-German political feelings, suggests stronger psychological and moral convictions than strictly intellectual ones. Gaston Paris also wanted to create a text that would be pedagogically useful: "Even assuming that here and there I have gone too far in attributing to the author of the *Alexis* one or another linguistic form to the exclusion of some other one, I think that it will indeed be recognized that the text of this poem, such as I am offering it to the public, offers an acceptable specimen of proper French language such as it must have been spoken and written in the middle of the eleventh century."[32] Paris needed to predigest the material he was presenting, simply because there was no real basis for his readership to fall back on.

This is of course no longer the case, and the profusion of literary histories, monographs, editions of all persuasions, even dictionaries, has obviated the need for the kind of prescriptive undertaking Paris envisaged. Furthermore, I am not sure whether it is appropriate to speak of an average reader (as does Roncaglia) for editions of medieval texts. The array of materials currently available, from modern language translations, to bilingual editions, to heavily annotated ones (for pedagogical purposes), to anthologies, has put the serious textual editor back in the position of writing for his professional colleagues of a philological or a critical bent. Accordingly, the special skills of the editor are necessary in order to mediate between the dispersion and frequent inscrutability of manuscript exemplars and the needs of the literary specialist. But instead of hiding or simply reducing the multiplicity of readings, the editor should attempt to make them available so that new approaches, new forms of reading—hopefully more appropriate to the medieval artifact—can be tested. Examples of such undertakings can be found in Jean Rychner's edition of *Lanval*, Professor Roach's monumental edition of the *Perceval* continuations, and the new edition of the fabliaux under the guidance of Willem Noomen and the late Nico van den Boogaard.

The profession of editing Old French texts in the 1980s is situated within a network of imaginative, academic, and antiquarian concerns. What is crucial about the editor's craft is its direct placement at that spot where modern concerns meet medieval ones in the very conception of the literary object. In this regard, it is im-

portant to keep in mind that editing is not simply prior to interpretation, it is consubstantial with it. The struggle between
Bédierists and Lachmannians, between scribes and authors, is
important for literary critics because it is a struggle within ourselves, a replaying of the necessarily agonistic relation between
literalism and interpretation, between history and genius. Not
only does this struggle characterize the creative moment, but it
both precedes and accompanies the interpretive voice. If, ultimately, it is either impossible or undesirable to settle the dispute
in text editing, it is perhaps because there is a scribe and an
author in all of us.

NOTES

1. The outline is reprinted in a note in Marcel Proust, À la recherche du
temps perdu, ed. Pierre Clarac and André Ferré (Paris: Gallimard [Éd-
itions de la Pléiade], 1954), xxv.
2. Marcel Proust, Correspondance, ed. Philip Kolb (Paris: Plon, 1984),
11:257 (letter of 28 October 1912 addressed to Eugène Fasquelle, Proust's
then publisher-to-be): "Comme je crois que vous ne me permettriez pas de
mettre 'I' sur le premier volume, je donne au premier volume le titre Le
Temps Perdu. Si je peux faire tenir tout le reste en un seul volume je
l'appellerai Le Temps Retrouvé. Et au-dessus de ces titres particuliers
j'inscrirai le titre général qui fait allusion dans le monde moral à une mal-
adie du corps: Les Intermittences du Coeur. Il serait à souhaiter que le premier volume fût le plus long possible, quand cela ne serait que pour faire
tenir en un seul volume (je ne suis pas certain que ce soit possible) la fin."
3. See Jean Milly, Proust dans le texte et l'avant-texte (Paris: Flammarion, 1985), 19–89.
4. Jerome J. McGann makes a strong case for this approach in his A Critique of Modern Textual Criticism (Chicago: University of Chicago
Press, 1983). Having noted a slightly weaker stance by James Thorpe ("The
work of art is thus always tending toward a collaborative status," quoted
on p. 43), McGann formulates his own argument as follows: "Authority is
a social nexus, not a personal possession; and if the authority for specific
literary works is initiated anew for each new work by some specific artist,
its initiation takes place in a necessary and integral historical environ-
ment of great complexity. Most immediately . . . it takes place within the
conventions and enabling limits that are accepted by the prevailing institutions of literary production" (p. 48).
5. XIV Congresso Internazionale di Linguistica e Filologia Romanza
(Napoli, 15–20 Aprile 1974). See Atti (Naples: Gaetano Macchiaroli, 1978),
1:509–11.
6. Atti, 1, 509, author's translation. [Là je crois qu'on est autorisé à choisir, et que si l'on ne choisit pas, on fournit un instrument de travail fautif
à ce lecteur moyen . . . Il faut éliminer un certain bruit, le bruit est con-
stitué par le planissa, mot banal, courant, tandis que le mot calmissa,

difficilement compréhensible par un copiste italien, est un mot technique, local . . . Si on lui (au lecteur moyen) donne un texte avec *planissa*,
on lui donne une idée plus banale du texte de Marcabru, que nous pouvons rejoindre avec raisonnement et interprétation.]

7. Ibid. [Ce n'est pas la méthode d'édition qui vous permet de choisir:
vous choisissez par votre goût!]

8. Ibid., 510. [Une édition critique est toujours perfectible, est toujours
un travail ouvert . . . (Karl Appel) n'avait pas suffisamment poussé en
avant l'interprétation. Et j'insiste encore que pour une édition critique
l'interprétation est essentielle . . . Et je crois qu'Appel lui-même, s'il était
là, reconnaîtrait la justesse de mon raisonnement et de mon choix.]

9. Ibid. [Rien ne prouve que la leçon *calmissa* ne soit pas la correction
d'un lecteur qui savait beaucoup de provençal. Vous ne pouvez pas le
prouver. Vous pouvez l'adopter parce qu'elle vous paraît meilleure, vous en
avez le droit. Mais rien ne prouve qu'elle soit plus authentique.]

10. Ibid. [Un copiste italien ne pouvait pas substituer à un mot qu'il com-
prenait, comme *planissa*, un mot provençal technique, local, qu'il ne com-
prenait pas. Or s'il a ce mot, il faut que ce mot soit dans le texte qui lui
a été transmis.]

11. Ibid. [Rien n'empêche que votre copiste italien pouvait avoir à côté de
lui un provençal, qui lui a glissé ce mot.]

12. The best and most succinct exposition of Lachmann's career and
editing methods (in the domain of classical texts) remains Sebastiano
Timpanaro's *La Genesi del metodo del Lachmann* (Florence: Felice Le
Monnier, 1963).

13. Bédier's *La Tradition manuscrite du Lai de l'ombre: Réflexions sur
l'art d'éditer les anciens textes* first appeared in article form in 1928 in the
journal *Romania*, and was published as a separate volume by Champion
in 1929.

14. This is clear from Bédier's remarks in *La Tradition manuscrite*, 3–4,
where in a note he expresses his ignorance as to the origin and development of the method.

15. See, for instance, the recent remarks made by Lee Patterson, largely
in defense of the Kane/Donaldson edition of *Piers Plowman:* "To be sure,
not editing has many different degrees, ranging from a diplomatic printing that candidly offers little more than the transcription of a single
manuscript to the traditional "conservative" edition that qualifies its critical commitments by privileging a single manuscript as its copy text"
("The Logic of Textual Criticism and the Way of Genius," in *Textual Criticism and Literary Interpretation*, ed. Jerome J. McGann [Chicago: University of Chicago Press, 1985], 88).

16. The strongest recent statement of this instance, based on the distinction between "meaning" and "significance," is that of E. D. Hirsch, Jr.,
Validity in Interpretation (New Haven: Yale University Press, 1967).

17. Patterson, "The Logic of Textual Criticism," 74.

18. See Ferdinand de Saussure, *Cours de linguistique générale*, based on
the collation of notes by Charles Bally and Albert Sechehaye, ed. Tullio de
Mauro (Paris: Payot, 1972). English translation by Wade Baskin, *Course in
General Linguistics* (New York: McGraw-Hill, 1966).

19. Saussure, *Course*, 14. [Elle est la partie sociale du langage, extérieure à l'individu, qui à lui seul ne peut ni la créer ni la modifier; elle n'existe qu'en vertu d'une sorte de contrat passé entre les membres de la communauté (*Cours*, 31).]

20. Saussure, *Course*, 15 [Nous ne parlons plus les langues mortes, mais nou pouvons fort bien nous assimiler leur organisme linguistique. Non seulement la science de la langue peut se passer des autres éléments du langage, mais elle n'est possible que si ces autres éléments n'y sont pas mêlés (*Cours*, 31).]

21. See, on this point, the cogent remarks of Giorgio Pasquali, *Storia della tradizione e critica del testo* (Florence: Felice Le Monnier, 1934), esp. 121–26.

22. See Jonathan Culler, *Saussure* (Hassocks, Sussex: Harvester Press, 1976), 80–84.

23. See Paul Zumthor's influential *Essai de poétique médiévale* (Paris: Seuil, 1972), 65–79; and for a revised formulation, *La Poésie et la voix dans la civilisation médiévale* (Paris: PUF, 1984), 110–15. On the relation between *mouvance* and textual criticism, see the excellent article by Mary B. Speer, "Wrestling with Change: Old French Textual Criticism and *Mouvance*," *Olifant* 7 (1980): 311–26.

24. Saussure, *Course*, 13. [L'Exécution n'est jamais faite par la masse; elle est toujour individuelle, et l'individu en est toujours le maître (*Cours*, 30).]

25. d'Arco Silvio Avalle, *Principî di critica testuale* (Padua: Antenore, 1972), 20, author's translation. [L'edizione critica . . . va intesa come un omaggio estremo alla verità nascosta, all'autografo scomparso.]

26. Joseph Bédier, *La Tradition manuscrite du Lai de l'Ombre*, 40, author's translation. [Ces légions de scribes, de remanieurs et de philologues qui, par distraction ou par ignorance, par fantaisie ou par pédanterie, ont altéré au cours des siècles les oeuvres non seulement de notre aimable ménestrel, mais de tous les écrivains profanes et sacrés de l'Antiquité et du moyen âge.]

27. Bédier, 10, author's translation. [Cessons, en effet, de considérer ces arbres qui n'ont jamais porté de fruits, les beaux fruits, d'un 'texte critique': arbres secs, figuiers stériles.]

28. Bédier, 54, author's translation. [Le raisonnement est fondé, sauf erreur, sur ce seul principe: deux frères doivent normalement se ressembler plus qu'ils ne ressemblent à un de leur cousins. Et ce principe est juste. Mais si l'un des deux frères s'est maquillé et travesti?]

29. Bédier, 71, author's translation. [À considérer la masse de ces contructions que l'on dénomme *Stemmata codicum* . . . presque toujours les principaux groupements de manuscrits y apparaissent déterminés de façon très juste, ceux qu'on aligne au bas du tableau: la base de la construction, le rez-de-chaussée, est solide. Mais il en va autrement des parties hautes.]

30. See, for instance, Cesare Segre's "Critica testuale, teoria degli insiemi e diasistema," in his *Semiotica filologica: Testo e modelli culturali*, (Turin: Einaudi, 1979), 53–70.

31. Hans Ulrich Gumbrecht, "'Un souffle d'Allemagne ayant passé':

Friedrich Diez, Gaston Paris, and the Genesis of National Philologies," *Romance Philology* 40, no. 1 (1986): 1–37.

32. Gaston Paris and Léopold Pannier, *La vie de Saint Alexis, poème du XIe siècle*, Bibliothèque de l'École des Hautes Études 7 (Paris: A. Franck, 1872), 135, author's translation. [Supposé même que çà et là je sois allé trop loin en attribuant à l'auteur d'*Alexis* telle ou telle forme de langage à l'exclusion de telle autre, je pense qu'on voudra bien reconnaître que le texte de ce poème, tel que je le livre au public, offre un spécimen admissible de la bonne langue française telle qu'elle devait se parler et s'écrire au milieu du XIe siècle.]

Raoul de Cambrai: The Illegitimacy of Writing

ALEXANDRE LEUPIN

Translated by Catherine Jolivet

Let us set out from the conception of the Other as the locus of the signifier. Any statement of authority has no other guarantee than its very enunciation, and it is pointless for us to seek it in another signifier, which could not appear outside this locus in any way. Which is what I mean when I say that no metalanguage can be spoken, or, more aphoristically, that there is no Other of the Other. And when the Legislator (he who claims to lay down the Law) presents himself to fill the gap, he does so as an impostor.

LACAN, *ECRITS*, P. 813

Thus, since the legislator can use neither force nor reasoning, he must turn to an authority of another order, which would direct without violence and persuade instead of convince.

ROUSSEAU, *DU CONTRAT SOCIAL*, 2.6

The Knighthood of Letters (la "Chevalerie de letreüre")

Throughout *Raoul de Cambrai*,[1] knighthood and its private wars are presented rhetorically: they are figures of the writing process generated by the text itself. This correspondence occurs as early as the narrator's exordium, in which the hero's father, Raoul Taillefer (a paradigm of the dead father whose heritage has to be preserved), is presented metaphorically as the "flower" of chivalry:

Chantet vous ont cil autre jogleor
Chançon novelle: mais ils laissent la flor,
C'est de Raoul; de Canbrai tint l'onour.

(4ff.)

(These other poets have sung
A new song for you, but they have left out the best,
It is about Raoul who had the fief of Cambrai.)

If knighthood is a flower of rhetoric, then rhetoric is a war, a verbal combat and, more specifically in our text, a feud or vendetta of words. Examples of this association abound: helmets and coats of arms (signifying masks that both reveal and conceal the signifier, the knight's body and face) are frequently studded with flowers and lapidary gems:

Li quens Raous fu molt de grant vertu.
En sa main tint le bon branc esmolu,
Et fiert Ernaut parmi son elme agu
Qe flors et pieres en a jus abatu.

(2857ff.)

(Count Raoul was of great courage.
In his hand he had a good sharp sword,
And he strikes Ernaut in the middle of his pointed helmet
So that the flowers and gems fall from it.)

Elsewhere:

Armes ot beles, paintes a flor de lis.

(4240)

(He had beautiful weapons, painted with lily flowers.)

Correlatively, lances and swords explicitly participate in a discourse that transforms them into metaphors of a murderous pen:

"D'or en avant el grant fer de ma lance
Est vostre mors escrite, sans faillance."

(1794f.)

("From now on, on the big blade of my lance
Your death is inscribed, without failure.")

"Au branc d'acier vos noterai tel lai
Dont ja n'arez a nul jor le cuer gai."

(5073f.)

("With this sword, I will write a poem for you
And your heart will never be gladdened by it.")

Thus, weapons are the vectors of a discursive demonstration, even of a *lectio* or a pseudotheological *sermo:*

"S'or n'avoit ci de ta gent tel fuison,
A ceste espée qi me pent au geron
T'aprenderoie ici pesme leçon
C'onques n'oïs si dolereus sermon:
Ja par provoire n'ariés confession."

(3982ff.)

("If there were not so many of your family members here,
With this sword that hangs at my side
I would teach you the harshest of lessons
For you have never heard such a painful sermon:
Never would your confession be heard by a priest.")

In this regard, the bloodshed brought on by verbal warfare can very well be considered the ink of the song itself, a song that obsessionally calls attention to the hemorrhagic character of its own writing:

Plaies ont grans, ne finent de saignier.

(5126)

(They have large wounds that don't stop bleeding.)

Raoul de Cambrai thus revives a well-known martyrologic and biblical topos that Curtius identified as "Blutschrift"[2]; allusions to the blood of Christ (1114) and to Longinus's lance (5300) function as discreet reminders of the topos. We may then presume that just as in the *Chanson de Roland*[3] (but with very different modalities), the stake of the feud is not only chivalric honor, prowess, or valor, but especially the production of a value that would be the value of the literary work itself, linked to the preservation of these feudal notions:

Dist Berniers: "Sire, molt aveiz grant poour.
Soiés preudoume et bon combateour:
Chascun remenbre de son bon ancesor.
Je nel volroie por une grant valour
Povre chançon en fust par gogleour."

(4140ff.)

(Bernier said: "My Lord, you were very afraid.
Be brave and a good warrior:
So that everyone can remember their courageous ancestor.
I would not want for a poet to make a bad song
About great valiance.")

From this standpoint, the writer's task is to insure that the writing in blood not be lost while spilling out of a dying body: lost on the soil (2865), in the grass (2985), in sand (3974), or even in water (4042). The writer must pose an obstacle between hemorrhage and its disappearance, an obstacle either visible in the fiction (such as a woman's body, with which paternal blood can produce an heir) or invisible to this same fiction (such as the page, where the hemorrhage coagulates into writing on the parchment).

However, no reading should stop at merely cataloguing the figures of textual reflexivity. First, since the phenomenon of reflexivity is very common in medieval literature, the commentator may compromise the text's specificity by simply enumerating its reflexive figures; the tautology "literature does nothing but speak itself" may be true, but it is always written in a different way. Next, a text reflecting on itself is never a neutral operation. Even if, as Geoffrey of Vinsauf claims, the textual mirror is an empty mirror,[4] it still has a dynamic role in determining meaning. This is why we must now scrutinize the stakes and symbolic economy particular to the writing of *Raoul de Cambrai*.

The Unlocatable Father

Above all, this text is a truly monumental effort at thinking the locus of the dead father in both symbolic and real senses; all the sons in the epic must bear this cross, sometimes to the point of being overwhelmed by it. Near the beginning of the text, Raoul reminds the Emperor Louis of this fact:

"Drois emperere, ge vos di tot avant:
L'onnor del pere, ce sevent li auquant
Doit tot par droit revenir a l'effant."

(699ff.)

("Just emperor, I declare to you:
That the honor of the father, everyone knows it
Must rightly go to the child.")

The fact that no one in the song is equal to the status of paternity shows us that the father in question is actually the Name-of-the-Father, and not the real or biological father. In this respect, it is not important that the contradictions in the feudal laws of heritage are either synchronic or anachronistic in relation to the time of the text's writing; digging into the archives here would be of no help for interpretation. However, the Lacanian parameters of the problem just raised must not obliterate the fact that the text submits the transmission of land to the symbolic determinations of its time.[5] In fact, in *Raoul de Cambrai* the right to inherit the Name-of-the-Father, or the fief that sustains this name, is very unstable, since two contradictory laws claim to establish it: on the one hand, there is the inheritance of land by the eldest son, and on the other the right of the sovereign (the ultimate figure of which is the emperor) to invest whomever he pleases. This second law is based upon the concept of royalty as a temporal figure of transcendental dimension: to distribute his vassals' lands, Louis must refer to a theological order. In other words, the feudal community as a whole must believe in and credit royal power with a divine origin, rethink it transitively as "God who made the laws" [Dieu qui fist les lois (731, 2150)]. Along the same lines, any word by which the king commits himself should ideally be *phatique* or self-fulfilling: committed by its very utterance to a realization that would verify it. From the moment that this transcendence of royal legitimacy is refused to the emperor, he is no longer the one chosen by God ["l'oint du Seigneur"], but only a pawn in a political chess game, and he maintains his leading position only through force or usurpation.[6]

This means that at a given moment any feudatory can claim the place of the father. An inverted confirmation of this fundamental illegitimacy is the fact that Louis must take an oath upon relics as a guarantee for his word of investiture (760). The oath in no way demonstrates the presence of a transcendental order in a position of power, but instead shows that the king's word has nothing self-fulfilling or sacred about it, and that it must therefore be guaranteed as strictly as possible.[7] Hence, his word of pseudorectitude, his "right," is absolutely inseparable from its opposite: "denunciation" [*desparler* (308)], "failure" (778), "verbal revocation" [*dé-dit* (948)], and "wrong" (777, 823, 5935). Giboïn le Manceaux's mistrust is therefore justified when he receives the fief of Cambrésis:

"Vos me donastes Cambrizis lés Artois;
Ne la poés garantir demanois."

(714f.)

("You gave me Cambrésis les Artois;
You cannot guarantee it immediately.")

Verbal revocation, which affects the entire text of the song, is most strikingly exemplified in the first verse, when the narrator promises the reader a joyful song:

Oiez chançon de joie et de baudor!

(1)

(Hear a song of joy and happiness!)

We know that it will not be so; therefore, the entire text must be examined as the antithesis of a contradiction.

This fissuring of "correct" discourse has the double effect of: 1) showing that any claim to legitimacy is a fiction; and 2) in a reflexive sense, making that claim vulnerable to any other discourse aiming for power. In no uncertain terms, Ybert de Vermandois drives this point home to the emperor:

"La me faucis: je faurai ci a toi."

(5944)

("You failed me then, I will fail you now.")

Raoul de Cambrai's character can be understood only in the light of this amphibology. It is noteworthy that the king disinherited him of Cambrésis and repaid him by giving him Vermandois. This implies that Louis, in order to affirm the locus of the father/sovereign by an act of speech, must engage in an endless substitution of fiefs, taking from one to compensate the other. As many passages of the text show, this is a voluntary strategy that would be advantageous if only he had the theological and military means to support it.

In a way, the song exists only because Raoul stubbornly abides by this word:

C'est la parole ou Raous ce tint tant,
Dont maint baron furent puis mort sanglant.

(697f.)

(This is the word Raoul held to so firmly,
For which many barons have died bleeding.)

And again:

"G'en pris le gant voiant maint chevalier,
Et or me dites q'il fait a relaissier!
Trestos li mons m'en devroit bien huier."

(2176ff.)

("I took the glove in the presence of many knights,
And now you are telling me that I have to give it up!
Soon everyone is going to look down on me.")

If Raoul accepts Vermandois, he then renounces his paternal heritage. Abiding by the king's word, he denies the place of the father; for his mother Aalais, this means that he lets himself be invested by death itself.[8] Moreover, Raoul's rigid adherence to royal investiture prevails only if he respects its premises: if he grants Louis absolute sovereignty and recognizes the theological order that supports such a prescription. However, he consistently transgresses his order. Very early in the narration he wants to burn down the churches of Vermandois (1211), and the text insistently amplifies his rejection of faith: in Origni he places a hawk, a symbol of chivalric pride, on the crucifix (1237), he leans against the holy cross, sleeps in front of the altar, and has the monastery nuns raped before slaughtering them. He breaks the sacred truce (1361, 1456), an act that will be repeated twice by his uncle Guerri le Sor (3289, 4742). To the horror of his lineage, who nevertheless follow him through feudal homage, Raoul does not observe the prescription of Lent (1567). His enemies see him as a Judas (1381) or as the devil (1913), and the portrait is accurate. As he is often warned (v. 1567, 3021), Raoul is above all a defier of God; in such theocentric times, his defiance amounts to signing his own death sentence. Guerri le Sor reminds him of this fact:

Si Diex te heit, tu seras tost finez.

(1276)

(If God hates you, you will die soon.)

For lack of space, I will not develop the problem of interpretation of the Saracen and Christian worlds that appears especially in the second part of the song. But there is one detail that provides the key to the "pagan" aspect of the text: the arms given by the emperor to Raoul when he becomes a knight:

Nostre empereres ama molt le meschin:
L'erme li donne qi fu au Sarrazin
Q'ocist Rolans desor l'aigue del Rin. . . .
En icel elme ot .i. nazel d'or fin;
.I. escarboucle i ot mis enterin,
Par nuit oscure en voit on le chemin.
Li rois li çainst l'espée fort et dure,
D'or fu li pons et toute la heudure,
Et fu forgie en une combe oscure.

(471ff.)

(Our emperor liked the young man a lot:
He gave him the armor that belonged to a Saracen

Whom Roland killed on the river Rhine. . . .
On this helmet, there was a gold nosepiece;
With a precious gem embedded in it,
Even when it was dark you could see the path.
The king gave him the mighty and strong sword,
The handle was made out of gold and so was the hiltguard,
And it had been made in a dark valley.)

Raoul is now invested with the glorious intertextuality of the *Chanson de Roland*, but the text symbolically inverts its elements; instead of repeating the motif of sacred warfare, the dubbing ceremony makes the weapons function as a sign of Saracen presence in the very heart of Christian feudalism. This pagan aspect has to be considered at the level of discourse: Raoul abides by a word without respecting its theological basis. In other words, by illegitimately claiming to be the origin and locus of meaning, he intends to be the only one occupying the place (of the father or of God) where all meaning begins. Like the emperor, he systematically assumes that if there is law, it originates with him; in this relation, Raoul may be considered one of the most radical figures of transgression in French literature.

In the song, the motif of the "juvenes"[9] (youth) is structured upon the refusal to recognize the place of the father. In the text's own words, Bernier and Raoul are fifteen-year-old "children"; the words of vengeance that involve the destiny of an entire lineage are uttered by three-year-old babies (4096). Thus, *Raoul de Cambrai* finds its narrative argument in a regressive discourse, a discourse that the text itself calls extreme, foolhardy, and outrageous. Moreover, no one seems able to impose a discourse of "paternal" wisdom; with little exception, all the characters invest themselves with the origin of meaning, and almost all of them are "children." Ybert's words to his son Bernier serve as a fitting example of this pervasive discourse without limits that disturbs the hierarchy of paternity and filiation:

"Fix," dist li peres, "preus estes et vaillans:
Li vostre sens va le mien sormontant."

(5977f.)

("My son," said the father, "you are brave and valiant:
Your intelligence surpasses mine.")

We are in the middle of the primitive tribe described in Freud's *Totem and Taboo*, where everyone can claim the place of the dead father for a moment; on this level, Emperor Louis draws the moral lesson of the fable when he declares:

"Qe, par celui qi en crois fu penez,
Chascuns en iert en fin deseritez."

(5441f.)

("For by him who was tormented on the cross,
Everybody will eventually be disinherited.")

("Except for me," he immediately hopes; but we know in advance
the futility of such a wish). The king thus tells us that they are all
illegitimate: this is why Bernier's character, in his illegitimacy,
emblematizes the imposture that poisons the song's discourse of
legitimacy. He is an exception only from the perspective of the
other characters, who take his illegitimate birth as a pretext to dismiss his discourse; for them, the condition of illegitimacy sabotages the ability of any discourse to usurp the words of the law.
Raoul confronts Bernier with this fact:

"Dire tel raison ne deüst bastars!"

(1660)

("A bastard should not say such things.")

Bernier's lack of a birthright thus makes him an alien ("un
estrange compaignon" [401]) within the feudal family. However, as
far as he is concerned, bastardy does not affect him in any way: he
is the only knight in the text to call upon a transcendental order
that justifies his illegitimacy:

"Q'il n'est bastars c'il n'a Dieu renoié!"

(1709)

("He who has not renounced God is not a bastard.")

In God's eyes, then, illegitimacy does not count, and could not be
imputed to Bernier; therefore, his character is the precise locus of
a radical inversion affecting the dialectics of legitimacy and illegitimacy. Correlatively, if there is indeed a bastard in *Raoul de Cambrai*, it is the title character of the song, who radically refuses to
respect Christian faith. However, this transcendental reference
presents Bernier with an insoluble problem. As he is reminded by
his mother Marsent, chivalry submitted to faith must above all
respect the ties that bind the vassal to his lord:

"Fix," dist la mere, "par ma foi, droit en as.
Ser ton signor, Dieu en gaaingneras."

(1386f.)

("Son," said the mother, "By God, Justice is on your side.
Serve your lord, and you will win God.")

But if Bernier obeys this law, by the same token, he threatens his own lineage, since Raoul, his sovereign, is at war with his father Ybert and his uncles to gain possession of Vermandois. Even worse, submitting to the law leads ultimately to the death of his own mother, who had told him to obey it, since Raoul finally has her burned at the stake in the Origni monastery. In this way, if Bernier wins God through submission to the king, he abdicates the place of the father, just as Raoul did. The only difference is that Bernier renounces it in the name of a transcendental order.

It is clear that the symbolic conflict between the paternity of the sovereign and the recognition of the dead father's rights is, explicitly or implicitly, the same conflict for all the text's characters. Though his name is assonant with law (lois), this conflict affects even the Emperor Louis, since he is recognized as only another "child" and not as "God's chosen one." The song is submitted to a law of generalized illegitimacy in which the place of the father is occupied only by a fundamental usurpation or by captivation in a phallic imaginary order. *Raoul de Cambrai* constantly denounces this imaginary order, thus exposing the nodal opposition of the epic. Contrary to what Bernier's son Julien thinks, this text shows that it is impossible to "find one's father" (8068).

By the same token, woman's place in the song becomes unthinkable to a certain extent; this fact derives directly from the systematic functioning of phallic signification as a mortal imaginary order. Initially, one might even believe that women are entirely at the mercy of the illegitimate principle governing land investiture by the king. In this light, they are nothing but a possession, a marketable commodity that can be given away, bought or stolen: Louis gives his sister Aalais to Giboïn le Manceaux (128), and gets his daughter Béatrix (against payment in goods) (6735) from Guerri le Sor, in order to give her to Herchambaut de Pontif, even though she is already married to Bernier. Women are thus submitted to what Béatrix calls the "prostitute law" [*pute loi*] of the father. The adjective she uses to qualify the law of the father denounces its illegitimate essence.[10]

However, this prostituted law is not the only one objectifying women; the transmission of land to the oldest son is another one. Aalais is the one who reminds her son of his own father's holdings:

"Molt m'esmervel del fort roi Loeys;
Molt longuement l'avez ore servi,
Ne ton service ne t'a de rien meri.
Toute la terre Taillefer le hardi,

Le tien chier pere qe je pris a mari,
Te rendist ore, par la soie merci,
Car trop en a Mancel esté servi.
Je me mervelg qe tant l'as consenti,
Qe grant piece a ne l'as mort ou honni."

(971ff.)

("King Louis surprises me a lot;
You have served him for a very long time,
And he has not rewarded your services.
All of Taillefer le Hardi's land,
Your dear father whom I married,
He should give you back now,
For Giboïn le Manceau has enjoyed it long enough.
I am surprised you have agreed to this for so long,
And that you haven't killed or disgraced him yet.")

Identifying itself with the Name-of-the-Father, feminine speech is thus linked to the writing of death. *If she were a man*, Aalais would prove her brother Louis wrong with a male's sword:

"Se je fuse hom, ains le sollelg couchier,
Te mosteroie a l'espée d'acier
Q'a tort iés rois, bien le pues afichier."

(5228ff.)

("If I were a man before the sun sets,
I would show you with a steel sword
That you are wrongfully a king, you can declare it.")

Moreover, castration underlies feminine discourse when its function is to preserve the rights of succession. When given to Herchambaut, Béatrix prevents all possible adultery by ingesting a magic root that makes it impossible for her kidnapper to know her sexually. In her mouth, she hides the principle of a phallic legitimacy (understood in both genealogic and discursive senses) that preserves her consecration to the Name-of-the-Father:

"Dont vins mes peres a la barbe florie
Si me livra au roi de Saint Denise
Qui me dona Herchambaut, cel traïte.
Le premier jor que je fui mariée,
Si vint .i. mie an iceste contrée.
Une tele herbe me dona a celée
Ne la donroie por l'or d'une contrée.

Quant je la tains an ma boche angolée,
Dont n'ai ge garde que soie violée."

(7219ff.)

("Then my father with a flowered beard
Gave me to the king of St. Denis
Who gave me Herchambaut, this traitor.
The first day that I was married,
A doctor came into the region.
He secretly gave me an herb
I would not give it up for the world.
When I hold it in my mouth,
I have no fear of being raped.")

Béatrix thus controls the adulterous desire of the male, and safeguards the legitimate link of her first marriage: she keeps Bernier's place as her one and only lord and master. No other symbol is a better illustration of the law's paradox than this root of inviolability: in other words, one can occupy the place of the law only through a recognition of castration. But further, since women are part of this law, they inevitably threaten that which they intend to protect. Let us read Béatrix's dream predicting Bernier's death (in *Raoul de Cambrai*):

"Quant vint ersoir, que prime m'endormi,
Sonjai .i. songe dont forment m'esbahis,
Que je veoie mon singnor revenir;
Guerris mes peres l'ot forment envaït
Que devant moi a terre l'abati;
Fors de son cors les .ii. . . . li toli,
Et moi meïsme le senestre toli."

(8468ff.)

("Last night, when I was falling asleep,
I had a dream that stunned me a lot,
I saw my lord coming back;
Guerri, my father, had violently attacked him
So that he was beaten to the ground before me;
He tore out his two . . .,
And pulled out my own left one [or,
And I myself pulled out the left one].")

Verse 8473 is missing a monosyllabic noun; editors have suggested "oilz" (eyes). Might we propose that this gap indicates a censorship of the male genitalia ("coilz" [testicles] would also fit)? In any case, it is striking to see Béatrix dream that either 1) she herself is submitted to castration, or 2) she is participating along with her father in Bernier's dismemberment. Though the suppleness of Old French syntax permits both of these readings, the text in no way corroborates this particular part of the dream. However, this passage does disclose the foundation of desire that subtends all writing in the song, and that desire is to reveal the assumption of power and the death of the other as castration. Ultimately, then, this means that all legitimacy is an illusion.

Moreover, woman, as a potential mother, the one whose status must be assured for the transmission of land, is wholly identified with the phallic imaginary order of heritage. When Béatrix wants to have her marriage to the bastard Bernier recognized, she confronts her father Guerri le Sor, insisting on the necessity of land transmission:

> "Mari vos qier dont je eüse .i. oir:
> Après vo mort vo terre maintendroit."
>
> (5780f.)

("I am asking you for a husband who could give me an heir: After your death, he would take care of your land.")

In addition to this, as long as woman's place in the feudal order is not fixed, she represents a powerful threat of instability: widowed or unmarried (and heiress to fiefs), she embodies a mobility capable of destabilizing the fragile system of alliances between lineages. Hence the text's compulsion to put her back in her place through marriage, and to submit her to the order of the father. As early as verse 127, Louis wants to marry his sister to Giboïn, Guerri approves of his daughter's bigamy, and so forth. Thus, on the level of writing, woman is the necessary instrument to the feud's continuation, since she gives birth to an heir who will preserve the father's honor when he has died: in this way, she reinforces the very economy of the song. On the other hand, she is also a figure of life: by allowing the union of her body with paternal blood and producing a son, she keeps hemorrhagic writing from losing itself. Moreover, since marriage can end private war by binding two enemy lineages together, woman symbolizes an appeasement of vendetta by marrying. This particular motif appears in the very first pages; Louis is among the first to mention it:

> "Mais, par celui qui fist parler l'imaige,
> Je quit sis dons li vendra a outraige:

> Se ne remaint par plait de mariaige,
> Mains gentix hom i recevront damaige."
>
> (901ff.)

("But, by him who made the image talk,
I think his gift will bring him shame:
If it is not maintained by a marriage contract,
Many gentlemen will be harmed by it.")

Béatrix uses a similar argument to seduce Bernier and to justify her desire to marry him:

> "Pren moi a feme, frans chevalier eslis:
> Si demorra nostre guere a toz dis.
> Soz ciel n'a home miex de vos soit servis.
> Veés mon cors com est amanevis:
> Mamele dure, blanc le col, cler le vis."
>
> (5696ff.)

("Take me as your wife, fair chosen knight:
This way, our war will end forever.
There is not a man under the heavens who would be better
    served than you.
See my body how it is appealing:
Firm breasts, white neck, fair face.")

Thus, marriage is an exact figure of the narrative pact itself, since it produces so many "legitimate" children or writers of death. At the same time, marriage is a possible end to the text in the silence that would follow the reconciliation of all the lineages, the appeasement of those feuds that furnish the narrative argument of *Raoul de Cambrai*.

Prolepses

In the song, all discourses are ambivalent or equivocal, existing only in the sense that they immediately refer back to an opposite. This is a fundamental economy of speech in the text, since all discourses credit themselves with the self-fulfilling and illusory "one" that would emerge from their enunciation. However, one type of enunciation escapes the general law of failure that affects "right" speech as soon as it is articulated, and that is the prolepse. Prolepse is the only discourse that is tenable and prevails, while all the others belie themselves. Discourses as diverse as the writing of death on the knights' swords (cf. *supra*), Aalais's premonitory dream foretelling Raoul's death (3515), Béatrix's dream (8493),[11] and their predictions concerning Raoul and Bernier's fates (990, 1006, 1202) fall into this category of *sustained* speech. The primordial instance of this sort of foretold discourse is undoubtedly Aalais's curse of her own son:

"Or viex aler tel terre chalengier,
Et qant por moi ne le viex or laisier,
Cil Damerdiex qi tout a a jugier
Ne t'en ramaint sain ne sauf ne entier!"

(1129ff.)

("Now you want to challenge this land,
And if you don't want to renounce it for me,
Let God who judges everything
Bring you back neither safe, sound, nor in one piece.")

The narrator immediately associates himself with this malediction:

Par cel maldit ot il tel destorbier
Com vos orez, de la teste trenchier.

(1134f.)

(Because of the curse, he had so much trouble
That he had his head cut off, as you will hear.)

This is not merely fortuitous, for the main function of the narrator's interventions is to predict fiction's course, to produce a prophecy, a *devinaille* that engages narrative destiny as a whole and belies, at the very beginning of the song, the promise made in verse one. For example:

As fils Herbert fist maint pesant estor
Mais Berneçons l' (Raoul) ocist puis a dolor.

(10f.)

(He attacked Herbert's sons many times
But Berneçon then dealt him (Raoul) a painful death.)

There are too many examples of this narrative prescription by the narrator to quote; they appear in a recurrent pattern in both parts of the song. Since it unfailingly keeps its promise of a realization through fiction, predictive discourse, as opposed to factitious, misrepresenting, or defective speech, seems to be the only one having a performative essence. One might say that it is not hard for a writer (even disguised as the figure of an implicit narrator) to predict his narrative's course and to respect his part of the narrative contract, especially after the fact. However, it is noteworthy that all proleptic promises concern the negative essence of a fundamentally defective discourse, in which the economy of death is inverted into the life of writing. Bertolai, a fictitious witness to the feuds, gives us testimony to this effect (and we remark that the moment when the song projects its own creation is also precisely the moment when that creation is inverted into an analepse):[12]

Bertolais dist que chançon en fera,
Jamais jougleres tele ne chantera.
De la bataille vi tot le gregnor fais
Chançon en fist, n'orreis milor jamais
Puis a esté oie en maint palais.

(2442ff.)

(Bertolai says he will compose a song,
Never will a poet sing such a song.
He saw all the greater exploits of the battle
And composed a song about them, you will never hear a better one
That has been heard since in many palaces.)

The prophecy, which is the only verbal form in the song to be fictively realized, is also linked to the implicit denunciation of all attempts to assume power since it foreshadows the only possible result of these attempts: death. Through the use of prolepse, the text does nothing but authorize itself, and thereby takes over the status and function of the representational authorities. This practice is very common in romance poetics; its first occurrence is found in the work of one of the earliest troubadours, Guillaume d'Aquitaine.[13] Raoul de Cambrai thus substitutes the mortal illegitimacy of all phallic pretentions with a discourse of authority based on the very emptiness of its own auto-reference.

Legacy and Attributions

Obviously, all figures linked with the law and the Name-of-the-Father are also metaphors of textual production and transmission. The question is: what can we conclude from this? First of all, since it inscribes itself in the dialectics of life and death, Raoul de Cambrai is potentially endless; in a way, its hemorrhagic writing reduces the other (any other) to silence:

"Molt par doit estre redoutés li siens brans:
Cui il ataint tos est mus et taisans."

(3915f.)

("His sword must be greatly feared:
He who is struck by it is mute and silent.")

Pushed to its limits, this economy threatens the text itself with extinction; the following passage suggests as much, since the hero's death on the field symbolizes the end of the poetic song:

Ne fust la coife del bon hauberc safré,
De par Gautier fust li chans afiné.

(4088f.)

(If it had not been for the strong gold helmet,
The song would have ended with Gautier.)[14]

On the other hand, once the father is dead, the song always manages to produce a son, grandson, uncle, or nephew who takes up the gauntlet and continues the feud. The genealogic dimension of the text is thus nothing but the metaphor if its own survival as a text. The transmission of the dead father's breath and blood[15] then becomes a figure for the renewal of writing, a figure that corresponds perfectly to one of the central symbols in Geoffrey of Vinsauf's *Poetria Nova:*[16] the rejuvenation of ancient topoi by a new writing. Two examples are illustrative here. The first, and perhaps most beautiful, is in the second part of the song, when Bernier's retinue escorts Raoul's dead body back to Origni. Enraged by Bernier's words, Guerri le Sor murders him, and thus inflames the old hostilities between Bernier's kin and the lineage of Cambrésis:

Si com il vinrent es prés sos Origni,
En celle place ou Raous fu ocis,
Li cuens Berniers fist .i. pesant sospir.
Li sor Guerris molt bien garde s'en prist;
Il li demande por quoi sospira il?
"Ne vous chaut, sire," Berniers li respondi,
Que maintenant me tient il au cuer si."
— "Jel vuel savoir," ce dist li sor Guerris.
"Jel vous dirai," Berniers li respondi.
"Ce poise moi quant il vous plait ainsi.
Il me remenbre de Raoul le marchis
Qui desor lui avoit tel orguel pris,
Qu'a .iiii. contes vaut lor terre tollir.

Vees ci le leu tout droit ou je l'ocis."
Guerris l'entent, par poi n'anraige vis,
Mais a sa chiere point de sanblant n'an fit,
Et neporquant a Bernier respondi:
"Par Dieu, vassal, n'este pas bien apris,
Qui me remenbres la mort de mes amis!"

(8371ff.)

(When they arrived near Origni,
In that place where Raoul had been killed,
Count Bernier sighed heavily.
Guerri the Red noted it well;
He asked him why he had sighed.
"It does not concern you, lord," Bernier answered,
"What I am feeling now."
"I want to know," Guerri the Red said.
"I will tell you," Bernier answered.
"It bothers me that you should be so pleased.
It makes me think of Marquis Raoul
Who was so vainglorious,
That he wanted to take the lands of four counts.
Here is the very place where I killed him."
Guerri listens to him and almost becomes mad,
But he showed nothing of it on his face,
However, he answered Bernier:
"By God, vassal, how ill-mannered of you,
To remind me of my kinsman's death.)

The second paradigm of this eternal return of the same (survival, emblematized either by a son or nephew who repeats the father's actions) and of the other (death) involves the organization of writing in the strictest sense, the writing for which this fiction's *rejuvenationes* are merely a figure. The song is divided into two parts: the first, up to laisse CCL, is rhymed; the second, from there to the end of the text, is in rhymed assonance. As always, the question to pose about these dual texts is not the one traditionally dictated by classical philology: what differentiates the first part from the second?[17] This question leads to hypotheses impossible to prove, hypotheses involving contrasts of "tone," "form," "spirit," or "intention" that end up projecting two distinct authorial identities. Above all, the question should be: what makes the oneness, the coherence of two forms of writing that simulate a dialogical dissemblance within one literary work?

It is possible to respond with a "philological" answer; however, the philology in question here is a renewed philology, one that takes stock of the material aspect of the manuscript, of the concept of writing exposed by the fictions, and of the intimate correlation between the two. The problem is presented as follows in the manuscript: the "first" hand that transcribed the text goes past the rhymed section up to laisse CCLXXIII (fol. 102, v. 6250); the "second" hand then completes the song but also writes the very first page in rhyme. Let us add that a rat, of unknown origin and era, collaborated on the text by eating a few leaves of parchment. Moreover, the second writing makes a palimpsest out of the first; according to the editors, "for one reason or another, the second writer, intending to take over the task of copying at a precise point, scratched out the preexisting text which extended to the bottom of the page (102) and apparently got rid of the quire's remaining pages."[18] Graphically, the text may be presented thus:

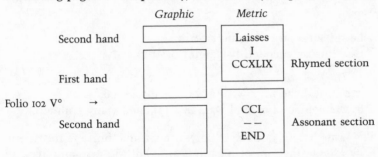

	Graphic	Metric	
Second hand		Laisses I CCXLIX	Rhymed section
First hand			
Folio 102 V° →			
Second hand		CCL – – END	Assonant section

The first hand changes metrical systems, going from rhyme to assonance. The second, in an inverted and reflexive pattern, uses assonance but can also rhyme, since it produced the first page. Moreover, with regard to the palimpsest, the instrument used to scratch out some of the manuscript's lines becomes the exact equivalent of the metaphorical death sword/pen, in addition to the second section's possibility of emergence upon a foundation of obliterated writing. On the material level then, the writing of the text bears witness to the "authors'" substitution and mirror play, to a circular reflexion that shows the text generating and authorizing itself. This reading hypothesis, both materialist and conceptual, remains valid even if one assumes that the text was written by only one scribe who was patient and perverse enough to practice two types of writing. However, this supposition tends to indicate a duality which the reader must take into account. Within the fiction, Raoul is the perfect emblem of this process: believing himself to be the only origin of meaning, his own authority [auctor], he dies, leaving behind his maternal nephew

Gautier to carry the torch for their name; he then reappears as the dead figure invoked in Bernier's sigh. Moreover, since he lets Louis take his father's land away from him in exchange for Vermandois, and because he denies the theological background that would make this second investiture legitimate, Raoul symbolizes the systematic destabilization of semantic authority promulgated by the text.

It is therefore impossible for the reader to ascribe paternal primacy to either of the two forms of writing in the text or to any of the characters that symbolize them in the fiction. They generate one another just as life and death do in the song, and are by turns in a position of authority or subjection, paternity or filiation, so that we can never decide the predominance of one position or the other. In this sense, the text is an orphan, similar to the children who are deprived of their fathers by Giboïn le Manceau during the feuds:

Le roi servi au bon branc acerin:
De pluisors gueres li fist maint orfenin.

(101f.)

(He served the king with a good steely sword:
In the course of several wars he orphaned many children.)

The issue here is not one of polysemy or of a limitless indeterminacy (dissemination) of meaning; instead, the text promotes an amphibology governed by precise laws. Textual paternity is not uncertain, but split, and this fact prevents it from affirming itself as one, as a paternity legitimized by a reference to only one name (the symbolic father's). Raoul and the other "children" of the fiction, like the assumed authors of the song, posit the autonomy of a writing without paternity (therefore denying the existence of God), in the sense that writing is self-generated and not transcendent. Correlatively, the text cannot be ascribed to an Oedipal metaphysics of writing, since it is sexually self-determined: female because of the page, and male because of the pen/sword, writing continually plays on the indifference of both its components.

The question remains: what assures the legitimacy of an interpretation in this text so blatantly given over to bastardy? To answer this, we must examine the figures of the last heirs (of meaning) who remain at the end of the text, because they are implicit fictions of a correct reading. Raoul's male descendents have been wiped out: his nephew Gautier has been killed by Bernier's son Julien; indubitably tired of his troublemaker role in a text made endless by his own desire for revenge, Guerri le Sor disappears from the horizon during a siege of Bernier's sons:

Quant il fu nuis, par verté le vous di,
Li sor Guerris de la cité issi,
Sor son cheval, si ala en escil,
Mais on ne set certes que il devint.
Hermites fu, ainsis con j'ai oït.

(8715ff.)

(At night, I am telling you in truth,
Guerri le Sor went out of the city,
He went into exile riding his horse,
But nobody knows what became of him for sure.
He became a hermit from what I heard.)

Bernier's sons Julien and Henri remain as masters of Arras, St. Quentin, and St. Gilles (the last two territories are also the war cries of the Vermandois lineage); they are true relics or remnants of the text and, in this regard, they embody the reader, taking over the fiefs of fiction. The inheritors of meaning descend from the only male character who renounces neither theological nor feudal law, Bernier.[19] Does this mean that as readers we can have access to the text only if we accept these laws? I think not. Instead, the text seems to say that among the many heirs who gloss over its meaning, it will eventually recognize its own. Moreover, the legacy of interpretation has nothing to do with the institution of any legitimacy, for the sons who survive the song of death are the only ones who originate from a lineage marked by Bernier's illegitimacy.

Two women, Aalais and Béatrix, also survive, with Aalais governing a land now deprived of male heirs. But the song doesn't breathe a word about it, and femininity disappears in an ellipsis: the women's absent survival shows that writing, in order to be transmitted, must go through the space and whiteness of silence. Therefore, as far as bastardy and ellipsis are concerned, we will draw only the obvious conclusions: first, the only heirs to the text, legitimate or not, are those who in some way earn it; next, meritorious readers must be silent when they come to the realization that their task is endless.[20]

NOTES

1. *Raoul de Cambrai*, ed. P. Meyer and A. Longnon (Paris: Société des Anciens Textes Français, 1882).

2. Ernst Robert Curtius, *Europäische Literatur und lateinisches Mittelalter* (Bern: Francke, 1948), 314, 348.

3. See Roland's exhortations to his companions in arms (*La Chanson de Roland*, ed. Joseph Bédier [Paris: L'Edition d'Art II. Piazza, 1930]):

"Tantes batailles en avum afinees!
Male chançun n'en deit estre cantee."

(1465f.)

("We have won so many battles!
A bad song must not be sung about it.")

"Pur Deu vos pri que ne seiez fuiant,
Que nuls prozdom malvaisement n'en chant."

(1516f.)

("By God, I beg you not to flee
So that no valiant man can sing a bad song about it.")

4. Geoffrey of Vinsauf, *Poetria Nova*, ed. E. Gallo (The Hague: Mouton, 1971), 48–49, 802–3; also see my "Absolute Reflexivity," in *Medieval Texts and Contemporary Readers*, ed. Laurie Finke and Martin Schictman (Ithaca: Cornell University Press, 1987), 138.

5. See P. Matarasso, *Recherches historiques et littéraires sur "Raoul de Cambrai"* (Paris: Nizet, 1962), esp. chap. 2, "Raoul de Cambrai et le monde féodal"; M. Combarieu du Grès, *L'Idéal humain et l'expérience morale chez les héros de chansons de geste* (Aix-en-Provence: Publications de l'Université de Provence, 1979); W. Calin, *The Old French Epic of Revolt* (Paris-Geneva: Droz, 1962); Marc Bloch, in *La Société féodale*, rev. ed. (Paris: Albin Michel, 1968), identified what he calls the "paradoxe de la vassalité" (325ff.) (paradox of vassalage); more than any archival document, *Raoul de Cambrai* sheds a somber light on this paradox and pushes its consequences to the limit.

6. See 5363, 5442, 6045. Verses 6445ff. are particularly revealing: Louis reaffirms his right of distribution of the land, even if it puts him in conflict with canon law; in this way, he sabotages the basis of his own power.

7. Louis has nothing to do with a historical figure: instead, he is related to a literary type developed by the cycle of Guillaume, particularly in the *Couronnement Louis:* he reactivates the Anchises complex: a weak son, unable to occupy the place of the symbolic father in a feudal hierarchy. Specifically, Charlemagne, presenting the imperial crown to Louis, urges him not to rob an orphan of his land and not to take advantage of widows. See *Le Couronnement Louis*, ed. Langlois (Paris: CFMA, 1966), 83–84; transgression of this paternal command will make him a "foolish" [*assoté* (2670)] king.

8. "Qi te dona Perone et Peronele
Et Ham et Roie et le borc de Neele,
Ravesti toi, biaux fix, de mort novele."

(1004ff.)

("He who gave you Perone and Peronele
And Ham and Roie and the town of Neele,
Invested you, my son, with a new death.")

9. See the works of George Duby on the subject, in particular *"Les 'jeunes' dans la société aristocratique,"* *Annales* 19 (1964): 835–46, and *Le Chevalier, la femme et le prêtre* (Paris: Hachette, 1981).

10. See

"Hahi!" dist elle, "pere de pute loi,
Con m'as traïe et mise en grant beloi!"

(6818f.)

("Alas," she said, "father of a prostitute law,
You betrayed me and put me in an unfair position.")

The motifs of illegitimacy and prostitution [*putainage*] are tightly linked in the text: Raoul reproaches Marsent with her "putainage" (1330).

11. Each time, the text stresses the truthfulness of the dream:

(Aalais) soinga . i . soinje qe trop li averi.

(3516)

([Aalais] had a dream that became very true for her.)

"Lasse" dist (Béatrix), "mes songe est averis."

(8493)

("Malediction is on me," said [Béatrix], "My dream has come true".)

In this sense, the text stresses the nature of her utterance as a death dream, one that only the text can make true.

12. Here, narrative temporality turns back on itself: I will return to this point in Legacy and Attributions.

13. Song 6 (*Les Chansons de Guillaume IX*, ed. Alfred Jeanroy, Les Classiques Français du Moyen Age 9 [Paris: Champion, 1927], 13) 6–7:

E puesc ne traire.l vers *auctor*
Quant er lassatz.

(my emphasis)

(And I can refer to the verse as an authority
After it has been bound together.)

14. This detail shows us one of the rhetorical functions of the armor: the preservation of life.

15. For example, Raoul's "aleine novele" (3698) (new breath). Death is often "novele" (new) or news in the text (900, 1002, 4692); moreover, it renews the text through war:

"Si m'aït Dix, tos revenroit la guere,
Car d'ome mort molt souvent renovele."

(5722f.)

("If God help me, war would come back soon
For it is often renewed by a man's death.")

And also

Car par aus fu la grant guere finée

Desc'a .i. jor qe fu renouvelée
Qe Gautelès la reprist a l'espée.

(5750ff.)

(For the great war was ended by them
Until the day it was renewed,
Because Gautelet started it again with his sword.)

16. See "Absolute Reflexivity," 124–133.

17. The bipartite structure of *Raoul de Cambrai* is not exceptional in Old French literature; cf. the ending of Chrétien de Troyes's *La Charrette* by "Godefroi de Lagni"; the continuation of *Perceval* by other writers; and the dual authorship of the *Roman de la Rose* by Guillaume de Lorris and Jean de Meung.

18. Introduction, lxxix.

19. He is the only character who repents having murdered:

"Baron," dist il, "por Dieu concilliés moi.
Pichiés ai fais dont je grant paor oi:
Maint home ai mort dont je sui en esfroi;
Raoul ocis; certes, ce poise moi.
Dusqu'a Saint Gile veut aler demanois;
Proierai li que plaidis soit por moi
Vers Damredieu qui sires est et rois."

(6588ff.)

("Baron," he said, "By God advise me.
I have committed sins and am afraid:
I killed many men and it frightens me;
I killed Raoul; indeed, this disheartens me.
I want to go to St. Gilles immediately;
I will pray that my cause be pleaded
Before God who is Lord and Master.")

In Bernier's discourse we may remark that God occupies the place of feudal lord and that St. Gilles is not a haphazard choice as the site of intercession, since it is the land that Julien will inherit.

20. This article has benefited from Vittoria Ardito's research; I am especially indebted to her remarks concerning Béatrix's dream of castration (Master's Thesis, Lousiana State University, 1987).

III

Literary Anthropology

Language and Incest in *Grisel y Mirabella*

MARINA S. BROWNLEE

"Discourse," as Michel Foucault observes, "was not originally a product, a thing, a kind of goods; it was essentially an act—an act placed in the bipolar field of the sacred and the profane, the licit and the illicit, the religious and the blasphemous. Historically, it was a gesture fraught with risks before becoming goods caught up in a circuit of ownership."[1] The liminal period referred to as the late Middle Ages explores the tension between these two types of discourse—the (potentially dangerous) social act and the literary commodity—in a variety of contexts.

In fifteenth-century Spain *Grisel y Mirabella* offers an illuminating case in point. This text by Juan de Flores continues his exploration of legal discourse begun in *Grimalte y Gradissa*. While *Grimalte* explores law in the (private, individual) amorous register, *Grisel* further problematizes the discourse of desire by placing it in the (public, universal) context of society. For in essence, *Grisel* examines the relationship between natural law and judicial law as they pertain to the discursive authority of their guarantor, the king.

As with *Grimalte*, here, too, a Boccaccian subtext tends to be posited but minimized, recognized but deemed unessential to an understanding of *Grisel*. Those who discount the orientation established by the first tale in day 4 of the *Decameron* locate Flores's concern either in a formal consideration—the preponderance of debate[2]—or a semantic concern with fifteenth-century feminism.[3] Both issues, however, stem from Boccaccio's discursive postulation of nominalism. *Grisel*, like its subtext, is about language, about naming, about the legitimacy of discourse per se.

In day 4 of the *Decameron* we find that Boccaccio orients our reading by devoting his Prologue to the topic of natural law—the indomitable power of desire. Being criticized not only for portraying so much sex, but for being totally obsessed by it at his advanced age, the author reminds his audience that "perché il porro abbia il capo bianco, che la coda sia verde" (although the leek's head is white, it has a green tail).[4] The inevitability of human desire is reinforced in the Prologue with the example of Filippo Balducci, the widower. Deeply distressed by the death of his beloved wife, Filippo decides to withdraw from the world by entering the service of God, taking his infant son with him. They live in a cave and the father "si guardava di non ragionare, là dove egli fosse, d'alcuna temporal cosa né di lasciarnegli alcuna vedere, acciò che esse da cosí fatto servigio nol traessero" (256) (took very great care not to let [his son] see any worldly things, or even mention their existence, lest they should distract him from his devotions [327]). As a consequence of this recast Platonic cave, the boy grows into manhood without ever having seen a woman, entirely ignorant of the second sex. At the age of eighteen, however, he sees women for the first time and is predictably awestruck. Asking the name of these wonderful creatures, Filippo deceptively identifies them as "goslings," indicating also that they are evil. Despite these words of caution, the son exclaims that: "Elle son piú belle che gli agnoli dipinti che voi m'avete piú volte mostrati. Deh! se vi cal di me, fate che noi ce ne meniamo una colà su di queste papere, e io le darò beccare" (257) (They are more beautiful than the painted angels [of the church] that you have taken me to see so often. O alas! If you have any concern for my welfare, do make it possible for us to take one of these goslings back with us, and I will pop things into its bill" [328]).[5] The moral of this story is obvious, yet Boccaccio leaves nothing to chance, saying to his inscribed female readers that:

> altra cosa dir non potrà alcun con ragione, se non che gli altri e io, che vi amiamo, naturalmente operiamo: alle cui leggi, cioè della natura, voler contastare, troppe gran forze bisognano, e spesse volte non solamente invano, ma con grandissimo danno del faticante s'adoperano. (260)

> (no reasonable person will deny that I and other men who love you are simply doing what is natural. And in order to oppose the laws of nature, one has to possess exceptional

powers, which often turn out to have been used, not only in vain, but to the serious harm of those who employ them. [331])

The dangers of denying one's offspring their sexuality—the pursuit of natural law—is also the focus of *Decameron* 4, 1. Tancredi, Prince of Salerno, "signore assai umano e di benigno ingegno" (261) (a most benevolent ruler, and kindly of disposition [332]), was, we are told, "as passionately fond of [Ghismonda], his daughter, as any father who had ever lived" (332). After waiting until she was several years past the marriageable age, Tancredi finally marries her, yet shortly thereafter she is left a widow. Ghismonda returns to her father's house, where, once again (as a result of his lustful inclinations) he is in "no hurry to make her a second marriage" (332). The father's repeated reluctance in letting his daughter go is the first sign of his incestuous desire. Realizing Tancredi's unwillingness to let her remarry, the beautiful daughter chooses a lover, a young valet in the service of her father named Guiscardo, "uom di nazione assai umile ma per virtú e per costumi nobile" (261) (a man of exceedingly humble birth but noble in character and bearing [333]). To make her intentions known to Guiscardo, Ghismonda composes a letter, concealing it in a (phallically suggestive) reed which she hands him, saying: "Fara'ne questa sera un soffione alla tua servente, col quale ella raccenda il fuoco" (262) (Turn it into a bellows-pipe for your serving-wench, so that she can use it to kindle the fire this evening [333]). This is the first in a series of images which function not only on a literal level, but on a metaphorical level as well—referring to her sexuality. Ghismonda's message is a phallic gesture not simply because she initiates the seduction, which comes in the form of a reed, but also because she has assumed the traditionally male role as writer (creator) who acts upon the passive female object of creation. The pen/phallus equivalence is a standard Western literary *topos* going back at least as far as Augustine. Derrida further elaborates this association when he explains that "the hymen is the always folded . . . space in which the pen writes its dissemination."[6] In essence, Ghismonda must take on this phallic role in order to counteract the tyranny of her own father's phallus.[7]

The metaphoric intent of this missive is obvious, once again illustrating Boccaccio's metalinguistic interest in this tale. Metaphor implies transference but at the same time usurpation of linguistic identity. For Ghismonda it is the rhetorical weapon by which she can counteract Tancredi's sexual usurpation, just as it serves his own transgressive desire. Guiscardo's correct deciphering of the message leads to a series of blissful trysts in Ghismonda's cave, the cave being an emblem of her female sexuality as well as the architectural space of her bedchamber, until, quite by accident, the discreet lovers are discovered by Tancredi. Here, too, it is significant that the father's discovery stems from his incestuous inclinations, as suggested by a descriptive detail which the narrator mentions but does not elaborate, namely, that "appoggiato il capo al letto e tirata sopra sé la cortina, quasi come se studiosamente si fosse nascoso"(263) (the concealed Tancredi rested his head against the side of [Ghismonda's] bed and drew the curtain round his body as though to conceal himself there on purpose [335]), as he often did while awaiting her return. At this point he falls asleep, concealed from the lovers' sight, but awakens to the sounds of their amorous ecstasy.

Substantiation of Boccaccio's interest in sexual metaphor abounds, as Guido Aimansi suggests. In the brief space of one paragraph, for example, we find the following concentration of suggestive details: The cave had been used "at some remote time in the past," i.e., during Ghismonda's first marriage. This concealed space was virtually forgotten until "Love reminded the enamoured lady of its existence" (the sexual awakening after the bereavement of her widowhood). The passage into the cave is "a secret staircase . . . but the way was barred by a massive door." In a futile gesture, Ghismonda resists this barrier "for several days" (in an attempt to forestall an illicit liaison). Within the side of the mountain there exists a *spiraglio* (shaft) which had been "almost entirely covered by weeds and brambles." It is through this narrow passageway that Guiscardo penetrates the cave, by means of a rope that he hitches to "a stout bush that had taken root at the mouth of the opening." He wears "a suit of leather to protect himself from the brambles."[8]

Having discovered the lovers, Tancredi feels totally betrayed by his daughter and his trusted valet. Guiscardo is abruptly seized and taken prisoner, remarking only that: "Amor può troppo piú che né voi né io possiamo" (264) (Neither you nor I can resist the power of Love [335])—recalling in a serious register the lesson of Filippo Balducci.[9] These words take on even greater significance since they are the only words uttered by Guiscardo in the entire novella. Tancredi is devastated and speaks of the "appalling dilemma" into which his daughter has cast him, oblivious of the fact that the dilemma stems from his own unnatural denial of her natural urge: "di te sallo Iddio che io non so che farmi. Dall'una parte mi trae l'amore, il quale io t'ho sempre piú portato che alcun padre portasse a figliuola, e d'altra mi trae giustissimo sdegno preso per la tua gran follia" (264) (God knows what I am to do with you. I am drawn in one direction by the love I have always born you, deeper by far than that of any other father for a daughter; but on the other hand I seethe with all the indignation that the folly of your actions demands [336]).

Although Tancredi condemns Ghismonda's actions, she pointedly asserts that her behavior stems directly from his unnaturally covetous behavior:

> a questo non mi indusse tanto la mia feminile fragilità quanto la tua poca sollecitudine del maritarmi e la virtú di lui. Esser ti dovea, Tancredi, manifesto, essendo tu di carne, aver generata figliuola di carne e non di pietra o di ferro. (265)

> (I was prompted to act as I did, not so much by my womanly frailty as by your lack of concern to marry me, together with his own outstanding worth. You are made of flesh and blood, Tancredi, and it should have been obvious to you that the daughter you fathered was also made of flesh and blood, and not of stone or iron. [337])

Her action—referred to as "natural peccato" (265)—is thus a natural response to his misguided *action,* and also to his *words* of high praise for Guiscardo: "Chi il commendò mai tanto, quanto tu 'l commendavi in tutte quelle cose laudevoli che valoroso uomo dee essere commendato?" (266) (For was it not you yourself who sang his praises more loudly than any, claiming for him all the qualities by which one measures a man's excellence? [338]). In his oblivious state, Tancredi never dreamed that his words would be interpreted by Ghismonda as they were, and would be the direct cause of her falling in love with Guiscardo. He is unaware of the power of words, or more precisely, of the distinction between word and context.

As Bakhtin explains, a unit of language is neutral, an utterance (a semantic context) is not. Thus, "depending on the context, the utterance, the sentence 'He died' can also reflect a positive, joyful, even a rejoicing expression. And the sentence 'What joy!' in the context of a particular utterance can assume an ironic or bitterly sarcastic tone."[10] Likewise, Tancredi's words of praise for Guiscardo as a worthy valet are understandably construed by Ghismonda as praise for a worthy lover—literally the last interpretation her father would wish to endorse.

The eloquent speech Ghismonda delivers to her father is notable for several reasons. Above all, because, despite her distressed state at realizing her father's vengeful inclination, and assuming that Guiscardo has already been killed, she maintains her composure and delivers an admirably conceived speech. This speech takes the form of a "verdictive," a statement of fact (not a "directive," designed to persuade Tancredi to be lenient): "né a negare né a pregare son disposta, per ciò che né l'un mi varrebbe né l'altro voglio che mi vaglia; e oltre a ciò in niuno atto intendo di rendermi benivola la tua mansuetudine e 'l tuo amore" (265) (I am resolved neither to contradict you nor to implore your forgiveness, because denial would be pointless and I want none of your clemency. Nor do I have the slightest intention of appealing either to your better nature or to your affection [337]).

The substance of Ghismonda's speech offers proof that she acts in accord with her words, whereas Tancredi does not. On the one hand, the father claims that her welfare was more dear to him than anything else, on the other, he denied her the right to amorous fulfillment, even within the chaste bonds of matrimony. This *action*—imprisoning her in his house while claiming in his *speech* that he is a benevolent and just ruler—is clearly a violation of his self-perceived benevolence. Along similar lines, Ghismonda takes issue with Tancredi's reproaching her "more bitterly not for committing the crime of loving a man, but for consorting with a person of lowly rank" (338). Boccaccio once more offers a meditation on metaphoric usage, as Ghismonda responds to the charge that Guiscardo is of low rank by differentiating between "titular" and "natural" nobility, according to which standards Guiscardo is a patrician (as Tancredi's earlier praise corroborates), whereas the titular nobles are noble in name only and plebeians in fact. Thus, Ghismonda repeatedly illustrates that Tancredi's actions do not conform to his words: "piú mirabilmente che le tue parole non potevano esprimere, non vedessi; e se pure in ciò alcuno inganno ricevuto avessi, da te sarei stata ingannata" (266) (I have seen him practice the very virtues for which you commended him, in a manner more wonderful than your words could express. So that if I was deceived in my estimate of Guiscardo, it was you alone who deceived me [338–39].)

Ghismonda's own case is precisely the opposite—her words unfailingly bear out her actions. In keeping with the behavior he has exhibited thus far, not only do Tancredi's words contradict his actions, but he disbelieves that his daughter's actions will bear out her words, that she will actually kill herself: "Conobbe il prenze la grandezza dell'animo della sua figliuola, ma non credette per ciò in tutto lei sí fortemente disposta a quello che le parole sue sonavano" (267) (Although Tancredi knew that his daughter had a will of iron, he doubted her resolve to translate her words into action [339]).

Feeling that his daughter deserves to be punished, but that she will recover from her sadness in due time, Tancredi devises what he perceives to be an exemplary punishment. And with a vindictiveness we might expect from a betrayed lover, rather than a father, he instructs a servant to present Ghismonda with a golden chalice containing the dead lover's heart.[11] Undaunted, Ghismonda kisses the heart repeatedly, praising it both metaphorically and metonymically: "Io son certa che ella è ancor quicentro e riguarda i luoghi de' suoi diletti e de' miei; e come colei che ancor son certa che m'ama, aspetta la mia, dalla quale sommamente è amata" (268) (I feel certain that his soul still lingers here within you, waiting for mine and surveying the scenes of our mutual happiness, and that our love for one another is as deep and enduring as ever [340]). Despite this eloquence (and unlike us, the readers) her ladies-in-waiting are unable "che volesson dire le parole di lei non intendevano" (268) (to make any sense of her words [341]), since they are entirely ignorant of the secret affair. When Ghismonda has eulogized the heart at length, clutching it to her breast, she pours a poison into the chalice and imbibes it, saying "Rimanete con Dio ché io mi parto" (269) (God be with you all, for now I take my leave of you [142]). With this venereal reenactment of holy communion, she becomes one in body as well as in spirit with Guiscardo—effecting the ultimate conjoining of her words and deeds.

Never having imagined that she would be faithful to her words, Tancredi is dismayed by her action. Too late he recognizes the validity of Ghismonda's claim to natural law—and his own linguistic transgression—by acceding to her desire to be buried next to Guiscardo, thus also making the affair public knowledge. The text ends in a scene of collective pathos, which Boccaccio describes as follows: "Tancredi dopo molto pianto, e tardi pentuto della sua crudeltà, con general dolore di tutti i salernetani, onorevolmente amenduni in un medesimo sepolcro gli fe' seppellire" (269) (As for Tancredi, after shedding countless tears and making tardy repentance for his cruelty, he saw that they were honourably interred together in a single grave, amid the general mourning of all the people of Salerno" [342]). Thus, the prince belatedly recognizes that the unfortunate affair was in fact his doing, stemming from his abuse of (natural) law. While the sacrifice of Guiscardo conformed to a societal norm of judicial law, Tancredi is invalidated as the agent of justice by his perversion of natural law—which is at the root of his linguistic perversion.[12]

From this outcome we see that much more than the configuration of the cave—the locus of Balducci's linguistic deprivation and Ghismonda's sexual deprivation—unites the two narratives. Each father figure, an old widower with a single child, misuses words in order to control his child's desire; each is blind to the natural impulse toward sexuality. At the same time, however, these two texts appear to be thematic opposites, as Giuseppe Mazzotta remarks in his important study of the Decameron: "At first glance, the two readings in terms of naturalism and incest are contradictory, for if one upholds the rights of nature, the other is a sharp refutation of the very assumptions of a naturalist ideology."[13] Mazzotta argues that this paradox is only an apparent one, that both texts are intended instead as an indictment of omniscient discourse: "In the world of Fortune's randomness, everyone's vision is impaired by blind spots. Claims of omniscient perspective by critics, lovers, prince or author are thus deflated by Boccaccio's text" (158). Accordingly, he sees Ghismonda as deteriorating into "madness and violence" (151) analogous to that of Tancredi. I would maintain, however, that the common (discursive) thematic which unites these two narratives involves not the existential misperception of omnipotence, but the linguistic perception of referentiality. For Ghismonda is—in an important discursive sense—the opposite of her father and of Balducci. While their words consistently contradict their deeds, hers never do. Their counterfeiting of language contrasts boldly with her linguistic integrity, whereby words and actions are mutually defining. Thus, the distinction is neither between naturalism and incest nor the vicissitudes of Fortune. Rather, what is at issue is nominalism—the arbitrariness of signs—of which Ghismonda and Tancredi are two extremes.[14]

Finally, the fact that it is Fiammetta who narrates this novella is significant, further valorizing a metadiscursive reading of it by means of typically Boccaccian irony. Namely, it is a narrative which punishes the linguistic transgression of Tancredi—the flaw of which Fiammetta herself was guilty—as her eponymous Elegia makes manifest. The thematic coincidence is not at all fortuitous.

Written in the 1480s, more than one hundred years after the Decameron, Grisel discursively complicates Boccaccio's basic structure significantly. Although this work departs from the usual first-person structure of the novela sentimental by offering instead a third-person account heavily laden with second-person debate, the work is in fact oriented by and inscribed within a letter. Consequently, the text is dominated from beginning to end by a first-person voice which, while implicit, is quite powerful.

The prefatory letter which precedes the text (labeled "Tractado compuesto a su amiga" [A Treatise Composed (by the Author) for his Lady])[15] tends to be ignored by critics although it is of seminal importance to interpretation here. Perhaps it is the atypical nature of this letter which results in its dismissal. For in it, Flores reveals himself to be quite neurotically insecure about his writing. He speaks for example of the "falta de [su] flaco juizio" (333) (poorness of [his] judgment), claiming to his lady that "sin esfuerço de vuestra ayuda no podiera hazer cosa que razonable fuesse" (333) (without your help I would never dare to undertake this difficult task). He explicitly claims, moreover, that he is nothing more than a *scribe* in this enterprise: "yo desto solamente soy scriuano," and that he has had the courage to write down this text because it serves to glorify womankind: "por la comunicacion de vuestra causa" (333) (to further your cause).

Yet he derives his strength not from the subject matter, the glorification of the lady he serves, nor from her passive acceptance of his labors—the normative male/female configuration. Instead, it is the promise of her *active* editorial participation which empowers him to write:

> Si vuestro fauor en ello no me ayudara: diera grande occasion ala riza y malicia delos hoyentes. y por esto lo enbio a vos senyora: como persona que lo malo encobrira: y lo comunal sera por mas de bueno touido. y si del todo fuesse inutil: que le dariades la pena que mereçen mis simples trebaios. porque non mas de a vos fuessen publicos mis defectos. pues es razon: que asi como haueys seydo causa de me dar soberbia: que seays reparo para la culpa dello. (333)

> (If you were to deny me your assistance, there would be cause for laughter and derision on the part of the listeners. For this reason, I am sending [my text] to you, my lady, since you will eliminate its weaknesses, and improve it. And, *if you decide that it is without merit, destroy it,* so that my defects will not be made public. It makes sense that since you have been the inspiration for my text, you should also be the remedy for its shortcomings.)

We see that Flores offers much more than the obligatory, reverential *captatio benevolentiae* required by the courtly idiom. This apology is quantitatively longer and qualitatively different as well. In place of the anticipated claim that his lady is beautiful, Flores praises her literary sensibilities. Such editorial complicity is striking within the *novela sentimental* corpus. Within the particular context of *Grisel*, I maintain, it is equally significant. By casting the anonymous *amiga* not simply as a muse figure (a passively inspirational woman) but as an active intellect, Flores adds a new virtue to the pro-feminist cause, which in turn leads us to expect *Grisel* to be an extended narrative encomium of female attributes. The fact that the text does not bear out the unproblematic, wholly laudatory orientation established in the prefatory letter is all the more striking. The letter establishes a generic expectation in the reader which will be calculatedly undermined during the course of the narrative itself. Flores's prefatory words claim one thing, unqualified pro-feminist adulation, but his extended discursive deed effects quite another—that is, the subordination of both pro- and anti-feminist discourse to the nature and function of discourse per se.

In keeping with Boccaccio's essential argument, Flores also portrays a victimized princess and daughter, Mirabella, who has a secret affair with Grisel because her father, the king of Scotland, denies her right to natural law—to amorous fulfillment—even within the context of lawful matrimony. The father's perversion of natural law will result in the deaths not only of the two lovers but of many other subjects as well. This causal relationship is established at the outset of the narrative proper:

> el Rey su padre por non tener hijos: y por el grande mereci-miento que ella tenia: era dell tanto amada: que a ninguno delos ya dichos la queria dar. y asi mismo en su tierra non hauia tan grande senyor a quien la diesse: saluo a grande mengua suya. de manera que el grande amor suyo era aella mucho enemigo. y como ya muchas vezes acaheçe quando hay dilacion en el casamiento delas mujeres: ser causa de caher en verguenças y yerros: assi a esta despues acahecio. (334)

> (The king, [Mirabella's] father, since he had no sons, and because she was so virtuous, greatly loved his daughter. Because he did not wish to give her to any of the knights who pursued her, and *since there was in fact no knight in his kingdom who deserved her, but rather a great lack of such a worthy person*, the king's intense love for his daughter was to her a great enemy. And as often happens when a woman delays in marrying, she falls into error, as happened with her. [My emphasis])

Because the king's incestuous desire prevents him from giving Mirabella in marriage, many knights vie for her hand, losing their lives in the process. It is as a consequence of military not familial considerations—these multiple deaths—that the king decides to remove his daughter from public view by locking her up in a tower. Flores chooses this architectural symbol of male sexuality—as opposed to Ghismonda's cave—advisedly, for it anticipates Grisel's more dominant role in the narrative by comparison with Boccaccio's Guiscardo. At the same time it is an emblem of Mirabella's imprisonment by her father's architectural, metaphorical phallus—a transparent, but logical substitution for Ghismonda's cave.

It is as a direct result of Mirabella's imprisonment that she ultimately becomes involved with Grisel. Had her father not kept her from getting married by exhibiting the "grande amor . . . a ella mucho enemigo" (great love which was a great enemy to her), the tragic sequence of events would never have occurred. What becomes apparent from the opening paragraph, therefore, is that Flores models the causality of his text after *Decameron* 4, 1—not after the *Chastelain de Coucy* (where a betrayed husband imprisons his adulterous wife, forcing her to eat her lover's heart) or other narratives involving a *coeur mangé*.[16] Like Prince Tancredi, the king of Scotland is reputed as "de todas virtudes amigo, y principalmente en ser iusticiero. y era tan iusto: como la misma iusticia" (334) (the friend of all virtues, especially justice, he being justice personified). Yet also like Tancredi, his impeccable commitment to judicial law is marred by his transgression of natural law which irreparably deforms his authority, both verbal and actantial.

Further discursive complication of Boccaccio's novella results from the narrator's evaluative remarks, such as his ironic remark that: "en su tierra non hauia tan grande senyor a quien la diesse" (334) (there was [in fact] no knight in the kingdom who deserved [Mirabella]), a value judgment which the text will boldly disprove. Beyond this type of metadiscursive device, and much more extensive, is Flores's reliance upon the structure of debate. Not one but four debates occur in the text: the first between Grisel and the unnamed other knight; the second between Grisel and Mirabella; the third between Torrellas and Braçayda; and the fourth between the queen and the king. Each debate has serious implications for the language theory posited by Flores.

The theme of the two friends—a traditional motif whereby each is willing to sacrifice his life for the other—is evoked as soon as we learn that the king has incarcerated his daughter. Grisel and the Unnamed knight—the two guards who have been assigned to protect Mirabella from potential suitors—are repeatedly described as "close friends." Both men not only guard Mirabella but in addition are captivated by her. One night each discerns a male figure descending an iron ladder leading to Mirabella's chamber, an intruder whom he attacks:

> firieron se el vno al otro muy fieramente. y los mantos enbraçados y las spadas sacadas conbatieron se hasta que en las aquexadas y secretas vozes se conocieron. y acordando se de su amistat strecha: y ahun por no ser dela casa conocidos: stuuieron quedos. retrayendo se en vn lugar apartado donde el vno al otro tales razones se dizen. (335)

> (Both attacked savagely, and hidden by their capes with their swords raised, they fought until by their complaints they recognized one another's voice and stopped fighting. Remembering their bond of friendship, and also not wanting to arouse the inhabitants of the house, they fell silent. Withdrawing to a safe distance they began to debate.)

The significance of the ensuing debate is that words fail to resolve the dispute over which man has the greater love for Mirabella. The unnamed knight says that since they are friends they should not argue the point. Instead he suggests the drawing of lots to determine the outcome. Grisel replies that this suggestion of lots is demonstration enough that his interlocutor does not love Mirabella, for if he did he would never jeopardize his love in such a fashion. In his defense, the unnamed knight claims that he had suggested lots because he knew he had right on his side, that God would guarantee his victory. To this conviction he adds that the suggestion was made in order to spare his friend from a tragic outcome in a duel. Grisel claims that this attitude itself is a further indication of his rival's lack of love, since for a true lover suffering is unavoidable. The unnamed knight therefore proposes a duel to determine the outcome, for God will surely resolve the dispute most equitably.

Surprisingly, the unnamed knight (who claims that God is on his side) loses the duel. This constitutes a notable departure from convention, for the judicial duel is meant to be an index of divine law, and those who invoke such adjudication tend to win, since "right equals might."[17] The reference here to transcendent order— a misreading of it—is, moreover, the first in a series of allusions to a Christian axiology. Likewise the claim made later on that

Grisel's death is a "miracle" (362), because it demonstrates that he is more guilty than Mirabella, represents a similar misappropriation of religious authority by society, whereas in fact Grisel commits suicide because of his altruistic passion. The attribution of the Apocalyptic darkening of the sun and sky (355) as a reflection of the queen's attitude toward the death sentence for Mirabella functions in a related (although opposite) manner. Whereas we would expect this meteorological phenomenon to be attributed to divine authority, it is explained instead as an instance of the "pathetic fallacy," whereby nature mirrors the human affect. These are three in number of examples of what might be termed negative religious evocation, designed to undermine not religion, but its human misinterpreters. This form of religious misrepresentation points to the global linguistic misappropriation exposed most visibly on the level of plot.

Mirabella accepts Grisel's love and the couple engages in "that battle which is more pleasurable than dangerous," until the king is informed of the affair, at which point the lovers are seized and incarcerated. In accord with the law of the land, the so-called "Law of Scotland,"[18] the initiator of the affair must be burned at the stake and the accomplice exiled for life, and it is this crucial degree of guilt which the king seeks to determine. This ambiguity which Flores generates is a pointed rewriting of the clear causality of Ghismonda's letter-laden reed. It is, we shall see, a way of turning the conflict of a particular father and daughter into a dramatization of linguistic usage in general. True to his reputation as "the most just ruler alive at that time," the king proceeds in an orderly manner by appointing judges. These men in turn mount an investigation, yet they fail to discover anything, since the affair was conducted with extreme discretion. Adopting a different strategy thereafter, they decide upon a debate in which the lovers will dispute their relative guilt. The judges interrogate both lovers, resorting even to torture—as the medieval judicial system allowed. However, since the lovers know that the more guilty party will die, they each claim total responsibility in order that the other's life be spared. In this debate, as in the first, between Grisel and the unnamed knight, words do not serve a heuristic function, failing to determine the appropriate action to be taken. Because of this judicial impasse, the judges decide that the issue of relative guilt can only be determined by a third debate, this time between one man and one woman, who will argue in general terms as to whether man or woman is more at fault in initiating seduction. The representatives chosen for this debate are forensic experts

with universal reputations. They are Torrellas, the notorious arch-
misogynist poet of fifteenth-century Spain, and Braçayda, the notable female apologist from the Trojan War, who has been resurrected for this occasion. To adjudicate this dialogic confrontation
twelve judges are selected: "los cuales fueron elegidos por per-
sonas de mucha conciencia y sin suspecha: con solennes iura-
mentos que fizieron de iuzgar segun fuesse su mas claro pareçer"
(343) (chosen as people of great conscience and impeccable reputation. With a solemn oath they vowed to judge impartially).

Debate is the form of verbal violence par excellence. Debates
were a tradition in medieval Europe in general, and in fifteenth-
century Spain in particular. Nonetheless, the debate in question
constitutes a departure from the norm and as such it is important
to interpretation of *Grisel*. First of all, the issues debated by these
two contestants have literally nothing to do with the attitudes projected by Grisel and Mirabella.[19] On the contrary, their self-
sacrificing, idealistic bond of love could not be more alien to the
thoughts, words, and ultimately deeds, of the cynical Torrellas
and Braçayda.

From its inception, this debate is semantically "overdetermined." That is, neither opponent can speak objectively. Torrellas
is an avowed misogynist and Braçayda a misandrist—pretending
to represent victimized females while having gained notoriety for
precisely the opposite reason—a victimizer of men, an archetype
of womanly infidelity.

Each contestant offers an arsenal of stock arguments to prove
the greater guilt of the opposite sex. Torrellas, for example, says
that since women are the daughters of Eve, they are obviously
guiltier than men, at which point Braçayda reminds him that
woman was created from Adam's rib.

Both participants are calculatedly unobjective. For this reason
they function as a cynical inversion of the king's unconscious lack
of objectivity. Yet at the same time they are in a fundamental
sense discursively analogous. Just as the king's discourse of regal
impartiality is invalidated by its context, so is their totally biased,
sexist discourse. Again the epistemological fissure separating *sig-
nans* from *signatum* is exposed. Flores emphasizes this point by
introducing a significant addition to the traditional compendium
of predictable sexist argumentation. Namely, in addition to their
denigration of the opposite sex, both Braçayda and Torrellas programmatically accuse each other (and the sex they represent) of
linguistic counterfeit—saying one thing while doing another. In
this way they make *explicit* what has, until now, been presented

implicitly, that is, the dangers of the word/deed dichotomy we first encountered in the case of Tancredi.

Of equal significance is the explicit admission by each debater that they believe the legal system to be just. Braçayda expresses confidence that she will win since "en tierra tan iusta stamos" (345) (we live in such a just land). This opinion is shared by Torrellas, who is confident of his own victory for the same reason, that this just land is inhabited by "tan magnifico Rey y Reyna y notables caualleros y damas" (351) (such a magnificent king and queen and notable knights and ladies). In this way, Flores entirely dissociates the debate from the causality of the king's incestuous inclinations, of which the kingdom is ignorant. In this way, Braçayda and Torrellas provide independent verification and an extreme example of the inescapably biased nature of *any* speech situation.

Torrellas wins the debate. We are told simply that the judges "fundaron por muchas razones ser ella en mayor culpa que Grisel" (355) (concluded, for many reasons, that Mirabella was guiltier than Grisel). The fact that no concrete reasons are given suggests that the decision of the jury—like the very premise of this judicial debate—is questionable to say the least. This too leaves us with the impression that unbiased, objective discourse is virtually unobtainable.

After the sentence has been passed, whereby Mirabella is consigned to death by immolation, Braçayda invokes God as the ultimate authority ("suberano iuez delos hombres" [355]), hoping that justice will prevail over what she considers to be, in retrospect, a prejudiced court. That Mirabella should die because a jury believes that women are the instigators of illicit love is incongruous, and we feel sympathy with Braçayda. Soon after this desperate divine invocation, however, she betrays our sympathies by advocating genocide. Because men are our enemies, she reasons, we should not further their cause:

> O malditas mujeres porque con tantos affanes de partos y fatigas quereys aquellos que en muertes y menguas vos dan el gualardon. o si conseio tomasedes en el nacimiento del hijo: dariades fin asus dias. porque non quedassen soietas asus enemigos. y alegre vida viuiessen. (355)

> (O cursed women, who with so many toils of childbirth and suffering you love those who reward you with death and strife. Oh, if only you would agree to kill your male children at birth, so that you would not be subject to your enemies, you would live happily ever after.)

In total frustration, Braçayda advocates that women cease dealing with men to any degree: "de aqui adelante ahun que los veamos morir: demos asus passiones disfauores por gualardon" (356) (henceforth, even if we see them dying: let us reward their passion with disfavor). The implications of this charge are quite horrifying. For were women to follow this advice, the human race would perish.

The final and briefest of the four debates occurs between the queen and the king. It is significant that here, too, words fail to convince and the ensuing action does not result from rational discourse. The queen pleads for Mirabella's life, yet the king refuses to spare her, despite the queen's valid assertion that "en virtud y nobleza consiste: perdonar a quien yerra: ante que dar pena a quien no la mereçe" (357) (Virtue and nobility consist of pardoning transgressors, rather than condemning one who does not deserve it). In desperation, the queen offers to sacrifice her own life so that Mirabella may live. And, as in the debate between Torrellas and Braçayda, here, too, we find an incongruous proposal. While maternal love can account for some of the queen's motivation, it is aberrant in terms of judicial logic that she should sacrifice herself for an illicit love committed by another woman. The king is moved by his wife's offer to spare their child by sacrificing herself, yet he is unwilling to accept the substitution because it would be unjust. He argues that "si en mi alguna virtud hay: de aquella me precio. ansi que pues sola iusticia es mi victoria: y lo mas loable en mi stado: no quiero perder aquello: que con tan grande studio y trabaio he ganado" (358) (If there is in me some virtue to be found, I value it. Thus, justice alone is my victory, and the most praiseworthy attribute for a king. I do not wish to lose that which I have attained by such long study and hard work).

Nonetheless, the king belies this discourse of regal impartiality, contradicting both his words and actions. Like his wife, he is himself so distraught that he offers to sacrifice his own life in place of his daughter's: "mi muerte si la quieres: yo la atorgo. mas biuo que ella biua es impossible" (358) (If you wish my death, I grant it. But as long as I am alive, she cannot live). These words not only fail to satisfy the queen, they cause her to break violently with the king: "el primero dia que te conoci fue la mi muerte ... plaze me que tu crueza pueda tanto: que en hun dia sin fijos y mujer quedes solo" (359) (the first day I met you was death for me ... It pleases me that your cruelty is so great that in one day you are left without children or wife—alone). Her aggressivity toward the king is quite unexpected because it departs from the norm of queenly decorum. Yet, of course, it is motivated by his own indecorous kingly comportment, his discursive counterfeit.

As Mirabella is being carried off to her horrible death (which 15,000 mourning virgins have assembled to witness), the lovers exchange their final words of love. To Mirabella's oath of eternal devotion, Grisel says that to outlive her "seria hombre perdido sforçado el que sin vos beuir quiziesse que alli podria bien dezir Braçayda. quexando se dela poca fe delos hombres" (361) (would be reprehensible indeed if he still desired life after Mirabella's death—an example which would prove the validity of Braçayda's lament concerning the faithlessness of men). Grisel's evocation of Braçayda's discourse on the faithlessness of men is one more unanticipated moment in the text. For Grisel is a paragon of faithfulness and amorous self-sacrifice. Having uttered these words, he demonstrates their integrity through his action by leaping into the fire intended for Mirabella so that her life might be spared. Mirabella lunges toward the fire to join her lover, but she is restrained by Braçayda and the other women, who "forcibly removed her from the flames." It is no accident that those who prevent Mirabella from joining Grisel are women incapable of understanding the power of love. For surely it would be a much crueller fate for Mirabella to outlive Grisel, just as he had perceived the impossibility of a meaningful existence without her.

The bond of Mirabella and Grisel serves as an idealistic paradigm which none of the people around them can comprehend, let alone imitate. Evidence of this is offered immediately thereafter, as the spectators claim to have witnessed a miracle: "del cielo vino por marauilloso milagro dar muerte a quien la merecia: que contra la voluntad de Dios no diesse pena a quien no la mereçe" (362) (a miracle came from Heaven in order to kill the one who deserved it. For no one is ever killed by the will of God except he who deserves to be killed). Except for Mirabella, no one understands Grisel's motivation, yet they are eager to designate him as the sacrificial victim (the obviously guiltier party deserving immolation) so that she may be spared. Similarly, the judges who had originally sentenced her to death are easily persuaded to revoke the sentence, since Grisel has died.

Just as Grisel's words to Mirabella were not understood by any of the spectators, likewise the spectators do not assume that Mirabella will kill herself, although she has explicitly indicated that she will do so (360). This incredulity is reminiscent of Tancredi's disbelief of Ghismonda's potential for suicide. Not only does Mirabella choose to end her own life, but the manner of her death is as violent as Grisel's, since she hurls herself into a den of lions where she is torn to shreds—*despedaçada* (363). The lion is not indigenous to Scotland, but there as elsewhere it is the emblem of regal authority. For this reason, it is very appropriate that she is destroyed by these symbols of her father's identity. It is, moreover, significant that these lions are anthropomorphically endowed with erotic sensibilities, being described as "each one sating his appetite with her delicate flesh" (363). She kills herself because life without Grisel has no meaning for her. And, although Mirabella has explained this fact *alta voce* to the assembled multitudes, they do not anticipate that she will guarantee the truth of her words by her actions. It is equally revealing that rather than serving an exemplary function of amorous and linguistic fidelity (as the deaths of Ghismonda and Guiscardo did for the city of Salerno), the deaths of Grisel and Mirabella are decidedly *un*exemplary for the Scottish kingdom, resulting in even greater violence.

The escalation of violence is precipitated by Torrellas's unexpected infatuation with Braçayda following the death of Mirabella. By means of a letter he declares his love to Braçayda, at the same time indicating that he realizes he is unworthy and is desirous of doing penance (365). The understandably incredulous lady shows the letter to the queen, who sees Torrellas's affective change as an excellent opportunity for revenge against the man responsible for her daughter's death. She thus instructs Braçayda to reply by feigning a reciprocal interest in him—a pretext designed to lure the unsuspecting poet to a grisly death.

For his part, Torrellas's passionate declaration appears motivated by lust rather than love, since he boasts to his friends that Braçayda will be an easy conquest. Upon arrival at Braçayda's chamber he is seized by the incensed and bloodthirsty females, bound with rope, fastened to a pillar, and gagged so that he can not utter any words. The *verbal violence* of the debate is now replaced by *physical violence* as he is tortured by "a thousand different torments." As some women burn him with tongs, others flirt with cannibalism, tearing him to shreds with their nails and teeth (369). After he has been so brutally abused that he seems on the point of death, the women stop tormenting him in order to partake of a sumptuous dinner. The banquet takes place in close proximity to the mutilated Torrellas, so that he can witness their enjoyment and so that they can abuse him verbally before returning to their physical abuse. When the supper is concluded the women resume the torture of Torrellas, described now in terms of food: "despues que fueron alçadas todas las mesas fueron iuntas a dar amarga cena a Torrellas. y tanto fue de todas seruido con potages y aues ... que non se como scriuir las differencias delas iniurias y offienças que le hazian" (369) (after the tables were cleared, the women went to give Torrellas a bitter supper. He was served such soups and birds ... that I am incapable of describing all the injuries and offenses which they caused him).

Two religious images are recalled by the treatment of Torrellas here, and they accord with the subverted religious motifs mentioned earlier. Martyrdom and the Last Supper are each being enacted here in a perverted form.[20] In addition, this supper constitutes a subversion of romance celebration. Rather than ending the text with the normative banquet in honor of the couple (in commemoration of order restored) we find instead a graphically lurid destruction of that ideal in the physical destruction of Torrellas's body. The manner of his death—the poet's gory dismemberment at the hands of outraged females—recalls the dismemberment of another infamously misogynistic poet, that of Orpheus in Book II of the *Metamorphoses*. He likewise dies the victim of women, whom he has spurned since the time of Eurydice's death, favoring the love of young boys instead. It is from this affective switch that Orpheus derived his fame in the Middle Ages as the father of homosexuality. By this subtextual reminiscence, Flores suggests that Torrellas's view of women was anything but objective. Two further observations should be made in this context. The *physical dismemberment*—a metaphor of Torrellas's *dismembered discourse*—is an inversion of the amorous eucharist which ultimately united the lives of Ghismonda and Guiscardo. Ghismonda's *metonymic* act of contiguity—her physical incorporation of Guiscardo's heart, as well as the common coffin they share—likewise contrasts sharply with Mirabella's (paradoxical) *metaphoric* act of substitution, her physical *dismemberment* as metaphor of spiritual *union*.

Torrellas is a love-martyr *in malo* (the opposite of Grisel and Mirabella), which is why the women burn his ashes and carry them in a pendant around their necks—in place of the traditional wearing of a locket containing a lover's portrait. Torrellas's martyrdom thus reflects as badly on him as it does on the bloodthirsty women who effect it.[21] Given the violent dissolution of the three relationships portrayed in the text (those of Grisel and Mirabella, the king and queen, and Torrellas and Braçayda), it is tempting to read the text as an illustration of René Girard's axiom that desire inevitably breeds disaster (rather than romance).

According to the Girardian view, the fault lies with the lovers who succumb to their passion, thus causing a chain reaction of multiple deaths and savage brutality that threatens the very fabric of society. It is because desire threatens society that the couple must be ritualistically eliminated. Ritual, as Girard explains, is nothing more than the exercise of "good violence."[22] The importance of ritual sacrifice is paramount, its absence cataclysmic:

> Mimetic desire is simply a term more comprehensive than *violence* for religious pollution. As the catalyst for the sacrificial crisis, it would eventually destroy the entire community if the surrogate victim were not at hand to halt the process and the *ritualized mimesis* were not at hand to keep the *conflictual mimesis* from beginning afresh. (148)

Such ritual sacrifice serves as a form of catharsis, as an affirmation of the rules upon which a given community is predicated. This is the reason why societies create laws to punish transgressors. It is not that the crime will be undone by the act of punishing the guilty individual, but that, because of the punishment, the crime will serve as an example of behavior which society will not tolerate.

What we see graphically depicted in *Grisel* is precisely the opposite. After the twelve judges (clutching their bloodstained swords) pronounce the death sentence for Mirabella (355), rather than reverting to the peaceful status quo of orderly behavior, Scottish society breaks down before our very eyes. This disintegration contrasts boldly with Boccaccio's more optimistic depiction of the city of Salerno, whose collective pathos serves to unify it. The only legitimate successor to the throne, Mirabella, kills herself. The queen not only becomes estranged from the king, she takes the law into her own hands, with the help of many other equally disaffected females. Braçayda's unnatural call for genocide—initially perceived as the passing rage of a provoked female—by the end seems to be within the realm of the possible. For his part, the king is incapable of stopping the murderous females, much less of bringing them to justice.

Given that the violence does not end with the sacrifice of Grisel and Mirabella, that society is not restored, it appears that it is not the lovers' desire which is at fault.[23] If it were, their deaths would have ended the chain of destruction, as Girard's phenomenology of sacrifice makes clear. One is tempted to conclude, therefore, that it is the law or, more precisely, the king as law-bearer, who is flawed. That, had he allowed his daughter to marry rather than preventing her from doing so out of his own incestuous desire, none of the tragedies would have occurred. The fact that this incestuously inclined king is not eliminated (as happens in the Arthurian world, for example), indicates that we are not reading a romance. If we were, the virtuous Mirabella would have inherited the kingdom from an equally virtuous father. Alternatively, they both would have perished as a result of their sexually transgressive behavior. But Flores is suggesting something different.

Like her Italian predecessor, Mirabella dies not, as we would expect, of infanticide (the anticipated resolution of an incestuous union), but as a result of *her own linguistic preference*. Given the etiology of incest that pervades the narrative, it is surprising — indeed shocking — that the father's incestuous urge does not achieve physical intimacy; the focus is not physical but verbal transgression. Unlike earlier medieval incest narratives, physical defilement is unnecessary. In fact, its elimination here is very revealing. For what is at issue is nothing less than a new attitude toward language. The text is a negative, nominalist recasting of the early medieval discursive principle whereby the continuity of language guarantees genealogical succession, as Isidore of Seville had posited.[24] Juxtaposing the new attitude operative in the later Middle Ages with the earlier attitude, Howard Bloch writes: "This [new] body of grammatical thought [the work of the speculative grammarians] is organized around synchronic categories; more committed to logical distinction than to chronological sequence, continuity and origins; less oriented toward the 'verticality' of the single word — etymology or definition — than toward 'horizontal' problems of syntax and signification."[25] A *metaphoric* attitude toward language thus replaces a *metonymic* one. This accords, moreover, with Roman Jakobson's observation of "the [diachronically] alternative predominance of one or the other of these two processes."[26] The absence of physical violation in *Grisel* discursively illustrates these two antithetical modes of signification (the etymological and the syntactic), foregrounding the ubiquitous threat of linguistic violation and its dangerous implications, irrespective of lineage. The extent of Flores's interest in rejecting the traditional teleology of lineage is also visible in that no words exchanged by the father and daughter are recorded in the text — a striking contrast to the case of Ghismonda and Tancredi. This also explains why so much of the Spanish text is devoted to the debates of other discursive pairs. The result is an illustration of the universality of linguistic transgression. Indeed, a new kind of incest text is revealed, that of linguistic incest. Language is "deprived of its hallowed function as support of the law, in order to become the cause of a permanent trial of [every individual] speaking subject."[27] For Kristeva, *poetic discourse* is incestuous in that it routinely trangresses codified forms of signification and social hierarchies of decorum.[28] In his text, Flores dramatizes the realization that not only poetic discourse but *all discourse* is inherently incestuous.

A further and related displacement of our generic expectations occurs in that the romance paradigm (on the model of Tristan) involves illicit love that shuns marriage. Here the situation is reversed. Mirabella and Grisel become furtively involved precisely because she is prevented by the king from marrying a vassal of his own choosing.[29] This reversal likewise signals Flores's very *un*romance axiology.

The text ends with the words "Thus the ladies triumphed over Torrellas's wickedness, and he received just payment." Given the behavior not only of Torrellas, but of his female torturers as well, the claim of "justice" is problematic indeed. It has even led some readers to argue that the negative portrayal of the women may have been inadvert and unintentional. Yet both the savage and protracted quality of this portrayal make it difficult to imagine that Flores was unaware of what he was doing. We recall, moreover, that his text has been necessarily scrutinized and approved by his own lady, by virtue of the fact that she did not destroy it as she was instructed to do if she found its portrayal of women objectionable.

The text is neither misandrist nor misogynistic — or rather it is both. What is wistfully celebrated in the text is the couple of idealistic lovers whose words guarantee their deeds — in other words, the determinacy of signs. This successful private relationship bears no connection to the public and its laws. The admirable love and death of Grisel and Mirabella does not function exemplarily for the godless society of Scots. The lovers' amorously motivated words and actions do not convince others to emulate them. They are, as it were, two displaced romance characters, adhering to a kind of paradoxically prelapsarian language model, lost in a novelistic world. What is denigrated is not the putatively destructive desire of Grisel and Mirabella, but the linguistic perversion of society itself, its lamentable ability to generate verbal ambiguity and distortion.

It is significant that the only exception to the linguistic perversion which pervades the Scottish kingdom is an extradiegetic one, namely, the couple represented by Flores and his lady. They perpetuate the philosophy of language projected by Grisel and Mirabella in an enduring verbal artifact, the eponymous text on which they collaborate. The discourse of dismemberment generated by the *verbally* incestuous Italian prince and Scottish king is finally ended, replaced by a linguistic integrity which exposes its devastating implications. In this way, Flores and his lady respond to the Foucaultian distinction with which I began. They offer a corrective to the potentially *destructive social act* in their own *creative literary act*. Does this also suggest that the creation of such linguistic integrity is largely a fictional pursuit? Perhaps.

What can be said with certainty, however, is that the text is much more than an illustration of the perennial conflict between law and desire, or misogyny and misandry. It is a parable of language.

NOTES

1. "What Is an Author?" in *Textual Strategies: Perspectives in Post-Structuralist Criticism*, ed. Josué Harari (Ithaca: Cornell University Press, 1979), 148.

2. Echoing Marcelino Menéndez Pelayo's comment, Carmelo Samonà characterizes *Grisel* as an "esile cornice narrativa che racchiude il nucleo dottrinale del debate" (*Studi sul romanzo sentimentale e cortese nella letteratura spagnola del quattrocento* [Rome: Carucci, 1960], 109.) Samonà is justified in underscoring the prominence of dialogue in this text since no less than three-fourths of it is taken up by debate. This dialogic structure is suggestively viewed by Samonà as having an undeniable impact on *La Celestina* (113).

3. Barbara Matulka sees *Grisel* as she saw *Grimalte*, namely as a stridently pro-feminist text. Thus Torrellas's death at the hands of outraged females is interpreted as exemplary: "In describing so minutely the cruel torture and death of Torrellas [Flores] seems to have adapted the punishment which the other famous misogynist, the Archpriest of Talavera, had suggested as a suitable vengeance of the irate ladies against whom he had thundered his violent abuse (B. Matulka, *The Novels of Juan de Flores and Their European Diffusion* [New York: Institute of French Studies, 1931], 116). Indeed, Matulka further asserts that Torrellas's minutely (i.e., "realistically") described death was not only accepted as just, but that "it was taken as a historical fact and set up as an example of the cruel fate that awaited the enemies of women" (166).

4. *Decameron*, ed. Cesare Segre (Milan: Mursia, 1974), 258. All references to the Italian are taken from this edition. *The Decameron*, trans. G. H. McWilliam (Harmondsworth: Penguin, 1972), 329. English translations are from this edition.

5. Balducci's words of caution not only fail to convince his son, but his metaphoric attempt at deception gets him into further trouble: "Io non voglio; tu non sai donde elle s'imbeccano!—e sentí incontanente piú aver di forza la natura che il suo ingegno" (258).

6. Jacques Derrida, *Of Grammatology*, trans. Gayatri Spivak (Baltimore: Johns Hopkins University Press, 1976), lxv–lxvi.

7. Milicent Marcus, in *An Allegory of Form* (Palo Alto: Anma Libri, 1979), 52ff., offers an illuminating series of examples of the reversed sex roles exhibited by Ghismonda's "virile" composure and Tancredi's "feminine" lachrymosity. I would add that this inversion is meant not simply to highlight Tancredi's unnatural love for his daughter, but also to emphasize the greater authority of her discourse, since she comports herself with the controlled, regal demeanor that the distraught prince lacks.

8. Guido Aimansi, *The Writer as Liar. Narrative Technique in the 'Decameron'* (London: Routledge and Kegan Paul, 1975), 141–42.

9. Several critics have commented on the fact that Guiscardo's words echo those of Francesca da Rimini in *Inferno* 5 of the *Divine Comedy*. Luigi Russo, for example, distinguishes Ghismonda from Francesca by saying that the latter exhibited an interest in spiritualized love, the former a carnal attraction ("Postura critica a Ghismunda e Guiscardo," *Il Decameron* [Florence: 1939], 379). By contrast, Marcus recalls that "Francesca makes the body the exclusive subject of her lament" (*Allegory of Form*, 48).

Yet is is important to note that Ghismonda is in fact morally superior to Francesca for two reasons. Firstly, because she chose Guiscardo as a result of her ethical concern for spiritual (as opposed to titular) nobility. Secondly, she initiated the relationship only because her father would not allow her to remarry. Francesca's motivation is quite another matter. She was married at the time, thus yielding to lust by her involvement with a married man (Paolo Malatesta), her husband's younger brother.

10. Bakhtin, *The Dialogical Principle*, trans. Tzvetan Todorov (Minneapolis: University of Minnesota Press, 1984), 51.

11. Aimansi, *The Writer as Liar*, 150.

12. Marcus speaks of Tancredi's "triumph"; at the time of their deaths he "gains ascendancy over the couple in his capacity as father and king" (*Allegory of Form*, 60). However, if he may be said to gain ascendancy, it is only after he has undergone a painful process of linguistic education, a kind of purgation whereby he finally must admit the referentiality of language, the all-important relationship of word to deed, by acknowledging his fault and publicly burying the lovers together.

13. G. Mazzotta, *The World at Play in Boccaccio's 'Decameron'* (Princeton: Princeton University Press, 1986), 134.

14. Marcus (*Allegory of Form*) focuses her interesting analysis of 4.1 on the significance of metaphor in the tale. Indicating that this figure of language characterizes Ghismonda's affair from its inception (59), Marcus sees its function here (as in Balducci's tale) as illustrating reality rather than masking it (51). I would argue, however, that it is not metaphor which conceals or reveals "truth," but the perspective of the enunciator and interlocutor is the issue. Although, for example, Balducci himself exploits metaphor to mask the truth, his son does not perceive it as such; for him metaphor does serve to illuminate the situation, in this case that the attractive creatures are called "goslings."

In this connection, Marcus's claim that Tancredi "violat[es] the terms of metaphor itself by presenting Guiscardo's heart to 'gli occhi della fronte'" (65) is relevant, for it illustrates, I would argue, that metonymy is as much an issue in this novella as is concretization of metaphor. Indeed, Tancredi's fundamental problem results from his metonymic misperception of his daughter; that she is not autonomous, but an inseparable part of his identity. The "correction" of this misperception occurs only at the tale's end, when the metonymic identification of Guiscardo and Ghismonda is definitively (and publicly) acknowledged by him. Not only does she clutch his heart to hers, but Guiscardo and Ghismonda are fixed in a perpetual metonymically contiguous posture by sharing the same casket. It is thus the referentiality both of his metaphoric and metonymic usage which Tancredi finally learns to correct at the expense of his daughter's life.

15. Text is from Matulka (my translation).

16. Although she analyzes *Grisel* in regard to *Decameron* 4.1, Matulka does not perceive the relationship of the Scottish king's linguistic transgression to that of his Italian predecessor.

17. As R. Howard Bloch explains, "the judicial duel belongs to the series of ordeals common to any primitive sense of justice in which legal process remains indistinguishable from divine law" (*Medieval French Literature and Law* [Berkeley: University of California Press, 1977], 18).

18. "In the [twelfth-century] lives of St. Kentigern we find very clearly explained an ancient 'Law of Scotland,' according to which the king carries out, against his own daughter, the penalty of death for illicit love while unmarried" (Matulka, 162).

19. That this debate is not just extraneous, but novel as well, is reflected in the title of an English adaptation of the Grisel story: *A Paire of Turtle Doves: or, the Tragicall end of Agamio, wherein (besides other matters pleasing to the reader) by way of dispute between a knight and a lady is described this never before debated question, to wit: Whether man to woman, or woman to man offer the greatest temptations and allurements unto unbridled lust, and consequently whether man or w[o]man in that unlawful act, be the greater offender.* See Everett Ward Olmstead, "Story of Grisel and Mirabella," in *Homenaje ofrecido a Menéndez Pidal: Misceánea de estudios lingüísticos, literarios e históricos* (Madrid: Hernando, 1925), 2: 371–72.

20. A. D. Deyermond notes this inversion in *A Literary History of Spain* (London: Ernest Benn, 1971), 165.

21. Patricia Grieve observes that Torrellas's death constitutes a recapitulation of all the other deaths: "At least one aspect of each of the other deaths can be found in the spectacular torture-murder of Torrellas. The knights die somehow because of an entrapment of Mirabella's beauty. Otro Caballero, like Torrellas, was slain during the night by a friend. His words were the cause of his death, since Grisel found offensive the suggestions made by Otro Caballero. Because of Torrellas's verbal debasement of women, resulting, ultimately, in Mirabella's suicide, the Queen sought his death. Grisel's suicide was a leap into the flames (like the flames of love), while Torrellas was tortured by "fieras llagas." After Mirabella's leap during the night into the courtyard, hungry lions devoured every inch of her flesh, leaving only her bones. Her mother and ladies-in-waiting metamorphosed by rage into lion-like creatures, clawed the flesh from Tor-

rellas's bones until none remained" (*Desire and Death in Fifteenth- and Sixteenth-Century Spanish Sentimental Romances* [Ph.D. diss., Princeton University, 1983], 106–7.

I would add that these reminiscences force us to compare each of the deaths to that of the calculating, professional misuser of language, Torrellas, and, ultimately, to linguistic usage itself. In so doing, what becomes apparent is that these multiple deaths reflect a number of different attitudes toward language.

22. René Girard, *Violence and the Sacred*, trans. Patrick Gregory (Baltimore: Johns Hopkins University Press, 1977), 37.

23. For an alternate reading see Grieve (113ff.), who views the text as an illustration of Girard's principle, a "demythification" of love and its destructive effects.

24. "Ex linguis gentes, non ex gentibus linguae exortae sunt" (Isidore of Seville, *Etymologiarum . . . Librixx*, ed. W. M. Lindsay [Oxford: Clarendon Press, 1966], 9:1, xiv).

25. Howard Bloch, *Etymologies and Genealogies* (Chicago: University of Chicago Press, 1983), 160.

26. Roman Jakobson, "The Metaphoric and Metonymic Poles," in *Fundamentals of Language*, ed. Roman Jakobson and Morris Hale (The Hague: Mouton, 1971), 92.

27. Julia Kristeva, *Desire in Language*, trans. Thomas Gora, Alice Jardine, and Leon S. Roudiez (New York: Columbia University Press, 1980), 137.

28. Kristeva's interest here is in "the intrinsic connection between literature and breaking up social concord: Because it utters incest, poetic language is linked with 'evil' (I refer to a title by George Bataille) [and] should be understood, beyond the resonances of Christian ethics, as the social body's self-defense against the discourse of incest as destroyer and generator of any language and sociality. This applies all the more as 'great literature,' which has mobilized unconsciousness for centuries, has nothing to do with the hypostasis of incest (a petty game of fetishists at the end of an era, priesthood of a would-be enigma—the forbidden mother); on the contrary, this incestuous relation, exploding in language, embracing it from top to bottom in such a singular fashion . . . defies generalizations [yet] still has this common feature in all outstanding cases: it presents itself as demystified" (*Desire in Language*, 139).

29. For a discussion of romance and the social threat it poses, especially in terms of the Tristan myth, see Denis de Rougement, *Love in the Western World*, trans. Montgomery Belgion (Princeton: Princeton University Press, 1983).

Transgression and Transcendence: Figures of Female Desire in Dante's *Commedia*

RACHEL JACOFF

For Diana Wilson

Dante's pilgrimage in the *Commedia* presents itself as a progress toward the congruence of legitimacy and desire, toward an Edenic situation defined precisely by the identity of the desirable and the permissible. When Dante arrives at the entrance to Eden, he is told by Virgil that he may, in fact that he *must* henceforth take his pleasure as his guide: "'lo tuo piacere omai prendi per duce'" (*Purg.* 27.131).[1] Dante discovers immediately upon entering Paradise that "molto è licito là, che qui non lece" (*Par.* 1.55) (much is permitted there that is not allowed here); in the Empyrean God's "etterna legge" (*Par.* 32.55) replaces both human and natural law: "dove Dio sanza mezzo governa, la legge natural nulla rileva" (*Par.* 30.122–23) (where God governs without intermediary, the law of nature in no way prevails). The pilgrim's desire and will are, in the poem's final lines, imagined as moving in perfect accord with this law of cosmic Amor. Because Dante is concerned with differing spheres of legitimacy and legality throughout the *Commedia*, it is revealing to track the usage of words such as *licito* and *legge*, and to note the varying contexts, human and divine, in which they are used. In this essay I want to articulate one such context as a way of rethinking the relationship between legitimacy and desire, and in particular, female desire.

Alice Jardine has recently argued that legitimacy is "part of that judicial domain which, historically, has determined the right to govern, the succession of kings, the link between father and son, the necessary paternal fiction, the ability to decide who is the father—in patriarchal culture."[2] From this perspective, notions of legitimacy traditionally lend themselves to—or derive from—gendered narratives, narratives which deal with the engendering and transfer of power. We can tease out one such narrative and its possible implications by focusing on three female figures or emblems in Dante's *Commedia*.

I begin with two legendary figures of female desire, Semiramis and Myrrha. These two women are, as it happens, the framing females of Dante's *Inferno:* Dante's strategic placement of Semiramis and Myrrha as the first and last female figures associated with particular sins suggests their iconic potential. Semiramis initiates the catalogue of the lustful in *Inferno* 5, while Myrrha interrupts Canto 30 in a brief appearance where she is paired with Gianni Schicchi as exemplary impersonators in the bolgia of the falsifiers. Although they are placed in different categories and widely separated in the poem, both Semiramis and Myrrha are, as all commentators note, primarily associated with incest. And although the issue is mother-son incest in the case of Semiramis, and daughter-father incest in the case of Myrrha, in each instance the locus of desire is assumed to be the female subject. Furthermore, as we shall see, both cases are represented in strikingly similar rhetorical and prosodic structures. Certain of these structures return in the concluding canto of the *Paradiso* where they are deployed—in a way that both suggests and evades scandal—in relation to the poem's ultimate and consummate female figure, the Virgin Mary.

Let us begin at the beginning, with the figure of Semiramis and her legend. Dante's major source was Orosius, usually identified with the soul described in the Heaven of the Sun as "'quello avvocato de' tempi cristiani / del cui latino Augustin si provide'" (*Par.* 10.119–20) ("that defender of Christian times, of whose discourse Augustine made use"). Dante himself made such use of Orosius's "Latin" that he virtually quotes his description of Semiramis as she who made lust legal in her law: "libito fé licito in sua legge" clearly translates Orosius's "ut cuique libitum esset liberum fieret."[3] Orosius's version of Semiramis's story is congruent with Augustine's brief but damning mention of her in the *City of God*, but it is Orosius who actually invents this particular charge, the charge which Dante foregrounds in her portrait and which makes Semiramis the model not only of lust but of self-exculpation as well. For Augustine and Orosius, Semiramis's transgressive sexuality is synecdochical for her total being.

In order to see how much this is the case, it is useful to look briefly at earlier portraits of Semiramis. The earliest sources, such as the Greek historian Diodorus Siculus (60 B.C.), depict Semiramis as a great heroine, a figure of extraordinary martial bravura and civic achievement. In Diodorus's "library of history" Semiramis is "the most renowned of all women of whom we have any record."[4] He retells the legend of her semidivine origin as the daughter of the Syrian goddess Derceto, a sirenic goddess who was half woman and half fish. Since she is rescued from death as a child by the care of doves, Diodorus connects both her name itself and her final metamorphosis into a dove at her death with this episode. He concentrates on her marvelous architectural operations, including the rebuilding of Babylon, and her daring and successful conquests; his account of her adventurous attempted conquest of India, complete with an entourage of camels disguised as elephants makes amazing reading. Her sexuality is mentioned briefly in relation to the charge that she consorted with her handsomest soldiers, whom she subsequently had killed. Neither in Diodorus nor in any of his sources, however, is there *any* mention of Semiramis's incestuous desire for her son.

The source of that particular detail is Justinus, a third-century historian whose Latin epitome of Pompeius Trogus's *Historiae Philippicae* was widely read throughout the Middle Ages. Justinius's reportage is much briefer than Diodorus's and he concludes Semiramis's story by claiming that she was murdered by her son after she sought to sleep with him: "Ad postremum cum concubitum filii petisset, ab eodem interfecta est."[5] This sentence is the source for Augustine's more vivid summary description of Semiramis in the *City of God:* "For the son of Ninus ascended the Assyrian throne after his mother Semiramis. It is said that she was killed by her son, because she, his mother, had dared to defile him by incestuous intercourse."[6]

Whereas the ancient historians thought of Semiramis as the founder of the empire which would ultimately be lost by Sardanapalus—in itself a suggestive pairing, insofar as she is represented as a woman of manly virtues and he as a man of effeminate comportment—Christian historians connected Semiramis with biblical history. In the Eusebius-Jerome chronicle, Semiramis's reign coincides with Abraham's history. In her summary of medieval readings of Semiramis, Irene Samuel says, "From Justinus and Jerome they knew Semiramis as the builder of Babylon; Orosius reminded them that it was the city Nimrod had founded, Augustine that it was the antitype of the City of God. . . . Augustine combined the parallelism of Jerome with the details of Justinus and added the censure that Orosius and many a churchman after him were to repeat"[7] and elaborate. While Diodorus had called Semiramis "the most renowned of all women," Dante's contemporary Giovanni Villani, echoing Brunetto Latini, could say that she "fu la più crudele e dissoluta femmina del mondo."[8]

This (im)moralized Semiramis is clearly present in Dante's description of her as "imperadrice de molte favelle" (*Inf.* 5.54) (empress of many tongues), an allusion both to her conquests and her legendary role as either founder or rebuilder of Babylon, the city whose very name was thought to signify confusion. Dante juxtaposes her political power and her transgressive sexuality, a juxtaposition more fully spelled out in Orosius, who condemns her lust for power quite explicitly and makes it both analogous to and prophetic of her disordered sexuality:

> This woman, not content with the boundaries which she had inherited from her husband, who, at that time, was the only warlike king and who had acquired these lands in the course of fifty years, added Ethiopia to her empire by war and drenched it with blood. . . . Such action at that time, namely to persecute and slaughter peoples living in peace, was even more cruel and serious than it is today, because, at that time there were neither the incentives for war abroad, nor such great temptation to exercise cupidity at home.[9]

Orosius immediately follows this condemnation of Semiramis's lust for power with a description of her lust, culminating in her incestuous desire and her legalization of it.

Dante extends the resonances of this conflation of political and sexual cupidities by grouping Semiramis with Dido and Cleopatra, legendary oriental queens whose stories, particularly in their Virgilian form, reveal the same constellation of political and erotic danger. The catalogue of lovers in *Inferno* 5 is based on the similar one in the *Aeneid* which precedes Dido's underworld appearance in Book 6. That catalogue, too, presents a figure of incestuous desire, Phaedra, as its leading lady.[10]

Semiramis acquires yet further emblematic resonance by Dante's heightened deployment of tropes of repetition in his portrayal of her. "Libito fé licito in sua legge" is, as we have seen, virtually a quotation from Orosius. But to Orosius's play on *libito* and *licito,* Dante adds the further alliteration in *legge;* and he calls attention to that word by placing it in rhyme position and by creating a *rima equivoca* on it.

"A vizio di lussuria fu sì rotta,
  che libito fé licito in sua legge,
  per tòrre il biasmo in che era condotta.
Ell' è Semiramìs, di cui si legge
  che succedette a Nino e fu sua sposa;
  tenne la terra che 'l Soldan corregge."

(*Inf.* 5.55–60)

("She was so given to lechery that she made lust licit in her law, to take away the blame she had incurred. She is Semiramis, of whom we read that she succeeded Ninus and had been his wife; she held the land the Sultan rules.")

Legge (meaning law) rhymes with *legge* (meaning read), enacting the problematic of identity and difference. Two identical words have different meanings, and must do so, according to the "law" of *terza rima;* insofar as rhyme is the formal marker of law in poetry, it enjoins obedience to the proper relationship between sameness and difference. Dante obeys this law rigorously throughout the *Inferno* and *Purgatorio,* but as we shall see, he constructs an exception to it elsewhere. In *Inferno* 5 the doubling of the notion of legality and reading is itself suggestive of hidden connections, since the law is what we read, and since reading becomes a thematic consideration later in the canto when Francesca attempts to legalize, or "authorize," her own lust in terms of the reading act: "'Galeotto fu 'l libro e chi lo scrisse.'" The alliterations on the letter "l" also bind the portrait of Semiramis to the word *lussuria* which defines the canto's explicit subject and which is the word used to characterize not only Semiramis, but Cleopatra as well, who is summed up by the adjective *lussoriosa.*

The high degree of alliteration in the portrait of Semiramis is only the first instance of what will quickly become the dominant stylistic feature of this canto. Canto 5 is saturated by tropes of repetition: alliteration, assonance, anaphora, paronomasia, and derivatio occur with such specific density that they acquire iconic status.[11] Figures of language become figures of thought; the phonemic becomes thematic in a canto which turns on the issue of imitation and repetition; as others have made clear, mimetic desire is dramatized both by Francesca da Rimini's putative imitation of Guinevere, and by the pilgrim's symbolic reenactment of Francesca's passion in his own compassion.[12] While Francesca attempts to collapse her life into literature, Dante momentarily collapses his life into his heroine's.[13] The obsessive and fundamental connection (and confusion) between *amor* and *morte* that governs all of the figures in the canto is reiterated in the canto's heavily alliterative concluding line: "E caddi come corpo morto cade."

The repetitions and potential confusions of words that are either identical with different meanings (*legge/legge*) or nearly identical (*libito/licito*) provide a lexical version of the larger issues of boundaries, confusions, and repetitions at stake in the dramatic and thematic matter of the canto. Furthermore, the repetitions of words such as *amor, ancora, morte* and of sounds (such as *or* and *a*) become functional in the rhetoric of ineluctability deployed in Francesca da Rimini's account of the law of love that legalizes her own lust. Francesca's self-presentation dramatizes the same confusions and self-exonerating strategies that were proleptically at work in Dante's description of Semiramis. Furthermore, the issue of incest taints Francesca as well, since Dante takes care at the opening of the canto to categorize the lovers as "i due cognati,"[14] thus reminding us of the fact that Francesca's lover and her husband are brothers.

The suggestive nexus of incest and alliteration recurs in Dante's brief description of Myrrha twenty-five cantos later. *Inferno* 30 opens with two great Ovidian images of grief and madness leading to human descent into animality; these powerful evocations of Athamas and Hecuba, parents either causing or responding to the death of children, prepare for the entrance of "due ombre smorte e nude, / che mordendo correvan di quel modo / che 'l porco quando del procil si schiude" (*Inf.* 30.25–27) (two pallid shades, that I saw biting and running like the pig when it is led out of the sty). One of the "due rabbiosi" is Gianni Schicchi, the other:

> "Quell' è l'*a*nima *a*ntica
> di Mirra scellerata, che divenne
> al padre, fuor del dritto *amore, amica*."
>
> (*Inf.* 30.37–39; my emphasis)

("That is the ancient spirit of infamous Myrrha, who became loving of her father beyond rightful love.")

Both Gianni and Myrrha are designated by the verb "falsificare," since both took on the form of another in order to achieve their illicit desires. The pairing of these two figures is puzzling until one considers that incest interrupts the normal descent of patriarchal power just as Gianni Schicchi's counterfeiting of a dying man was designed to shortcircuit the transfer of goods from parent to child. Myrrha, "falsificando sé in altrui forma," and Gianni, "testando e dano al testamento norma," violate norm and form, sabotaging the legitimate social construction of kinship and property. The connection between Myrrha and Gianni Schicchi, thus, goes beyond the fact that they both resort to disguises to satisfy their desires. In both cases, their very desires are destructive of structures of legitimacy in terms that are crucial to its function within patriarchal culture.

The pairing of Myrrha and Gianni presumes a linkage between the incest prohibition and the social construct, a linkage whose theoretical centrality we have come to understand from Lévi-Strauss's argument that the prohibition of incest demarcates the intersection of biology and society. According to him, "the rules of kinship and marriage are not made necessary by the social state. They *are* the social state itself, reshaping biological relationships and natural sentiments, forcing them into structures implying them as well as others, and compelling them to rise above their original characteristics."[15] For Augustine, too, the prohibition of incest is necessary to the extension of social sympathy that makes society possible. In Book 15 of the *City of God*, he explains that in the earliest times all extant humans were derived from our first parents, necessitating the marriage of brothers and sisters. As soon as a sufficient number of persons existed, the prohibition against such unions went into effect in order to guarantee the spread of charity in social life.

> The aim was that one man should not combine many relationships in his one self, but that these connections should be separated and spread among individuals, and that in this way they should help to bind social life more effectively by involving in their plurality a plurality of persons. "Father" and "father-in-law," for instance, are names denoting two different relationships. . . . Adam was compelled to be, in his one self, both father and father-in-law to his sons and daughter.[16]

The Edenic situation is necessarily incestuous, but only provisionally so. In Augustine's discussion of the incest prohibition, he, like Orosius in his condemnation of Semiramis, identifies incestuous desire with geopolitical lust: "For if it is wicked to go beyond the boundary of one's lands in the greed for increasing possession, how much more wicked is it to remove a moral boundary in the lust for sexual pleasure!"[17]

Augustine's analysis of the social consequences of the same person playing more than one kinship role at a time is reminiscent of a particularly strong passage in Myrrha's monologue from

Ovid's *Metamorphoses*, Dante's source for the figure of Myrrha. In her anguished debate with herself, Myrrha focuses on the problem of names:

> et quot confundas et iura et nomina, sentis!
> tune eris et matris paelex et adultera patris?
> tune soror nati genetrixque vocabere fratris?
>
> (10.346–48)[18]

(Think how many ties, how many names you are confusing! Will you be the rival of your mother, the mistress of your father? Will you be called the sister of your son, the mother of your brother?)

Like Augustine, Ovid's Myrrha understands that the very use of language is somehow dependent on a plurality of persons to occupy the plurality of kinship roles. These meditations on names and roles call to mind Lévi-Strauss's extraordinary insight that the incest prohibition and exogamy are necessary to move from biological to social organization and are, from this point of view, functionally identical to language itself.[19] The role of the incest prohibition in effecting the transition from nature to culture makes incest the equivalent of that which is not human; but once this happens, the "not human" is no longer seen as natural, but rather as bestial. This is exactly the point made by Ovid's Myrrha when she attempts to rationalize her desire in terms of the behavior of animals.

> coeunt animalia nullo
> cetera dilectu, nec habetur turpe iuvencae
> ferre patrem tergo, fit equo sua filia coniunx,
> quasque creavit init pecudes caper, ipsaque, cuius
> semine concepta est, ex illo concipit ales.
> felices, quibus ista licent! humana malignas
> cura dedit leges, et quod natura remittit,
> invidia iura negant.
>
> (10.324–31)

(Other animals mate as they will, nor is it thought base for a heifer to endure her sire, nor for his own offspring to be a horse's mate; the goat goes in among the flocks which he has fathered, and the very birds conceive from those from whom they were conceived. Happy those who have such privilege! Human civilization has made spiteful laws, and what nature allows, the jealous laws forbid.)

Myrrha attacks the "malignas leges" and "invidia iura" which divide animals from humans, nature from culture, in terms of the incest prohibition—even though later in this very speech she herself refers to the prohibition as a law or contract (*foedus*) of "great nature" (10.352–53) itself.

Dante reaffirms the link between incest and bestiality in his presentation of Myrrha by associating her with Hecuba and Athamas, humans who descended into bestiality, and, again, in the simile of the "porco quando del porcil si schiude." But he does so even more powerfully through another mythological paradigm, Pasiphaë, who (also in disguise) mated with a bull and who is also the mother of Phaedra.[20] Dante makes Pasiphaë the negative exemplum on the terrace of the lustful in Purgatory where, although the penitents, as far as we can tell from those named, are all male, she serves as the negative type for those whose sin was unbridled lust:

> "Nostro peccato fu ermafrodito;
>   ma perché non servammo umana legge,
>   seguendo come bestie l'appetito,
> in obbrobrio di noi, per noi si legge,
>   quando partinci, il nome di colei
>   che s'imbestiò ne le 'mbestiate schegge."
>
> (Purg. 26.82–87)

("Our sin was hermaphrodite: but because we observed not human law, following appetite like beasts, when we part from them, the name of her who bestialized herself in the beastlike planks is uttered by us, in opprobrium of ourselves.")

By reiterating the *rima equivoca* on *legge/legge* which distinguished the description of Semiramis, Dante in effect "rhymes" Pasiphaë with Semiramis, bestiality with incest. Furthermore, the fact that male penitents figure their transgressive desire in a female emblem suggests that the female *is* the very *figura* of such desire. This extreme assertion finds corroboration in the circle of Venus in *Paradiso* where we find, among the three souls named, two women, Cunnizza and Rahab, and a male poet, the only "professional" poet of the whole *cantica*, who describes his youthful, lustful, self in terms of predominantly female figures of erotic transgression.

> "ché più non arse la figlia di Belo,
>   noiando e a Sicheo e a Creusa,
>   di me infin che si convenne al pelo;

né quella Rodopëa che delusa
    fu da Demofoonte, né Alcide
    quando Iole nel core ebbe rinchiusa."

(Par. 9.97–102)

("for the daughter of Belus, wronging both Sichaeus and Creusa, burned not more than I, as long as it befitted my locks;
nor yet the Rhodopean maid who was deluded by Demo-
phoön, nor Alcides when he had enclosed Iole in his heart.")

Throughout the *Metamorphoses* incest is not only associated
with the bestial, but also with the divine. The permissive bestial
model of incestuous union cited by Myrrha recalls an analogous
permissive divine model used by Ovid's other incestuously desirous heroine, Byblis.[21] Byblis justifies her illicit desire for her
brother by noting that such love is permitted among the gods;
Ovid himself makes the same point frequently throughout the
Metamorphoses and the *Fasti* by having Juno proudly claim that
she is both Jupiter's sister and his wife. This intersection of the
sacred and the scandalous, however, is hardly unique to pagan
mythology; Christianity can be seen to manifest a comparable
doubleness at the heart of its own theology of generation. Recent
work by Marina Warner and Julia Kristeva attempts to interrogate
the psychologically problematic content of Mary's role in incarnation theology. Warner calls attention to the extraordinary multiplicity of roles played by the Virgin, and their contradictory
implications.[22] Kristeva goes even further in explicating the normally transgressive terms of Mary's role reversals and assumptions. Apropos of the iconography of what is called the Dormition,
Kristeva notes the way that Mary is represented at her "death" as
if she were a little girl in the arms of her son who thenceforth
becomes her father; "she reverses her role as Mother into a
Daughter's role for the greater pleasure of those who enjoy Freud's
'Theme of the Three Caskets.' Indeed *mother* of her son and his
daughter as well, Mary is also, and besides, his *wife*; she therefore
actualizes the threefold metamorphosis of a woman in the tight-
est parenthood structure."[23] Kristeva cites Dante's prayer to the
Virgin from the last canto of the *Paradiso* as the apotheosis of this
"gathering of the three feminine functions (daughter-wife-mother)
within a totality where they vanish as specific corporealities
while retaining their psychological functions."[24] (Kristeva's erroneous assertion makes one aware that in fact Dante suppresses the
perfectly traditional category of spouse in order to foreground the
mother and daughter roles.)

What Kristeva calls the vanishing of specific corporealities is the key to the transition from the potentially transgressive to the transcendent. But this is a very problematic move in an incarnational theology or poetics.[25] The trace of transgression nonetheless remains in the very insistence of the oxymoronic language in which Dante foregrounds the logical and linguistic "impossibility" of the Incarnation.

> "Vergine Madre, figlia del tuo figlio,
>   umile e alta più che creatura,
>   termine fisso d'etterno consiglio."
>
> *(Par.* 33.1–3)

("Virgin Mother, daughter of thy son, humble and exalted more than any creature, fixed goal of the eternal counsel.")

The term "Virgin Mother" is, in any other context, merely catachresis or, as Alan of Lille would put it, a solecisim; furthermore, the idea of "figlia del tuo figlio" subverts not only kinship terminology, but the very temporality of filiation.[26] This is, of course, precisely what Dante wants us to understand, just as elsewhere he insists on the paradoxical spatial situation of the Virgin whose womb both contained Christ and is simultaneously contained by Him *(Par.* 23.103–8). The virgin mother, like the squared circle, forces us to the limits of language in order to communicate that which is beyond the human: "Trasumanar significar *per verba/ non si poria" (Par.* 1.70–71). It is not the use of *verba,* but rather their "misuse" which points to the reality of divinity. In the prayer to the Virgin, Dante reveals and revels in the potential intersection of transgression and transcendence; his consummate version of orthodox theology displays, compresses, and masters the paradoxes at the heart of language and theology.[27]

The relation between the sacred and the sacrilegious is spelled out in a much cruder—and therefore even more revealing—way in the exegetical tradition that connected Mary with, of all people, Myrrha. Myrrha's connection with the myrrh tree and the importance of myrrh in a number of biblical passages[28] set into motion a play of the signifier that led ultimately to the two figures being compared. Pierre Bersuire glosses the Myrrha story both *in malo* and *in bono; in bono* "she is the blessed virgin who conceived through the father and was changed into myrrh, that is bitterness and into the fragrance of scent." Bersuire cites Ecclesiasticus 23, "I give a swete odour as the best myrrhe," and explicates Myrrha's parturition as a figure of the Virgin's uncontaminated motherhood: "She therefore conceived a son by her father: that is, Christ: and she contained him within the wood and bark, that is, within a pure and untouched womb without corruption, and afterwards she bore him, existing not as flesh but as wood, that is not a carnal being but as a perpetual virgin."[29] The author of the *Ovide moralisé* goes even further in allegorizing Myrrha as a figure of Mary and her pregnancy as emblematic of the Incarnation; Adonis thus becomes a type of Christ.[30]

Dante, of course, never makes any such explicit connection; he wishes to keep the figures of Myrrha and Mary utterly separate in our consciousness.[31] Nonetheless, what brings the figures of transgressive desire (Semiramis and Myrrha) into relation to the exemplum of transcendence is the insistence on the language of kinship confusion both in its negative versions and in its unique positive hypostasis. In any literal reading of the Incarnation as an incest story we would have to reactivate just those specific corporealities that Kristeva had argued were to be left behind. This is exactly what Milton will do in Book 2 of *Paradise Lost* in order to create a demonic generation myth meant to parody the Trinity, whereby Sin's incestuous union with Satan, another rewriting of Ovid's Myrrha story, produces Death.[32] Just as cannibalism is a literalist perversion of the sacramental nature of communion,[33] incestuous union is a literalist perversion of incarnation theology. Yet such "perversions" are important reminders of the violence which attends origins and subtends the promise of their transformation. "The Eucharist does not make us forget cannibalism—rather it keeps reminding us to *remember to forget* cannibalism."[34] The rules of temporality and filiation are violated by the Incarnation, but they are also reaffirmed by the exception, just as the "law" of *terza rima* could be said to "depend" on its unique exception, the identical rhyming on "Cristo," permitted in the *Paradiso*, which "grounds" the law of which it is the exception.[35]

What distinguishes Mary from Myrrha, and from other female subjects as well, is her status as pure vessel: she is quintessentially *ancilla dei*, or as Dante puts it, "albergo del *nostro* disiro" (*Par.* 23.105). In the perfection of her passivity, in the perfect absence of her own desire, she is worthy to be Mother of God. This much is clear. But where are we to find paradigms that suggest other possibilities? We are told that the penitents on the circle of lust celebrate "wives and husbands who were chaste, even as virtue and marriage enjoin" (*Purg.* 25.133–135), but the lack of specificity is startling; no one is named. We have been taught to appreciate Dante's brilliant critique of the ways literature might be conducive to desire in *Inferno* 5, but perhaps the opposite point needs to be made both about the *Commedia* and about its culture and ours. What theology, and literature, too, make it difficult to uncover is an image of female desire that is not in and of itself transgressive.[36] For this reason, Semiramis, Myrrha, and Pasiphaë—like the emblematic Siren in Dante's central purgatorial dream—appear to be icons not only of transgressive female desire, but of the nature of all female desire, and, ultimately, perhaps of desire itself—any desire, that is, which is reluctant to relinquish "specific corporealities."[37]

NOTES

1. All citations from the *Commedia* are from the text and translation in the edition of Charles S. Singleton, Bollingen Series 80 (Princeton: Princeton University Press, 1970–75). The accuracy of Virgil's identification of Dante's actual moral condition at this state in the journey has rightly been called into question by Christopher J. Ryan in "Virgil's Wisdom in the *Divine Comedy*," *Medievalia et Humanistica* 11 (1982): 1–38.

2. Alice A. Jardine, *Gynesis: Configurations of Woman and Modernity* (Ithaca: Cornell University Press, 1985), 24.

3. Orosius, *Historiarum adversum paganos libri septem*, 1.4.4.8. The passage is quoted in Singleton's Commentary to *Inferno*, 78. The early commentators immediately recognized this borrowing, and most of them cite Orosius for their own information about Semiramis. Landino is the first to cite Justinus.

4. Diodorus of Sicily, *The Library of History of Diodorus of Sicily*, trans. C. H. Oldfather (London: Heinemann, 1953), 2.3.4:357. In some legends Semiramis is connected with Ishtar; this is implied in Diodorus's account of her mythical origins and death. Cf. W. W. How and J. Wells, *A Commentary on Herodotus* (Oxford: Clarendon Press, 1928), 143. How and Wells are also the source of the frequently invoked image of Semiramis as "a sort of Assyrian Catherine II, distinguished equally in war and for sensuality."

5. Justinus, *Epitoma Historiarum Philippicarum Pompei Trogi*, ed. Otto Seel (Leipzig: Teubner, 1935) 1.2:5.

6. Augustine, *City of God*, trans. Henry Bettenson (London: Penguin, 1972), 18, 2:764. Augustine makes it clear that Semiramis's incestuous desire for her son justifies his matricide. This point is reiterated in Boccaccio's discussion of Semiramis in *De Claris Mulieribus*, 2, although Boccaccio gives other possible readings of the story. Boccaccio's version is strategically rewritten by Christine de Pizan in *The Book of the City of Ladies*, where Semiramis replaces Eve as the first woman in the catalogue of famous women, and where she is represented as an exemplary ruler and, like Christine herself, a resourceful widow. On Christine's rewriting of the legend, see Liliane Dulac, "Un mythe didactique chez Christine de Pizan: Semiramis ou la Veuve Héroïque," *Mélanges de Philologie Romane offerts à Charles Camproux* (Montpellier: Centre d'Estudis Occitans,

1978), 1:315–43; and Patricia Phillippy, "Establishing Authority: Boccaccio's *De claris mulieribus* and Christine de Pizan's *Le Livre de la Cité des Dames*," *Romanic Review* 77 (1986): 167–93. Boccaccio and Christine (and Petrarch as well) show awareness of non-Christian sources, while Dante does not.

7. Irene Samuel, "Semiramis in the Middle Ages: The History of a Legend," *Medievalia et Humanistica* 2 (1944), fasc. 2:35.

8. Quoted by Samuel, 41.

9. Orosius, *The Seven Books of History Against the Pagans*, trans. Roy J. Deffair (Washington, D.C.: Catholic University of America Press, 1964), I, 4:22.

10. As R. G. Austin notes in his commentary on *Aeneid* 6 (*P. Vergili Maronis Aeneidos Liber Sextus* [Oxford: Clarendon Press, 1977]), the catalogue is "strange and disturbing" since it includes "an incestuous woman, a notorious traitress, a woman of unnatural lust, a bizarre man-woman, a jealous and suspicious wife, a devoted wife, and a loving woman" (161–62). This "schiera di Dido" is so peculiar that it serves, as Austin says, to deepen the enigma of Virgil's attitude toward Dido. The seven women are: Phaedra, Procris, Eriphyle, Pasiphaë, Evadne, Laodamia, and Caenus.

11. See Francesco Tateo's *voce* "allitterazione" in *Enciclopedia dantesca* (Rome: Istituto della Enciclopedia Italiana, 1970), 1: 168–69, on the "ampia funzione espressiva" of alliteration in a variety of contexts in the *Commedia*. Curtius treats alliteration in terms of mannerism in *European Literature and the Latin Middle Ages*, trans. Willard R. Trask (New York: Harper and Row, 1953), 282–84. Paolo Valesio (*Strutture dell'allitterazione: grammatica, retorica e folklore verbale* [Bologna: Zanichelli, 1967]) discusses alliteration as both a metrical and rhetorical phenomenon; his analysis of Francesca's speech on Amor is resolutely technical (74–75) and ignores the thematic implications of its dependence on repetition.

12. See Renato Poggioli, "Paolo and Francesca," in *Dante: A Collection of Critical Essays*, ed. John Freccero (Englewood Cliffs, N.J.: Prentice Hall, 1965), 61–77, and René Girard, "The Mimetic Desire of Paolo and Francesca," in *"To Double Business Bound": Essays on Literature, Mimesis, and Anthropology* (Baltimore: Johns Hopkins University Press, 1978), 1–8.

13. The theme of idolatry of one's own work is surely at stake here and has important connections with the theme of incest. Ovid makes this connection by placing the Myrrha story immediately after that of Pygmalion. Cinyras and Myrrha are Pygmalion's descendants and, as Eleanor Leach notes, "The incestuous love of child for father is only a reversal of Pygmalion's passion for the woman he has created by his art" ("Ekphrasis and the Theme of Artistic Failure in Ovid's *Metamorphoses*," *Ramus* 3 [1974]: 123). Leach and others remark the echo of the word *similis* from Pygmalion's prayer to Venus for a "coniunx . . . similis mea eburnae" (*Metamorphoses* 10.275–76) in Myrrha's announcement to her father that she seeks a suitor like him, "similem tibi" (10.364) and her wish that he feel a "similis furor" (10.355) to her own; "Ista tua est," says the nurse as she brings Myrrha to her father, ironically calling attention to her status as

his "creation." The confusion between creature and creator is endemic to both idolatry and incest, while the love of that which is "similis" or identical to oneself brings incest and narcissism into the same orbit. I think it no accident that Dante's one overt Infernal allusion to Narcissus comes in the same canto as Myrrha. Roger Dragonetti writes provocatively on the metaliterary implications of incest in "The Double Play of Arnaut Daniels' *Sestina* and Dante's *Divina Commedia,'* in *Literature and Psychoanalysis: The Question of Reading,* ed. Shoshana Felman (Baltimore: Johns Hopkins University Press, 1982), 227–52, esp. 242–46. And cf. Julia Kristeva, *Tales of Love,* trans. Leon Roudiez (New York: Columbia University Press, 1987), 129–30.

14. Whether the connection between romantic love and incest is in any sense structural, it does recur in some of the most famous literary works; Tristan, for example, is Mark's nephew as well as his subject. The suggestion of incest seems to trope the inherent forbiddenness of the love in such cases, while in others the sense of the lovers' identity is communicated by the suggestion that they are brother and sister.

15. Claude Lévi-Strauss, *The Elementary Structures of Kinship,* rev. ed., trans. James Harle Bell, ed. John Richard von Sturmer and Rodney Needham (London: Eyre and Spottiswoode, 1969), 490. Lévi-Strauss characterizes the incest prohibition as the "fundamental step because of which, by which, but above all in which, the transition from nature to culture is accomplished" (24), and the means by which "nature transcends itself" (25). The conceptual centrality of theories about incest in our century owes much, of course, to Freud as well as to Lévi-Strauss; while Lévi-Strauss assumes the universality of the prohibition, Freud assumes the universality of the desire. For a provocative discussion of these and other theories about incest, see Robin Fox, *The Red Lamp of Incest* (New York: E. P. Dutton, 1980).

16. Augustine, *City of God,* 15.16:623. Cf. Dante's address to Adam in *Par.* 26.91–93: "O pomo che maturo / solo prodotto fosti, o padre antico / a cui ciascuna sposa è figlia e nuro."

17. Ibid., 624.

18. Citations from the *Metamorphoses* are from the text and translation by Frank Justus Miller in the Loeb Classical Library Ovid (Cambridge: Harvard University Press, 1971).

19. "What is more, if the incest prohibition and exogamy have an essentially positive function, if the reason for their existence is to establish a tie between men which the latter cannot do without if they are to raise themselves from a biological to a social organization, it must be recognized that . . . exogamy and language . . . have fundamentally the same function— communication and integration with others . . . The incest prohibition is not a prohibition like the others. It is *the* prohibition in the most general form, the one perhaps to which all others . . . are related as particular cases. The incest prohibition is universal like language." (*Elementary Structures,* 493). The role of women as signs in this symbolic economy is clear, but Lévi-Strauss attempts to complicate the issue in the book's final pages by claiming that "woman could never become just a sign" (496). Nonetheless Lévi-Strauss does not give examples of woman as "generator of signs."

20. In this figuration of the linkage between incest and bestiality Dante follows a literary tradition rather than a theological one. St. Thomas separates the two, linking incest with other sins against right reason, and bestiality with other sins against nature. See *Summa Theologica*, 2a 2ae, quest. 154, art. 9, on incest, and art. 12, in which bestiality is characterized as the greatest of sins against nature, "since it does not observe the due species."

21. On the relationships between the stories of Byblis and Myrrha see Betty Rose Nagle, "Byblis and Myrrha: Two Incest Narratives in the *Metamorphoses*," *Classical Journal* 78 (1983): 301–15. Nagle's main interest is in the differences between the two stories as they reflect the different narrators who tell them: Ovid "himself," and Orpheus.

22. Marina Warner, *Alone of All Her Sex: The Myth and the Cult of the Virgin Mary* (New York: Knopf, 1976). See Geoffrey Ashe, *The Virgin* (London: Routledge and Kegan Paul, 1976) for another overview of materials and myths concerning Mary.

23. "Stabat Mater," in *The Kristeva Reader*, ed. Toril Moi (New York: Columbia University Press, 1986), 169.

24. Idem. Dante's suppression of the Virgin as spouse is, I would argue, consistent with the poem's effort to sublimate the erotic into the maternal. See my "The Tears of Beatrice," *Dante Studies* C (1982): 1–12.

25. Dante seems more aware of the problems than Kristeva does. Particularly in the *Paradiso* he insists on the importance of the body, although, to be sure, he also distinguishes between the mortal body and the glorified body. Cf. especially the extraordinary conclusion to *Par.* 14. In the "Stabat Mater" essay Kristeva seems more preoccupied with the psychic comfort associated with the Virgin and the "social anguish" attendant on the diminishment of her importance in contemporary culture. This is, in fact, an oddly "conservative" argument, one perhaps well suited to the rhetoric of the current Marian year. Since this is only the second Marian year in church history, its proclamation merits serious study. (The other one was 1594.)

26. The subversion of temporality characteristic of cross-generational incest makes its symbolic potential very different from that of sibling incest.

27. Erich Auerbach ("Dante's Prayer to the Virgin and Earlier Eulogies," *Romance Philology* 3 [1949]: 1–26) traces the precedents for Dante's prayer and the ways in which Dante fuses a number of traditions (classical, biblical, early Christian, Franciscan) to create "something entirely new and different. He uses all the material of the tradition, historical, dogmatic, and figurative, but he condenses and organizes it" (23). Cf. Alan of Lille, *Anticlaudianus* 5.471–500 for another poetic version of Marian theological paradoxes.

28. The key biblical passages are Matt. 2.11, Mark 15.23, and John 19.39–40. Myrrh is glossed in a variety of contexts in the *PL*, as a perusal of the indexes makes clear. An extended meditation on myrrh may be found in Bernard de Clairvaux's sermons on *The Song of Songs*, especially Sermon 43. Myrrh's bitterness of taste and sweetness of odor give it antithetical properties which are used suggestively by the exegetes, while its use in

embalming allows them to connect it with the Resurrection.

29. *Metamorphosis ovidiana moraliter* . . . (Paris, 1515), fol. 83. I am using the translation by Noam Flinker in "Cinyras, Myrrha, and Adonis: Father–Daughter Incest from Ovid to Milton," *Milton Studies* 14 (1980): 63. Flinker traces the exegetical traditions of the Myrrha story very succinctly. One reason that Myrrha's story could be read both *in bono* and *in malo* is that Ovid himself sees Myrrha from two quite differing perspectives. Orpheus begins her tale by salaciously calling attention to her impiety, but from the moment Myrrha is discovered by her father and must flee, she is treated with great sympathy and compassion. The Mary-Myrrha connection is explored by Sarah Spence in "Myrrha, Myrrha in the Well: Metonymy and Interpretation in *Inferno* 34" *Dante Studies* 103 (1985), 15–36.

30. Cf. *Ovide moralisé: Poème de commencement du quatorzième siècle,* ed. C. de Boer, (Amsterdam: Müller, 1936), 4.10.3684ff., 98–99. Flinker ("Cinyras, Myrrha, and Adonis," 65) cites Colard Mansion's French prose paraphrase of the *Metamorphoses* (1484) for an even more explicit version of the Myrrha-Mary identification; "This virgin, then, conceived a son with her father, that is to say, Jesus Christ, and bore him between the wood and the bark." Another Renaissance text which plays with this connection is, as Diana Wilson has shown, Cervantes's last work, the *Persiles.* See her "Uncanonical Nativities: Cervantes's Perversion of Pastoral," in *Critical Essays on Cervantes,* ed. Ruth El Saffar (Boston: G. K. Hall, 1986), 189–209, esp. 199–201.

31. Myrrha is, after all, one of the images of "wicked Florence" in Epistle 7, Dante's letter urging Henry VII to come to Rome. "Florence is the name of this baleful pest. She is the viper that turns against the vitals of her own mother; she is the sick sheep that infects the flock of her lord with her contagion; she is the abandoned and unnatural Myrrha, inflamed with passion for the embraces of her father Cinyras [haec Myrrha scelestis et impia, in Cinyrae patris, amplexus exaestuans] . . ." Later Dante says of Florence, "Verily she burns for the embraces of her own father, when she wickedly and wantonly seeks to compass a breach between thee and the supreme Pontiff, who is the father of fathers." (*Epistolae,* ed. Paget Toynbee, 2d ed. [Oxford: Clarendon Press, 1966], 104).

32. See Flinker, ibid., 32.

33. See John Freccero, "Bestial Sign and Bread of Angels: *Inferno* XXXII and XXXIII," in *Dante: The Poetics of Conversion,* ed. Rachel Jacoff (Cambridge: Harvard University Press, 1986), 152–66.

34. John Kleiner, comment on an early draft of this essay. The proximity of the sacred and the sacrilegious is brilliantly analyzed by Mary Douglas in *Purity and Danger: An Analysis of the Concepts of Pollution and Taboo* (London: Routledge Kegan Paul, 1966; reprinted 1985). See esp. 169–179, where Douglas's discussion of the Lele Pangolin cult has an uncanny relation to the argument I have been making.

35. See John Freccero, "The Significance of Terza Rima," in *Dante: The Poetics of Conversion,* 267.

36. This argument is congruent with Luce Irigaray's reading of the "impossibility" for women of the discourse of their own pleasure, as it is

discussed in *This Sex Which Is Not One*, trans. Catherine Porter (Ithaca: Cornell University Press, 1985), and *Speculum of the Other Woman*, trans. Gillian Gill (Ithaca: Cornell University Press, 1985). And cf. Jessica Benjamin, "A Desire of One's Own: Psychoanalytic Feminism and Inter-subjective Space" in *Feminist Studies, Critical Studies*, ed. Teresa de Lauretis (Bloomington: Indiana University Press, 1986), 78–101.

37. This paper owes much to discussions with Diana Wilson, John Kleiner, Renato Rosaldo, Robert Harrison, John Freccero, and Andrea Wilson. I am also very grateful to the Stanford Humanities Center, which gave me the time and the perfect ambiance in which to explore these issues.

Dante's Sexual Solecisms: Gender and Genre in the *Commedia*

JEFFREY T. SCHNAPP

> The comic poet dares to show us men and women coming to . . .
> mutual likeness.
>
> GEORGE MEREDITH, "AN ESSAY ON COMEDY"

> *Dante's* Divine Comedy *is without fate and without a genuine
> struggle, because absolute confidence and assurance of the reality
> of the Absolute exist in it without opposition, and whatever oppo-
> sition brings movement into this perfect security and calm is
> merely opposition without seriousness of inner truth.*
>
> G. W. F. HEGEL, *NATURAL LAW*

Licit and Illicit Solecism

In the opening meter of his *De Planctu Naturae*, the twelfth-
century poet and theologian, Alan of Lille, denounces the practice of homosexual love through the description of an illicit verbal transference or *translatio* cultivated by certain contemporary
grammarians. Choosing to couple *hic* with *hic*, the masculine
gender with the masculine gender, these grammarians substitute
woman for man and man for woman, thereby upsetting the natural subordination of female to male, predicate to subject, passive
to active.[1]

Se negat esse virum Nature, factus in arte
  Barbarus. Ars illi non placet, immo tropus.

Non tamen ista tropus poterit translatio dici.
In vicium melius ista figura cadit.

(1.21–24)

(Becoming a barbarian in the art of grammar, he [the deviant grammarian] denies the manhood bestowed upon him by Nature. [As a result], the art of grammar does not find favor with him, but rather, finds in him a trope. Yet this transposition cannot truly be referred to as a trope, for [t]his figure falls more exactly under the rubric of [grammatical] vices.)

The unnatural conversion of one gender into another, Alan insists, is nonproductive. It yields a trope that is not really a trope, a figure that is not really a figure. What, then, might one call this grammatical nonentity? Alan's response is that it belongs to that null grammatical category known as "verbal vices" or "defects of speech." Yet one is still left wondering *which* defect or vice. Technically speaking, it cannot truly be referred to as a "barbarism" because it is not a foreign body surreptitiously introduced into the pristine natural body of Latinity. Generated from within that body, it must instead be defined as a "solecism," a "sexual solecism" to be exact.[2] To quote another twelfth century grammarian on the subject (one who, I might add, is not intentionally alluding to the grammar of homosexual love):

Si demonstrando virum dicimus *hanc*, aut demonstrando mulierem dicimus *hunc*, fit soloecismus . . . Sed soloecismus est vicium inexcusabile. Ergo in talibus sermonibus erit vicium inexcusabile, non ergo figura.[3]

(If in designating a man we say *hanc* [or *her*] or if in designating a woman we say *hunc* [or *him*], we are committing a solecism . . . But a solecism is an inexcusable error. Therefore an inexcusable error, not a figure of speech, will be evident in all such manners of speaking.)

Harsh as it is, this vilification of the practice of sexual solecism is relatively mild when contrasted with that found in Alan's *prosimetrum*. For Alan, it is not a mere lapse in verbal decorum that is involved, but rather deceit—the concealment of a monstrous origin: "nulla figure honestate illa constructionis iunctura vicium poterit excusare sed inexcusabili soloecismi monstruositate turpabitur" (10.55–57) (this [unnatural] bond and union will not be able to pass off its defect as if it were some sort of honest [or respectable] figure, but will bear the stain of monstrous and impardonable solecism).

Whence the vigor of this exclusion of a "dishonest" figure from literary practice? Whence this language of moral indignation in the sphere of grammar? In responding to such questions, it is not enough to simply rehearse the point that beneath the veil of Alan's grammatical analysis—thin as it is—there lurks the discourse of a homophobic moralist. For the relative ease with which both Alan and his contemporary interweave the moral and the grammatical suggests another answer: that *from the beginning* morality and grammar were never entirely distinct in the Latin tradition. Even in its late medieval form, Latin rhetorical and poetic theory had remained a resolutely prescriptive and normative system in which all speech acts were defined as embedded in a "natural" ontological and social hierarchy. Committed to conserving this order it had sharply restricted the use of ornamented speech and could only conceive of deviant tropes and figures as vicious and morally defective. Lacking in comeliness or taste and hence bearing the signature of those least empowered to speak— that is, of the lowest social stratum composed of foreigners, women, slaves, and prostitutes—and of their various vernaculars, these grammatical deviants were viewed as a menace to the laws of identity, propriety, and natural property. Like the beautiful maiden joined by a horse's neck to the body of a fish covered with multicolored feathers who presides over the opening of Horace's *De Arte Poetica*, they were seen as the progeny of licentious and indiscriminate verbal couplings: that is, as literary monsters.[4]

More than a mere violation of verbal decorum, then, sexual solecism is for Alan "monstrous and impardonable" inasmuch as it attacks one of the fundamental links in Nature's hierarchical chain: the subordination of female to male. It thereby threatens to contaminate not only the grammatical relation of predicate to subject, but also the entire network of parallel relays extending from the base to the exalted, the physical to the metaphysical, the passive to the active, the slave to the master, and, most important of all, man to God. Once male is confused with female and female confused with male, nature's vertical scaffolding must necessarily come tumbling down, leaving nothing but a horizontal ruin: a world of masks, a world of phenomena ungrounded in any noumenon. This is to say that, within the context of Latin rhetorical and poetic theory, the appearance of sexual solecism marks the advent of carnival.

Affirming the bond between solecism and this carnivalesque cosmogony, Alan binds his own Menippean satire to the conservative tradition of such Roman predecessors as Juvenal and Horace, as well as to such contemporaneous satirical texts as the *carmina burana*. Yet the extraordinary lavishness of his play in the *De Planctu Naturae* on the intersection of grammar and sexuality also marks Alan's distance from these traditions, revealing the utter seriousness which he brings to the study of grammar. It is this seriousness that firmly plants him in the midst of the intellectual revolution of his time—the so-called "renaissance" of the twelfth century—with its debates on "natural" and "ethical" grammars, its efforts to build upon Anselm's grammar of God, and to rethink the relation between theology, rhetoric, and grammar.[5]

Moreover, Alan's poetic engagement with sexual solecism can only remind one of that *other* great revolution of the twelfth and thirteenth centuries: the revolution which, in her influential books *Jesus as Mother* and *Holy Feast and Holy Fast*, Caroline Walker Bynum has termed the "feminization of religious language."[6] To a hitherto unprecedented extent, Alan's era had placed both traditionally feminine values and actual women at the center of Christian religious practice. Whether manifesting itself in the form of the canonization of ever-increasing numbers of female saints, an expanding corpus of mystical writings by women, or a growing emphasis among scriptural exegetes on the *Song of Songs*, this event brought to the theology of the early Middle Ages, with its generally distant and omnipotent God, a new insistence upon the carnal immediacy of Mary and Jesus. It accelerated the development of a highly codified Mariolatry which construed every event in Mary's life as a reenactment of an event in her son's biography, while elaborating in turn a new Christology which emphasized Jesus's so-called "feminine" side: his passivity and suffering, his approachability and affectivity.

To cite one example, the climactic event of the Christ story, the crucifixion, came increasingly to be seen not as a proleptic enthronement of Jesus the *eschaton* and judge, but rather a precise double of Mary's act of giving birth. Accordingly, Jesus on the cross was a pregnant mother enduring the longest and harshest of labor pains. I quote from the Carthusian prioress Marguerite of Oingt: "for when the hour of your delivery came you were placed on the hard bed of the cross . . . and your nerves and all your veins were broken. And truly it is no surprise that your veins burst when in one day you gave birth to the whole world."[7] Considered alone, such views might seem to do little more than expand upon certain well-established patristic *topoi* dating back at least to the time of Augustine. Yet considered in relation to the Cistercian cult of the abbot as mother and to cults like that of Francis of

Assisi, focused on the "feminine" attributes of affectivity and nur-
turance, they mark a decisive epochal shift. They put forward a
new paradigm for the exercise of authority that is at once paternal
and maternal.

So, paradox of paradoxes, in the course of the twelfth and thirteenth centuries the very grammatical practice that Alan had
identified with a "monstrous and impardonable" vice had already
become a central attribute of the language of the holy. Indeed, sexual solecism, or the play of gender substitutions, is so abundant
in the theological writings of authors such as Anselm, Bernard of
Clairvaux, Albert the Great, and Bonaventure, that contemporary
feminist thought has come to view it (sometimes incorrectly) as
the mark of their modernity.[8] Although characterized primarily
by the feminization of the masculine, this phenomenon may well
be modeled after the masculinization of the feminine practiced in
an earlier period of medieval piety, but which continued through
Dante's era. One may think in this regard of the somewhat obscure
Carolingian cult of the bearded Mary, of the many hagiographic
and monastic tales in which female cross-dressing is viewed as a
sign of spiritual advancement, and of the ongoing celebration of
the martial heroism of female martyr-saints such as Perpetua,
Catherine, and Joan of Arc.[9]

Now whatever the larger historical meaning of this other revolution, one thing is certain: by insisting on the most radical implications of incarnational theology—namely, that through Christ
and Mary the exalted becomes the base and the base becomes
exalted—it transforms the entire edifice of Classical metaphysics
and offers a powerful alternative to the patriarchal culture of the
Romans (reflected in turn in the theology of Byzantine Christen-
dom). Sexual solecism, a scandal within the system of Roman
rhetoric, inextricably tied to the debased body, becomes the privileged sign of the sacred body, inaugurating what I should like to
call, for reasons of contrast with Alan's carnivalesque cosmogony,
a "paradisiac masque."

But to return from this new perspective to the *De Planctu Naturae*, there arises the question of how it is possible for Alan to rec-
oncile the defense of Latin grammar against the improper translation of gender with God's regular recourse to this "impardonable
and monstrous" error. As it turns out, I have been a bit unfair to
Alan and to the Latin tradition, for they do have a ready answer:
solecism, they assert, does not *necessarily* have to be a vice. In certain exceptional circumstances it can indeed become a figure or
trope, but only when employed by an author of sufficient stature

who is striving to say something inordinate and striking. The grammarian Marius Victorinus, for instance, writes: "nunquam ergo soloecismus excusari potest: si a nobis per imprudentiam fiat, vitium est; si a poetis vel oratoribus affectate dicatur, figura locutionis et appellatur graece *skema*" (solecism can never be excused [and] if used by us out of ignorance is a defect of speech. But if employed in ornamented [or affected] speech by poets or orators, it is a figure of elocution and is referred to in Greek as a *skema*).[10]

The point is replicated, but this time in an explicitly theological setting, in Alan's rhythmic poem, the *De Incarnatione Domini*, where the incarnation is figured as the unnatural—which here means *super*natural—grammatical *copula* that undoes every grammatical and poetic law:[11]

Novus tropus in figura / Novus fit constructio
Novus color in iunctura / Nova fit translatio.
In hac Verbi copula / Stupet omnis regula.

(A new [strange, uncanny, unforeseeable] trope is created [by God] in this figure of speech, a new composite. A new rhetorical color appears in this conjoining, a new metaphor. In this verbal coition, every rule is struck senseless.)

The incarnation is the solecism to beat all other solecisms, an exercise in poetic license so inordinate and striking that only one truly possessed with authorial authority, such as God, could get away with it. Instituting the Son's new law, it abrogates the laws of the fathers. Converting the exalted into the base, it transforms the base into the exalted.

I arrive now at the heart of my subject: Dante's role as the heir to this double tradition. What I should like to propose is that the astonishingly free play with gender inversions which characterizes Dante's entire literary *opus* represents a quantum expansion and transformation of the conventional polarity between licit and illicit sexual solecism. Dante explores the infernal carnivalesque of the Latin satirical tradition. He also explores both the female to male and male to female vectors of the "paradisiac masque" of twelfth-century piety, masculinizing such figures as Beatrice and Mary, while feminizing Virgil and the *Commedia*'s final guide, Bernard of Clairvaux. But I will argue that in the *Commedia* he takes one additional revolutionary step, elaborating a middle ground between licit and illicit solecism: a place where the exchange of masculine and feminine attributes serves to redefine the relation between Latin and vernacular, between the historical persons of Virgil and Beatrice, and between the literary genres of epic and lyric, or history and love poetry.

Let it be said from the outset that limitations of space will not allow me to adequately emphasize the conservative underpinnings of Dante's theory of gender. Nor will I be able to offer an exhaustive account of Dante's play with gender identity.[12] Instead, my emphasis will be selective. I will begin with a brief excursus on Dante's contact with the two traditions which I earlier defined. Then, I will shift to an analysis of gender transference at the beginning, the midpoint and the end of Beatrice's career in Dante's writings. This survey will serve, in turn, as an introduction to what I have just proposed as Dante's central innovation in this area: the elaboration of a middle ground where issues of secular authority are worked out via recourse to sexual solecism. Finally, I should like to close with a brief examination of the matter of genre as it relates to sexual solecism in the *Commedia*. What I will be proposing is that Dante's extensive play with sexual substitutions constitutes a strategy to articulate the intersection between the "feminine" world of vernacular lyric and the "masculine" world of Latin epic, the world of Beatrice and the world of Virgil. Only by approaching, however tentatively, the figure of the textual androgyne, can Dante come to grips with the *Commedia*'s status as an impure linguistic artifact and generic hybrid.

Julius Caesar as Queen

Of Dante's allusions to the "infernal carnivalesque" one example shall have to suffice, though it must stand for other episodes which also involve gender reversals such as that of Paolo and Francesca. On the seventh terrace of Mount Purgatory where sins of erotic excess are ritually purged through the exchange of chaste kisses of peace, souls are seen wheeling about in two contrary directions, one clockwise and one counterclockwise. The task of explaining this dual rotation belongs to the vernacular love poet Guido Guinizelli. Guido states that those who turn in a counterclockwise direction were "hermaphrodites" (or heterosexual) in their sin. Those who instead follow a clockwise motion were "sodomites": they "'offended in that [sin] for which Ceasar in his triumph once heard "Queen" cried out against him'" ["offese / di ciò per che già Cesar, trïunfando, / 'Regina' contra sé chaimar s'intese" (*Purg.* 26.76–78)].[13]

The triumph alluded to is that recorded in Suetonius's *De Vita Caesarum* (1.49.1–4) which followed Julius's final victory over the last of the republican forces. During his processional entry into Rome, finally the uncontested ruler of the empire, Julius was said to have been greeted by jeers calling him to task for his having committed sodomy with King Nicomedes of Bithynia. Shouted by his soldiers according to Suetonius, by the populace according to Uguccione of Pisa, the cries that Caesar heard were of "Ave rex et regina!" (Hail, O King and Queen), and "Aperite portas regi calvo et regine Bitinie!" (Open the gates for King Baldy, the Queen of Bithynia!). King for a lifetime, Caesar's fate, it seems, was to be queen for a day. Indeed the saturnalian tone of these jeers is fitting with the tenor of the occasion, for Uguccione, who was perhaps aware of the etymological link between the Latin *triumphus* and the Greek *triambos* (or hymn to Bacchus), insists that on such days "anyone could say anything he wished to the person who was having a triumph."[14]

The Crucified As Mother

If the brief description of Julius's mock coronation reveals Dante's proximity to the world of Alan's illicit solecisms, the presentation of the crucifixion in *Paradiso* II makes clear Dante's investment in the feminization of the holy. Earlier I have referred to a well-established tradition, linked to the cult of Jesus as mother, which viewed the crucifixion as a scene of childbirth. In the heaven of the sun, Dante's surrogate, Thomas Aquinas, would seem to echo this tradition. Thomas introduces his lengthy account of the birth of the Franciscan and Dominican orders with the description of a holy matrimony between Christ and the Church. Providence, he tells us, "in order that the Bride of Him [Christ] might go to her delight, secure within herself and also more faithful to Him who with high cries wedded her with His blessed blood, ordained two princes who on this side and that [on the side of Spain and on the side of Italy] might serve as her guides":

La provedenza . . .
però che andasse ver' lo suo diletto
  la sposa di colui ch'ad alte grida
  disposò lei col sangue benedetto,
in sé sicura e anche a lui più fida,
  due principi ordinò in suo favore,
  che quinci e quindi le fosser per guida.

(Par. 11.28–36)

What is perhaps most striking about this passage is that, although ostensibly concerned with the consummation on the cross of a blood wedding between Jesus and the Church, it makes use of the phrase "high cries" or "alte grida" in describing Jesus's final plea: "'Eli, eli, lamma sabacthani'" ("Father, Father, why have you forsaken me?" [Matt. 27.46]). While "high cries" may appear a close enough transcription of the Vulgate's "clamavit voce magna" (he cried out with a loud voice), the phrase has a technical valence for Dante that is often overlooked. It is associated with the cries of mothers giving birth, as in Canto 15, its only other appearance in the poem, where Cacciaguida describes how, in the course of his own birth, Mary "'gave him up,'" (that is, granted him egress into this world), "'called on with high cries'" by his mother ["Maria mi diè, chiamata in alte grida" (*Par.* 15.133)].

What Thomas, then, is describing in Canto 11 can only be an act of masculine childbirth, with God the Father playing the part of Mary as the facilitator of the birth. The dying Jesus gives birth not only to the whole world, as Marguerite of Oingt would have it, but also to two princes who, released into this world by the celestial Father, will inherit their progenitor's kingdom as well as the cure of his ailing widow and wife. While I am willing to admit that this reading verges on the scandalous, it is perhaps worth recalling that in his great essay on Saint Francis in the *Commedia*, Erich Auerbach has argued forcefully that scandal and outrage are central to the poetic strategy of this canto.[15]

The narrative which follows Thomas's speech would seem to confirm the point, presenting the parallel tales of Francis and Dominic as reenactments of this scene of male parturition. Like Christ on the cross, each of the two princes will wed and then give birth, fathering (and, indeed, *mothering*) a purely masculine line of descent: the Franciscan order in the case of Francis, the product of his marriage with Lady Poverty; the Dominican order in the case of Dominic, the product of his marriage with Lady Faith. By way of a transition to the analysis of Beatrice, it is also worth noting that this implicit transposition of the genders of Francis and Dominic is consistent with one of the founding principles of Dante's poetic universe: the principle that guides, as authority figures, are especially subject to gender reversals. This is true, of course, not only of these two princes ordained by Providence to guide *Mater Ecclesia*, but also of Virgil, who is repeatedly figured as the mother, muse, or nursemaid of Dante and Statius; of Beatrice, who appears as an admiral, confessor, and judge; and of Bernard of Clairvaux, who is consistently viewed as a double of Mary.

Beatrice and Sexual Solecism — 1

So much for the polarity of illicit and licit solecism. Let me now focus on the figure of Beatrice, in whom the possibility of a dynamic middle ground is first disclosed. From her very first appearance in Dante's work to her final disappearance, Beatrice is characterized by a generic doubleness which in turn reflects upon her dual identity as the historical flesh and blood Beatrice Portinari, Dante's preteen Florentine sweetheart, and as the Christ-event in his spiritual biography. On the one hand, Beatrice is linked inexorably to the affective world of the vernacular lyric and to a Christian latinity which is inseparable from the "feminized sacred" of the Virgin Mary. On the other hand, she is associated with classical latinity and with masculine authority, in both its sacred and secular forms.

At the moment Beatrice makes her first bow on the stage of world literature — Chapter Two of the *Vita Nuova* — she is accompanied by an elaborate string of quotations which define her nature as sexually ambivalent. The first of these, presented in Latin (and hence an interruption of the text's vernacular prose), is in the masculine gender and describes her as a conquering masculine god: "Ecce deus fortior me, qui veniens dominabitur michi" (Here is a god — *deus* and not the feminine *dea* — stronger than me, who has come to master me). The second, also in Latin, identifies her instead with beatitude, a word of feminine gender closely associated with the figure of the Virgin Mary: "Apparuit iam beatitudo vestra" (She who has appeared is your beatitude). The third extends this shifting of gender boundaries even further and is a quotation from book twenty-four of the *Iliad*, familiar to Dante via a Latin translation of Aristotle's *Ethics*. In the Homeric original the verse had evoked the memory of the vanquished Hector, son of Priam and hero of the Trojan war, saying of him: "he did not appear the son of mortal man, but of a god" (*Iliad* 24.258), or in the medieval Latin, "vere hic homo filius dei erat" (*Nicomachean Ethics* 7.1).[16] Dante's redaction, however, is not in Latin (as were the two prior epithets), but rather in the vernacular and hence is assimilated into the linguistic body of his text. Even more striking is the fact that Dante inverts the gender of Homer's sentence. Converting Hector into Beatrice, Greek epic into vernacular lyric, he writes: "*ella* non parea figliuola d'uomo mortale, ma di deo" (*she* did not appear the daughter of mortal man, but of a [masculine] god).

Thus from the very outset, while Beatrice's principal ties are to the "feminine" value-sphere of *stilnovist* lyric, she is also marked as "other," as a being who exceeds the boundaries of this world by her affiliation and identification with masculine authority figures from Christian doctrine [God] and classical epic [Hector]. To make matters more complex, the authority of the epic world finds itself transposed into the humble vernacular as well as filtered through the feminized sacred of thirteenth-century Christian piety. In Beatrice, Latin and Greek *grammatica* crosses over into Tuscan *Umgang* and *Muttersprache*.

Beatrice and Sexual Solecism — 2

I suppose that one might be tempted to attribute some of this to inattention on Dante's part, if it were not for the reappearance of the same configuration of gender substitutions in Canto 30 of the *Purgatorio*. In this unforgettable passage of the *Commedia*, after a nearly twenty-five-year absence from Dante's writings, Beatrice makes her return on the chariot of the Church. But, unlike Caesar, she is not greeted in her triumph by cries of "Regina." Rather, she is hailed as "Christus Rex" in a succession of events whose beauty and intricacy I can only begin to do full justice to here.

The canto opens with the singing of a verse from the *Song of Songs:* "'Veni, sponsa, de Libano'" (*Purg.* 30.11) ("Come from Lebanon, my bride"). This first anticipation of Beatrice's impending advent seems appropriate because it looks forward to the coming of a woman: a woman who, according to the verse's concluding word, *coronaberis*, is coming to be crowned. No less appropriate seems the implicit identification of Beatrice with the bride of the *Song of Songs*, a figure conventionally allegorized as the Church or the soul. So far so good. But the next Latin phrase reverses this implicit allegory, identifying Beatrice not with the bride, but with the *bridegroom* or, according to the conventional allegoresis, Jesus Christ.[17] Shouted out by the blessed throng gathered in the Garden of Eden at the very instant of Beatrice's epiphany, it transforms the ironic cry heard as Christ enters Jerusalem to be crucified, "'Benedictus qui venit in nomine Domini'" (Matt. 21.9) ("Blessed is he who comes in the name of the Lord") into the more direct but no less masculine: "'Benedictus qui venis'" (*Purg.* 30.19) ("Blessed are *you* who come").

This shift from feminine to masculine, from bride to bridegroom, is startling enough. But Dante appends to it a full Latin verse cited from Book Six of Virgil's *Aeneid*, whose meaning as well as gender it reverses: "'Manibus, oh, date lilia plenis'" (*Purg.*

30.21) ("Oh, let me scatter lilies with full hand"). Pronounced at the moment of greatest pathos in Virgil's text—the moment at which the tragic price to be paid to found Rome has come most fully into view—the verse had originally referred to the scattering of funerary lilies over the corpse of the young Marcellus, history's victim and the symbol of Rome's dashed hopes. Dante has us revisit this Virgilian verse from the perspective of the crucifixion, showing how Christ's victimage at Golgotha transforms irony into allegory, classical tragedy into Christian comedy, Virgilian despair into Dantean hope. Beatrice returns from the dead, thus, to what were once the funerary flowers of Marcellus, now revealed as the eternal lilies of the Virgin Mary.

The scene is of course a succession scene, and this first juxtaposition of Virgil's Latin text with the text of the Vulgate gives way to a flurry of vernacular transcriptions of the *Aeneid* at the very moment at which Virgil has disappeared. Confronted by the imposing spectacle of Beatrice as the Bridegroom, the pilgrim is now seen as the Bride or *anima*. He feels "the great power of ancient love" [d'antico amor sentì la gran potenza (*Purg.* 30.39)]. He experiences the same "'tokens of the ancient flame'" ["conosco i segni de l'antica fiamma" (*Purg.* 30.48)] as the tragic lover of *Aeneid* 4.23 ("agnosco veteris vestigia flammae"), playing Dido to Beatrice's Aeneas, powerless before the latest onslaught of love's flame.[18] Filled with terror, he is infantilized, turning "to the left with the anxious uncertainty of a little child who runs to its mother when it is afraid or it is afflicted" [volsimi a la sinistra col respitto / col quale il fantolin corre a la mamma / quando ha paura o quando elli è afflitto (*Purg.* 30.43–45)].

But mother Virgil has already vanished and in her place stands a Beatrice who, throughout the concluding cantos of the *Purgatorio*, will remain a predominantly masculine presence. She first appears "like an admiral who goes to stern and bow to inspect the men that are serving on other ships, and encourages them to do well" [quasi ammiraglio che in poppa e in prora / viene a veder la gente che ministra / per li altri legni, e a ben far l'incora (*Purg.* 30.58–60)]. Next she is seen as regal and stern in mien, in the role of judge (*Purg.* 30.67–75); then as a mother who is harsh to her child, forcing him to taste the stern *pietas* of the Roman patriarchy: "d'amaro / sente il sapor de la pietade acerba" (*Purg.* 30.80–81) (bitter is the flavor of [her] stern piety). In the concluding portion of Canto 30 she will play the part of Dante's confessor: a role, it is worth remembering, strictly reserved for the male priesthood.

Beatrice and Sexual Solecism — 3

If Beatrice in both the *Vita Nuova* and the Garden of Eden is, then, like Alan of Lille's Christ, a new and uncanny trope that strikes every grammatical rule senseless, a solecism that is a trope and figure, the same is no less true of her appearance in the celestial rose. In that high court where Christ is a Roman and Mary reigns as Augusta, Beatrice will complete Dante's transcendental masque by giving way in the last instance to a masculine guide, Bernard of Clairvaux. And Bernard, in turn, will lead the pilgrim to a final vision of what is, despite its abstractness, a masculine God. Yet this ultimate shift towards the masculine and away from the feminization of the holy does not end Dante's specular play with gender identity, as revealed by the symmetrical seating arrangements in the rose.

Dante's celestial amphitheater is organized along a number of

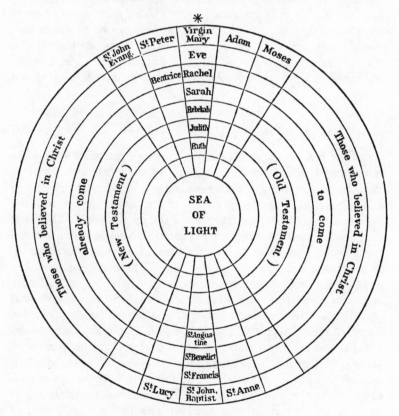

The Seating Arrangement of Dante's Celestial Rose

radial axes extending upward and outward from its center, where there is a pool of light, to its circumference (see Figure 1). A single sex grouping of beatified souls is seated along each of these axes, as, for example, along one of the rose's two central radii, the group made up of Ruth, Judith, Rebekah, Sarah, Rachel, Eve, and finally, Mary (who occupies the highest point at the structure's edge). Facing it across the rose is a group composed of members of the opposite sex: in this case a group including Augustine, Benedict, Francis of Assisi, and, at the outermost/uppermost edge, John the Baptist. This law of symmetrical opposition knows no exception: just as Mary is seated exactly opposite John the Baptist, Adam (who is to Mary's left) sits diagonally across from Lucy, and Peter (who is to Mary's right) sits diagonally across from Anne. No exception, that is, with *the exception of Beatrice*, who alone is seated in the same grouping of souls as a man, thereby disrupting the entire numerical and structural equilibrium of the rose (at least insofar as it is presented to us).[19] The man in question is none other than the apostle Peter and there can be no doubt that this alignment is strategic, for it places her alongside Rachel, the symbol of the contemplative life, while at the same time identifying her with the authority of Christ and the Church, both vested in Peter.

Genre and Gender

I arrive now at my conclusion by posing a question which has remained implicit throughout much of the present discussion: namely, why is it that Dante feels impelled to extend the field of gender reversal to encompass a dynamic middle zone between the pure and the impure, the sacred and the sacrilegious? What is it that conditions this extension of sexual solecism to such a broad spectrum of figures as Virgil, Statius, the pilgrim-poet himself, Bernard, and Beatrice? Although I cannot here address the issue as fully as I might wish, let me hazard a partial response; Dante is driven to do so by constraints which are no less theological than they are literary and linguistic. The key text in this regard is Virgil's *Aeneid*, an epic whose male-dominated (and, indeed, *male-haunted*) world Dante must somehow sublate into the "feminine" value-sphere of *stilnovist* lyric, if a hybrid genre such as Christian *comedy* is to become possible. The problem, I repeat, is not that of expelling the Virgilian model, but instead of transforming it through incorporation into the *Commedia*'s poetic world, of rewriting the *Aeneid* as if it were an epic love story.

Within this framework, sexual solecism becomes a powerful tool:

a. for reconceptualizing the relationship between fathers and sons, ancients and moderns, authorities and subjects, "major" and "minor" literary genres;
b. for figuralizing or sublimating the erotic/corporeal sphere; and
c. for articulating a critique of classical epic values which situates the principle of feminine mediation at the center of the epic world.

I begin with the first of these strategies, whose emblematic gesture is the feminization of the masculine, a "feminization" which involves recourse to maternal language in framing the relation between literary fathers and sons.[20] Such is the case when, in *Purgatorio* 21, Dante has Statius affirm the *Aeneid*'s maternity with respect to the *Thebaid* and, by extension, the *Commedia*: "'mamma / fummi, e fummi nutrice, poetando'" (*Purg.* 21.97–98) ("it was as a mother and a wetnurse to me in poetry"). Here the Oedipal drama is averted via an imaginary regression to a stage of development which might best be described as "pre-oedipal": a situation of apparent plenitude in which, absorbed into the maternal term, the father is no longer present, leaving the son in sole possession of a mother to whom he is now bound by intensified ties of affection and dependency. By means of this operation (in which, it is worth recalling, Statius and his epic play the role of "front men"), Dante is able to place Virgil, the *Aeneid*, and its Latin *grammatica* in a more intimate relation to himself, his *Commedia*, and its agrammatical vernacular; a relation where metaphors of suckling, nurturing, and corporeal oneness can cover over the underlying reality of difference, rivalry, and conflict. In the process, the ancients' authority is restricted, while, in a simultaneous move, their symbolic distance from their medieval descendants is greatly reduced.

The efficacy of this maternalization of the literary father is ensured by an additional detail which, for the sake of clarity, I have momentarily overlooked. In the above-cited speech, Statius did not conclude his paean to Virgil merely with the proclamation of the *Aeneid*'s maternity with respect to his *Thebaid*. Rather, he went on to interpose a surrogate mother figure, the wetnurse, into the now dissolved Oedipal triangle, reinvesting in her the authority of the mother: "mamma fummi, e *fummi nutrice, poetando.*" While it is not entirely clear whether Dante intends to differentiate mothers from wetnurses, this semantic and syntactical *dédoublement* of the mother is, nonetheless, powerfully suggestive. It blocks any simple identification of the literary father with the figure of the mother, suggesting that Virgil's role is no less akin to that of the mother's helper, her wetnurse. Figuralizing the mother/child bond in the very act of restating it, it quite emphatically opens up the maternal term to a potentially infinite play of substitutions.

The uncertainty is productive because it structures a complex network of gender reversals in which male epic poets are associated with the figure of the Muse, who is now revealed as the true mother/wetnurse of *all* poets, irrespective of whether they are ancient or modern. The Muses, accordingly, are described as "'our wetnurses'" ["le nutrice nostre" (*Purg.* 22.105)], a conceit which, I believe, is unique to Dante. They are the "holy virgins" [sacrosante Vergini (*Purg.* 29.37)] whose Parnassian springs are so confused with the overflowing *ubertas* of Mary's breast that they inspire poetic discourse by filling the tongues of bards with only the sweetest of milks: "se mo sonasser tutte quelle lingue / che Polimnïa con le suore fero / del latte lor dolcissimo più pingue" (*Par.* 23.55–57).[21] The bards themselves are but their collaborators and doubles: Homer is "'that Greek / whom the Muses suckled more than any other'" ["quel Greco / che le Muse lattar più ch'altri mai" (*Purg.* 22.102)]; Virgil is "our greatest muse" [nostra maggior musa (*Par.* 15.26)]; Dante belongs among them [o sante Muse, poi che vostro sono (*Purg.* 1.8)]; and the epic heroes of the heaven of Mars are of such "'great fame / that any muse [that is, epic poet] would be rich with them'" ["fuor di gran voce / sì ch'ogne musa ne sarebbe opima" (*Par.* 18.32–33)].

Implicit throughout this texture of allusions is a portrayal of the entire epic tradition as a matrilinear succession in which surrogate mothers (earlier poets) give suckle to their figurative infant daughters (later poets), all *equally* under the aegis of the true mother, the lactating Muse. The result is a reconceptualization of literary genealogy that carves out a privileged space for the vernacular epic by recasting literary authority in the image of the Virgin Mary, whose power is manifest in acts of intercession and overflowing charity: acts which mark her not as distant, but as readily available and accessible.

It is as if the burden had now shifted over onto the shoulders of the ancients. It is *they* who must reach out to embrace their modern followers and not the contrary; *they* who must intercede in order to resolve the crisis at the opening of the *Inferno*; *they* who must light the path, not for themselves, but for those who are to follow. In the course of Dante's poem, the central icon of Roman *pietas* will thus find itself inverted, maternalized, and merged with the iconography of the Christian *pietà*. No longer Aeneas carrying the aged Anchises over his back out of the swirling fires of a vanquished Troy, *pietas* will now be figured by Virgil, the father of Roman poetry, who bears a Christian poet upon his breast "like a mother who is roused by the noise and sees beside her the raging flames, and seizes up her child and flees, and more concerned for him than for herself, does not pause even to put on a shift" (*Inf.* 23.38–42).[22]

At this juncture, it is necessary to proceed from Dante's feminization of the masculine to a brief consideration of the inverse procedure, which is no less pervasive. The two operations are, in my view, largely complementary, because when Dante masculinizes a figure such as Beatrice, he is merely attempting to further collapse the distance between his own literary *opus* and various forms of secular and sacred authority. The emblematic gesture in this regard is not so much the inscription of Beatrice within the *paternal* sphere—which in the last instance stands above and beyond the play of gender substitutions—as her inscription within the sphere of the *son*. More often than not, then, Beatrice figures as the double of Virgil or of Christ, exercising an authority that is best defined as sternly "fraternal," particularly in the monastic sense of the word.

This is not to deny that, upon occasion, Beatrice is also identified with the power of the father. A case in point would be the extended allusion in *Paradiso* 21–23 to the story of Semele, where she assumes the part of Jove, while the poet-pilgrim is figured as Semele. When such an identification does take place, however, it is usually provisional. Its function is to extricate Beatrice from a too "lyrical" or overtly erotic relation to the poet-pilgrim: a relation associated with states of paralysis and hypnotic fixation which are always rapidly overcome in the name of narrative and spiritual progress. Yet, even in these special cases, it would seem that paternal attributes—the same is true of Mary—are usually filtered through the relatively ambivalent images of the teacher and authoritative mother. In the process, paternal prohibitions are wont to give way to maternal permissions.[23]

I arrive now at the final part of my tripartite conclusion, which is concerned with how this attempt to escape certain Oedipal dynamics and to sublimate or, at least, displace the erotic, must be viewed as part and parcel of Dante's critique of classical epic values. In the *Paradiso* (which will have to stand here for the whole of Dante's poem), this critique is articulated from two different but complementary perspectives. The first comes from beyond the borders of the Roman tradition and is represented by the vernacular lyric and by its privileging of what I have referred to, for lack of a better term, as "the feminine value-sphere." The second comes from within the Roman tradition and is marked by the regular recurrence of the writings of Ovid at the precise moment at which Virgil has exited from Dante's narrative. Both target the issue of feminine mediation or, to be more exact, its absence as a sign of the marginality of romantic love in the world of Virgil's epic.[24]

I begin with the first. It is striking enough that Dante should have made Beatrice the central figure of his epic of love, but no less so is the fact that the literary genre most closely associated with Beatrice—the lyric—should figure as the *telos* of his epic. What I mean is that Dante's poem reaches its rhetorical climax in a scene which takes us back to Beatrice's poetic origin in the *Vita Nuova:* the scene of Bernard's recitation of the prayer to the Virgin in *Paradiso* 33. Sung by Beatrice's double, the poet-courtier of Mary's celestial court, this prayer brings an end to the *Commedia's* epic cycle inasmuch as it marks the first sustained eruption of the vernacular love lyric—to be sure, an intensified vernacular lyric crossbred with the Latin of the Church.

Heretofore in the *Commedia,* the vernacular love lyric had either surfaced as a fragmentary tag line cited to link Dante's own biography to that of figures like Bonagiunta da Lucca (*Purg.* 24.51) and Charles Martel (*Par.* 8.37), or been rejected because of its ties to discredited modes of reception: the case of the songs of the siren and Casella, and of Francesca da Rimini's self-presentation as the victim of Love.[25] In the celestial rose, however, it is finally given full rein and permitted to take over Dante's poem. And this within the fold of an eminently vernacular and lyric auditorium: a structure which is the icon of sublime erotic love and receptivity adapted from the poetic world of the *Roman de la Rose,* a structure of feminine gender ruled over by a mother and populated equally by infants, women, and men; a structure where there are no horses, arms, or engines of war; in short, a structure that might be said to reverse both the gender and genre of its classical prototype—Virgil's Elysium.

I arrive now at my second and final point: the resurgence of Ovid in Dante's final canticle. What I have in mind is that the apparent subversiveness with respect to the *Aeneid's* epic values of Ovid's *Metamorphoses* (and to an even greater degree, of works such as the *Heroides* and the *Ars Amatoria*) may have been important to Dante because of the centrality of feminine mediation in his Christian epic. Ovid's writings, while frequently identifying themselves in rather mocking fashion with the Latin epic tradition, launch a spirited assault on the absolute authority of the Roman patriarch—the origin and end of the key Virgilian virtue of *pietas*. This they accomplish, first, by rendering the central myths of Rome's historical origins as secular narratives, empty of the preternatural mystery and tragic power they enjoy in Virgil's epic; second, by intermingling them with variegated tales of Greek extraction, so dislodging them from the privileged heights they occupy in Augustan propaganda; third, by overtly debunking them in certain cases, as in *Ars Amatoria* 1.101–134, where the rape of the Sabines is presented not as a model of the "hard golden age" celebrated by Virgil and Horace, but as a brutal gang rape carefully orchestrated by none other than Rome's founding father, Romulus.[26]

It is not my intention here to trope Ovid's presentation in the *Tristia* of certain of his works as parricides, the killers of those that fathered them.[27] Such a reading could, I am certain, be grossly reductive. Yet what I do wish to signal is a possible opening in Ovid towards the "feminine." Whether it takes the form of an affirmation of the values of playful self-creation and romantic love over and against the cult of the Roman war machine, or, rather, of an assertion of the superiority of contemporary Roman society, with all of its luxury and frivolity, to the rigors of the golden age, this opening is distinctly non-Virgilian.[28] It is buttressed by the fact that when Ovid has occasion to invoke legitimate spiritual authority, such authority is regularly associated with various female avatars of the *Magna Mater* (The Great Mother).[29] The Venus of the *Fasti* is, thus, like the Mary of the celestial rose, the empress of her own Olympian court: "she sways, and well deserves to sway, the world entire; she owns a kingdom second to that of no god; she gives laws to heaven and earth and to her native sea and by her laws keeps every species in being." She is the builder of the *civitas*, not its disrupter: "she first stripped man of his savage garb" and taught mankind the virtues of *cultus*; she is the mother of invention and "of one thousand arts."[30]

Here in Ovid's spirituality, with its opening towards woman and the world of love, Dante may have perceived a pre-Christian model for his own insistence upon the decisive importance of feminine and, especially, *maternal* mediation in overcoming the central threats of the epic world: the threats of wayward eros and of oedipal violence. As such, I should like to envision the specter not only of the vernacular lyric, but also of Ovid's texts, looming in the background of Dante's translation of Roman *pietas* into Christian *pietà*.

NOTES

I would like to thank my colleagues in the Dartmouth Dante Institute, and particularly Rachel Jacoff and Kevin Brownlee, without whose intellectual stimulus and generosity the present essay could not have been written.

1. All quotations from Alan's *De Planctu* are from Nikolaus M. Häring's text, published in *Studi Medievali*, 3d ser., 19.2 (1978): 797–879. My English translations are based on *Alan of Lille: The Plaint of Nature*, trans. and comm. James J. Sheridan (Toronto: Pontifical Institute of Mediaeval Studies, 1980).

2. Although the phrase "sexual solecism" is of my own coinage, gender reversals are fundamental to the theory of solecism as put forward by the Latin grammarians. In his brief *excursus* on solecism at the beginning of the *Institutio Oratoria*, Quintilian writes: "Sed id quoque, quod schema vocatur, si ab aliquo per imprudentiam factum erit, soloecismi vitio non carebit. In eandem specie sunt sed schemate carent, ut supra dixi, nomina feminina, quibus mares utuntur, et neutralia, quibus feminae" (I must however point out that a figure, if used unwittingly, will be a *solecism*. In the same class, through they cannot be called figures, come errors such as the use of masculine names with a female termination and feminine names with a neuter termination (*Institutio Oratoria*, 1.5.53–54; text and translation from the Loeb Classical Library edition, ed. H. E. Butler [London: Heinemann, 1980]).

3. The passage, from Charles Thurat, ed., *Notices et extraits de divers manuscrits latins pour servir à l'histoire des doctrines grammaticales au moyen âge* (Paris: 1869; repr. Frankfurt, 1964), 264, is cited in Jan Ziolkowski, *Alan of Lille's Grammar of Sex: The Meaning of Grammar to a Twelfth Century Intellectual* (Cambridge, Mass.: Medieval Academy of America, 1985), 38. The English translation is by Ziolkowski.

4. "Humano capiti cervicem pictor equinam / iungere si velit, et varias inducere plumas / undique collatis membris, ut turpiter atrum / desinat in piscem mulier formosa superne" (If a painter chose to join a human head to the neck of a horse, and to spread feathers of many a hue over limbs picked up now here now there, so that what at the top is a lovely woman ends below in a black and ugly fish" [*De Arte Poetica* 1–4; trans. H. R. Fairclough, Loeb Classical Library (London: Heinemann, 1932)].) The key issue for Horace is that poets must make responsible use of the special freedom they are granted to diverge from the ordinary and unornamented use of language. This means that the exercise of "poetic license" in elaborating both fictions and ornate discourses must be moderate and

guided at all times by nature's laws. Cf. the later discussion of Alan's *De Incarnatione Domini*, which suggests how, in the Christian view, God's poetic license is such that he alone can overturn the laws of nature (via the Incarnation) without lapsing into the practice of illicit solecism.

5. On the links between Alan's satirical use of sexual solecism and contemporaneous developments in theology and philosophy see Ziolkowski, *Alan of Lille's Grammar of Sex*, esp. 77–144.

6. Caroline Walker Bynum, *Jesus as Mother: Studies in the Spirituality of the High Middle Ages* (Berkeley: University of California Press, 1982), see in particular chapters 4 and 5, 110–262; and *Holy Feast and Holy Fast: The Religious Significance of Food to Medieval Women* (Berkeley: University of California Press, 1987), the concluding chapter (pp. 277–93), which links up with a number of themes from the earlier study.

7. This passage from Marguerite's writings is quoted by Bynum in *Jesus as Mother*, 153. Jewish literature had long employed metaphors of childbirth in describing the advent of the messianic kingdom, a practice imitated in such New Testament *loci* as Matt. 24.8 and John 16.21.

8. For a succinct overview of Bonaventure's positive evaluation of the feminine as contrasted with Thomistic views of gender see Joan M. Ferrante, *Woman as Image in Medieval Literature from the Twelfth Century to Dante* (New York: Columbia University Press, 1975), 101–8.

9. See Jo Ann McNamara, "Sexual Equality and the Cult of Virginity in Early Christian Thought," *Feminist Studies* 3, 3/4 (1976): 145–58; John Anson, "The Female Transvestite in Early Monasticism: The Origin and Development of a Motif," *Viator* 5 (1974): 1381–94; and Evelyne Patlagean, "L'Histoire de la femme déguisée en moine et l'évolution de la sainteté féminine à Byzance," *Studi Medievali*, 3d ser., 17.2 (1976): 597–623.

10. The extract from Marius Victorinus's grammatical fragments is from Heinrich Lausberg, *Elemente der literarischen Rhetorik* (Munich: Max Heuber Verlag, 1967), par. 108.

11. This passage from stanza three is also employed by Ziolkowski, 135–36, whose translation I have slightly modified.

12. Dante's views regarding women and their relationship to the views of his contemporaries and predecessors are surveyed in Ferrante, *Woman as Image in Medieval Literature*, 129–52. Of particular relevance to my argument is her suggestion that Dante makes ambiguous use of his pronouns throughout the *Commedia*. In the first canticle, such confusion of gender boundaries is, according to Ferrante, "the price that souls pay for their sins because they have succumbed to their lower impulses and surrendered to their weaknesses" (142); in the second, "it serves a different purpose from the shame it carries in Hell" (142); in the third, it "contributes to the sense of mankind as one, of the union or fusion of male and female" (142).

13. This satirical use of "regina," a bivalent Latin/vernacular word, is unique in Dante's poem. In all its other occurrences, with only three exceptions, the word is the exclusive property of the Virgin Mary, who is addressed in song as "regina" in *Purgatorio* 7.82 and *Paradiso* 23.128 and 33.34; and who is described as: "regina del cielo" (*Par.* 31.100), "la regina / cui questo regno è suddito e devoto" (*Par.* 31.116–17), and "la nostra regina"

(*Par.* 32.104). In the three other usages of the term "regina" refers either to earthly queens violating or upholding their sacred duties (*Purg.* 17.35, *Par.* 6.133) or to Hecate, the queen of the underworld (*Inf.* 9.44).

14. Uguccione, Dante's primary source on matters of etymology, writes: "In illa die licebat cuilibet dicere in personam triumphantis quicquid vellet, unde Cesari triumphanti fertur quidam dixisse, cum deberet induci in civitatem: 'Aperite portas regi calvo et regine Bitinie,' volens significare quod calvus erat, et quod succuba extiterat regis Bitinie; et alius de eodem vitio: 'Ave rex et regina!'" (On such a day anyone could say anything he wished to the person who was having a triumph. Thus the story is told that when Caesar was being led into the city in triumph, someone said: 'Open the gates for King Baldy and the Queen of Bithynia!' This referred to the fact that he was bald and that he had lain with the King of Bithynia. Another, with the same vice in mind, said: 'Hail, King and Queen!'" [from Paget Toynbee, *Dante Studies and Researches* (London: Methuen, 1902), 113]).

15. Erich Auerbach, "Saint Francis of Assisi in Dante's *Commedia*" in *Scenes from the Drama of European Literature* (New York: Meridian Books, 1959), 79–88; reprint, Minneapolis: Univ. of Minnesota Press, 1984.

16. The passage in the *Nichomachean Ethics* is particularly suggestive since it introduces a discussion of vice, incontinence, and brutishness by briefly contrasting these moral states with their positive counterparts: superhuman excellence, heroic discipline, and divinity. It is in this context that Aristotle cites Priam's speech from the *Iliad* (24.258), arguing that the appearance of this triad of virtues in Hector marks him as that rarest of types which the Spartans called "the godlike man." After this, Aristotle turns to the analysis of the "effeminate" vices, known as incontinence and "softness," which are negatively contrasted with the virile attributes of continence and endurance. Given this feminization of vice and masculinization of virtue, it would appear that Dante's reversal of Hector's gender also implicitly reverses the Aristotelian gendering of moral states.

17. A more detailed analysis of this entire sequence of events can be found in Charles S. Singleton, *Dante's Commedia: Elements of Structure* (Baltimore: Johns Hopkins University Press, 1977), 44–60.

18. It is worth noting that Dante's representation of Dido in *Inferno* 5 as "she . . . who broke faith with Sichaeus's ashes" [colei che . . . ruppe fede al cener di Sicheo (61–62)] suggests a more extended parallelism, since the confession scene of cantos 30 and 31 will focus on Dante's broken vows to his own ancient love: the Beatrice of the *Vita Nuova*.

19. It might be objected that Dante offers the reader no detailed indications as to the overall seating arrangement of the blessed in the rose. The placement, for instance, of Bernard de Clairvaux is never elucidated; nor is there any explicit indication that the principle of sexual segregation obtains beyond the central axis. Yet what little Dante does describe suggests an attention to structural and numerical symmetries that lends strong credence to the view that every detail of the arrangement is symbolically charged (and especially so the asymmetrical placement of Beatrice). To cite but a single example: the rose's demography. Just as the

number of souls saved before the advent of Christ (ancients) is to equal
those saved after his advent (moderns), so the number of males and
females whom the reader encounters appears equal: there are ten (9 + 1)
females (Lucy, Mary, Anne, Sarah, Rebekah, Rachel, Judith, Ruth and Eve,
plus a recent arrival, Beatrice); and ten (9 + 1) males (Bernard, Francis, Benedict, Augustine, John the Evangelist, Peter, John the Baptist, Moses and
Adam, plus the most recent arrival, Dante himself).

20. On this general subject see Rachel Jacoff's "Models of Literary Influence in the *Commedia,*" in *Medieval Texts and Contemporary Readers,*
ed. M. Schichtman and L. Finke (Ithaca: Cornell University Press, 1987),
158–76.

21. The classic study of the role of the Muses in the Western literary tradition is still E. R. Curtius's *European Literature and the Latin Middle
Ages,* trans. W. R. Trask, Bollingen Series 36 (Princeton: Princeton University Press, 1973), 228–46.

22. The original passage reads:

Lo duca mio di sùbito mi prese,
   come la madre ch'al romore è desta
   e vede presso a sé le fiamme accese,
che prende il figlio e fugge e non s'arresta,
   avendo più di lui che di sé cura,
   tanto che solo una camiscia vesta;
e giù dal collo de la ripa dura
   supin si diede a la pendente roccia,
   che l'un de' lati a l'altra bolgia tura.
Non corse mai sì tosto acqua per doccia
   a volger ruota di molin terragno
   quand' ella più verso le pale approccia,
come 'l maestro mio per quel vivagno,
   portandosene me sovra 'l suo petto,
   come suo figlio, non come compagno.

(*Inf.* 23.37–51)

Its full implications can only be grasped when contrasted with *Aeneid*
2.707–743. Virgil's procession out of Troy had, after all, become a celebrated symbol of Roman *pietas* because of its insistence upon a spatial
hierarchy, both vertical and horizontal, which corresponded to the
Roman social pyramid. As the genuine *pater familias,* Anchises occupies
the highest position in Virgil's scene. He rides high on Aeneas's shoulders
and bears the family gods. As the genealogical link between the Trojan
past and the Roman future, Aeneas is the pivotal figure and occupies the
middle position in the leading group. He guides his first-born son, Ascanius, by the hand, whose inferior position is marked by the fact that,
because of his shorter legs, he somewhat trails his father and grandfather.
In the footsteps of the leading group one might expect Creusa, Ascanius's
mother and Aeneas's wife, but in her place we find the *famuli* or household servants. Situated behind them and at the rear of the pack is Creusa,
who is twice distanced ("et longe servet vestigia coniunx" [2.711], "pone
subit coniunx" [2.725]), such that, in the end, she will vanish entirely so
that she may be rediscovered in Lavinia. My point is that the maternali-

zation of the father figure in Dante's redaction of this scene reinserts into the Roman concept of *pietas* that which had been rigorously excluded or projected outward into a distant future: namely, the feminine and the maternal. The result is a transformation of the pious gesture itself. Carrying Anchises above him and leading Ascanius below him by the hand, Aeneas had affirmed his strict obeisance to the maintenance of a properly hierarchical relation between ancestors and descendants. Carrying Dante "sovra 'l suo petto" like a suckling babe, the Virgil of the *Commedia* instead affirms a less hierarchical version of piety founded in the virtue of compassion, the special province of Mary.

23. In the case of Dante's reenactment of the Semele/Jove story in *Paradiso* 21, this means that a vision that had initially been the subject of an absolute prohibition ("se non si temperasse, tanto splende, / che 'l tuo mortal podere, al suo fulgore, / sarebbe fronda che trono scoscende" [10–12]), becomes permissible only two cantos later ("possente / se' fatto a sostener lo riso mio" [*Par.* 23.47–48]), through the agency of Christ and Mary, who have appeared in the intervening moments. The pagan injunction that no mortal may gaze upon the father in his full celestial splendor and survive thus gives way to a Christian invitation to look directly into Beatrice's fulgurant and transfiguring smile. On this passage, see Kevin Brownlee's seminal essay, "Ovid's Semele and Dante's Metamorphosis: *Paradiso* 21–23," *MLN* 101 (1986): 147–56.

24. On Dante's christianization of Virgilian epic see my own *The Transfiguration of History at the Center of Dante's Paradise* (Princeton: Princeton University Press, 1986).

25. The major exception would appear to be Arnaut Daniel, who in *Purgatorio* 26.140–47 identifies himself by reciting eight verses in Provençal. Yet it must be said of Arnaut's song that, far from being a joyous celebration of love or of the lyric voice, it is a lament of his *passada folor*. As such it appears as an act of literary contrition, retracting the content of Arnaut's earlier writings, and rejecting their cult of stylistic complexity, for here the master of the *trobar clus* sings (and cries) a lament of the utmost transparency.

26. For a somewhat divergent view of Ovid's relation to Virgil and to the Augustan project, see G. Karl Galinsky (*Ovid's Metamorphoses. An Introduction to the Basic Aspects* [Berkeley and Los Angeles: University of California Press, 1975]): "to construe Ovid's intentions as a deflation or 'undercutting' of Vergil's epic is both unduly narrow and misleading. Rather, Ovid's aim was to present a successful alternative to Vergil's adaptation of myth and to suggest that the narrative possibilities of myth . . . were by no means exhausted. Ovid's playfulness, which is so characteristic of the *Metamorphoses*, is not only essential to his revivification of myth, but also to preserving his poetic and creative independence vis à vis the otherwise inhibiting influence of Vergil's achievement" (247–48).

27. "Tres procul obscura latitantes parte videbis,— / sic quoque, quod nemo nescit, amare docent. / hos tu vel fugias, vel, si satis oris habebis, / Oedipodas facito Telegonosque voces. / deque tribus, moneo, si qua est tibi cura parentis, / ne quemquam, quamvis ipse docebit, ames" (*Tristia*, Loeb Classical Library, ed. and trans. A. L. Wheeler [Cambridge: Harvard

University Press, 1975] 1.1.111–16). Ovid is, of course, referring to the sentence of exile that resulted from the celebrity attained by such works as the *Amores, Remedia Amoris,* and *Ars Amatoria.*

28. In *"Femina Virtus!* Some New Thoughts on the Conflict Between Augustus and Ovid," A. W. J. Holleman (*Acta Conventus Omnium Gentium Ovidianis Studiis Fovendis* [Bucharest: Bucharest University Press, 1976]) adopts a similar stance concerning the representation of the "feminine" in Ovid's art: "while Catullus in his Lesbia and Virgil in his Dido had warned that *amor* must lead to *otium* which turns out to be destructive to Roman *virtus,* Ovid will show that *amor* as occasioned and conditioned by *otium* can lead to a new *virtus:* namely *cultus,* which for obvious reasons is preeminently a matter of woman's concern" (348).

29. What seems particularly striking about the Dante/Ovid confrontation is that in both authors one senses that the feminine, whether *Magna Mater* or *Vergine Madre,* serves as the emblem of consummate artistry. Writing of the *Ars Amatoria,* Molly Myerowitz (*Ovid's Games of Love* [Detroit: Wayne State University Press, 1985]) observes: "paradoxically, the female emerges as the inferior *amator,* the superior *cultor,* enjoying an artist's *otium,* perhaps unenviable yet superior in that detachment to which the male *artifex* only can aspire. She is, in the words of Joyce, totally 'the artist, like the God of creation, [who] remains within or beyond or above his handiwork, invisible, refined out of existence, indifferent, paring his fingernails.' She may devote herself completely to art, 'the human disposition of sensible or intelligible *matter* for an aesthetic end'" (128). In the case of Dante, Bernard's oration to the Virgin in *Paradiso* 33 makes it clear that she alone is able to create and recreate God, giving him body without subjecting him to the imperfections of matter.

30. "Illa tenet nullo regna minora deo, / iuraque dat caelo, terrae, natalibus undis, / perque suos initus continet omne genus / . . . prima feros habitus homini detraxit: ab illa / venerunt cultus mundaque cura sui. / . . . mille per hanc artes motae; studioque placendi / quae latuere prius, multa reperta ferunt" (*Fasti,* trans. J. G. Frazer, Loeb Classical Library [Cambridge: Harvard University Press, 1976], 4.92–114). Cf. F. Altheim's remark that "Göttinnen haben durchaus den Vorzug vor den männlichen Bewohnern des römischen Olymp" (Throughout [Roman religion] goddesses are granted priority over the male inhabitants of the Roman Olympus [cited in Holleman, 351]).

Semiotics and Power: Relics, Icons, and the *Voyage de Charlemagne à Jérusalem et à Constantinople*

EUGENE VANCE

During the last few years, a renewed perception of the importance of history to the understanding of literary texts has begun to influence contemporary critical thought.

At the same time, certain historians question the legitimacy of modern historiographical discourse that ignores the relativity of its own models of understanding.[1]

Both developments have quite naturally generated new interest in what we call medieval culture, when the discourses of both secular historiography and vernacular literature first emerged.

The new medievalism evolving in France, Germany, and North America is not a uniform movement, but it does have certain common denominators.

First, it has developed out of—or rather, away from—a set of structural and poststructural preoccupations of the past twenty-five years that did not hold up literary texts (medieval or otherwise) as products of a specific culture, but rather as embodiments of universals. Such language-centered, generalist movements as narratology, semiotics, psychocriticism, and grammatology were either indifferent to the historical discursive matrix of literary texts, or, in the case of certain strains of Marxism, caricatural, at least concerning the Middle Ages.[2]

Second, the new medievalism tends to respect the inherent poetics of a literary text, yet to stress the interaction between the constitutive discourse(s) of literature and those other discourses (the scientific, the theological, the judicial, the political, the historio-graphical, etc.) coinhabiting a given cultural context.

This context includes those conscious theories of sign, discourse, and culture that might have informed the production and reception of medieval texts and artifacts in their own time.

The "problem of history" is therefore not a documentary one of directly relating a given poem to a given event in time. Rather, it is one of understanding: first, how social events are coded or even dictated by discourse; second, how social events cluster themselves (for instance, the simultaneous rise of literacy, capitalism, and urbanism in the twelfth century) to produce new *interdiscursive* configurations specific to this or that cultural moment and its texts.

The new medievalism is a science not of things and deeds, but of discourses; it is an art, not of facts, but of *encodings* of facts. Such priorities are quite consonant with those of medieval intellectual life itself, whose curriculum was dominated during a span of nearly 1,000 years by the three "arts of discourse" [*artes sermocinales*] of the *trivium:* grammar, rhetoric, and logic.[3] Moreover, medieval rhetoric itself, while weak in dealing with questions of genre and form, was strong as a pragmatics of discourse. It is not surprising that Andreas Capellanus's treatise on courtly love is above all a treatise about different modes of uttering one's love across boundaries within a social hierarchy. Not only did rhetoricians after Cicero and Augustine insist upon the multiplicity of discourses constituting the body politic, but upon the stylistic features and semantic fields specific to each. The thirteenth-century theoretician of preaching, Humbert of Romans, discerned 100 distinct discourses constituting the body politic: the perfect preacher must master them all.[4]

As an example of the kind of historical and theoretical problem that summons new critical paradigms, I shall deal with certain semiotic concerns of the anonymous twelfth-century antiepic, *Le voyage de Charlemagne à Jérusalem et à Constantinople* (hereafter abbreviated *VC*). Specifically, I shall suggest that the humor of this poem, which has proved troublesome to many orthodox critics,[5] is closely bound to two gestures: first, a radical disjunction of relics as motors of spirituality from the discourse of theocratic power in Capetian France; second, the poet's depiction of a crisis of spirituality and of political law as the expression of a yet deeper crisis of male sexual identity in the Latin West. I shall argue that a combination of several historical events in mid-twelfth-century

Capetian France nurtured the humor of a poem whose effect is to unmask the dehumanizing arbitrariness of the sign-making powers of a patriarchal hegemony of church and monarchy.

Politics, Gender, and Representation

Few would deny that the apogee of that hegemony occurred in the twelfth century at St.-Denis, whose most privileged relics were a nail from the cross and Jesus's crown. Suger's conception of the French crown, as it is described by Erwin Panofsky, includes perspectives central to the *VC:*

> For he was convinced of three basic truths. First, a king, and most particularly the king of France, was a "vicar of God," "bearing God's image in his person and bringing it to life"; but this fact, far from implying that the king could do no wrong entailed the postulate that the king must do no wrong ("it disgraces a king to transgress the law, for the king and the law—*rex* et *lex*— are receptacles of the same supreme power of government"). Second, any king of France, but quite especially Suger's beloved master, Louis le Gros, who at his coronation in 1108 had divested himself of the secular sword and had been girded with the sword spiritual "for defense of the Church and the poor," had both the right and the sacred duty to subdue all forces conducive to internal strife and obstructive to his central authority. Third, this central authority and, therefore, the unity of the nation were symbolized, even vested, in the Abbey of St.-Denis which harbored the relics of the "Apostle of all Gaul," the "special and, after God, unique protector of all the realm."[6]

That the *VC* is concerned less with specific people than with relationships of power and gender, especially with regard to the symbol-making processes of a political and spiritual hegemony, is clear from the opening scene. Before an assembly of his highest vassals at St.-Denis, Charlemagne takes up his crown and his sword, symbols of his divinely instituted kingship and authority. He addresses his wife with the "fulness of his speech" [*De sa pleine parole*][7] in order to compel her admiration, not simply of his personal magnificence, but of his aptitude as a symbol-bearer, that is, as the mediator of a transcendental power:

> "Dame, veïstes unkes hume dedesuz ceil
> Tant ben seïst espee, ne la corune al chef?"

(9–10)

("My Lady, did you ever see a man under heaven to whom the
sword was more suited, or the crown on his head?")

But the Queen, the poet clearly tells us, is not *sage*, and to the
scandal of the emperor, she answers in folly [*folement* (12)]:

"Emperere, dist ele, trop vus poez priser.
Uncore en sai jo un ki plus se fait leger
Quant il porte corune entre ses chevalers:
Kuant la met sur sa teste plus belement lui set!"

(13–16)

("Emperor," she said, "you hold yourself in too high esteem. I
do know of someone more jaunty when he bears the crown
amongst his knights: when he puts it on his head, it is more
beautiful on him.")

Whether in a theological or ideological perspective, this queen of
an emperor is out of line in answering the very vicar of Christ in
such a way, especially before a secular assembly of knights where
(as in *King Lear*) a king's divided identity can only produce
further political division. As Paul put it, man is "the image and
glory of God, but woman is the glory of man. (For man was not
made from woman, but woman from man. Neither was man
created for woman, but woman for man.)"[8] Having seen himself
through a queen darkly, Charlemagne threatens that if the joking
queen has not spoken truly, he will cut off her head; if she has
spoken truly, he will share his crown with the unknown other.

In a human perspective, Charlemagne's silly conduct deserves
only the response that it gets, and throughout the poem there will
be a contest between dogma and common sense that will leave a
stupid emperor and his dogma arbitrarily on the top, and a smart
woman prostrate in abjection. However, if I may anticipate my
conclusions, we will be brought to see that this hierarchy is sanctioned by a mendacious, Gallo–phallocentric God, and that it is
the twin fetishism of the relic (the Latin word for relic, *pignus*,
means "money") as money of the soul and of the harder money of
the political world that will make His lies true.

The principal characters here are Charlemagne and his joking
queen, and the setting is St.-Denis, where, we are told, Charlemagne quarrels with his wife under a palm tree. This impossible
combination of persons, plants, and place has evinced enormous
scholarly commentary, too diverse to rehearse here, except to say
that any reasonably informed audience of the twelfth century
would have known that St.-Denis was the burial place of the

French kings and hardly the seat of Charlemagne's power, and much less a palm grove. Some of the poem's audience might also have recalled that even the identity of St.-Denis's patron saint was something of a fiction: as Abelard had so imprudently disclosed (at the cost of imprisonment), its founding saint was not at all Dionysius the Areopagite, but another Dionysius, bishop of Corinth. However, as for Charlemagne's equally fictitious Byzantine rival for the queen's admiration, King Hugon le Fort, a St.-Denis-Constantinople rivalry was thriving in the middle of the twelfth century, centered in the mutual ambivalence between Louis VII and Manuel Comnenus, the powerful and cultivated emperor of Byzantium.[9]

Two details will illustrate that ambivalence on the part of the French. On the positive side, St. Bernard's secretary, while preparing the Second Crusade, could in the most unctuous terms recommend the young Henri, son of the powerful Thibaut de Blois and future Count of Champagne, to Manuel to be knighted:

> The magnificence and glory of your name, which has spread far and wide across the face of the earth, has come to us . . . I am therefore scarcely worthy to send to the throne of your glory the bearer of the present letter, a youth of great nobility, in order that you administer to him the oaths of knighthood, and that you gird him with the sword against the enemies of the cross of Christ, and against those who raise up their head in pride against him. This young man might aspire to attain the highest honors, but by my better advice we sent him to the special glory of your empire that he might remember all the days of his life from what hand he had received the dignity of military art.[10]

On the negative side, the same splendor of Manuel's Constantinople was a mote in Abbot Suger's eye. The Bishop of Laon had told him that the treasures of St. Sophia were vaster than those of St.-Denis, but Suger reassured himself, on the basis of testimony from travelers, that they probably were not. But if the Bishop were right, Suger reasoned, and if, because of their rusing nature [astucia], the Greeks were hiding their treasures instead of using them for the Mass, then the Greeks should be blamed.[11]

The Byzantines, too, had ambivalent attitudes toward the Latin barbarians. Drawing upon Manuel's contemporary biographer Cinnamus, Michael Angold writes,

> For his part Manuel was much attracted by the prowess of western knights and sought to outdo them. His German em-

press was constrained in full senate to admit that she drew
her descent from a great and warlike race, but out of all them
she never heard of any who boasted so many feats in a single
year as her husband Manuel. Manuel insisted on using 'a
lance incomparable in length and size', customarily known as
an 'eight-footer'. He showed it to that paladin, Raymond,
prince of Antioch, who was apparently most impressed. (206)

However, there are deeper cultural forces subtending the thematic surface of the opening scene, and these become more apparent
as the poem unfolds. Alexandre Leupin evokes them well, though
in Lacanian terms: first, Leupin says, there is a concern in the *VC*
with the vitiating power of writing as a mode of representation;
second, there is a sexual dimension of the problem of representation which valorizes the link between the true and the naked;
third, there is a link between the quest for truth in speech and the
potency of an absent master-signifier [*maître-signifiant*], which is
the phallus, in the Lacanian sense of that term. According to Leupin, Charlemagne, with his *parole pleine*, aspires to be a figure "of
the Divine thing" [*du Réel divin*] who wields the phallic master-
signifier, while the queen, as the *parole folle*, lays bare the inade-
quacy of the king and thereby provokes the voyage of the story
itself, which is the story of a cover-up:

> Mettant en doute *la vertu* de Charlemagne (sa puissance,
> dans tous les sens du terme—v. 56), le discours de la reine en
> a dévoilé le manque constitutif, l'obligeant à entamer le voy-
> age du récit lui-même. Ainsi, la parole folle est-elle la cause
> profonde du récit; cause profonde, mais inavouable: car l'em-
> pereur lui substitue un pèlerinage qui la recouvre; la quête
> des reliques est asservie, mensongèrement, à la confrontation
> esthétique.[12]

Leupin's terms are not *merely* Lacanian. That the powers of writing and representation were vital problems in the cultural context
of the *VC* is amply borne out by M. L. Clanchy, Brian Stock, and
others.[13] Moreover, with regard to an evolving *poetics* of textuality, I have proposed elsewhere that one may consider the *Chanson
de Roland* (which was a strong subtext of the *VC*) as the embodiment of a painful transition of French culture from orality to writing. Roland, I have proposed, is a hero of the outcry, an oral poet's
hero of power and presence. Charlemagne, from the start, is an
emperor of silence who becomes, after the carnage at Ronceval,
the first reader of the *Chanson de Roland* and the first insti-

gator of sanctuaries, of monuments, and of inscriptions.[14] The twelfth century was a time when not only the *techné* of writing altered the workings of mind, but so, too, did the new modalities of silent reading.[15] We are dealing with questions that involve not only a textual poetics, but a visual poetics as well. Linda Seidel has studied the dialogue between Roman imperial art and Romanesque façades in Aquitaine,[16] and Stephen G. Nichols, Jr., has studied the evolution, in Romanesque art, of Carolingian notions of history as *theosis*, with the Holy Sepulchre as a fulcrum.[17] Perhaps for the sake of brevity, Leupin moves his focus directly from St.-Denis to Constantinople, considered as the "place" of artistic representation—or of what I will call the power of iconic signs. However, we may deepen some of Leupin's intuitions about the *VC* by dwelling some more on St.-Denis, on its modes of thought and its treasures, and then by speaking of Charlemagne's visit to Jerusalem before we follow him to Constantinople.

Of Signs and Sanctuaries

Let me begin the discussion of St.-Denis with a word about Charlemagne. It is clear that "Charlemagne" is not the name of a literary "character" in the romantic sense of that term. Nor is Charlemagne a clear-cut historical *persona*, since everyone who could read this poem would have known that Charlemagne's seat of power was Aachen, while St.-Denis was the burial-place of French monarchs and therefore the *locus* of a French ecclesiastical and monarchical hegemony. Nor is "Charlemagne" the name of a "myth," understood as a popular story whose cognitive functions outweigh its factor of truth. "Charlemagne" might be more aptly construed as the name of a "legend," in the twelfth-century sense of *legenda*, as that which must be "read," in the same sense that "agenda" means the things that must be "done." However, "legend" is now too easily construed as "myth." To the extent that "legend" is akin to the Greek *legein* and *logos* ("to speak" and "discourse"), let us consider "Charlemagne" as the name of a written *discourse*, though in the sense that Michel Foucault and, more recently, Timothy Reiss give that term: not only as an *epistémè*, or mode of understanding, but as a productivity of actions or things (e.g., a crusade, a university, a church, an empire).[18] Proper names (e.g., Socrates, the Stoics, Descartes, Marx, Freud) often serve as markers not of people and places, but of methods and discourses.

The ideological discourse named "Charlemagne" constituted

itself largely in eleventh- and twelfth-century Europe as a discourse of origins, power, truth, unity, and of sanctity.[19] It was a discourse of empire that the Germans were trying to monopolize, even with the aid of such false documents as the Pseudo-Turpin. The higher the truth value of a discourse, the falser its documents may be. The German Emperor Frederick I canonized Charlemagne in 1165.

But "Charlemagne" was a discourse that the French also wished to appropriate, and with false documents of their own: such are the powers of writing, of *legenda*, things you must read. Already before the first crusade, a spurious story entitled the *Descriptio* had been composed, which told how Charlemagne, at the request of the patriarch of Jerusalem and of the emperor of Constantinople, liberated Jerusalem from the Turks. Returning by Byzantium, he was given numerous relics, including the crown of thorns and a nail of the cross. The relics were taken to Aachen, where they remained until Charles the Bald, Charlemagne's grandson, emperor, and the first king of the French, gave the crown and the nail to St.-Denis.[20] The "legend" of Charlemagne in the eleventh and twelfth centuries seems to have swarmed with documents both true and false, validating the presence, in different places, of relics which were themselves perhaps no less true or false. Relics allied to names of the great, both of which carry "true" stories, and the prestige of written texts all reinforced each other's truth value. For instance, in the so-called *Liber de constitutione*, compiled in the first half of the twelfth century, the monks of Charroux claimed to have received from Charlemagne not only some wood of the cross, but Christ's foreskin, miraculously bestowed upon the emperor by the boy-Messiah during a visitation.[21] In order to emphasize the genealogical ties of the French monarchy to Charlemagne, Suger himself became a creative archeologist. He opportunely discovered and dusted off, for instance, a decree of Charles the Bald (whom he calls *Karolus imperator tertius*) that the king be buried amongst the relics of St.-Denis "for the protection of his soul and body:"

> But, since these injunctions of so great an Emperor, though sanctioned by documents sealed with the golden seal, had partly cooled off, owing to the envious mutability of hoary time, and partly fallen into disuse altogether, we zealously endeavored, having deliberated our intention with our brethren, to revive and restore them for the love and honor of God and of the sacred relics, and also for the salvation of the soul of our Lord the Most Serene and August Charles.[22]

Aside from the ashes of saints, there were at St.-Denis the severed arms of saints James the Less, Stephen, and Vincent. If, as Peter Brown has recently said, the early dissemination of relics throughout the Latin West involved an effort of the primitive church to constitute a new Christian infrastructure,[23] inversely, we may see the distribution of relics alleged to Charlemagne by eleventh- and twelfth-century ideologues as attempts to forge (in more than one sense of the word) new national political identities.

However, relics as a class of sign involve specific cognitive processes, and an esthetic as well—that of passing from the apprehension of an abject fragment marked with the violence of dismemberment, roasting or flaying of human bodies, to the vision of a resplendent, resurrected whole. Hence, Suger's careful presentation of martyrdoms (for instance, the Martyrdom of St. Vincent on a roundel of a window at St. Denis[24]) and his production of extraordinary reliquaries. The experience of transcendence of what is abject through the effect of beauty is what Suger calls the *anagogicus mos*. Its paradigm was the Plotinian ecstasy of union with the One as that theory had been expressed in the writings of Pseudo-Dionysius the Areopagite himself.[25] Moreover, there is a clear homology of the idea of the *many* absorbed into the spiritual *one* with the idea of the Carolingian empire as a totality. That is to say, the ideological claims of Carolingianism as a discourse of unity, truth, sanctity, and power are *esthetic* categories as well. For example, consider how Suger contemplates the Escrin de Charlemagne, an elaborate five-tiered reliquary of precious metal and gems whose crest jewel was a crystal showing a portrait of Julia, daughter of the Roman Emperor Titus, perhaps reinterpreted as the Virgin Mary.[26] By its very form, this artifact is a visual template for a spiritual ascent from being to non-being, from place to non-place (Utopia), from Eve to Mary, from the many to the indivisible One:

To those who know the properties of precious stones it becomes evident, to their utter astonishment, that none is absent from the number of these (with the only exception of the carbuncle), but that they abound most copiously. This, when—out of my delight in the beauty of the house of God— the loveliness of the many-colored gems has called me away from external and worthy meditation has induced me to reflect, transferring that which is material to that which is immaterial, on the diversity of the sacred virtues: then it seems to me that I see myself dwelling, as it were, in some

strange region of the universe which neither exists entirely in
the slime of the earth nor entirely in the purity of Heaven;
and that, by the grace of God, I can be transported from this
inferior to that higher world in an analogical manner. (*De
administratione*, 62–5)

Such an esthetic had failed to materialize in the *Song of Roland*.
If "Charlemagne" is the name of a discourse, and if we may consider "Roland" as the name of a *poetic* discourse, already in the
earlier poem we may observe a tragic drift from the perception of
a divine imperialistic force fiercely immanent in Roland's sword
(which contains in its pommel a tooth of St. Peter, some of St.
Basil's blood, and some of Mary's clothing) to a perception of the
empire as a fragmented, rebellious wasteland painfully remote
from the spiritual unity of paradise where French martyrs are
gathered into the mystical body of the resurrected Christ.

The Quest for Symbols

If Charlemagne's political rebuke by the queen is also a sexual
rebuke, both occur primarily as denials of *symbolic* power.
Though in his list of subjacent cultural problems in the *VC* Leupin does not mention that of wealth as a symbolic representation
of power, it is important to note that the queen unwisely tries to
soothe her outraged master by making a distinction between his
martial power and the superior wealth of his rival:

"Emperere, dist ele, ne vus en curucez!
Plus est riche d'aver et d'or et de deners,
Mais n'est mie si pruz ne si bon chevalers
Pur ferir en bataille ne pur ost encaucer!"

(26–29)

("Emperor," she said, "don't be angry. He's richer in possessions, in gold and in money than you, but is not at all as brave
or as good a knight when he strikes in battle or chases
armies.")

However, at a time when social relationships were being textualized, so, too, were they being monetarized, as Georges Duby has
made it clear,[27] and as we see from Suger's own writings, where
the exchange value of so many objects and services in the world of
St.-Denis is precisely quantified in monetary terms. If money
could easily be melted into precious artifacts in order to ransom

human souls, clearly money now could rival the sword as the master-signifier.[28]

The queen's rebukes call, therefore, for a quest for restored symbolic power. Thus, the emperor of France sets out for the Holy Land, not with the sword of a crusader, but with the humbler staff and sack of the penitent pilgrim, and mounted not on a war-horse, but a mule. His twin purposes, he says, are to venerate the cross and Holy Sepulchre and to seek out the rival king of whom the queen has spoken. As a sexually and economically intimidated emperor, Charlemagne is the opposite of the crusading Charles of the *Descriptio*.

From History to Story

What, we may ask, brought about such dire inflections in the discourse of empire named "Charlemagne," now the privileged discourse of Capetian power? Hard evidence for the dating of the *VC* is lacking, but it seems to me that the convergence of several events in the mid-twelfth century during the reign of Louis VII go very far in explaining the combination of factors in Charlemagne's humiliation.[29]

Most obviously, there were the disastrous consequences of the Second Crusade, preached by Bernard and led personally by Louis VII, in the company of his 25-year-old queen, Eleonore of Aquitaine.[30] Otto of Friesling recounted that just before setting out on the crusade, Louis received a mysterious letter, written perhaps by God himself, prophesying that his conquests would extend so far to the east that his initial L would be changed to C: Louis would incarnate, in other words, not just *C*harlemagne, but *Constantine* himself.[31] In the summer of 1147, the crusading army left for the East. After visiting Constantinople, then in its apogee of material splendor and literary culture under a hospitable Manuel I Comnenus, the crusaders continued to Antioch. There the queen became so infatuated with her uncle Raymond of Antioch that she tried to repudiate her marriage with Louis VII on the grounds of consanguinity so that she could remain in Antioch. Eleonore was compelled to resume her journey to Jerusalem.[32] After the defeat of the crusaders at Damascus and their return to France in 1149, criticisms of the crusade abounded, but were countered by accusations by such people as Otto of Friesling, Bernard of Clairvaux, and Peter of Blois that the crusaders had been justly punished. William of Newburgh claimed they were punished not only for their greed, but for their debauchery: the camps of the army, *castra*, he reasons, instead of being free of debauchery as the word *castra* indicates they should be, succumbed to licentiousness.[33] Thus, Louis VII's misfortunes in the Second Crusade could be perceived as a humiliation of several sorts: military, sexual, spiritual, and economic. Moreover, within two years after his return, Eleonore fell in love with Henry Plantagenet of England and divorced Louis. Louis thereby lost Aquitaine to Henry, and much wealth with it.[34] To a sexual humiliation was added poverty. Louis is reported to have said to one of Henry's subjects,

> "As for your prince, he lacks for nothing: valuable horses, gold and silver, silken fabrics, precious stones, he has them all in abundance. At the court of France we have only bread, wine and gaiety."[35]

Nor was the discourse of Capetian Carolingianism reinforced by the election, in the same year as Louis's divorce in 1152, of the true Holy Roman Emperor and strongman Frederick I Barbarossa to the German throne. On his side, Frederick reinforced his link to Charlemagne by commissioning a hagiographic *Vita sancti Karoli*, in order to "bring into the full light, with the help of God, this sun that shadows had hidden for 351 years . . . Charles is to the Church as the sun is to the moon."[36]

The Poetics of Impotence

The mid-twelfth-century was a time of crisis, therefore, in the reign of a weak Capetian king, and this nexus of events explains very well why in the *VC* a pilgrimage east to the Holy Sepulchre might not promise to be the panacea for the humiliations suffered by Charlemagne at the hands of his wife. Since Charlemagne's quest is for symbolic grandeur, he brings neither arms nor supplies but seven hundred Persian camels loaded with gold. Pausing en route to solicit once again admiration of himself from Bertram — this time as a leader of multitudes — he confides thus to Bertram:

> "Veez cum gens cumpaines de pelerins erraund!
> Hitantes milies sunt el premer chef devant:
> Ki ço duit et governet, ben deit estre poant!"
>
> (95–98)
>
> ("See what a company there is of wandering pilgrims. There must be eighty thousand of them up ahead. The man who leads and governs them must be very powerful!")

At his arrival in Jerusalem, Charlemagne and his barons wander by
chance into a monastery that seems to be a vague amalgam of several different churches of the Holy City, including Christ's tomb,[37]
but whose ornamentation and iconography (for instance, the seat
of Christ and the twelve chairs of the apostles, the depictions of
martyrs, the sumptuous painting) strike chords recalling the splen-
dors and dodecimalism of Suger's St.-Denis, on whose façade was a
scene of the Christ in Majesty surrounded by the apostles.[38]
Although Charlemagne is impressed with the scene (Mult fu let
Karlemaine de cele grand bealté [123]) he draws a cognitive blank as
to the significance of this setting of the Last Supper and plops himself down in the sealed chair of Christ, with his twelve peers beside
him. When a Jew enters the church and sees Charlemagne sitting
there like a Christ in Majesty of the Apocalypse, with his twelve
peers in the seats beside him, the Jew nearly faints with fear and
rushes to the patriarch to inform him that God himself and the
twelve apostles have returned to earth. Given the ancient charge
that the Jews merited punishment because of their refusal to
recognize Christ, and given Suger's own concerns to orchestrate
anagogical epiphanies in art, Charlemagne's dullness of mind is
spectacular. Worse, it is totally incommensurate with the honor
that the patriarch now bestows on him as he crowns him Charles
the Great [Charlemaine], supreme among all kings. At a time
when the controversy between nominalism and realism was hot,
this bestowal of an empty name by an overcredulous patriarch on a
weak king must have seemed especially ironic:

> "Sire, mult estes ber!
> Sis as en la chaere u sist meïmes Deus:
> Aies non Charlemaine sur tuz reis curunez!"
>
> (156–8)

("My Lord, you are very noble. You are sitting in the chair that
God himself sat in. Be crowned with the name of Charlemagne over all other kings.")

While it is true that Charlemagne is besting his wife, nothing
could be less deserved than this pure accident of political glory.
This glimpse of the arbitrariness both of Charlemagne's personal
destiny (not to speak of that of the Holy Roman Empire) flies in
the face of Bernard's vigorous theology of predestination as
expounded in his De gratia et libero arbitrio, composed before
1128. Moreover, if Charlemagne has the right name and all the
luck, his first reflex is to solidify them with the power of relics:

E dist li emperere: "Cin cenz merciz de Deu!
De voz saintes reliques, si vus plaist, me donez,
Que porterai en France qu'en voil enluminer!"

(159–61)

(And the emperor said, "Five hundred thanks to God; now, if
you please, give me some of your holy relics so that I may
carry them back to illuminate France.")

In a swift-moving poem of 870 lines whose story carries us from
France to Jerusalem and Constantinople and back to France, the
ensuing list of relics and their virtues is conspicuously long—
more than fifty lines.[39] The overabundance of the patriarch's charity heightens the scandal of Charlemagne's blind luck. The list
names not only such prestigious relics as the Holy Shroud, some
of Mary's milk, her shirt, and St. Peter's beard, but also relics that
were actually at St.-Denis: a nail from the cross, the crown of
thorns, and remains from the martyrs Simeon and Steven. In his
closely argued article, John L. Grigsby treats the three groups of
relics implicit in this list, and also their *number*, which he calcu-
lates to be thirteen, and which corresponds to the number of Charlemagne and the twelve peers and to the number of *gabs* (jokes)
performed by the French. If Grigsby is right, we may see the *VC*
as a scandalous parody of salvation history.[40] In any case, so powerful is this monstration of relics that a paralytic leaps to his feet
in perfect health. "Les reliques sunt forz, Deus i fait grant vertuz"
(192) (The relics are strong; God has shown his great power). The
emperor now prepares a *chasse* for the relics made from 1,000
marks of gold, far outstripping Suger's most extravagant orna-
ments, and this loaded *chasse* will become Charlemagne's chief
weapon in the forthcoming testicular war with Hugon le Fort,
emperor of Constantinople. As Charlemagne leaves Jerusalem,
not having even seen Christ's tomb, the good patriarch spontaneously offers Charlemagne the rest of his treasures (a hundred
mules loaded with gold), in return for which Charlemagne agrees
to wage war on Saracens, even in Spain—where, the poet volun-
teers, Roland and the twelve peers did indeed perish. The *VC* is a
poem whose comic vision presupposes a reading of its tragic subtext, the *Chanson de Roland*.[41]

Still obsessed with the queen's *gab*, Charlemagne sets out again
on his mule for Constantinople. Doubtless a reflection of Louis
VII's arrival in Constantinople during the Second Crusade,
Charlemagne's own arrival there provides exactly that display of
intimidating wealth that the French most feared.

However, it is the uncanniness of Hugon's power that is most confusing to the French, who first encounter the Greek emperor plowing a field with a golden plough. We quickly see that Hugon's realm has realized the highest ideals of the classical city: peace, agricultural skill, prosperity, and civic order.[42] Elaborately described, Hugon's golden plough is a triumph of technology and of opulence, two social goals ardently cultivated by the French in the mid-twelfth century as they began to improve agricultural and manufacturing techniques and to build their gothic cathedrals. Leupin has expounded the nexus of meanings of the plowing king very well: recalling Alain de Lille's phallic metaphors of the plow-share and the pen, Leupin suggests (p. 6) that the field with its straight lines is also a figuration of the text. Certainly the tradition of the field-as-text goes back at least to Augustine,[43] as does the motif of the phallic tongue and pen, so Leupin is on firm terrain here. The plough-king Hugon le Fort represents not only the phallic element lacking in the emperor of France, but he embodies a whole cluster of enviable productive powers—economic, cultural, and artistic. Hugon's courtesy is real, but fraught with scents from the barnyard: "Or dejundrai mes beos pur la vostre amistet" (316) (Now I will unhitch my oxen for your friendship). The French hero of other epics, Guillaume d'Orange, is less friendly: if this were France, he exclaims, and if his friend Bertram were there, they would smash it with hammers. Such is the logic of epic, now becoming obsolete, where beautiful things and people are destroyed; but it is not the logic of the courtly romances shortly to come, where opulence and sexual fulfillment are the natural ends of the heroic quest.

However, the most intimidating aspect of Hugon's wealth is not, finally, its abundance, nor even the technological ingenuity of a royal palace that turns in the wind like a wheel on an axle; rather, it is the statues of two boys, each of which holds an ivory horn to its mouth. When the wind strikes them, the statues sound their horns together, and then they even turn and look laughingly at each other. So realistic are they that they actually seem to be alive. These statues are perfect icons, fashioned by the hand of man. It is at this moment when art perfectly represents life itself that Charlemagne is decisively overwhelmed, or should we say undercut, by the truth of his wife's *gab:*

Cil corn sunent e buglent e tunent ensement
Cum taburs u toneires u grant cloches qui pent:
Li uns esgardet l'altre ensement en riant,

Que ço vus fust viaire que tut fussent vivant.
Karle vit le paleis et la richesce grant;
La sue manantise ne priset mie un guant.
De sa mullier li membret que manacé out tant.

(358–64)

(The horns sound and bugle and resound together, like drums, or thunder, or a great ringing bell. One looked laughingly at the other such that it seemed that they were perfectly alive. Charles saw the palace and the great wealth. He did not esteem his own possessions more than a glove. He remembered his wife, whom he had threatened so much.)

Indeed, the music of these icons [*imagenes* (373)] is a perfect reproduction of the harmony of Paradise itself. Hugon's power is that of a divine artist who has transcended the difference between matter and spirit, between the mortal and the divine:

L'un halt, li altre cler, mult feit bel a oïr:
C'est avis qui l'ascute qu'il seit en paraïs.
La u li angle chantent e suëf e seriz!

(375–7)

(One high, the other bright, it was beautiful to hear. It seemed to anyone who listened that he was in paradise, where angels sing so beautifully and so delicately.)

The rivalry between Charlemagne and Hugon le Fort began as a sexual and political affront; now it involves conflict between two distinct sign types—relics and icons—which correspond to two different modes of mediating divine power. This is a comic reduction of a centuries-old historical division over icons between East and West that had been apparent in the *Roland*, where the icon [*image*] of Apollo was joined to the pagan trinity of Mahomet and Tervagan, and where the Saracens behaved as idolators until they overthrew and defiled the idols after their defeat by the relic-bearing French.[44] On a more historical note, the Grecophobic French chronicler of the Second Crusade, Odo of Deuil, twice spoke snarlingly of Manuel as that Constantinopolitan "idol."[45]

The confrontation between Charlemagne and Hugon has serious political overtones, but this Charlemagne is traveling on a mule and is unarmed except for his pilgrim's staff and sack, so warfare is out of the question. Given that this is a poem about symbolic aggression, not raw *gesta*, joking is appropriate.

It is interesting that what is perhaps the first comic poem in the

French language should so lucidly explore the genesis and ends of joking, indeed, of comedy itself. We are shown a sexually frustrated man who seeks out a rival unknown to him with the purpose either of besting him or of making him an ally. Joking [*gabber*] is the vehicle of his aggressive energy, and exactly one half of the *VC* is devoted to the production and reception of *gabs*. It is not difficult to see sketched out here an etiology of tendentious humor quite similar to Freud's as developed in his *Jokes and Their Relation to the Unconscious*,[46] though with this difference, crucial to a perception of the difference between medieval and modern culture: Freud is concerned with the workings of the inscrutable human unconscious, the *Id;* the medieval text is concerned with the workings of the ineffable mind of God himself, the *Idipsum.* Thus, Hugon, Charlemagne's rival and future ally, will not be converted to this second role through his own laughter at Charlemagne's tendentious *gabs:* rather, thanks to the supernatural powers of the relics, God himself will become Charlemagne's ally and will perform true miracles for his false French heroes in order to compel Hugon into submission.

The sequence of events is as follows. After a banquet where the French eat and drink too well, they are ushered to their lodging with yet more wine to finish off the evening. But Hugon is a rusing Greek, and he plants a spy in the French quarters to overhear them, while he himself sleeps with his wife. Supposedly amongst themselves at last, the French vent their envy and their frustrations:

> E dist li uns al altre: "Veez cum grant beltet!
> Veez, cum gent palais e com forz richetet!
> Pleüst al rei de glorie de sainte majestet
> Carlemaine mi sire les oüst recatet
> U cunquis par ses armes en bataile champel!"
>
> (448–52)

(They said to one another, "Look at the great beauty! Look at the noble palace and the powerful riches! May it please the king of glory and his holy majesty, my lord Charlemagne that he buy them out or conquer them by arms on the battlefield!")

In his impotence, Charlemagne's response is to launch a round of *gabs* ("'Ben dei avant gabber'" [453] ["I will joke first"]). However, Charlemagne's *gab* is to imagine himself armed with his sexual rival's sword in pitched battle, striking an epic swordblow whose superlatives are an overelaboration of Roland's already hyperbolic swordblows at Ronceval, especially the plunge of the phallic sword deep into the bowels of the earth:

"Li reis Hugun li Forz nen at nul bacheler,
De tute sa mainee, qui tant seit fort membré,
Ait vestu dous hoabers e dous heaumes formet,
Si seit sur un destrer curant e sujurnet;
Li reis me prest s'espee al poin d'or adubet:
Si ferrai sur les heaumes u il erent plus chers,
Trancherai les haubercs et les heaumes gemmez,
Le feutre avec la sele del destrer sujurnez;
Li branc ferrai en terre: si jo le lès aler,
Nen ert mès receüz par nul hume charnel
Tresqu'il siet pleine haunste de terre desteret!"

(454–64)

("King Hugon the Strong has no young knights in his whole domaine whom—no matter how strong their members, or whether on a rapid or fresh horse—so long as the king lends me his sword garnished with its golden tip, I will not strike on the helmets where they are most rich, and I will split the hauberks and the gemmed helmets, and the lance-crutch and the saddle of the fresh horse; the sword will bite into the ground and never be recovered by a living man until it is unburied from a depth the length of a lance!")[47]

The end of the French *gabs*, like that of all tendentious humor, is clearly to discharge frustration through laughter at fantasies of potency, sexual and otherwise. Though the *gab* is a way of avoiding direct aggression that the French are in no position to undertake, the presence of Hugon's spy causes the tendentious humor of the Franks to backfire into a life-or-death situation, according to the very same law that Charlemagne had invoked with regard to his joking queen. Each of the twelve peers divulges his own fantasy of power, and the spy responds with the proper degree of astonishment to each. Roland says that he will take Hugon's horn, blow down the whole city, blow off Hugon's beard, and burn up his furs with his breath.

It is Oliver's *gab*, however, that becomes the main pivot of the poem: Oliver boasts that he will take the king's daughter to his bed, and if he cannot prove that he has possessed her one hundred times during the night,

"Demain perde la teste, par covent li otrai!"
"Par Deu, ço dist il eschut, vus recrerez anceis!
Grant huntage avez dit: mais quel sacet li reis,
En trestute sa vie mès ne vus amereit!"

(489–92)

("Tomorrow, I will lose my head: so I swear it!"
"By God," says the spy, "you'll take that back! You've spoken
very shamefully, but the king will know it, and never in his
life will he love you!")

The following morning, when the French must account for their
gabs, Charlemagne now quite properly fears for his life. He holds
a hasty council, and summons the relics to invoke divine protection against Hugon. An angel rebukes them for their *grant folie*,
but promises divine protection. The first *gab* to be tested is of
course Oliver's. Hugon sends him to bed for the night with his
daughter, "si la beisat .iii. feiz" (715) (and he had her three times).
With ninety-seven turns of the screw ahead of him, a spent Oliver
suddenly offers clemency to the young woman along with his
pledge of love to her in exchange for her false testimony in his
behalf the next morning. She accedes, and Hugon is astonished.
When two more French *gabs* are fulfilled by Damne Deu and
Jhesu, Hugon decides he has been bested. He agrees to become
Charlemagne's vassal, and when the two kings appear together
with their crowns, Hugon's "being a little lower" because Charlemagne is (again by mere chance) one foot three inches taller, the
French know that "Ma dame la reïne folie dist et tord: / Mult par
est Karle ber pur demener esforz" (813–14) (Madam the queen
spoke in folly and error; Charlemagne is very great because of his
high deeds). This is the third of three ridiculous coronation
scenes which form the architectonics of this well-wrought story.[48]
As the French embark, Hugon's daughter, who had trusted in
Oliver's covenant and had both perjured and dishonored herself
for him in good faith, asks to follow him back to France:

La fille al rei Hugun i curt tut a bandum:
La u veit Oliver, sil prent par sun gerun:
"A vus ai jo turnet m'amistet e m'amur!
Car m'enportez en France: si m'en irrai od vus!"
—Bele, dist Oliver, m'amur vus abandon:
Jo m'en irrai en France od mun seignur Carlun!"

(852–57)

(King Hugon's daughter runs frantically to Oliver, and seizes hold of his hem: "I gave you my friendship and my love; now take me away to France, and I will accompany you!" "Lovely woman," says Oliver, "I leave my love to you. I will return to France with my lord Charles!")

Few, I imagine, have laughed at this last French trick. Indeed, Oliver's conduct far exceeds the angel's earlier injunction: "Ne gabez ja mès hume, ço cumandet Christus!" (676) (Let man never joke: thus Christ commands!). However, the French not only depart unscathed from Hugon and his grieving daughter, but return triumphantly to St.-Denis, where Charlemagne deposits the nail and the crown on the altar and distributes other relics through his kingdom. When the queen falls contritely at his feet, Charlemagne forgives her, with consummate hypocrisy, "out of love for the sepulchre that he had adored" (870).

The conclusion of this mordant poem leaves us with a perception of Capetian political power as a tissue of illusions whose ultimate guarantors are the privileged relics of St.-Denis, a nail and Christ's crown. They and the texts about them are what make what is false true, what is wrong, right. The closure of this tightly structured poem is more than just artful: it *dis*closes the scandalous arbitrariness of those discourses of church and state in the Latin West that determine gender relationships as well—right to the present day, if we may take the papal encyclical *Redemptoris Mater* of 25 March 1987 as an example. I shall not speculate about the gender of the author of this anonymous poem, but I would find more than credible the proposition that it was a woman. In any case, the *VC* has carried us some distance from the blind conviction of the *Chanson de Roland*, whose hero cries out, on the threshold of death, to God, "*Veire Patene, ki unkes ne mentis*" (2384) (True Father, who never lies). Indeed, in this poem's ironic homage to a lying, rascal God, theology itself has become one of the West's darkest jokes.

NOTES

1. See, for example, Bernard Guenée, *Histoire et culture historique dans l'Occident médiéval* (Paris: Aubier, 1980); Paul Veyne, *Comment on écrit l'histoire* (Paris: Le Seuil, 1978); Jacques Le Goff, *L'imaginaire féodal* (Paris: Gallimard, 1986).

2. For example, see Cesare Segre, "What Bakhtin Left Unsaid: The Case of the Medieval Romance" in *Romance: Generic Transformations from Chrétien de Troyes to Cervantes,* ed. Kevin Brownlee and Marina Scordi-

lis Brownlee (Hanover, N.H.: University Press of New England, 1985),
23–46.

3. For a recent survey of the history of the *trivium*, see *The Seven Liberal Arts in the Middle Ages*, ed. David L. Wagner (Bloomington: Indiana University Press, 1983). On the *trivium* in the twelfth century, see Jean Jolivet, *Arts du langage et théologie chez Abélard* (Paris: Vrin, 1969), and Rolf Köhn, "Schuldbildung und Trivium im lateinischen Hochmittelalter und ihr möglicher praktischer Nutzen," *Schulen und Studium im sozialen Wandel des hohen und späten Mittelalters*, ed. Konstanzer Arbeitskreis für mittelalterliche Geschichte (Sigmaringen: Jan Thorbecke, 1986), 203–84. For a study of the *trivium* and twelfth-century poetics, see Eugene Vance, *From Topos to Tale: Logic and Narrativity in the Middle Ages* (Minneapolis: University of Minnesota Press, 1987).

4. Maria Corti, "Structures idéologiques et structures sémantiques dans les *sermones ad status* du XIIIe siècle," in *Archéologie du signe*, ed. Lucie Brind'Amour and Eugene Vance (Toronto: Pontifical Institute of Medieval Studies, 1982), 144–63.

5. To mention only the two most thorough critics of the poem, Jules Coulet (*Études sur l'ancien poème français du* Voyage de Charlemagne en orient [Montpellier: Coulet, 1907]) considers it "un poème moral du XIIe siècle" (454) whose poet was "un artiste conscient, qui, voulant donner une idée de ce qu'était Jérusalem au temps de Charlemagne, s'est uniquement attaché à lui en présenter une image aussi simplifiée et aussi vraisemblable que possible" (453). Jules Horrent (Le pèlerinage de Charlemagne. *Essai d'explication littéraire avec des notes de critique textuelle* [Paris: Belles Lettres, 1961]), considers the poem "un conte à rire sans sortir des préceptes moraux courants de la conception chrétienne de son époque, conception fervente, naïvement optimiste, libre d'allure familière et qui se permet certaines privautés innocentes avec le divin et le sacré (124). Le poème est comique et non satirique" (125).

6. Erwin Panofsky, *Abbot Suger*, ed. Gerda Panofsky-Soergel (Princeton: Princeton University Press, 1979), 2; see also Sumner McKnight Crosby, *L'abbaye royale de St.-Denis* (Paris: Paul Hartman, 1953), 6–10.

7. *Le voyage de Charlemagne à Jérusalem et à Constantinople*, ed. Paul Aebischer (Geneva: Droz, 1965), v. 8. All references to the text are to this edition, and all translations in this article are my own, unless indicated otherwise.

8. 1. Cor. 11.8–9.

9. Michael Angold, *The Byzantine Empire 1025–1204. A Political History* (London: Longman, 1984), 161–243.

10. Nicolas of Clairvaux, in the name of Bernard, to Manuel Comnenus, letter 168. Bernard of Clairvaux, *Opera omnia*, ed. Migne, *Patrologia latina* 182, col. 673.

11. Suger, *De administratione*, ed. and trans. Erwin Panofsky (Princeton University Press, 1979), 65. After the Second Crusade, hostility toward the Byzantines became shrillest, as we see in Odo of Deuil's account of the crusade, *De profectione Ludovici VII in orientem*, ed. and trans. Virginia Gingerich Berry (New York: Columbia University Press, 1948).

12. Alexandre Leupin, "La compromission (sur *Le voyage de Charle-*

magne à Jérusalem et à Constantinople)," *Romance Notes* 25 (1985): 5.

13. M. T. Clanchy, *From Memory to Written Record. England, 1066–1307* (London: Edward Arnold, 1979). Brian Stock, *The Implications of Literacy. Written Language and Models of Interpretation in the Eleventh and Twelfth Centuries* (Princeton: Princeton University Press, 1983). Eugene Vance "Medievalisms and Models of Textuality," *Diacritics* 15 (1985): 55–94.

14. Eugene Vance, *Mervelous Signals. Poetics and Sign Theory in the Middle Ages* (Lincoln: University of Nebraska Press, 1986), 51–85.

15. Paul Saenger, "Silent Reading: Its Impact on Late Medieval Script and Society," *Viator* 13 (1982): 367–414.

16. Linda Seidel, *Songs of Glory. The Romanesque Façades of Aquitaine* (Chicago: University of Chicago Press, 1981). "I have suggested that the abstract, architectural forms of Romanesque façades in Aquitaine deliberately utilized a group of triumphal and commemorative motifs of Roman imperial invention that had been transformed into a sacred Christian vocabulary in Carolingian times. In their new location, these liturgical shapes monumentalized and publicized the Church-sponsored concept of salvation and triumph through death to which each knight possessed direct access and which he was urged to exercise." (82)

17. Stephen G. Nichols, Jr., *Romanesque Signs. Early Medieval Narrative and Iconography* (New Haven: Yale University Press, 1983): "By the late tenth century . . . we have evidence for a legendary homologization of Charlemagne to the Holy Sepulchre where the figure of Constantine serves at once as the mediating principle and source of the authority now claimed for Charles . . . By the later tenth century, then, to mention the Holy Sepulchre no longer automatically called up the sole image of Constantine, but also, and perhaps even rather, Charlemagne" (73).

18. Timothy Reiss, *The Discourse of Modernism* (Ithaca: Cornell University Press, 1982), 27–30.

19. Robert Folz, *Le souvenir et la légende de Charlemagne dans l'empire germanique médiéval* (Paris: Belles Lettres, 1950).

20. "Descriptio qualiter Karolus magnus clavum et coronam Domini a Constantinopoli Aquisgrani detulerit qualiterque Karolus Calvus hec ad S. Dionysum retulerit," ed. G. Rauschen, *Die Legende Karles des Grossen im XI un XII Jahrhundert, Publikationen der Gesellschaft für rheinische Geschichteskunde* 7 (1890): 45–66, 121–25.

21. The full title is *Liber de constitutione, institutione, consecratione, reliquiis, ornamentis et privilegiis Karrofensis cenobii*. See L.-A. Vigneras, "L'abbaye de Charroux et la légende du pélerinage de Charlemagne," *Romanic Review* 32 (1941): 121–29.

22. Suger, *Ordinatio A.D. MCXL vel MCXLI confirmata*, ed. and trans. Erwin Panofsky, 131.

23. Peter Brown, *The Cult of the Saints. Its Rise and Function in Latin Christianity* (Chicago: University of Chicago Press, 1981), 92–105.

24. Panofsky, *Abbot Suger*, fig.17.

25. Ibid., 21.

26. Ibid., fig. 24. For connections between the monumental arch of Titus in Rome and Romanesque art, see Seidel, 58, 73.

27. Georges Duby, *Hommes et structures du moyen-âge*. (The Hague: Mouton, 1973), chap. 2 and 4.

28. On the overlapping economies of money, gems, and salvation, Suger's conception of the golden crucifix at St. Denis (for which 80 marks of gold were melted) is revealing: "For when I was in difficulty for want of gems . . . (for their scarcity makes them very expensive): then, lo and behold (monks) from three abbeys of two Orders . . . entered the little chamber adjacent to the church and offered us for sale an abundance of gems such as we had not hoped to find in ten years, hyacinths, sapphires, rubies, emeralds, topazes. Their owners had obtained them from Count Thibaut for alms; and he in turn had received them, through the hands of his brother Stephen, King of England, from the treasures of his uncle, the late King Henry, who had amassed them throughout his life in wonderful vessels. We, however, freed from the worry of searching for gems, thanked God and gave four hundred pounds for the lot, though they were worth much more" (*De administratione*, 59).

29. In what follows, I shall not reiterate the lengthy debate about the dating of the *VC*, but shall assume that the poem was composed after 1152 and before 1165. My convictions that the poem indirectly reflects the failure of the second crusade and the divorce of Eleonore from Louis VII have been shared by other critics, especially Theodor Heinermann, "Zeit und Sinn der Karlsreise," *Zeitschrift für romanische Philologie* 56 (1936): 497–562. A useful (though polemical) summary of the different "historical" interpretations of this poem over the past century will be found in Jules Horrent, *Le Pèlerinage de Charlemagne. Essai d'explication littéraire avec des notes de critique textuelle* (Paris: Belles Lettres, 1961).

30. Elizabeth A. R. Brown, "Eleonore of Aquitaine: Parent, Queen, and Duchess" in *Eleonore of Aquitaine. Patron and Politician*, ed. William W. Kibler (Austin: University of Texas Press, 1976), 14.

31. Folz, *Le souvenir*, 206.

32. Brown, 14.

33. William of Newburg, *Historia rerum anglicarum*, 1.20, as mentioned by Mabillon in his notes to Bernard of Clairvaux, *De consideratione*, trans. L'Abbé Charpentier, *Oeuvres complètes de Saint Bernard* (Paris: Vivès, 1866), 2:789. See also Elizabeth Siberry (*Criticisms of Crusading, 1095–1274* [Oxford: Clarendon Press, 1985]), who traces the interpretation of the defeat as the divine judgment of an angry God (77–81).

34. For a study of Eleonore's relationship to Louis's patronage of St.-Denis, see Eleanor S. Greenhill, "Eleanor, Abbot Suger, and Saint-Denis," in *Eleonore of Aquitaine*, ed. Kibler, 81–113.

35. As quoted (without reference) by R. H. C. Davis, *A History of Medieval Europe from Constantine to Saint Louis* (New York: McKay, 1957), 302.

36. Folz, *Le souvenir*, 214.

37. Horrent, *Le Pèlerinage de Charlemagne*, 32–34.

38. Suger, *De consecratione*, 97, 105. See E. Jane Burns, "Portraits of Kingship in the *Pèlerinage de Charlemagne*," *Olifant* 4 (1984–85): 171.

39. For a suggestive classification of these relics and its parallelism with the narrative and iconographical structure of the *VC*, see John L.

Grigsby, "The Relics' Rôle in the *Voyage de Charlemagne*," *Olifant* 9 (1981): 20–34.

40. Grigsby, "The Relics' Rôle," 20–34.

41. Guido Favati, ed. *Il "Voyage de Charlemagne."* Biblioteca degli "Studi mediolatini e volgari" (Bologna: Palmaverde, 1965), 4:51.

42. These are the ideals of the classical city, as expressed, for example in Aristotle's *Politics* and Virgil's *Georgics*. See Michael C. J. Putnam, *Virgil's Poem of the Earth. Studies in the Georgics*, (Princeton: Princeton University Press, 1979). Burns ("Portraits of Kingship") believes that Hugon's Constantinople is "the image of visionary kingship," and that the text leads to "an apotheosis of Charlemagne into a king beyond judgment, a ruler who will judge others from a seat of perfectly balanced power: the throne of the crusading monarch and the plow of the pious pilgrim" (180). Burns does not discuss the *gabs* or Hugon's sending his daughter to bed with Oliver.

43. Vance, *Mervelous Signals*, 15.

44. *Chanson de Roland*, ed. Joseph Bédier (Paris: L'Edition d'Art H. Piazza, 1930) 3267–68. As Michel Zink has shown, Apollo was cast as a supreme idol well into the thirteenth century. See "Apollin," in *La Chanson de geste et le mythe carolingien. Mélanges René Louis* (Mayenne: Floch, 1983), 1:503–9.

45. Odo of Deuil, *De profectione Lodovici*, 71.91.

46. Sigmund Freud, *Jokes and Their Relation to the Unconscious*, trans. James Strachey (New York: Norton, 1963).

47. Cf. *Chanson de Roland*, laisses 93 and 104.

48. Burns, 163. See also Burns's apt criticism (in her note 4) of John D. Niles's attempt ("On the Logic of *Le pèlerinage de Charlemagne*," *Neuphilologische Mitteilungen* 81 [1980]: 208–16) to account for the structure of the *VC* in terms of Proppian folktale morphology.

IV

Authority and History

The Problem of Faux Semblant: Language, History, and Truth in the *Roman de la Rose*

KEVIN BROWNLEE

The *Roman de la Rose* constitutes one of the most important literary meditations on the status of language produced during the French Middle Ages. On the broadest structural level, the work is a "dialogue" between two texts: the ostensibly uncompleted 4,000-line poem of Guillaume de Lorris (dating from the late 1200s) was continued and ultimately "finished" forty years after Guillaume's death by a second poet, Jean de Meun, whose continuation amounted to more than 17,000 lines. On the level of plot, the Lover's quest for the rose involves almost exclusively a series of linguistic encounters with personification characters each of whom embodies a different discursive practice, a different poetics. In a very real sense, the "meaning" of the *Rose* as a whole results from the interactions among these mutually contradictory positions as perceived by the reader. Again, a dialogic model is operative. In addition, Jean's part of the poem consistently foregrounds what might be called the diegetic speech situation: direct discourse becomes the dominant mode as each of the major personification characters engages in an extended speech. Indeed, the very identities of these characters are defined by—are coterminous with—their discourse. Thus, the ways in which discursive interaction takes place within the context of the story line constitute a fundamental part of Jean's overall narrative strategy.

Given both the structure of the *Rose* and its insistent focus on problems of discourse and meaning, two key Bakhtinian concepts are particularly relevant to a global interpretation of the thirteenth-century poem: dialogism and polyphony. While I do not here propose a "Bakhtinian reading" of the *Rose*, my approach owes much to the perspective of Bakhtinian linguistic theory, with its emphasis on speech context and historical context.[1] This perspective is particularly fruitful to my primary present concern: a consideration of the *Rose*'s single most problematic figure, Faux Semblant.

There are a variety of reasons for Faux Semblant's uniquely problematic status.[2] First, his long speech seems to be radically extraneous to the romance's plot and subject matter: it simply does not treat either Amant's quest for the rose or, indeed, the subject of love in general. Further, this same speech involves the radical intrusion of history into Jean de Meun's poetic text: for it explicitly and repeatedly refers to the conflict between the secular masters and the mendicant orders for control of the University of Paris that took place between 1252 and 1259.[3] Finally, Faux Semblant personifies the power of duplicity—both linguistic and behavioral—in ways that problematize both Jean de Meun's use of poetic language and the status of love as poetic subject matter.[4]

Three kinds of questions are at issue then: Faux Semblant's narrative or diegetic status; his historical subtext; and his linguistic-poetic significance. In my view these three aspects of the problem of Faux Semblant are intimately related and must be considered together. The present essay will attempt such a consideration by focusing selectively on several key aspects of the Faux Semblant episode. I will begin by looking briefly at the way in which Faux Semblant is first introduced into the poem and then move on to a more detailed consideration of the dialogic structure of his speech to the God of Love. Next, I will turn to the function, within Faux Semblant's speech, of two "historical" texts which were central to the mid-thirteenth-century struggle at the University of Paris. In all of these cases, I will be particularly interested in the complex relationship between the God of Love and Faux Semblant, who functions, in the words of Sylvia Huot, as Love's "parodic double."[5] At the same time, I will necessarily be treating questions of truth and textual authority in Jean de Meun's *Rose*. Finally, I will consider the broader implications of Jean de Meun's inscription of history into the conjoined *Rose* text at the precise moment when an ostensibly authoritative restatement of courtly codes seems to have effected a definitive exclusion of historical consciousness from the poem. This will involve considering the status of Faux Semblant as the emblem of a necessarily polyphonic—and dangerous—discursive system within the global po-

THE PROBLEM OF FAUX SEMBLANT   255

etic economy of the *Rose* as a whole. In terms of the focus of the present volume, what is at issue in all of these aspects of the problem of Faux Semblant is the way in which Jean de Meun's *Roman de la Rose* both stages and questions its own legitimacy as a poetic *summa*.

Faux Semblant the character appears in the *Rose* for the first time in connection with the reappearance of the God of Love near the midpoint of Jean de Meun's conjoined text. Having ascertained the Lover's current impasse in the quest for the rose, the God of Love summons his barons to lay siege to the Castle of Jealousy. The poet-narrator proceeds to name Amours's barons in sequence, ending with Faux Semblant (10,459)[6] who appears as the consort of Contrainte Astenance (10,458). This double début constitutes a shocking and dangerous surprise on many levels. For the courtly linguistic and behavioral system established by Guillaume de Lorris, and (ostensibly) continued by Jean de Meun, by definition excludes Faux Semblant. This exclusion is, as it were, dramatized in the opening sequence of Guillaume's poem as the figure of Papelardie (407–441)—the only possible avatar of Faux Semblant's language and behavior found in the first *Rose* text—is painted on the *outside* wall of Deduit's garden and is thus explicitly rejected from the idealized courtly world in which Guillaume's love quest takes place. Faux Semblant's first appearance in Jean's *Rose* is thus marked with a series of glosses. First, the poet-narrator intervenes to give his genealogy:

> Baraz engendra Faus Semblant,
> Qui va les cueurs des genz emblant;
> Sa mere ot non Ypocrisie,
> La larronesse, la honie,
> Cete l'alaita e nourri,
> L'ort ypocrite au cueur pourri,
> Qui traïst mainte region
> Par abit de religion.
>
> (10,467–474)

(Fraud engendered False Seeming, who goes around stealing men's hearts. His mother's name is Hypocrisy, the dishonored thief who suckled and nursed the filthy hypocrite with a rotten heart who has betrayed many a region with his religious habit.)

Next, Amours articulates his own (and the reader's) surprise at Faux Semblant's presence in this company:

Quant li deus d'Amours l'a veü,
Tout le cueur en ot esmeü:
"Qu'est ce?" dist il, "ai je songié?
Di, Faus Samblanz, par cui congié
Iés tu venuz en ma presence?"

(10,475–479)

(When the God of Love saw him, his whole heart was dis-
turbed within him. "What is this?" he asked. "Am I dreaming?
Tell me, False Seeming, by whose leave have you come into
my presence?")

In answer to these questions, Astenance Contrainte explains that
she has brought Faux Semblant, who is essential to her existence
and honor. She begs the God of Love not to be displeased at this,
stating that it is important to her that Faux Semblant "be called
a good man and a saint" [preudon e sainz (10,490)].

Having been introduced into the poem in this striking and suggestive manner, the "problem" of Faux Semblant is then deferred,
as the God of Love almost immediately thereafter launches into
his famous speech to his assembled troops (10,495–10,678).[7] It is in
this speech that the poetic genealogy of the *Roman de la Rose* as
a whole is explicitly articulated and authorized. The two authors
are named (for the only time in the work) and a poetics of continuation is set forth. Guillaume de Lorris is to begin and leave
unfinished a work that continues the love service of the Latin
poets Gallus, Catullus, Tibullus, and Ovid. Jean de Meun will continue and complete Guillaume's unfinished poem, expanding its
scope and fulfilling its promise. Guillaume's *Roman de la Rose* is
thus retitled the *Mirouer aus Amoureus* (10,651). It is important to
note that the God of Love has presented a purely literary author-
ization for the conjoined *Rose* text, by his exclusive use of the
closed system of courtly discourse. The Latin elegiac poets are radically "misread" in retrospect: it is as if they constituted, collec-
tively, a courtly poetic tradition in the French vernacular which
Guillaume and Jean renewed and brought to definitive culmination. The first-person lyric mode is not only valorized, it is presented as a kind of ultimate authority. What is most strikingly
excluded from Love's speech is history. The self-authorizing poetics of continuation he articulates is effectively sealed off from
any awareness of—or vulnerability to—contemporary historical
reality. Furthermore, the fact that Love writes history out of the
diegetic presentation of the genesis of the conjoined *Rose* text, at
its structurally significant midpoint, seems to imply authorial

collusion. Amours seems to be speaking for Jean de Meun even as he inscribes the author figure into his own text. For Love ends his speech with a double request of his barons: that Guillaume qua lover-protagonist be helped in his quest to win the rose and that Jean qua poet-narrator be helped in his "quest" to write the romance.

In their affirmative reply, his barons beg the God of Love to give over his anger against Faux Semblant and to consider him as one of their number (their "baronie" [10,925]). It is this request and Amours's immediate agreement that introduce Faux Semblant into the poem directly, speaking in his own voice:

"Par fei," dist Amours, "je l'otrei.
Des or vueil qu'il seit a ma court,
Ça, viegne avant." E cil acourt.

(10,928–930)

("By my faith," said Love, "I grant this permission. From now on I want him to be in my court. Here, come forward." And False Seeming ran forward.)

Faux Semblant's long speech (10,931–12,014), 1,086 lines, is actually an extended dialogue with the God of Love. The dialogic structure of Faux Semblant's self-presentation constitutes an essential and unique part of his identity. None of the other major "discursive" characters in the poem (Raison, Ami, La Vieille, Nature, Genius) involve this kind (or this degree) of dialogue. In a very real sense, Faux Semblant is presented as a "function" of his interlocutor: the God of Love himself. This involves important structural and thematic implications for the poem as a whole, as well as for the figure of Faux Semblant. Two dialogic models are simultaneously at issue: 1) the scholastic examination; and 2) the personal confession. Two discursive modes are thus simultaneously—and paradoxically—operative: 1) the new dialectic mode of late-thirteenth-century philosophical debate, associated with the Dominicans; and 2) the new self-revelatory mode of late-thirteenth-century spiritual narrative, associated with the Franciscans.

The dialogue between Love and Faux Semblant involves a series of seven questions posed by Love, who thus plays the role of examiner/confessor. Faux Semblant's seven answers constitute, on the one hand, a penetrating and polemical discussion of certain doctrinal matters in the context of contemporary practices and abuses: in particular, poverty, abstinence, and mendicancy. On the other hand, Faux Semblant's answers involve an extended self-

definition as character and as language. As character, Faux Semblant is a kind of archetypal religious hypocrite whose disguise is
the role of a mendicant friar. As language, he embodies a radical
detachment of sign from referent, a systematically duplicitous discourse which is ungrounded in, unguaranteed by any extralinguistic or transcendent "truth." The dialogic structure of the sequence
is such that Love's identity is also modified and expanded, most
especially in terms of discursive possibilities. In the context of
Jean's *Rose* as a whole, this means a significant widening of the
scope of poetic discourse as such.

Let us now turn to a brief, schematic consideration of the dialogue between Love and False Seeming in structural and thematic
terms.[8] As will be seen, an overall pattern of shifting is involved
in the relations between questions and answers, as well as in the
identities of the two interlocutors. This is because the status of
the "truth" that emerges from the dialogue is a function of the
evolving speech situation, which is dramatized as such. In linguistic terms, there is a continual shifting of appropriateness conditions; the cooperative principle is repeatedly redefined in order
for the dialogue to continue.[9]

Before the dialogue proper begins, however, there is a brief preliminary passage in which Love articulates the essence of Faux
Semblant's identity, which is thus presented as a given, known in
advance of the systematic interrogation that is to follow:

"Senz faille, tu iés maus traïtres
E lierres trop desmesurez;
Cent mile feiz t'iés parjurez."

(10,940–942)

("Without fail, you are a wicked traitor and an unrestrained
thief. You have perjured yourself a hundred thousand times.")

Love's first set of questions (10,943–951) is posed on behalf of the
assembled host and involves the issue of semiotic recognition: by
what signs can Faux Semblant be known and in what places can
he be found? Faux Semblant's answer (10,952–983) involves a systematic evasion: He has "mansions diverses" (10,952) which he cannot reveal in detail because of his fear of his companions, who
want their whereabouts to be kept a secret.

Love's second set of questions (10,984–998) repeats and elaborates the first set, stressing that Faux Semblant must now tell the
truth because he is one of Love's barons. The emphasis is on revelation, on the uncovering of what is normally hidden. Love de-

mands that Faux Semblant name his various "mansions" and that he explain his mode of life. Faux Semblant's reply (10,999–11,082) introduces the motif of clothing as disguise in a context in which seeming and being are radically separated. Clothing as sign is presented as fundamentally unreliable in a religious context. Thus, Faux Semblant explains that he is lodged among the "'faus religieus / Des felons, des malicieus, / Qui l'abit en veulent vestir / E ne veulent leur cuers mestir'" (11,023–026) ("the false religious, the malicious criminals who want to wear the habit but do not want to subdue their hearts"). In terms of his "service," Faux Semblant declares that "'nule rien fors barat n'i chaz'" (11,067) ("I pursue nothing except Fraud"). Both his clothes and his words deceive qua signs.

Love's third question (11,083–090) involves the reverse side of the sign/referent dichotomy in the context of religious clothing. Love asks if one can find true religious faith in secular clothes. Faux Semblant's reply (11,091–222) begins by affirming that clothing as sign is not reliable in this direction either. He then goes on to characterize his own identity as an infinitely expandable series of disguises which involves the effective nullification of social, age, and gender distinctions, through the manipulation both of language (11,194–195) and of clothing, most especially in the context of religion. Finally comes a somewhat paradoxical self-revelation:

"En tele guise
Come il me plaist je me desguise.
Mout est en mei muez li vers,
Mout sont li fait aus diz divers."

(11,219–222)

("I disguise myself in whatever way pleases me. I'm not what I seem to be; my acts are very different from my words.")

Love's fourth question (11,223–237) is an elaboration: "'Di nous plus especiaument / Coment tu serz desleiaument'" (11,227–229) ("tell us more especially in what way you serve disloyally"). Appearance and reality, word and deed, sign and referent are contrasted in three related ways. When Love tells Faux Semblant that he *seems* to be a "sainz ermites" (11,231), the reply is: "'mais je sui ypocrites'" (11,232). When Love says that Faux Semblant preaches "astenance" (11,232), the latter's acknowledgement is combined with an affirmation of gluttony. Finally, when Love states that Faux Semblant preaches poverty (11,237), the response is a long disquisition on the meaning of poverty and the status of begging that constitutes Faux Semblant's fourth extended answer to Love's systematic interrogation (II,238–406). Having once again affirmed the disjunction between sign and referent in terms of his purely external devotion to poverty, Faux Semblant launches into an extended discussion of the Bible's treatment of the subject of mendicancy. The primary focus is on the Gospels and St. Paul (Luke 18:20; I Cor. II:29; 2 Cor. 8:9, and I Thess. 4:II–12), as Faux Semblant interprets the New Testament to mean that begging was systematically prohibited for Christ and the Apostles. It is important to note that here Faux Semblant speaks the "truth." His Biblical interpretations are valid.

Love's fifth set of questions (II,407–413) involves an important elaboration of these theological and exegetical concerns, as he asks when a sincere religious vocation can legitimately include begging. Significantly, Love's questions here presuppose a truthful interlocutor, and Faux Semblant's fifth answer (II,414–524) is in accord with this presupposition. The truthfulness of Faux Semblant's discourse at this juncture is guaranteed by the first *explicit* inscription of history into the dialogue. He introduces his long list of the special cases in which mendicancy is permissible by recalling the extratextual, historical moment during which the debate on this subject between the secular masters and the mendicant orders was raging in Paris (II,425–430). The special cases themselves all come from a treatise written by the key spokesman for the secular masters at the height of the debate: the *Responsiones*[10] of Guillaume de Saint-Amour, which in turn had cited the authority of St. Augustine's *De Opere monachorum*. In a kind of inscribed *translatio* of (legitimate) Christian authority, Faux Semblant explicitly identifies Guillaume de Saint-Amour as *his* authority (II,488). What follows is an encapsulated biography of Guillaume (II,489–508), who is presented as a martyr to the truth. In a significant shift of perspective, Faux Semblant himself bears witness to this truth:

> "Car je ne m'en tairaie mie
> Se j'en devaie perdre vie,
> Ou estre mis contre dreiture,
> Come Sainz Pos, en chartre ocure,
> Ou estre baniz dou reiaume
> A tort, con fu maistre Guillaume
> De Saint Amour, qu'Ypocrisie
> Fist esseillier par grant envie."

(II,501–508)

("For I would not keep silent about it if I had to lose my life, or, like Saint Paul, be put unjustly into a dark prison, or be wrong-fully banished from the kingdom, as was Master William of Saint-Amour, whom Hypocrisy, out of her great envy caused to be exiled.")

The degree to which Faux Semblant's perspective has shifted is further emphasized by the fact that the personified Hypocrisy whom he condemns here had been presented as his own mother when Faux Semblant first appeared in the text (10,468–470).

Faux Semblant only shifts back into character when speaking (11,513ff.) of Guillaume de Saint-Amour's single most important book, the *Tractatus brevis de Periculis novissimorum tempo-rum*,[11] which he describes as a threat to his own way of life as a hypocritical mendicant.

There is a corresponding shift in Amours's perspective as inter-locutor when he poses his sixth set of questions, for he reacts only to what Faux Semblant has turned back into, expressing shock at the latter's "'granz desleiautez apertes'" (11,527) ("great and open dis-loyalty") and asking: "'Don ne crains tu pas Deu?'" (11,528) ("Don't you fear God then?"). Faux Semblant's sixth answer (11,528–618) begins with an extensive self-revelation in which his activities as deceiver and hypocrite are described in detail: "'Mais je, qui vest ma simple robe / Lobant lobez e lobeeurs, / Robe robez e robeeurs'" (11,550–552) ("But I wearing my simple robe, duping both the duped and the dupers, rob both the robbed and the robbers"). Special em-phasis is placed on his exploitation of his status as a confessor. Indeed, this entire passage involves Faux Semblant articulating in the first-person as a self-description a set of charges made against hypocritical mendicants in the *De Periculis*. Next, Faux Semblant again shifts perspective, as he turns to a discussion of how these deceiving criminals [*felons* (11,599)] can be recognized [*aperceivre* (11,599)]. What is at issue is once again the status of signs and the question of how to "read," how to interpret them correctly. It is thus highly significant that Faux Semblant's response is to turn to the one text whose signs never deceive: the Bible. For he launches into a detailed paraphrase and gloss of Matt. 23: 2–4, the *locus clas-sicus* on the subject of hypocrisy.

It is in the midst of this sequence of Biblical exegesis that Love asks his seventh and final question (11,619), a brief and specific query about the meaning of Matt. 23:4. At this point in their dia-logue, Love plays the role of student to Faux Semblant as master exegete. Once again, the shifting appropriateness conditions opera-

tive in this sequence of the *Rose*'s diegetic speech situation implicitly present Faux Semblant as a locus of truthful discourse. Faux
Semblant's seventh answer (11,619–976) begins by confirming this
status, as he finishes the gloss on Matt. 23:4–8 with exemplary
Christian exegetical insight. What follows is another abrupt shift
in perspective, as Faux Semblant resumes his "mendacious identity" in order to make further disclosures concerning his deceitful
activities as a religious hypocrite whose words and dress belie his
true nature. It is at this point that Faux Semblant returns once
again to history (and to "truth"), in a long disquisition (11,791–896)
on the episode of the *Evangile Pardurable*,[12] which from the
moment of its appearance in 1254 played a key role in the struggle
between the mendicant orders and the secular masters of the University of Paris. Faux Semblant's narrative of the debate over this
controversial book is basically presented from the perspective of
the secular masters, and the same is true of his extended interpretation of the work, including a detailed gloss of a key passage.
Indeed, Faux Semblant speaks almost exclusively here as an avatar of Guillaume de Saint-Amour. His perspective changes once
again, however, as he returns to the topic of self-description
(11,897–968). His systematic deployment of deceptive discourse is
again detailed in a variety of specific contexts, including that of
his long-term alliance with the Beguines. It is important to note
that repeated shifts in perspective occur quite frequently throughout this section, as Faux Semblant alternately praises and condemns the code of hypocrisy, adopting in turn the viewpoint of
Antichrist and the viewpoint of God. In light of this kind of
repeated interpretative instability that is built into Faux Semblant's discourse at every level, it is fitting that he conclude by
focusing explicitly on the truth status of his discourse in the context of this specific speech situation:

> "Mais a vous n'ose je mentir;
> Mais se je peüsse sentir
> Que vous ne l'aperceüssiez,
> La mençonge ou poing eüssiez;
> Certainement je vous boulasse,
> Ja pour pechié ne le laissasse;
> Si vous pourrai je bien faillir
> S'ous m'en deviez mal baillir."

(11,969–976)

("But to you I dare not lie. However, if I could feel that you
would not recognize it, you would have a lie in hand. Cer-

tainly I would have tricked you, and I would never have held
back on account of any sin. And I will indeed betray you even
if you treat me badly for it.")

We end then with an articulation of the inherently ambiguous
nature of Faux Semblant's discursive practice. There is by definition no external guarantee for the truth of what he says. And the
problem of credibility is placed entirely with the receiver of his
discourse.

The problematic is, as it were, dramatized in the scene immediately following, as the God of Love "officially" takes Faux Semblant into his service, now that their interrogation cum dialogue
is over. In response to Love's question: "'Me tendras tu ma couve-
nance?'" (11,985) ("Will you keep your agreement with me?"), Faux
Semblant gives an emphatically affirmative answer: "'Oïl, jou
vous jur e fiance; / N'onc n'orent sergenz plus leiaus / Vostre peres
ne vostre aiaus'" (11,986–988) ("Yes, I swear it and promise you;
neither your father nor your forefathers ever had more loyal ser-
geants"). But because of the nature of Faux Semblant as speaking
subject, all of his words are by definition untrustworthy. Love is
thus obliged to question the validity of the very words he most
desires to hear. Faux Semblant's response is significant:

"—Metez vous en en aventure,
Car, se pleges en requerez,
Ja plus asseür n'en serez,
Non veir se j'en baillaie ostages,
Ou letres, ou tesmoinz, ou gages."

(11,990–994)

("Take your chances on it, for if you demand pledges, you will
never be more sure, in fact, not even if I gave hostages, letters,
witnesses, or security.")

What Faux Semblant is saying, then, is that no extralinguistic
guarantee is possible for his discourse. Yet this is not tantamount
to characterizing it as consistently mendacious. Rather, Faux
Semblant's discursive practice is fundamentally and radically
ambiguous with regard to "truth." For if on the one hand it is self-
defined as a string of empty signifiers detached from any referent,
it is also capable of articulating historical and religious truths of
the greatest import, as we have already seen. Love is thus obliged
to accept Faux Semblant into his army on the only terms possible:
"'Or seit, je t'en crei senz plevir'" (12,010) ("So be it, I believe you
without guarantee").

By this point in the text, the figure of Faux Semblant has emerged as a kind of emblem of multivoicedness. At the most obvious level, this ostensibly unified speaking subject involves a series of conflicting voices which are repeatedly played off against each other: the voice of the hypocritical friar (linked to the generic discourse of the *fabliau* and the *Roman de Renart*); the voice of the Biblical exegete and moralizing social critic (linked to the persona of Guillaume de Saint-Amour and—to a somewhat lesser degree—to the anticourtly subgenre of *trouvère* political satire, as exemplified by Rutebeuf); and the voice of the radical Joachite prophet (linked most specifically to the *Evangile Pardurable*). Furthermore, Faux Semblant's polyphonic discourse cannot be effectively interpreted (or judged) from an internal point of view. This is perhaps most obvious with regard to the complex question of the "truth content" of what Faux Semblant says as related to the constantly shifting voices and perspectives that constitute his speech. In terms of discourse analysis, the "truth" of Faux Semblant's language is a function of context, of the (diegetic) speech situation, which is itself also changing constantly. For the relationship between Faux Semblant and Amours as interlocutors is profoundly dialogic. Multiple perspectives are built into both speaker and addressee, in such a way as to give an inescapable "doubleness" to their individual utterances as these participate in a temporally evolving speech situation that alone confers meaning upon their discourse. In order to account for this kind of complexity in a literary context that foregrounds and thematizes the speech situation as such, the relatively static model of the "classic" illocutionary act is, I would suggest, inadequate.[13] In the context of medieval France's most complex literary treatment of the dialogic status of language, a more powerful interpretive tool is provided by Oswald Ducrot's revisionist "theatrical" model of a fundamentally "polyphonic" speech act.[14]

As we have seen, both the narrative context in which Faux Semblant appears and the dialogic structure of his extended speech link him to the God of Love. In addition, a number of suggestive parallels are established between the discourse of Amours and that of Faux Semblant in terms of the self-presentation and self-authorization of Jean de Meun's conjoined *Rose* text.

Like Amours's speech to his barons, Faux Semblant's speech deals at length with the questions of authority of writing and the process of literary continuation. This is accomplished in large part through Faux Semblant's discussion of two books: one by a Guillaume; the other associated with a Jean. Both of these books,

as we have already noted, played key roles in the historical struggle between the secular masters and the mendicant orders for control of the University of Paris in the mid-1250s.

The first to be mentioned by Faux Semblant was in fact the second to be published: Guillaume de Saint-Amour's *De Periculis*,
which appeared in Paris in 1255. It contained the single most sustained, learned, and powerful attack against the Dominicans and
the Franciscans to have appeared in the entire course of the conflict. A particularly important part of this attack involved Guillaume de Saint-Amour's response to a book published in Paris
during the preceding year (1254) and entitled the *Evangelium Eternum sive Spiritus Sancti*. This was the work of a Franciscan "dis-
ciple" of Joachim de Fiore named Gerard de Borgo San Donnino,
though the Friars' enemies ascribed it to Jean de Parme, the General of the Franciscan Order, thus ultimately causing his downfall. The *Evangelium Eternum* consisted of a *Liber Introductorius*
by Gerard and a glossed version of Joachim de Fiore's *Liber Concor-
die*. The core of Gerard's message was that with the imminent
advent of Joachim's Age of the Holy Ghost (or third *status*) the
Old and New Testaments were fulfilled, displaced and succeeded
by the Eternal Gospel of the Holy Ghost contained in the works
of Joachim.[15] This is the second book mentioned by Faux Semblant, who gives its title as the *Evangile Pardurable* (11,802).

These two books may be said to represent the two extremes of
the opposing sides in the conflict. Historically speaking, the dialogic confrontation between the books (as contained in the *De Periculis*) represented the conflict itself. Within the context of Faux
Semblant's speech, on the other hand, the conflict is figured, both
in the text and in history, as a confrontation between these two
books. At the same time, Faux Semblant's treatment of each of
the books individually involves a commentary on and a reworking of the God of Love's presentation of the *Roman de la Rose* in
his speech to his troops, in terms of an authoritative poetics of
continuation. Important questions of textual and discursive authority are at issue here. Their implications can best be considered by examining Faux Semblant's treatment of each of the two
books in sequence.

Guillaume de Saint-Amour's *De Periculis* is by far the most
important subtext for Faux Semblant's speech. An extraordinarily
high percentage of the subjects treated, the arguments employed,
the perspectives adopted and the very words used by Faux Semblant are visibly based on the text of Guillaume de Saint-
Amour.[16] This is clear long before Faux Semblant first cites "cil de

Saint Amour" explicitly as an authority (II,488). By the time "maistre Guillaume"'s (II,506) "nouvel livre" (II,513) is mentioned, it is clear that an important change has already been effected in Jean de Meun's intertextual strategy. In a very literal sense, Guillaume de Saint-Amour has replaced Guillaume de Lorris in the Faux Semblant episode. It is this *new* Guillaume who now provides the model text for Jean de Meun's simultaneous rewriting and continuation. This is the first time in the 6,000 lines of Jean's poem up to this point that Guillaume de Lorris ceases to function as privileged model and point of departure. All the major characters and episodes in Jean's continuation until now have been generated out of elements in Guillaume's kernel text by a systematic use of *amplificatio*.[17]

The implications of this substitution, or displacement, are quite profound. For a new, supplementary, point of departure is being suggested for Jean's poetic enterprise. Guillaume de Lorris's literary, courtly romance text is here displaced by a work of religious and political polemic situated in contemporary history. The initial set of *romance* oppositions with which Guillaume de Lorris's text had begun — appearance/reality, lies/truth — is here redeployed in a historico-religious context. The result of this recontextualization is twofold. On the one hand, there is an increase in the seriousness, the prestige, the importance of the *Rose*'s subject matter. On the other hand, there is a dramatic emphasis on the *dangers* of treating this subject matter in terms of, by means of, poetic discourse.

Both of these matters are further elaborated in Faux Semblant's treatment of the *Evangile Pardurable* (II,791–896). This work is presented as involving a negative, a diabolical version of the poetics of continuation. For what it claims to continue, to complete, and to fulfill is nothing less than the Gospels:

"La trouvast par granz mespreisons
Maintes teles comparaisons:
Autant com par sa grant valeur,
Seit de clarté, seit de chaleur,
Seurmonte li solauz la lune,
Qui trop est plus trouble e plus brune,
E li noiaus des noiz la coque,
Ne cuidiez pas que je vous moque,
Seur m'ame le vous di senz guile,
Tant seurmonte cete evangile

Ceus que li quatre evangelistre
Jesu Crit firent a leur titre."

(II,811–822)

("In this book [were] found many such grossly erroneous com-
parisons as these: as much as by its great worth, in brightness
or in heat, the sun surpasses the moon, which is much more
dark and obscure, as much as the nut surpasses its shell —
don't think I am making fun of you; on my soul I am speaking
to you without guile — so much this gospel surpasses those
which the four evangelists of Jesus Christ wrote under their
names.")

The *Evangile Pardurable* thus appears as a monstrously distorted
image of the God of Love's presentation of the *Rose*, involving the
ultimate dangers posed by human language ungrounded in "truth":
1) blasphemy; and 2) linguistic idolatry. To the degree that the
parallels between Love's *Rose* and Faux Semblant's *Evangile Pardurable* are functional, the validity of poetic discourse as such is
called into question.

In addition, there is an important historical dimension to Faux
Semblant's presentation of the *Evangile Pardurable*, involving a
second negative version of continuation, and based on the following citation: "Tant com Pierres ait seignourie / Ne peut Johans
montrer sa force" (II,856–57) (As long as Peter has lordship, John
cannot show his power). Faux Semblant's gloss elucidates the historical implications of this claim:

"Or vous ai dit dou sen l'escorce,
Qui fait l'entencion repondre,
Or en vueil la moële espondre:
Par Pierre veaut le pape entendre
E les clers seculers comprendre,
Qui la lei Jesu Crit tendront
E garderont e defendront
Contre touz empeescheeurs;
Par Johan, les preescheeurs,
Qui diront qu'il n'est lei tenable
Fors l'Evangile pardurable,
Que le Sainz Esperiz enveie
Pour metre genz en bone veie.
Par la force Johan entent
La grace don se va vantant

Qu'il veaut pecheeurs convertir
Pour les faire a Deu revertir."

(II,858–74)

("Now that I have told you the rind of the sense, which hides
the intent, I want to explain its marrow. By Peter, it wants to
signify the Pope and to include the secular clergy, who will
keep, guard and defend the law of Jesus Christ against all
those who would impede it. By John, it means the preachers,
who will say that there is no tenable law except the Eternal
Gospel, sent by the Holy Spirit to put people on the good way.
By the force of John is meant the favor by which he goes
around vaunting himself because he wants to convert sinners
to make them turn back to God.")

The *Evangile Pardurable* thus predicts that the present historical
epoch (that of Peter) will be succeeded and fulfilled by a second
and superior one (that of John). This historical model of succession (based on Joachim de Fiore's concept of the third *status*) is
explicitly identified as a failure:

"Lors comanderont a ocierre
Tous ceus de la partie Pierre,
Mais ja n'avront poeir d'abatre,
Ne pour ocierre ne pour batre,
La lei Pierre, ce vous plevis,
Qu'il n'en demeurt assez de vis,
Qui toujourz si la maintendront
Que tuit en la fin i vendront,
E sera la lei confondue
Qui par Johan est entendue."

(II,881–90)

("Those of John's party will order all those of Peter's party to
be killed; but they will never have the power to overcome the
law of Peter, either to kill or to punish; I guarantee you this,
since there will not be enough of them remaining alive to
maintain it forever so that in the end everybody will come to
it; and the law that is signified by John will be overthrown.")

The *Evangile Pardurable* thus embodies a double linguistic failure: as religious prophecy and as historical prophecy. In both
cases, an unsuccessful and diabolical succession is at issue, significantly associated with the name *Jehan*. On a variety of levels,
then, the *Evangile Pardurable* is presented as an inscribed, nega-

tive version in miniature of Jean de Meun's book. As such, it functions in tandem with Faux Semblant's presentation of the *De Periculis* simultaneously to expand the scope of the *Rose* as literary-poetic enterprise and to problematize the very terms of this enterprise, both structural and linguistic. This expansion and this problematization both involve Faux Semblant (as character and as discourse) being played off against the God of Love as a kind of negative double. Thus, Love's structural model of continuation for the *Rose* appears as potentially dangerous, when seen from Faux Semblant's new "historical" perspective. And Love's discourses, both amatory and poetic, appear as inescapably duplicitous when viewed in tandem with Faux Semblant's linguistic practice. Finally, the textual self-presentation of Jean de Meun's new literary enterprise, written into the central sequence of the conjoined *Rose*, results in large measure from the dialogic interaction between the God of Love and Faux Semblant, between the discourse of courtly poetry and the discourse of history.

NOTES

1. See the lucid presentation by Tzvetan Todorov in his *Mikhail Bakhtin: The Dialogical Principle*, trans. Wlad Godzich (Minneapolis: University of Minnesota Press, 1984), esp. chap. 4, "Theory of the Utterance," 41–59. See also M. M. Bakhtin, "Discourse in the Novel," in his *The Dialogic Imagination: Four Essays*, trans. Caryl Emerson and Michael Holquist (Austin: University of Texas Press, 1981), 259–422; and David Carroll, "The Alterity of Discourse: Form, History, and the Question of the Political in M. M. Bakhtin," *Diacritics* 13, 2 (1983): 65–83. It should be added that Bakhtin's own views of literary history led him in large part to neglect medieval literature, which in fact provides a particularly fertile field for interpretive analysis from a Bakhtinian perspective. An excellent recent example is Cesare Segre, "What Bakhtin Left Unsaid: The Case for the Medieval Romance," in *Romance: Generic Transformation From Chrétien de Troyes to Cervantes*, ed. K. Brownlee and M. S. Brownlee (Hanover, N.H.: University Press of New England, 1985), 23–46.

2. For important recent treatments see Richard Emmerson and Ronald B. Herzman, "The Apocalyptic Age of Hypocrisy: Faus Samblant and Amant in the *Roman de la Rose*," *Speculum* 62, 3 (1987): 612–34; Pierre-Yves Badel, *Le "Roman de la Rose" au XIVe siècle: Etude de la réception de l'oeuvre* (Geneva: Droz, 1980), 52–53 and 207–12; Jean-Charles Payen, *La Rose et l'utopie* (Paris: Éditions sociales, 1976), 79–104; Jean Batany, *Approches du "Roman de la Rose"* (Paris: Bordas, 1973), 97–110; Daniel Poirion, *Le "Roman de la Rose"* (Paris: Hatier, 1973), 167–73. See also William W. Ryding's suggestively entitled "Faus Semblant: Hero or Hypocrite?" in *Romanic Review* 60 (1969): 163–67; and Alan M. F. Gunn, *The Mirror of*

Love: A Reinterpretation of "The Romance of the Rose" (Lubbock: Texas Tech Press, 1952), 158–64.

3. For a comprehensive study of these events see M.-M. Dufeil, *Guillaume de Saint-Amour et la polémique universitaire parisienne, 1250–1259* (Paris: Picard, 1972). See also Daniel Poirion, "Jean de Meun et la Querelle de l'Université de Paris: Du libelle au livre" in *Traditions Polémiques. Cahiers V.L. Saulnier 2* (Paris: École Normale Supérieure de Jeunes Filles, 1984), 15–19.

4. Cf. Armand Strubel's suggestive remark that Faux Semblant "incarne la limite de l'écriture allégorique" in *La Rose, Renart et le Graal: La littérature allégorique en France au XIIIe siècle* (Paris: Champion, 1989), 221.

5. In "Vignettes marginales comme glose marginale dans un manuscrit du *Roman de la Rose* au quatorzième siècle (B.N. fr. 25526)," in *La Présentation du livre,* ed. E. Baumgartner and N. Boulestreau (Paris: Centre de Recherche du Département de Français de Paris X-Nanterre, 1987), 173–86.

6. All citations from Guillaume de Lorris and Jean de Meun, *Roman de la Rose,* ed. Ernest Langlois, 5 vols. (Paris: Firmin Didot, 1914–24). Translations are from Charles Dahlberg, *The Romance of the Rose* (Princeton: Princeton University Press, 1971).

7. See Kevin Brownlee, "Jean de Meun and the Limits of Romance: Genius as Rewriter of Guillaume de Lorris" in K. Brownlee and M. S. Brownlee, eds., *Romance,* 114–19; and Karl D. Uitti, "From *Clerc* to *Poète:* The Relevance of the *Romance of the Rose* to Machaut's World" in *Machaut's World: Science and Art in the Fourteenth Century,* Annals of the New York Academy of Sciences 314 (1978): 212–15.

8. Cf. Lee Patterson's suggestive structural analysis of Faux Semblant's speech as embodying the paradox of the "truthful hypocrite," in his important article "'For the Wyves love of Bathe': Feminine Rhetoric and Poetic Resolution in the *Roman de la Rose* and the *Canterbury Tales,*" *Speculum* 58 (1983): 672.

9. For an extremely useful treatment of appropriateness conditions and of the cooperative principle in the context of literary analysis see Mary Louise Pratt, *Toward a Speech Act Theory of Literary Discourse* (Bloomington: Indiana University Press, 1977), 81–91, 125–32, and 214–23. See also H. Paul Grice, "Logic and Conversation" in *Syntax and Semantics III: Speech Acts,* ed. Peter Cole and Jerry L. Morgan (New York: Academic Press, 1975), 41–58.

10. See Edmond Faral, ed., "Les *Responsiones* de Guillaume de Saint-Amour," *Archives d'Histoire doctrinale et littéraire du moyen âge* 18 (1950–51): 337–94.

11. Ed. Vlastimil Kybal, in *Regulae Veteris et Novi Testamenti,* ed. Matthias de Ianov, 3 vols. (Innsbruck, 1908–11), 3:252–314.

12. See P. Heinrich Denifle, "Das *Evangelium aeternum* und die Commission zu Angani," *Archiv für Literatur und Kirchengeschichte des Mittelalters* 1 (1885): 49–142.

13. See J. L. Austin, *How to Do Things with Words* (Cambridge: Harvard University Press, 1962), 98–131; John R. Searle, *Speech Acts: An Essay in the Philosophy of Language* (New York: Cambridge University Press, 1969),

22–25 and 54–71; John R. Searle, "Classification of Illocutionary Acts," *Language in Society* 5 (1976): 1–23.

14. As described in "Esquisse d'une théorie polyphonique de l'énonciation" in *Le Dire et le dit* (Paris: Minuit, 1984), 171–233.

15. See Marjorie Reeves, *The Influence of Prophecy in the Later Middle Ages. A Study of Joachimism* (Oxford: Clarendon Press, 1969), 63–64.

16. For a detailed treatment of this close textual relationship see the Langlois edition, 3: 316–25 and Guillaume de Lorris and Jean de Meun, *Le Roman de la Rose,* ed. Félix Lecoy, 3 vols. (Paris: Editions Honoré Champion, 1965–70), 2: 280–290.

17. Manuscript evidence offers an interesting commentary on Jean's substitution of Guillaume de Saint-Amour for Guillaume de Lorris as primary subtext in the Faux Semblant episode. Several thirteenth-, fourteenth-, and fifteenth-century rubricators confuse the two Guillaumes, some going so far as to attribute to Saint-Amour the authorship of the first part of the *Rose* (see MSS B.N. f.fr. 1569 and 804, as well as Bibl. Mazarine 3873), a phenomenon tellingly discussed by Badel (208–10). The name "Saint-Amour," of course, is particularly appropriate for this kind of confusion and, indeed, from this point of view might seem to be an invention, a fiction of Jean de Meun. It is entirely in keeping with Jean's provocative strategy of juxtaposing literary with historical discourses that Saint-Amour is doubly anchored in extratextual "reality," having a double historical referent: both Guillaume the man and the village (in the Jura) where he was born and died.

Allegory and the Textual Body: Female Authority in Christine de Pizan's *Livre de la Cité des Dames*

MAUREEN QUILLIGAN

In their massive study of the woman writer and the nineteenth-century literary imagination, Sandra Gilbert and Susan Gubar not only ask such impish questions as—If a pen is a metaphorical penis, with what metaphorical organ does a woman write?—they also revise Harold Bloom's influential thesis about the profound anxiety there is in all literary tradition and argue that for a woman writer the question is not so much an anxiety of influence as an "anxiety of authorship." For a woman to pick up a pen and write is laden, in the nineteenth century, with fears of madness and impropriety.[1]

To cite work by twentieth-century literary critics about nineteenth-century literature as a way of introducing the practice of a medieval woman's radical revision of her male precursors may be allowed its own legitimacy—beyond the hint it provides that the question of authorial gender maintains a certain intractable (if metaphorical) physicality throughout all literary periods. Post-structuralist French feminist theorists, such as Hélène Cixous and Luce Irigaray, who ground their definition of "l'écriture féminine" in the female body, as well as the controversy such an "essentialist" position has caused in Anglo-American feminist theory, may offer some more theoretically coherent terms in which to address the problem of the body in Christine de Pizan's allegory.[2] However, Gilbert and Gubar's arguments about female authority in the nineteenth century, when novels by female authors became an accepted part of the popular and therefore "literary" canon, also usefully remind us that the legitimacy of any period in literary history depends upon the formation of a body of works deemed characteristic for that period. To argue for the insertion of a previously marginalized text into the canon necessarily destabilizes that canon and calls into question the means by which it was previously fixed.

If Christine de Pizan is herself a canonical fifteenth-century French author because she remains taught in our curricula as a lyric poet, her prose is less well known. Although female, she was not completely marginalized by her society; rather she worked at the center of cultural production in her period, a privileged member of the French court.[3] However, the first pro-woman polemic, the first female-authored history of women, the *Livre de la Cité des Dames* (1405), is not itself a canonical text, although it has been taken up as a possible starting point for a whole new canon of female writing.[4] As a marginal female author, Christine takes a master discourse and makes it speak of her own concerns, explicitly commenting on her own process of rewriting her tradition. This is, of course, no more or less than the practice of medieval poetics in general, with its assumptions about the necessity for the citation of *auctores*. Yet we cannot understand what Christine is doing without making some attempt to discover what her culture assumed her *auctores* were doing. By grounding our reading of Christine's revision of her precursors in the materiality of their manuscript texts—that is, by also looking at some illuminations—we may be in a better position to assess just how idiosyncratic Christine's rewrite of a masculine tradition of textuality may be.[5]

The text first mentioned in the reading scene generic to medieval allegorical narrative, with which Christine appropriately opens her *Cité des Dames*, is Mathéolus, a virulently misogynist tract. But Christine's real target, as she makes absolutely explicit, is Jean de Meun's far more authoritative *Roman de la Rose*.[6] In the "Querelle de la Rose," Christine had objected not only to Jean's misogyny, but to his vulgar language; in telling the story of Saturn's castration by Jupiter, Jean had made his Lady Reason use the slang term for testicles, "coilles."[7] This moment was a favorite one for illuminations of manuscripts of the *Rose*, and the illuminations are usually as explicit as Jean's very explicit language (Fig. 1).[8] Christine's point was that the vulgar term for such a human body part derogated the sacred function of sexuality and was, furthermore, most inappropriate to a character such as Lady Reason.

Christine's critique of Jean has drawn much criticism over the

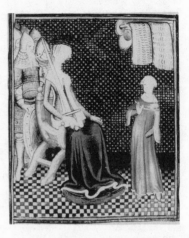

1   Jupiter castrating Saturn.

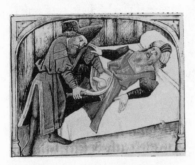

2   Semiramis and Ninus.

3   Reason directing Christine's
removal of misogynist opinion
from the "field of letters."

4   Cornificia in her study.

SOURCES

1. *Le Roman de la Rose* (Oxford: Bodleian, Ms. Douce 195, f. 76v). 2. *Des Cleres et Nobles Femmes* (London: British Library, Ms. Royal 20 C V, f. 8v). 3. *De Lof der Vrouwen* (London: British Library, Ms. Add 20698, f. 17). 4. *De Lof der Vrouwen* (Ms. Add 20698, f. 70.)

centuries, but her objection to the language of the castration story pinpoints her greatest move against Jean in the *Cité de Dames*— as well as her remarkable swerve away from the authority of her second major *auctor* in the *Cité*, Boccaccio, with particular reference to his *De Mulieribus Claris*. Her rewrite of her *auctores* goes straight to the heart of a castration anxiety which may be said to be the originary moment for the misogyny in the texts of both the *Rose* and the *De Claris*.[9] Reason's impolite language in Jean's text is the cause for which the lover dismisses Lady Reason as a figure of authority and rejects her kind of love: the lover specifically asks for "quelque cortaise parole," and thus Jean anticipates the kind of response readers like Christine would have and makes it part of his text. The rejection of Lady Reason because of her uncourtly speech, however, motivates the rest of the plot. In rejecting Reason, the lover turns to all the other dramatis personae of the poem. A number of other attempts are made in the *Rose* to explicate the story of Saturn's loss of his genitals; one may say, without much exaggeration, that Jean's text is slightly obsessed with getting the story and its implications of idolatry understood aright.[10]

The dismemberment of the male father god, through which erotic love is born, is not, of course, Jean's creation. But the myth and its crucial dismemberment of the male body underwrite the superficially polite but obscene tropes in which Jean describes— at epic length and in great (and hilarious) detail—a single act of sexual intercourse. Christine also appears to have understood the connection between the two, for she objected to the "unnaturalness" of such language with just as much vehemence as she argued against Jean's vulgarity.[11] And of course Jean's images for this final, culminating act of sexual intercourse are all drawn from the euphemisms Lady Reason explains she *could* have used instead of "coilles" to refer to genitals (especially "reliques"— indicating the primary problem of idolatry).

There is no explicit dismemberment of the male body in the opening of Boccaccio's *De Mulieribus Claris*. However, the second story he tells (after the story of Eve) is of Semiramis. A glorious and ancient queen of the Assyrians, Semiramis, on the death of her husband Ninus, cross-dressed and masquerading as her young son, took over the rule of the realm and led the army on to great victories. After proving herself, she revealed her true identity, causing great wonder, Boccaccio says, that a mere woman could accomplish so much. In her own person she not only maintained her husband's empire, but added to it Ethiopia and India. She restored the city of Babylon and walled it with ramparts, Boccaccio stresses, of marvelous height. Boccaccio takes care to tell of one particular incident when Semiramis, having her hair braided, was interrupted by the news that Babylon had rebelled. Vowing to wear her second braid undone until she had subdued the city, she soon vanquished it and brought it to good order. A bronze statue was erected in Babylon of a woman with her hair braided on one side and loose on another, a reminder of Semiramis's brave deed.[12] The usual illumination of the moment in manuscripts of the French translation of Boccaccio's text, however, emphasizes the infamous side of Semiramis's story. Not only was she a great warrior queen and city builder, she also practiced mother-son incest. Boccaccio makes clear the terrifying sexual ambiguity such an action causes.

> But with one wicked sin this woman stained all these accomplishments . . . which are not only praiseworthy for a woman but would be marvelous even for a vigorous man. It is believed that this unhappy woman, constantly burning with carnal desire, gave herself to many men. Among her lovers, and this is something more beastly than human, was her own son Ninus, a very handsome young man. As if he had changed his sex with his mother, Ninus rotted away idly in bed, while she sweated in arms against her enemies.[13]

A representative illumination of this aspect of Semiramis's story reveals the distinctly uncomfortable position in which his mother's martial power places the young son Ninus (Fig. 2). Boccaccio's figurative sense of Ninus's exchange of sex with his mother implies an emasculation the illumination also hints at in Ninus's posture: the truncated hand, stuffed (protectively?) into the young boy's placket in the general area of the genitals, all too clearly answers the menace of Semiramis's remarkably large sword. Doubtless the sword is meant to represent Semiramis's great martial courage and achievements; but juxtaposed with the figure of Ninus, it represents the young man's effeminization (his unworn armor hangs on a rack above him). That Semiramis's sword also bisects the head of one of the armed soldiers standing behind her to the left of the miniature may imply that her martial prowess menaces more than Ninus.

"Oh," Boccaccio laments, "what a wicked thing this is! For this pestilence flies about not only when things are quiet, but even among the fatiguing cares of kings and bloody battles, and, most monstrous, while one is in sorrow and exile. Making no distinction of time, it goes about, gradually seizes the minds of the unwary and drags them to the edge of the abyss." In order to cover her crime, Semiramis decreed "that notorious law" [*legem insignem*] which allowed her subjects to do what they pleased in sexual matters. According to some, Semiramis invented chastity belts. According to others, her end was not good. "Either because he could not bear seeing his mother with many other lovers, or because he thought her dishonor brought him shame, or perhaps because he feared that children might be born to succeed to the throne, Ninus killed the wicked queen in anger." Ninus's distinctly overdetermined matricide raises questions about the connection between the legend of Semiramis and the first story Boccaccio tells, concerning Eve, the mother of us all. More importantly, Boccaccio's humanist uncertainty about Ninus's motives underscores the problematic nature of textual transmission. He offers many endings for Semiramis's story because the authorities conflict.[14]

Astonishingly, Christine makes Semiramis the first story lady Reason tells in the building of her city of ladies. "Take the trowel of your pen and ready yourself to lay down bricks and labor diligently, for you can see here a great and large stone which I want to be the first placed as the foundation of your City" (p. 38, revised).[15] Christine's Semiramis is more of a city builder than Boccaccio's—the first empire was a dual achievement of the elder Ninus and Semiramis together, who no less than her husband campaigned in arms. Upon the husband's death, Semiramis does not cross-dress, but simply continues in her role of ruler and conqueror, adding Ethiopia and India, and fortifying Babylon. Christine retells the incident of the Babylonian rebellion, the braid left undone, and the statue, this time bronze and richly gilt. Where Boccaccio begins his descant on incest, Christine acknowledges: "It is quite true that many people reproach her—and if she had lived under our law, rightfully so—because she took as husband a son she had had with Ninus her lord" (p. 40). Where Boccaccio spends time guessing as to Ninus's possible motives in killing his mother, Christine points out the reasons Semiramis may have had for taking her son as husband. First: she wanted no other crowned lady in the realm, and this would have happened if her son had married; and second, no other man was worthy to have her as a wife except her son. What troubles Christine most is that "de ceste erreur, que trop fu grande, ycelle noble dame fait aucunement a excuser" (2.680) (But this error, which was very great, this noble lady did nothing at all to excuse) (40). Why? Because "adonc n'estoit encore point de loy escripte" (there was as yet no written law). Indeed, then, Christine reasons, people lived according to the law of Nature, where all people were allowed to do whatever came into their hearts, without sinning. Where Boccaccio's Semiramis decrees a law, Christine's lives before any such thing exists. That this law prior to which she lives is a *written* law, is, I think, significant. It subtly recalls all of the previous conversations between Christine and Reason about the written authorities of the misogynist tradition that Christine finds so daunting in the generic reading scene of this allegory. The only authority Christine has to oppose to the "grant foyson de autteurs," which are like a surging fountain and which have all denigrated women, is "moy meisme et mes meurs come femme naturelle" (2.618) (my self and my conduct as a natural woman).[16] That is, until the three crowned ladies appear and give her a lesson in allegorical reading.[17] Reason further undermines the authority of such texts when she wittily announces that any argument against women was not authorized by *her*. Such a tradition grows in part simply because "in order to show they have read many authors, men base their own writings on what they have found in books and repeat what other writers have said and cite different authors." This undermining of textual, written authority, makes Christine sound distinctly modern, much like Francis Bacon inveighing against the mindless quibblings of scholastic philosophy. A miniature from the late-fifteenth-century Flemish translation of the *Cité* illuminates the moment when the detritus of misogynist opinion is cleared from the "field of letters" before the foundations for the city are dug (Fig. 3). Christine's removal of such a written tradition is of a piece with her revision of Boccaccio's legal detail: by means of the speaking presence in the text of a visionary female figure of authority, who persistently says she speaks prophetically, and whose textual gender is made more literal by its coherence with the author's own, Christine appears to establish her specific, female authority on oral and prophetic grounds, different from a mere textual tradition. Christine suppresses Boccaccio's worry about textual transmission at the same time as she suppresses Semiramis's ignoble end.

We do not need to invoke any anthropological argument (or authority) to see the priority granted oral experience in Christine's story of Semiramis—though it is intriguing that, for instance, Derrida's discussion of the violence of writing focuses on a scene that involves little girls divulging to Lévi-Strauss the secret names of the tribe.[18] Christine's own authority in the *Cité*

is, however, at the same time markedly scripted: Reason is constantly reminding Christine of what she has written in her own
prior texts, so that Christine's own corpus forms part of the
authorities to which Reason, Rectitude, and Justice appeal. Yet
the ultimate claim of female authority is to a nonscripted, prophetic mode, grounded in a realm of discourse that is made to
stand as far outside the textual as anything within a text can get.

In a sense, Christine's emphasis on a prior unscripted freedom
that would authorize mother-son incest as acceptable and even
honorable is of a piece with her criticism of Jean de Meun's vulgar
terms for body parts and also his euphemism in describing the act
of sexual intercourse: the relations between language, written and
oral, become most crucial in naming body parts. If her two *auctores* founded their texts on stories that underscore the originary
problem of castration anxiety, her objections—overt against Jean
and silent against Boccaccio—react not only to their terms but
also to the fundamental importance of the problem. One does not
need to invoke Freud to see the peculiar emotional burdens
revealed by the manuscript illuminations of the two moments in
Jean's and Boccaccio's texts. Christine's city is built with a foundation stone (the story of Semiramis) and written in the language of
an allegory that refuses to recognize this peculiar terror as being
first or, finally, very significant. The body upon which Christine
focuses, both early and late, is, not surprisingly, the female body.
And it is a body which also relentlessly, almost monotonously,
refuses to be dismembered.

It is important to notice at the outset that the physical body
which first bears mention in the text is Christine's own. The physicality of this body—and its essential femaleness—makes its
appearance very subtly in the first paragraph of the text of the
Cité. In the midst of the reading scene, just as Christine comes
across the volume of Mathéolus while searching through the
shelves for a volume of poetry, Christine's mother calls her to supper. (Imagine anyone calling any of the protagonists of allegorical
dream visions to supper just after he has picked up the text which
will be his authority in the subsequent journey.) That it is
Christine's *mother* who calls her to supper is not only pertinent
in terms of the continuum of female authorities Christine is
going to supply in her text, it signals the humdrum domesticity of
the scene. (Christine's mother did in fact live with her; one of the
figures of authority in the *Cité* talks about this real, down-to-
earth mother who had not wanted her daughter to get the education her father had given her.[19]) Unlike Dante (or Chaucer, or the

narrator of the *Rose*), Christine takes time out to eat and does not
have a "dream" such as most allegorical dream-visions insist.
Rather, she has a waking vision, much like Dante's (whose authority in this she does follow, having explicitly preferred him to Jean
de Meun in the Querelle de la Rose[20]). The next morning and
most importantly, however, Christine's response to reading Mathéolus is revulsion against her own female body:

> "Alas God, why did you not let me be born in the world as a
> man, so that all my inclinations would be to serve you better,
> and so that I would not stray in anything and would be as per-
> fect as man is said to be? . . . " I spoke these words to God in
> my lament and a great deal more for a very long time in sad
> reflection, and in my folly I considered myself most unfortu-
> nate because God had made me inhabit a female body in this
> world. (5)[21]

The vision begins with the arrival of the three ladies immediately
after this lament; but Christine further specifies the exact physical position in which she sits in her chair.

> So occupied with these painful thoughts, my *head* bowed like
> someone shameful, my *eyes* filled with tears, holding my
> *hand* under my *cheek* with my *elbow* on the pommel of my
> chair, I suddenly saw a ray of light fall on my lap, as though
> it were the sun. (6; revised; emphasis added)[22]

Given the fact that the description of the position follows directly
upon Christine's lament about her "corps femenin," however, the
specific mention of body parts is striking. In an earlier text, the
Mutacion de Fortune, Christine had said that Fortune changed
her into a man so she could take the helm of her foundering ship,
but in the *Cité*, this gender change is distinctly disallowed.[23] The
three women arrive to chastise her for being like the fool in the
story who was dressed in women's clothes while he slept; "because those who were making fun of him repeatedly told him he
was a woman he believed their false testimony more readily than
the certainty of his own identity" (6). The woman who will later
be identified as Reason, specifically by the mirror she holds — anyone who looks into it will achieve clear self-knowledge — specifically argues that all the misogynist argument which has tempted
Christine to feel self-disgust for her femaleness, is like the fire
which tries gold:

Fair daughter, have you lost all sense? Have you forgotten that when fine gold is tested in the furnace, it does not change or vary in strength but becomes purer the more it is hammered and handled in different ways. Do you not know that the best things are the most debated and the most discussed? . . . Come back to yourself, recover your senses, and do not trouble yourself anymore over such absurdities. (7–8)

Such an insistence on the senses may simply be metonymic reference to the alternative authority of "experience" Reason wishes to stress against the scripted authority of misogynist tradition. The problematic relationship between the experience of the physical female body and the bookish tradition may be seen in a miniature in the Flemish translation. Figure 4 shows a despondent Cornificia, hand on cheek, elbow on chair, surrounded by books. The small detail of the knife on her desk beneath her left hand, used for correcting scribal errors, itself pointing to the books to Cornificia's left, may suggest that the illuminator understood the point quite well about the need to correct the written tradition.[24] (The same miniaturist painted the scene of digging as a representation of Reason's command to clear away misogynist opinion from the "field of letters"; the two pictures, then, make the same point.) Chaucer's Wife of Bath had announced her preference: "Experience though none auctoritee / Were in this world is right enough for me." Chaucer's portrait of the antimisogynist Wife also underscores a similar conflict. The Wife's deafness is caused when her fifth husband, the clerk Jankyn, hits her on the side of the head after she has ripped out some pages from his misogynist book. Does the deafness, one wonders, speak to the problematic orality of a female tradition that is necessarily opposed to the clerkly scripted tradition?

Of course, most of what gets said by the three figures of authority in the *Cité des Dames* comes out of books. The very building of the city is the writing of the *book* of the city of ladies. Christine cannot, nor, as an allegorist, would she wish to, escape textuality. As Jane Gallop has usefully reminded us, no writing can evade textuality, even that which would strain most resolutely to ground the difference between male and female writing in the biological differences between male and female bodies:

At the very moment when she would proclaim the shift from metaphor to fact, the feminist critic cannot help but produce metaphors . . . this moment recurs in various texts . . . when, in reaching for some nonrhetorical body, some referential body to ground sexual difference outside of writing, the critic produces a rhetorical use of the body as metaphor for the non-rhetorical.[25]

It may be easier, however, to specify a distinctly female practice in writing that does not run into the contemporary modern dilemma of "essentialism" by focusing on a medieval female author's practice. Untouched by a biologism constructed by a modern "scientific" discourse, Christine's approach to the historical actuality of female bodies, translated into a transcendent textuality, is empowered by a long-lived ideology of fleshly sacrifice, which paradoxically insists upon the power of the word made flesh.[26] The very presence of the third section of the Cité, narrated by Justice, in which Christine provides an abbreviated female martyrology taken from Vincent of Beauvais, insists upon the centrality of the female body to her project. Of course, including a martyrology is also her greatest resistance to her auctor Boccaccio who had insisted that the stories of pagan and Christian women should not be told together. Boccaccio rests his claim to humanist originality in the De Claris (and his own difference from Petrarch) on the distinction between the oft-told tales of saints' lives and the fact that the merits of pagan women "have not been published in any special work up to now and have not been set forth by anyone."[27] Christine is remarkably attentive to Boccaccio's representation of his own authority, as her inclusion of the martyrology attests. By including it, she aims to revise at the point where he bases his own greatest claim for originality. She further chooses to name him as her auctor for the first time when she retells his story of the Roman woman Proba, notable for having rewritten the stories of Scripture, from Genesis to the Epistles, in the verses of Virgil, "that is . . . in one part she would take several entire verses unchanged and in another borrow small snatches of verse, and, through marvelous craftsmanship and conceptual subtlety" she was able to narrate the Bible in Virgil's poetry (p. 66). As David Anderson has very interestingly suggested, Boccaccio's praise of Proba's achievements indicates some of his own practice of imitation in rehearsing Statius's Thebaid in the Teseide, as well as, of course, his own use of sources in the De Claris.[28] Proba's practice proleptically stages the very problem the Renaissance would find so tricky to solve. Suffice it to say that at least one fifteenth-century reader noticed the significance of Boccaccio's story, if not for his practice, then for her own; Christine names him as her auctor, and quotes him verbatim with an acknowledgment for the first time. What Proba did to Virgil, so Christine does to Boccaccio.[29]

Christine's greatest difference from Boccaccio, however, is her three-part structure and its allegorical frame, through which she analyzes and thematically organizes the materials she has taken from him. Through the allegorical frame she also stages her own authority and, in effect, turns herself into her own figure of authority.[30] By positing herself [moi mesme] as a "natural" woman at the center of her text, she literalizes the gender that has been implicit in all female figures of *auctoritas*, itself a feminine noun that would require a female figure for its personification. The famous illuminations of the *Cité* instructively indicate the nature of the wordplay on which Christine's allegorical metaphor rests: although the text of the *Cité* has been very little read, its illuminations are some of the best known in the history of art—having been done by the hand which Millard Meiss has termed the "Cité des Dames Master."[31] They are important not merely for their artistic merit, but because of their close replication of authorial intention. In a brilliant study of the different political programs for two separate manuscripts of Christine's *Epistre Othéa*, Sandra L. Hindman has shown that Christine not only herself wrote the manuscript of the text that is presently collected in the volume known as Harley 4431 in the British Library, she also indicated in special rubrics in purple ink specific instructions for the illuminator.[32] The illuminations of the *Cité* are from the same Harley two-volume collection of Christine's work. Although the text of the *Cité* does not bear the same authority as the text of the *Othéa*, its illuminations are so close to the copy, which probably was overseen by Christine, that they will serve for our purposes.[33]

The first thing that strikes the eye about the incipit illumination to the *Livre de la Cité des Dames* (Fig.5) is the femaleness of the enterprise. Christine's illuminator represents her as an author already; the text opens in Christine's book-filled study. The three crowned ladies holding their duly explained emblems are Reason, in the back, holding her mirror; Droiture, or Rectitude, holding her ruler, in the middle; and Justice in the foreground, holding her measuring vessel. To the right we see the actual construction of the city under way, with Reason handing Christine a building block, while Christine holds her trowel—or her pen. The coequal activity of the figure of authority and the author collapses their authority; it replicates the insistence in the text that the three

5   Christine in her study confronted by Reason, Droiture, Justice; Reason and Christine building the City of Ladies.

8   Justice receiving the Virgin Mary into the City of Ladies.

6   Droiture welcoming the sibyls into the partially constructed City of Ladies.

7   Justice receiving the Virgin Mary and other saints into the City of Ladies.

SOURCES
5. *Le Livre de la Cité des Dames* (London: British Library, Ms. Harley 4421, f. 290). 6. *Le Livre de la Cité des Dames* (Ms. Harley 4421, f. 323). 7. *Le Livre de la Cité des Dames* (Ms. Harley 4421, f. 361). 8. *Le Livre de la Cité des Dames* (Paris: Bibliothèque Nationale, Ms. F. fr. 1171, f. 95v).

ladies share with Christine the opposition to the tradition against which she reacts. In an echo, I suspect, of Dante's cry that he was neither Aeneas or Paul to undertake such a journey, Christine complains that she is not Thomas the apostle to build in heaven a city for the king of India. When she complains that furthermore she has a weak female body, Reason tells her that she will carry materials on her own shoulders (much like father Virgil carries Dante over some difficult spots). Together they construct both a book and a city that will become a haven for women safe from further misogynist attack. Christine has the books, Reason provides the bricks. The two sides of the illumination are held together by a textual pun. Each of the three figures continually tells Christine that they will "livrerons" the material for her city: "Thus, fair daughter, to you is given the prerogative among women to make and build the City of Ladies. For the foundation and perfection of which, you will take and draw from us three living water as from clear fountains, and we will deliver [te livrerons] enough material, strong and more durable than any marble with cement could be. So will your city be very beautiful without parallel, and of perpetual duration in the world" (II, revised).[34] The "livre" and the "cité" are written and built simultaneously, with the delivery of the same "matiere."[35] Thus, every story narrated in the first section is another "pierre" laid in the walls of this edifying edifice.

The opening of the second section of the Cité is illuminated by another miniature (Fig. 6). Droiture receives into the city the ten sibyls, famous prophetesses whose authority is greater than all the Old Testament prophets; their stories begin the completion of the internal palaces.[36] In this section, Droiture tells the story of the Sibyl Almathea; in her oral and prophetic authority, Droiture has more accurate knowledge than even the tradition of Virgil. Justice takes over for the third and final section of the Cité. She is shown welcoming Mary into the city as its queen (Fig. 7). A later illumination rereads the figure of Mary, substituting a baby for the book (Fig. 8). Such a book/baby translation is a legitimate and interesting reading of the corporeal textuality of the hagiography of the third section. It is not merely a conventional substitution as the earlier, more careful count of ten sibyls in the miniature for the second section attested. Before we consider how sensitively poised this body/book tension is in the last section, it will be useful to consider how the female body is represented in Boccaccio's text, at least as that text was read by Christine's contemporaries. There is a persistent vision of the display of violence against the

9 Nero having his mother
Agrippina cut open so he may
see the womb from which
he was born.

10 The martyrdom of Pope
Urban.

12 St. Christine refuses to
worship pagan idols.

11 The martyrdom of
St. Marcienne.

SOURCES
9. *Des Cleres et Nobles Femmes* (London: British Library, Ms. Royal 20 C V, f.
139. 10. *Miroir Historial* (Paris; Bibliothèque Nationale, Ms. F. fr. 313, f. 166). 11.
Miroir Historial (Ms. F. fr. 313, f. 276). 12. *Miroir Historial* (Ms. F. fr. 313, f. 236v).

female body throughout the illuminated manuscripts of the *Des Cleres et Nobles Femmes;* such violence in Boccaccio's text may have provided another reason for Christine's inclusion of a martyrology in the *Cité.* Figure 9 is a fairly representative miniature, showing Nero having his mother Agrippina cut open so he may see the womb from which he was born.[37]

Christine's text incorporates and rewrites this violence against the female body by authorizing it as hagiography. In switching genres in her change of *auctores,* she not only rejects Boccaccio's decision not to write about martyred Christian women, she also selects a genre which insists upon a parity between male and female passion.[38] Both male and female saints are tortured and die in similar ways. Furthermore, the representations of such torture in the illuminations often insist upon the sexlessness of the saint's body. Two representative miniatures, one of Pope Urban, a male saint, and of Marcienne, a female saint, in a late fourteenth-century manuscript of Vincent of Beauvais's *Miroir Historial* illustrate the gender-neutral body of the saint (Figs. 10 and 11). The lack of genitals and the parallel musculature insist that in this moment of physical suffering the experience of martyrdom is sexless (in both senses of the term).

Christine, of course, in only telling of female saints' lives in the *Cité,* changes the pattern of parallelism. She further regenders the body and changes its social contexts by including a number of different details; her revisions of Vincent of Beauvais, her *auctor* for the last section, are thus similar to her subtle suppressions and corrections of Boccaccio. She also uses a similar maneuver to her well-timed naming of Boccaccio when she cites Vincent as her *auctor,* just before Justice recounts the story of St. Christine, Christine's own patron saint.

> If you want me to tell you all about the holy virgins who are in Heaven because of their constancy during martyrdom, it would require a long history, including Saint Cecilia, Saint Agnes, Saint Agatha, and countless others. If you want more examples, you need only look at the *Speculum historiale* of Vincent de Beauvais, and there you will find a great many. However, I will tell you about Saint Christine, both because she is your patron and because she is a virgin of great dignity. Let me tell you at greater length about her beautiful and pious life. (234)

In naming Vincent just before she tells the story of her own patron saint, Christine distinguishes her own authority from his;

she also implies that the story she tells will be necessarily different. One reads Vincent; we hear Justice speak.

The largest difference between Christine's and Vincent's versions of St. Christine's story is the treatment in the *Cité* of the
saint's parents. In the *Miroir,* it is both pagan parents who separately attempt to persuade their headstrong daughter to sacrifice
to their pagan gods. In Vincent's text, St. Christine's father Urban
has shut her up in a tower with some ladies-in-waiting so she may
worship his gods (Fig. 12).[39] When the young female companions
tattle on her, revealing that she has not been worshiping the idols
but rather looking out the window to pray to a single celestial
god, her father has her tortured. As soon as her mother finds out
about this torture, she comes to visit her daughter to try to dis-
suade her from being so obstinate. Vincent's mother is a study in
hysterical pathos:

> And then her mother, wife to Urban, hearing that her
> daughter had suffered so great pain, tore her clothes and put
> ashes on her head and went to the prison and threw herself at
> her daughter's feet and, crying, said, "My only daughter, have
> pity on me who nursed you at my breasts and make it clear
> why you worship a strange god."[40]

St. Christine harshly answers: "Why do you call me daughter; for
you have no one in your lineage who is called a christian [*crestiene*]. Do you not know that I have my name from Christ my
savior? He is the one who tests me in celestial chivalry and has
armed me to conquer those who do not understand." The mother,
hearing this, returns to her house, reveals all, and denounces her
daughter to her husband.

In the *Cité,* St. Christine has no mother. Urban is sole parent,
and it is before him, both father and first torturer, that Christine
abjures her parentage.

> "Tyrant who should not be called my father but rather enemy
> of my happiness, you boldly torture the flesh which you
> engendered, for you can easily do this, but as for my soul
> created by my Father in Heaven, you have not power to touch
> it with the slightest temptation, for it is protected by my
> Savior, Jesus Christ." (235–36)

Christine's suppression of the saint's mother depicted in Vincent's
text is of a piece with the *Cité*'s persistent emphasis on patriarchal control exercised by earthly fathers (as well as surrogate tyrant figures) in a number of other lives; it is equally consistent

with an emphasis on the generous and loving relations between earthly mothers and daughters.

In both texts, Urban has St. Christine stripped naked, beaten by twelve men, tied on a wheel over a fire, and rivers of boiling oil poured over her body. Angels break the wheel so that the virgin is delivered "healthy and whole," while in the meantime more than a thousand treacherous spectators who had been watching this torture without pity are killed. Urban decides to drown her; a great stone is tied around her neck and she is thrown into the sea, but angels save her and she walks on the water with them. Praying, she asks that the water be for her the holy sacrament of baptism, which she has greatly desired, "whereupon Jesus Christ descended in His own person with a large company of angels and baptized her and named her Christine from His own name" (236) [la baptisa et nomma de son nom Christine (2.1005)]. However, in the *Miroir*, the waters are only a "signacle de beptesme," while a voice from heaven merely announces her prayer has been heard, as a cloud and a purple star descend on her head, representing the glory of Jesus Christ. While the notion of the name in the *Miroir* is the wedge between mother and daughter—and is present, if at all, only in a fairly unstressed use of the word "crestiene"—the granting of the baptismal name "Christine," from Christ's own name, in the *Cité* is nowhere mentioned in the *Miroir*; neither is the baptism a literal sacrament in the *Miroir*, as it is in the *Cité*, and Vincent also does not reiterate Christine's loyal suffering for Christ's "nom." Christine revises Vincent to make the baptism a literal event that underscores the naming of the saint by the divine son himself, with his own name. He is, of course, the baby who substituted for the book, the Logos who suffered a fleshly sacrifice. The baptism is one of two central events—both intricate conflations of verbal and physical issues—in the *Cité*'s version of Christine's story; the other also concerns the physical fact of language.

Yet a third judge, named Julian, takes a different and very interesting tack in his torture. After having set some snakes upon her, which merely nurse at her breasts, he decides to have her breasts cut off, whereupon milk and blood issue forth. Then he commands that her tongue be cut out. In the *Cité*, Julian's decision is precisely motivated: "because she unceasingly pronounced the name of Jesus Christ." She has already told him that he is blind: "if your eyes would see the virtues of God, you would believe in them." Her tongue is duly "coupee," but she goes on speaking more clearly than before of divine things. God speaks to her again, praising her for upholding the name of Christ. Hearing this voice, Julian charges the executioners to cut her tongue so short that she cannot speak to her Christ, "whereupon they ripped out her tongue and cut it off at the root" (239). Immediately thereafter:

> She spat this cut-off piece of her tongue into the tyrant's face, putting out one of his eyes. She then said to him, speaking as clearly as ever, "Tyrant, what does it profit you to have my tongue cut out so that it cannot bless God, when my soul will bless Him forever while yours languishes forever in eternal damnation. And because you did not hear my words, my tongue has blinded you, with good reason." (239-40)

The French makes the witty connection between *langue* and *parole* more obvious: "'Et pource que tu ne congnois ma parolle, c'est bien raison que ma langue t'ait aveugle'" (2.1009).[41] In the *Miroir*, the saint has a less witty if far more grisly denunciation:

> "Je te condamne mengier en tenebras les members de mon corpse. Tu les avois destruez & tua trenchee ma langue qui beneissoit dieu. Et pource as tu droicturierment perdue sa veue." (f. 485)

> ("I condemn you to eat in hell the parts of my body. You have destroyed them and have cut off my tongue which blessed God. And therefore you have rightfully lost your sight.")

In the *Cité*, this body is not accessible to a metaphorical infernal punishment. While in both texts, it is the physical, literal tongue which puts out the literal physical eye, only Christine calls attention to the metaphorical blindness that has been the problem all along.[42] One senses that the saint's curse in the *Miroir* has a literal, Dantesque character—a contrapasso punishment of the tyrant's eating the body parts of the saint he has so hideously dismembered. Christine de Pizan sacrifices this wittiness to stress her own sense of the relations between the power of the saint's fleshly, physical tongue to speak the truth in its continuing and miraculous confession of Christ's name and its power to make people see that truth—thousands have been converted by the saint's virtue. The dismembered tongue is capable of making a political intervention.

In the *Miroir* the story ends with the remark that "ung home de son lignage" writes the saint's legend. In the *Cité*, an ungendered "parent" takes "le saint corps et escript sa glorieuse legende" (2.1009). The body and its scripted legend are kept more closely connected, not consigned to an infernal region, but remaining a sainted flesh-form, apparently resurrected and still coextensive with the saint herself. Breaking into her own text for the only time, Christine directly addresses a prayer to St. Christine.

"O blessed Christine, worthy virgin favored of God, most elect and glorious martyr, in the holiness with which God has made you worthy, pray for me, a sinner, named with your name, and be my kind and merciful guardian. Behold my joy at being able to make use of your holy legend and to include it in my writings, which I have recorded here at such length out of reverence for you. May this be ever pleasing to you! Pray for all women, for whom your holy life may serve as an example for ending their lives well. Amen." (240)

If the authorities of Reason, Rectitude, and Justice may be said to be merely allegorical representations of Christine's own female authority, this prayer stands finally outside the fiction of the text, in a "real" appeal to a functioning saint. St. Christine is one of the citizens who will dwell in the *Cité*—but of course she already dwells in the *civitas dei*, transtemporally accessible to the author in this prayer. One could say that the details of the legend of Christine are exquisitely suited to representing a female anxiety of authorship. Christine did not make up the detail of the dismembered tongue; she does, however, save St. Christine's physical body in her text, against the witty authority of her *auctor*. The literal prayer, fully functional as active language, collapses distinctions between saint's legend, author's "escriptures," and the instrumental effect Christine hopes her text will have on her female readers in the political present of the French court in 1405 and in the future. Christine de Pizan remakes herself as her own figure of authority, punningly calling attention to the divine authority of her own name by dramatizing the naming of her patron saint.

Stephen G. Nichols has recently argued that hagiography is a mediated scripted genre controlled by the institution of the church, designed to marginalize unauthorized prophetic voices that would subvert central institutionalized authority, most specifically the voices of women. The only body that speaks in a hagiographical text is a dead body; it speaks, moreover, by having been turned into a text.[43] Christine's rewrite of Vincent's details, I have tried to suggest, reinvests the body with a living instrumentality, even as it is being dismembered. The mediated, interpreted events of St. Christine's legend in Vincent's rendition are made literal, present events in Christine's revision of her *auctor*. Mere signs become actual events. The prayer to St. Christine also functions to bring the possibilities of a present power into the text, which, while it remains a mere record, makes contact with a transtemporal and prophetic present. Christine's revisions of Vincent begin to turn hagiography into prophecy and connect the saints' legends of the last section of the *Cité* with the persistent emphasis on prophecy in the first two.

At the end of her life Christine de Pizan took to actual prophecy. After having retreated to a convent before the Burgundian invasion of Paris, and having remained silent for eleven years, Christine wrote the last poem of her life, the *Ditié de Jehanne D'Arc*, finishing it on July 31, 1429. It was the only poem to have been written about Joan during her lifetime. Christine nowhere mentions her own earlier texts in this poem; she does not call attention to her former persistent arguments about female virtue, her political treatises on peace, or on the arts of war, or any of her other writings. She does, however, begin with her formulaic "Je, Christine," which may function as an authoritative sign for the existing corpus of texts.[44] It has always seemed like a peculiarly appropriate accident of history that Joan should appear on the scene of the Hundred Years' War in time for Christine to write about her and to welcome her as an (at that point) unambiguous sign of God's special love for the female sex: "Hee! quel honneur au feminin Sexe! Que Dieu l'ayme il appert" (265–66). As far as I know, no one has asked if there might not be a connection between the two unique occurrences, the presence of a prominent female author, the first professional woman of letters who made public and constant arguments for the virtue of women at the French court for over twenty years, and the acceptance by that court, a generation later, of a low-born female teenager as the martial savior of her country. To suggest a possible causal connection may be to do no more than to question whether or not the practice of a prominently placed author contributed to the "discursive possibilities" of a culture.[45] Criticism is now more comfortable with thinking of literature in its potential social instrumentality—how, in fact, the practice of an individual author may be seen as an "intervention" in the ideological constructs of a society. This was certainly Christine's stated intention in the *Livre de la Cité des Dames*, as well as in a number of her more overtly didactic manuals. With the *Ditié's* specific address of the king, the soldier, Joan herself, the city of Paris, and the nation at large, Christine certainly intended a prophetic and immediate intervention for this particular poem, as she apparently also assumed, from her first critique of the *Roman de la Rose*, that literature had real moral impact.

Her radical insertion of her gender-specific authority into a misogynist tradition proceeds in the case of her three different, explicitly named *auctores* in an almost textbook-like demonstration of how it should be done. That she in the process creates an almost monolithically stable subjectivity in her persona as female author defies our current notions of the historical progress in the construction of the modern "subject." Her seeming modernity, predicated, as I have tried to show, on the most "medieval" practice of authorial citation and revision, her explicit and implicit scrutiny of a misogyny driven by what can be termed various oedipal anxieties, as well as her focus on the problematic relations between oral and written traditions of authority in the representation of the female body would seem to place her at the center of a number of late twentieth-century critical concerns and therefore in a position somewhat anachronistic to her late medieval moment. However, her not entirely coincidental overlap with Joan of Arc negates such an ahistorical accounting for her career. Christine doubtless wrote the text of the *Ditié* with a simple pen, but she appears to have written it with a sense of the political instrumentality of literature that we are only now beginning to appreciate. If the laws decreeing the legitimacy of the Middle Ages do not at the moment account for her political practices, need it be said that they should perhaps be rewritten?

NOTES

1. Sandra Gilbert and Susan Gubar, *The Madwoman in the Attic: The Woman Writer and the Nineteenth-Century Literary Imagination* (New Haven: Yale University Press, 1979).

2. A quick overview of the various positions taken by various French theorists may be found in Susan Suleiman, "(Re)Writing the Body: The Politics of Female Eroticism," in *The Female Body in Western Culture: Contemporary Perspectives,* ed. Susan Suleiman (Cambridge: Harvard University Press, 1986) 7–29.

3. For a recent study which places Christine in the context of the French court, see Sandra L. Hindman, *Christine de Pizan's "Epistre Othéa": Painting and Politics at the Court of Charles VI* (Toronto: Pontifical Institute of Mediaeval Studies, 1986).

4. Although a modern edition of the French text by Monica Lange has been forthcoming since 1971, the *Cité* has yet to be printed. The more obviously conservative *Trésor de la Cité des Dames (Le Livre des Trois Vertus)* was published in three early printed editions in 1497, 1503, and 1536; the *Cité* remains the only major text by Christine never to have been printed. See Angus J. Kennedy, *Christine de Pizan: A Bibliographical Guide* (London: Grant and Cutler, 1984).

5. Although a miniature can provide no sure check on textual interpretation, because visual evidence can be as easily misinterpreted as texts, the two were assumed to be coherently readable together. Early fifteenth-century understandings of the similar moral impact of both picture and text thus offer some historical legitimacy to taking pictures as evidence of possible interpretations. Jean Gerson, for instance, questions: "Mais qui plus art et enflemme ces ames que paroles dissolues et que luxuryeuses escriptures et paintures?" (But what burns and enflames these souls more than dissolute words and libidinous writings and paintings?) *Le Débat sur Le Roman de la Rose*, ed. Eric Hicks (Paris: Éditions Honoré Champion, 1977), 68.

6. "Et la vituperacion que dit, non mie seullement luy mais d'autres et mesement le *Rommant de la Rose* ou plus grant foy est adjoustee pour cause de l'auctorité de l'auteur" (2.624) (As for the attack . . . made not only by Mathéolus but also by others and even by the *Romance of the Rose* where greater credibility is averred because of the authority of its author). Citations are to "The 'Livre de la Cité des Dames' of Christine de Pisan: A Critical Edition," ed. Maureen Curnow, 2 vols. (Ph.D. diss., Vanderbilt University, 1975); English translations are from Christine de Piyan, *The Book of the City of Ladies*, trans. Earl Jeffrey Richards (New York: Persea Books, 1982).

7. Hicks, 13–14, 117–18. For English translations of the documents see *"La Querelle de la Rose": Letters and Documents*, ed. J. L. Baird and K. R. Kane (Chapel Hill: University of North Carolina Dept. of Romance Languages, 1978); Guillaume de Lorris and Jean de Meun, *Le Roman de la Rose*, ed. Félix Lecoy, 3 vols. (Paris: Éditions Honoré Champion, 1965), 1: 5507.

8. The miniature is from Douce 195, Bodleian Library, Oxford; it was done in the late fifteenth century for Louise of Savoy and the Count of Angoulême, parents of Francis I. For a peculiarly full illustration of the whole story, showing the birth of Venus from the dismembered genitals as well as the castrated body, see John V. Fleming, *The Roman de la Rose: A Study in Allegory and Iconography* (Princeton: Princeton University Press, 1969), fig. 33: the Valencia MS Fleming prints may have been illuminated by one of the miniaturists Christine used, causing her—so Charity Canon Willard guesses—greater consternation about the vulgarity of the text. See Willard, *Christine de Pizan: Her Life and Works* (New York: Persea Books, 1984), 229–30, n. 24.

9. When Lady Reason explains that Ovid turned to writing attacks on women only after he had been punished for his political and sexual transgressions by being "diffourmez de ses membres" (i.e., castrated), Christine would appear to point to this origin (*Cité* 2:648; Richards, 21). The argument about Ovid was, of course, conventional, but in the context of the *Cité*'s rejection of the whole misogynist tradition, Christine would appear to anticipate a series of modern feminist critiques of Freudian theories about the oedipal complex and female sexuality. See Hélène Cixous, "The Laugh of the Medusa," *Signs* 1 (1976): 875–93, and Luce Irigaray, *Speculum of the Other Woman*, trans. Catherine Porter (Ithaca: Cornell University Press, 1986).

10. For further discussion of the perhaps defensible tactic Jean de Meun uses and his revision of his precursors, see my "Allegory, Allegoresis, and the Deallegorization of Language: the *Roman de la Rose*, the *De planctu naturae*, and the *Parlement of Foules*," in *Allegory, Myth, and Symbol*, ed. Morton Bloomfield (Cambridge: Harvard University Press, 1981), 163–86.

11. Willard quotes Christine's basic argument: "If you wish to excuse him by saying that it pleases him to make a pretty story of the culmination of love using such images [figures], I reply that by doing so he neither tells nor explains anything new. Doesn't everyone know how men and women copulate naturally?" See Hicks, 20. Christine makes clear in a later document in the "Querelle" that her objections to the words are, in essence, political. Having argued that "the word does not make the thing shameful, but the thing makes the word dishonorable," Christine explains to Pierre Col that the "thing" in question is not precisely the physical body part (made by God, although polluted by the Fall), but the speaker's "intention" in using the word: in contrast to Christine's own use of a polite term, for instance, whereby "la fin pour quoy j'en parleroye ne seroit pas deshonneste," a use of the proper name would be shameful because "la premiere entencion de la chose a ja fait le non deshonneste" (Hicks, 117). Christine's ultimate objection to the *Rose* was to Jean's authorial misogyny: "lui, seul homme, osa entreprendre a diffamer et blasmer sans excepcion tout un sexe" (Hicks, 22). Her quarrel with his choice of words would appear to take aim at the bawdiness of a discursive practice which underwrote the overall misogyny. For a discussion of Christine's essentially political objections to the *Rose*, see Pierre-Yves Badel, *Le Roman de la Rose au XIVe siècle: Étude de la Réception de l'Oeuvre* (Geneva: Librairie Droz, 1980), 411–47, esp. 428.

12. The four-part incipit miniature in a manuscript of the French translation of the *De Claris*, the *Des Cleres et Nobles Femmes*, probably done by Laurent de Premierfait in 1401, reveals the importance of Semiramis's story in the fourteenth-century French reading of the text. The episode of the messenger's arrival while Semiramis is having her hair braided is represented in the lower left quadrant, just beneath the author portrait in the upper left quadrant (British Library, London, MS Royal 20 C.V, f. 1). The only text of the *Cité* to have any of its internal stories illustrated, the late fifteenth-century Flemish translation *De Lof der Vrouwen* (MS Add 20698 in the British Library) also illuminates this moment, for it is a signal event in Christine's version of the story as in Boccaccio's (f. 41).

13. Giovanni Boccaccio, *Concerning Famous Women*, trans. Guido A. Guarino (New Brunswick, N.J.: Rutgers University Press, 1963), 6. [Ceterum hec omnia, nedum in femina, sed in quocunque viro strenuo, mirabilia atque laudabilia et perpetua memoria celebranda, una obscena mulier fedavit illecebra. Nam cum, inter ceteras, quasi assidua libidinis prurigine, ureretur infelix, plurium miscuisse se concubitui creditum est; et inter mechos, bestiale quid potius quam humanum, filius Ninias numeratur, unus prestantissime forme iuvenis, qui, uti mutasset cum matre sexum, in thalamis marcebat ocio, ubi hec adversus hostes sudabat in armis (*De Mulieribus Claris*, ed. Vittorio Zaccaria, *Tutte Le Opere di Giovanni Boccaccio*, ed. Vittore Branca, 12 vols. [Mondadori, 1967], II:36).

14. For a discussion of Christine's and Boccaccio's different relations to textual tradition, see Liliane Dulac, "Semiramis ou la Veuve héroïque," in *Mélanges de Philologie Romane offerts à Charles Camproux* (Montpellier: C.E.O. Montpellier, 1978), 315–43.

15. Sy prens la truelle de ta plume et t'aprestes de fort maçonner et ouvrer par grant diligence. Car voycy une grande et large pierre que je veuil qui soit la premiere assise ou fondement de ta cité (2.676).

16. Susan Groag Bell ("Christine de Pizan [1364–1430]: Humanism and the Problem of a Studious Woman," *Feminist Studies* 3, 1 [1976]) points out that whereas Boccaccio denigrates women's traditional pursuits, Christine ignores his deprecations in her rewrites of his stories. Bell also notices that in the sequel to the *Cité*, the *Trésor de la Cité des Dames* or *Le Livre des Trois Vertus*, Christine does not counsel women to study letters but rather gives practical advice on how to gain power under the current social conditions; Bell concludes that this demonstrates Christine's assumption that "it was 'woman's work' that kept the fabric of society intact" (181).

17. It is possible that Christine knew Alain de Lille's *De planctu naturae*, in which Lady Nature gives a long explanation of reading "per antiphrasim"; in the *Cité* Lady Reason explains that we are to read by "the grammatical figure of *antiphrasis*" (7). In the debate over the *Rose*, Gerson had specifically taken Jean de Meun to task for plagiarizing Alain, pointing out, however, that, after having reread Alain, he can state unequivocally that Alain never speaks as Jean does, but consistently condemns vices against nature (Hicks, 80).

18. For a discussion of this moment in Lévi-Strauss's texts see Jacques Derrida, *Of Grammatology*, trans. Gayatri Spivak (Baltimore: Johns Hopkins University Press, 1976), 101–40.

19. Motherhood is one of the more immediate stances for female authority; Christine was herself a mother of three children, and she uses this authoritative position in the *Enseignemens moraux* to address her son, Jean Castel (*Oeuvres poétiques de Christine de Pisan*, ed. M. Roy, 3 vols. [Paris: Firmin Didot, 1886], 3:27–44). The significant importance of her own mother, however, in the opening pages of the *Cité*, calls up large questions about the relation of real mothering to any female's identity as author or otherwise. Recent feminist discussions of female authors writing in later periods make interesting use of the object relations theory of mothering outlined by Nancy Chodorow in *The Reproduction of Mothering: Psychoanalysis and the Sociology of Gender* (Berkeley: University of California Press, 1978). At base, it is more difficult for a female to detach from the first love object, the mother, and to create a separate identity because of their shared gender as well as their shared sociological role. The fact that Christine's mother is still feeding her (calling her to supper) also broaches notions of orality retained from infant attachments, and would need to be taken into account in a fuller discussion of the problematic relations of an oral, prophetic, and specifically female tradition by which Christine in the *Cité* "corrects" a written male tradition.

20. Hicks, 141–42: Dante's poem is a "hundred times better written"; there is "no comparison."

21. Helas! Dieux, pourquoy ne me faiz tu naistre au monde en masculin sexe, a celle fin que mes inclinacions fussent toutes a te mieulx servir et que je ne errasse en riens et fusse de si grant parfeccion comme homme masle ce dit estre? . . . Telz parolles et plus assez tres longuement en triste penssee disoye a Dieu en ma lamantacion si comme celle qui par ma foulour me tenoye tres malcontente de ce qu'en corp femenin m'ot fait Dieux estre au monde. (2: 621)

22. "En celle dollente penssee ainsi que j'estoye, la *teste* baissiee comme personne honteuse, les *yeulx* plains de larmes, tenant ma *main* soubz ma *joe acoudee* sur le pommel de ma chayere, soubdainement sus mon giron vy descendre un ray de lumiere" (2:621-22; emphasis added). Richards translates "joe" as "armrest" which is possible; however, I think the main burden of Christine's list of body parts in his description would tend to make the "joe" a human cheek rather than the side-part of an armchair. For "joe" as "joue," specifically as "cheek," see A. J. Greimas, *Dictionnaire de l'Ancien Français* (Paris: Librairie Larousse, 1968). See also fig. 12.4

23. Suzanne Solente, ed., *Le Livre de la Mutacion de Fortune*, 4 vols. (Paris: Éditions A. & J. Picard, 1959-66), 1, 9-12, vv. 51-156. See Willard (108) for a discussion of the transformation in the *Mutacion*.

24. A number of different miniaturists worked on this manuscript; it may be that the picture of Cornificia was originally scheduled by the second illuminator, the "Dresden Master," to be his author-portrait of Christine especially because it so closely adheres to the description of her posture in the text. For a discussion of this miniaturist see Bodo Brinkman, "Der Meister des Dresdener gebetbuchs und sein Kreis: Leben und Werk eines burgundischen Buchmakers zwischen Utretcht, Brugge und Amiens" (Diss., Free University, Berlin, 1990). I am indebted to Prof. Eugene Vance for the reading of the knife.

25. Jane Gallop, "Writing and Sexual Difference: The Difference Within," in *Writing and Sexual Difference*, ed. Elizabeth Abel (Chicago: University of Chicago Press, 1980), 287.

26. Hélène Cixous (*The Newly Born Woman*, co-authored with Catherine Clément, trans. Betsy Wing [Minneapolis: University of Minnesota Press, 1986]) assumes a relationship between the female body and "writing" as she conceives it: "woman is body more than man is. Because he is invited to social success, to sublimation. More body hence more writing" (95). Punning on the French word "voler," Cixous provides a double metaphor for a specifically female writing: "To fly/steal is woman's gesture, to steal into language to make it fly" (96). Christine not only shares the wordplay with such a theorist, who assumes a continuity between writing and the body, she also would appear to have anticipated the antioedipal stance of such a theorist as Luce Irigaray, who bases her description of "écriture féminine" on a critique of Freud's too oedipally based sense of female sexuality. See, in particular, Irigaray's "Psychoanalytic Theory: Another Look" in *This Sex Which Is Not One*, trans. Catherine Porter with Carolyn Burke (Ithaca: Cornell University Press, 1985) as well as the title essay.

27. Nullo in hoc edito volumine speciali . . . et a nemine demonstrata, describere, quasi aliquale reddituri premium (*De Mulieribus Claris*, 28).

28. David Anderson, unpublished manuscript.

29. For further corroboration, see Richards's note, 262.

30. Sandra L. Hindman (*Christine de Pizan's "Epistre Othéa"* [Toronto: Pontifical Institute of Mediaeval Studies, 1986], 57) argues for a similar conflation of the authorities of Christine and the figure of Othea through the epistolary form. The *Cité* makes the conflation a part of the dramatic dialogue as the three figures dictate the stories to Christine as named author.

31. Millard Meiss, *French Painting in the Time of Jean de Berry: The late XIVth Century and the Patronage of the Duke*, 2 vols. (London: Phaidon, 1967).

32. Hindman, 75–89. Hindman also discusses Christine's naming of a female border painter (69–70).

33. Paris, Bibliothèque Nationale, f. fr. 607; the MS was a presentation copy for the Duc de Berry.

34. "Ainsi, belle fille, t'est donné la prerogative entre les femmes de faire et bastir la Cité des Dames, pour laquelle fonder et parfaire, tu prendras et puiseras en nous trois eaue vive comme en fontaines cleres, et te livrerons assez matiere plus forte et plus durable que marbre . . . Si sera ta cité tres belle sans pareille et de perpetuelle duree au monde" (2: 630).

35. Such wordplay is typical of allegory. For the function of puns in William Langland's *Piers Plowman*, see my *The Language of Allegory: Defining the Genre* (Ithaca: Cornell University Press, 1979), esp. 58–79.

36. A later fifteenth-century illumination counts their uncanonical number more carefully—Christine says there are ten rather than nine; Paris, B.N. f. fr. 1177, f. 45.

37. In a miniature illustrating even so chaste a story as that of Penelope, the violence of the suitors seems implicitly directed at the exemplary wife rather than at each other (Royal 20 CV, British Library, f. 61v).

38. The incipit illumination of Jean de Vignay's translation of Vincent of Beauvais's *Miroir Historial* (Paris, BN, f. fr. 313, f. 1) is split down the middle; on the left is a group of male saints standing before a monk seated in a high chair writing; on the right is a group of female saints standing before a monk seated in a slightly lower chair, also writing. While the difference in the size of the chairs, the placement of the figures (the floor of the males' side is higher than the floor of the females'), and the use of a nimbus around one male saint's head but no corresponding haloes for the females, all suggest a hierarchical gender division, the miniatures are the same size and use the same format. The overall effect is of perfect parallelism.

39. The sexuality implicit in this miniature of the clothed St. Christine, opposed to the naked pagan idols, one white, one darker in color, contrasts with the sexless nature of other martyrs painted by the same hand. The idols are not nude, but naked, their shields covering genitals that must be present as a menace to the virgin saint. The color code of the pagan idols suggests that the threat of idolatry is both without and within, signed as a cultural other in the darker figure, but as the same in the lighter. Both, of course, as male, represent idolatry as a sexual threat to the female saint, who bends away from them with hand gestures that cover her own genital areas (though this is a typical placement for female hands even when there are no contextually present sexual implications).

40. Et donc sa mere femme Urben ouyante q'sa fille avoit suffert si grant

peine derompit ses vestemens & mist cendres sus son chief & ala chartre
et cheust aux pieds dicelle a pleur disant. Ma seule fille ayez pitie de moi
qui alaictas mes mammelles qui ta len fait pour quoi tu aoures ung
estrange dieu. (Paris, 1495, f. 483.)

41. Greimas notes that "langue" as meaning "langage parlé ou écrit" is
rare in *ancien français*; however, if it ever slips into this meaning, it does
so here.

42. The question of sightedness and blindness curiously recurs in a
number of different father-daughter relations in other saints' lives. The
stories of two cross-dressed saints, Euphrosine and Marine, both of whom
become monks, are told in sequence by both Christine and Vincent. However, Christine transfers the miraculous ability of St. Euphrosine's dead
body to St. Marine's, whose dead body, when kissed by a monk who has
lost the use of one eye, restores his sight. The signal difference between
the two saints is that Euphrosine fled to the monastery to escape her
father's attempt to marry her to an unwanted suitor, while Marine goes to
the monastery after being called there by her father, who misses her too
much after he has turned monk. Why Christine should suppress the
power to restore eyesight in rebellious Euphrosine's case and grant it to
the dutiful daughter Marine is, to say the least, suspicious; what seems to
be shifting about in this floating eyeball is a weird marker of oedipal relations. Vincent's text allows the initially hostile father of Euphrosine to
"see" his daughter again before her death; she is—like the monk's eyesight—"restored" to him. Christine's text insists upon this father's further
suffering, and his death. In Christine's text Euphrosine's dead body tenaciously holds the script that identifies it as female until the father can
read it; this script-holding body does not restore sight.

43. Stephen G. Nichols, paper presented at the University of Pennsyl-
vania, spring 1987.

44. Christine de Pisan, *Ditié de Jehanne d'Arc*, ed. Angus J. Kennedy
and Kenneth Varty (Oxford: Society for the Study of Mediaeval Languages
and Literature, 1977), 28. The specification of the eleven years' lamenta-
tion spent in an "abbaye close," since the time that Charles was forced to
flee Paris, not only coordinates the present moment of the poem with contemporary history, but also establishes Christine's signature biography,
which marks the peculiarly specific authority of her texts. The poem is
a part of history, but it is also a part of the writings of a speaker, who persistently names herself.

45. There is doubtless some social coherence in the mistaken assumption that Jean Gerson, Christine's companion in arms during the Querelle
de la Rose, was the author of a Latin tract defending Joan's transvestism,
dated 14 May 1429, titled *De Mirabili Victoria Cujusdam Puellae*, as well
as of the *Breviarum Historiale*, which describes the meeting at Chinon
and compares Joan to Deborah, Esther, and Penthesilea. The Dauphin
Charles who gave Joan further men of arms after their famous but rather
mysterious meeting at Chinon, was the youngest son of Isabeau of Bavaria
(if not the mad king), for whom Christine had made the presentation edition of her works, the present Harley 4431. Marina Warner (*Joan of Arc:
The Image of Female Heroism* [New York: Knopf, 1981]) makes a very inter-

esting argument about Joan of Arc's name having less to do immediately with the family name than with the subterranean Amazonian message it carries, the "arc" being the bow the famous warrior women carried (198–200). Christine had discussed the Amazon Kingdom at length, though she was not the only writer to do so. Christine devotes two huitains of her poem to a discussion of the trial at Poitiers, at which clerks and learned men investigated Joan's "fait" before the battle of Orleans; but Christine also "proves" Joan's legitimacy by prophecy, including a "Sebile" in the usual list of Bede and Merlin. Although Christine herself does not call La Pucelle an amazonian warrior, her presentation of Joan as authorized by sibylline prophecy connects her to the sibyls prominent in the *Epistre Othéa* and the *Cité des Dames*.

Intertextuality and Autumn / Autumn and the Modern Reception of the Middle Ages

HANS ULRICH GUMBRECHT

Translated by Michael Schultz

The Cancioneros *of the Fifteenth Century from a Dialectical Perspective*

Cancioneros are collections of texts in metrical form that were usually written in the century preceding their compilation. These texts originated more often than not during the fifteenth century in the Iberian kingdoms of Aragon, Castile, and Portugal, and were preserved until the last quarter of the fifteenth century, mostly in handwritten codices, after which time they were handed down primarily in printed versions. Many *cancioneros* present their individual texts in groups based on a variety of organizational principles. Thus, the term "intertextuality," when used in reference to this genre, characterizes *the relationships present in the overall corpus among series of individual texts.* The concern here is, at least primarily, neither the extent to which the forms of specific texts were determined by various other texts, nor the relationship to such outside texts, which were not available to the reading public in the same collection.

The field of Hispanic Studies has until now concerned itself with the *cancioneros* from three perspectives. First, there is a plentitude of those paleographical and codicological evaluations, produced in the spirit of positivism, which can be relied upon by a pragmatically oriented literary history. Second, literary histories of a general nature have usually discharged their duty to mention and characterize briefly the *cancionero* genre by stating that the act of compilation underlying the *cancioneros* was the manifesta-tion of an epigonous attitude; such a statement can only be made against the background of a trivialized romantic aesthetic. Third and last, whenever literary scholars devoted to the "art of interpre-tation" concerned themselves with the *cancioneros,* they were inclined to concentrate on individual texts; they naturally singled out examples that were atypical for the genre, since only to such paradigms could originality be ascribed. To summarize, the genre *cancionero* will remain an awkward subject as long as (literary-) historical interest in it is coupled with the obligation to demon-strate its lasting aesthetic value. But what genres would not seem awkward wherever this injunction is taken seriously?

Paul Zumthor's book *Le masque et la lumière*[1] offers a poten-tial line of inquiry for realizing this literary-historical subject. Zumthor states by way of introduction that he considers the *grands rhétoriqueurs* and the *cancioneros* to be parallel phenom-ena, so that an application to the *cancioneros* of the perspective he has developed for analyzing the texts of the *grands rhéto-riqueurs* is certainly justified. What the *grands rhétoriqueurs* wrote — just like the texts of the *cancioneros* — is on the one hand clearly dependent on high-medieval precedents with respect to the development of forms and motifs. On the other hand, these precedents are so far removed from their primary pragmatic con-texts, in both the works of the *grands rhétoriqueurs* and the texts of the *cancioneros,* that this observation — taken together with the emergence in the period of the *grands rhétoriqueurs* and the *cancioneros* of metrical texts with completely different forms — can be reinterpreted as signifying *the literary-historical "autumn" and soon-to-follow end of the Middle Ages.*

Our intention is to differentiate Zumthor's perspective into two specific lines of inquiry; the prospects for their respective resolu-tions are dialectically connected. The first of these two inquiry perspectives is based predominantly on textual and communica-tion theory: Can a connection — first of all on the level of a "non-binding" typology — be made plausibly between late medieval court culture, which Huizinga designates with the term *"Herbst des Mittelalters,"*[2] as a pragmatic context and that specific form of intertextuality that the *cancioneros* embody? In other words, we want to define the vague concept of intertextuality on the basis of textual pragmatics. The second line of inquiry, however, involves a primarily literary-historical interest that is not re-stricted to Spain and the *cancioneros*: Does a refined understand-ing of that type of intertextuality characterizing the *cancioneros*

lead to elucidation of the intellectual-historical preconditions—
the interests and attitudes—to which the reactualization and ob-
jectification of the cultural past can be attributed? To be specific,
the point of reference for our second question is a problem of literary historiography, which has to consider whether it wants to
see—as Huizinga does—the context of "reception of the Middle
Ages" in Western Europe in the fourteenth and fifteenth centuries
as *still* late-medieval or *already* the beginning of the modern history of reception of medieval literature. Let there be no misunder-
standings: the objects of literary history will not in themselves
present us with any solutions, no matter how exactingly and in-
tently we may look at them.

Individual Texts / Textual Configurations / Cancionero

The *Cancionero de Baena* was compiled around 1450 at the
court of Juan II—in the last years of this king's reign—by the converted Jew Juan Alfonso de Baena[3]; in the prologue the compiler
names himself

escriuano e seruidor del muy alto e muy noble rey de Castilla
Don Johan . . . (4)

(scribe and servant of the very lofty and noble king of Castile
Don Juan)

and emphasizes his Jewish heritage, probably because it was considered a title of honor in all cultural matters in Castile until near the
end of the fifteenth century. However, a closer investigation of these
particulars concerning the pragmatics of the corpus will be post-
poned to the next section of our discussion, where they will serve
as the basis for a response to our two main questions.

Let us first of all examine the individual texts composing the
Cancionero de Baena and the modes of their configuration. If it
can be established that these individual texts—with the exception of the bucolic scenario—cover *all* thematic areas that were
current in Castilian culture (and not only Castilian culture of
Christian origin) until the middle of the fifteenth century, then
that may point to a possibility for the historiographic structuring
of late-medieval literature that we have suggested elsewhere.[4]
Numerous texts of the fourteenth and fifteenth centuries show a
similar thematic richness, and their relation to other systems of
meaning, even culturally institutionalized ones, can be described
as *purely recursive negation:* in such texts *all* elements of mean-

ing that were characteristic for each of the other systems of meaning of the same period can appear, without losing any of the
senses that belonged to various other systems of meaning. Such
texts (or images or festivals: we had correlated purely recursive
negation with Bakhtin's concept of "carnival culture") can on the
one hand be seen as *symptoms of crisis,* as the result of the evolu-
tionary weakness of social systems (including systems of meaning) and institutions of the early and high Middle Ages in a
changed world. On the other hand, the chaos of meaning (that of
the "carnival texts," for example) that results from purely recursive negation is also the necessary precursor, often even the anticipation, of that characteristic of the early modern period which
is most important from the point of view of intellectual history:
the fullness of meaning, no longer restrained by the traditional
social systems and institutions, requires the subjective individual
as a flexible judge of selection and interpretation. A classic example in this regard was the *Libro de buen amor* (from the middle of
the fourteenth century), in which the first-person narrator (who is
also the protagonist) functions as the point of integration for
heterogenous fields of meaning.[5]

The case of the *Cancionero de Baena* is more complicated. Not
only because such tensions between individual precedents of
meaning and the point of convergence of their selection were
hardly a matter of everyday concern anymore in Castile around
1450 (even though broad areas of practical education and of com-
merce were not to be permeated by the subject-centered style of
establishing meaning until the following decades). Above all, it is
remarkable that the individual texts of the *Cancionero de Baena*
are configured in small text groups, instead of finding their place
in a comprehensive overall structure. Let us from the first four of
these textual configurations induce *textual configuration types,*
in the process of which we will make use of the titles of the individual texts—which were not infrequently expanded into brief
commentaries—in order to distinguish the isotopic levels specific
to individual configurations.

The first four individual texts are attributed to a single author,
the troubadour Maçias, who is supposed to have lived in the second half of the fourteenth century (and later became one of the favorite protagonists of the Spanish romanticists); in *all* cases we are
dealing with *cantigas* in Galician-Portuguese, which *all* evoke the
situation of unrequited love [*trabajo*]. Such monotony is broken
by the heading of the third text (which indicates that the text can
be read not only as an invective against the cruel nature of love,

but also, by allegorical extension, as an allusion to the Castilian king Pedro el Cruel, who was a contemporary of Maçias) as well as by the headings of the fourth and fifth texts (which draw attention to their perfect adherence to meter and rhyme scheme). The homogeneity of this text group depends on the attribution of all the individual texts to one author, whose name was probably already in the fifteenth century inseparably associated with the scenario of high-medieval courtly love. All this makes possible the playful representation of the past that is so typical for the "autumn of the Middle Ages," without, as we have seen, necessarily excluding direct references to personalities of the present and a fascination with the author's virtuoso command of the language.

The second text group encompasses either five or six individual texts, according to one's perspective. These, too, are attributed to a single author of the fourteenth century, Arçidyano de Toro. The situations in which the fictional first-person narrator appears are, by contrast, manifold. As in the case of his contemporary Maçias, four *cantigas* are found at the head of the group attributed to Arçidyano de Toro. The fourth *cantiga* is, according to its heading, supposed to have originated shortly before the death of the author. Eventually there follows—after the transition to the fourth *cantiga*, which is set off as an independent text—a fictional testament reminiscent of Villon and formulated in the new and complex meter of the *arte mayor*. In the case of this second type of textual configuration it is striking that the ordered plurality can fade into the beginnings of a biographical structure. In the context of this rudimentary biographical structure the word *arcidyano*, which as a designation for a career role and a social rank is part of the name of the author, develops a connotational potential that was certainly intensified among much of the reading public by association with the author name "Arcipreste de Hita," which was connected with the *Libro de buen amor* (still highly popular a hundred years after its origin).

Six individual texts constitute the third text group. Once again one author's name surfaces in all of the headings to the texts: Don Pedro Veles de Guevara. The configurational type that can be inferred from this text group lies between the two configurational types previously indicated. For all these texts produce one situational paradigm: the first-person narrator who has been written into the text addresses a textually immanent figure, which (with the exception of the fifth text, which is constructed in the manner of a turning to God), is given a name of (grammatically) feminine gender. In the two introductory hymns to the Virgin Mary, this figure is the mother of God; then it is Juana, the queen of Navarre; in the fourth text it is (from an allegorical perspective) the city of Seville, from which the narrator is expelled; and finally it is a lady at the court of the infante Fernando, who was "very old," so that

> non avya en el rreyno quien quisyese con ella cassar, tanto era ffea e de vyeja e de pobre, non enbargante que era dueña de muy buen linaje. (699)

> (there was not in the kingdom anyone who wanted to marry her since she was so ugly, old and poor, in spite of the fact that she was a lady of very good lineage.)

On the other hand, the recurrent situational paradigm of the first-person narrator and the female figure he addresses is filled in very different ways: prayer, praise of women, allegorical complaint, *contemptus mundi*, consolation. By means of the headings, which have been regularly expanded to commentaries, the third configurational type, with its individual texts, approaches a level of semantic differentiation and sequencing characteristic of a biography, without allowing for a unification of the individual texts to any extent whatsoever in a single identity-figure. Here (as in the case of the second text group) one gets the impression that the fascination with biographical detail stands in a latent relationship of mutual exclusion to the interest in textual variation and perfection: for only in the heading to the first text of the third group is it pointed out that a *cantiga* is "well organized"—and this in spite of the employment of extremely complex metrical patterns from the third to the sixth text.

The eight texts of the fourth text group are attributed to three different authors: to Diego Martines de Medyna, to Fray Lope de Monte, and to a *frayle*. Together the *cantigas e preguntas e desires* of this series constitute—not in spite of, but rather owing to the plurality of authors—a single situation: the situation of the theological disputation. The disputation is a fourth (and in the overall corpus a very frequent) textual configuration type of the *Cancionero de Baena*. In the fourth text group, where it appears for the first time, the disputation consists of questions and answers on the theological theme of the "Immaculate Conception," which (probably by way of the semantic isotopic bridge of "unconsummated love") in the last two texts of the group is blended into the problem of the consequences of that "Platonism" which was made obligatory by the rules of courtly love. As "fas-

cinating" as these questions may have been for authors and reading
publics of the fifteenth century (*fasinado* occurs in the sixth text of
the fourth group), it is noteworthy that the commentaries of the
headings specify not only the origins and allegiances to religious
orders of the questioners and answerers to whom the texts are attributed; frequent references are made, even within the framework
of the disputation situations, to linguistic aptitude and to the symbolic value of this competence with regard to society:

> Diego Martines de Medyna . . . el qual era vn omme muy onr-
> rado e muy discrepto e bien entendido, asy en letras e todas
> çiençias commo en estillo e platica de corte e mundo. (701)

> (Diego Martines de Medyna . . . who was a man of great honor,
> discretion and judgment, as much in letters and science as in
> his bearing and speech at court and in society at large.)

Although the uniformity of the individual text groups in the *Cancionero de Baena* is most evident, it is also possible to answer pos-
itively the question of whether there is a coherence among these
groups. Of course, one cannot name a basic principle of coherence
that would encompass all text groups; however, the concept of
"family relationship" may come to mind if one observes that there
is usually an isotopic bridge between the final texts of a specific
text group and the first texts of the following group, even though
these texts are not always on the same phenomenal plane. All
four texts of the first group are *cantigas* in Galician-Portuguese,
and this proves likewise true for the first four texts of the second
group; the form of the *cantiga*, which is also dominant in the second text group, once again forms the bridge to the third text
group, which begins with two *cantigas* in honor of the Mother of
God (although no isotopy is to be perceived between the last text
of the preceding group, the fictional testament, and the first text
of the following group). However, it is to be suspected that a *continuity of content*, especially for medieval readers, can be discovered between the last text of the third group, the consolation to
the unmarried lady, and the topic of the first text of the fourth
group, the Immaculate Conception. The consistency between the
fourth and the fifth text groups lies in the fact that one of the
three disputants in the fourth text group was Diego Martines de
Medyna, while all texts of the fifth group are attributed to Gon-
çalo Martines de Medyna.

At this point it must be emphasized that such consistencies,
both internal and external to the groups, were created by compil-

ers of the *Cancionero de Baena*. This may also, with some exceptions, be valid for the associations between individual texts and
names of authors (it would be interesting, for example, to investi-
gate whether the myth, still alive in Spain to this day, of the unrequited love of the troubadour Maçias could possibly have fed on
precedents other than the connection of his name with four *cantigas* on this same subject in the *Cancionero de Baena*). The structure of intertextuality of the various configurational types is in all
probability the result of a consciously executed allegorization.
Certainly we do not know whether the structure of the *Cancionero de Baena* as we have it is really the one established by Juan
Alfonso de Baena. For the list of texts at the end of the oldest preserved codex (after 1462) does not agree with the configuration of
individual texts found therein and partially described by us here.[6]
It is therefore conceivable that we owe this register, but not the
organizational structure handed down to us, to the court scribe of
Juan II. In no case, however, is the structure reproduced in the
modern editions the result of accidental arrangement. However,
as an intended structure (no matter by whom), it is characteristic
of the use of the *cancioneros* around the middle of the fifteenth
century—regardless of the specific identity of the compiler.

The Codex in the Solemn Routine of the Court

What can the practical application[7] of this *cancionero*, which
originated at the court of Juan II of Castile, have been? Against
the background of the reception practices common today, our finding regarding the structure of the *cancionero* will at first suggest
no relevant hypothesis as to its function, but will instead only
leave us perplexed. For, on the one hand, the relationships among
the individual texts are more complex than we are perhaps accustomed to from anthologies; on the other hand, the sequence of
the individual texts is quite far from fitting neatly together into a
narrative plot structure or thematic unity.

We will attempt to come closer (nothing more can be hoped for
in this brief sketch!) to a solution of our unusually difficult question of functional history by concentrating on the relationship between the textually immanent roles and the reception attitudes
suggested by the texts. In this regard a text group at the end of the
Cancionero de Baena provides insight; the individual texts of this
group, according to the commentaries of the headings, were all
written on the occasion of the birth of Juan II in 1405. The wording of these commentaries follows:

Este desir fiso el dicho Miçer Françisco Ynperial, natural de Jenoua, estante e morador que fue en la muy noble çibdat de Seuilla; el qual desir fiso al nasçimiento de nuestro señor el rey Don Juan, quando nasçio en la çibdat de Toro, año de MCCCCV años; e es fecho e fundado de fermosa e sotil invençion e de limadas diçiones. (413)

(This *desir* was composed by Miçer Françisco Ynperial, a native of Genoa, a citizen of the noble city of Seville; who composed this *desir* on the occasion of the birth of our king, Don Juan, when he was born in the city of Toro in the year 1405; and it is made with a subtle invention and polished words.)

Este desir fiso el maestro Fray Diego de Valençia, de la orden de Sant Françisco, en rrespuesta d'este otro desir e de ençima que fizo el dicho Miçer Françisco al nasçimiento del rrey nuestro señor; el qual desir el dicho maestro fizo por los consonantes qu'el otro primero, e en algunos lugares rretrato al otro. (434)

(This *desir* was written by Fray Diego de Valençia, of the Order of Saint Francis, in response to the one referred to above, composed by Miçer Françisco on the birth of our king; this *desir* was written by Fray Diego using the consonant rhymes of the first and recasting parts of it as well.)

Este desir fiso Bartolome Garçia de Cordoua, frayle que agora es en el monesterio de Frex de Val en Burgos, quando nasçio el rrey nuestro señor en la çibdat de Toro, del qual desir se pago mucho el señor rey Don Enrryque su padre. (449)

(This *desir* was made by Bartolome Garçia de Cordoba, a friar who now resides in the monastery of Frex de Val in Burgos, on the occasion of our king's birth in Toro. Don Enrique, the king's father, was very pleased by this *desir*.)

Este desir fiso . . . quando nasçio el rrey nuestro señor en la çibdat de Toro, el qual desir es bien fecho e bien escantado, segunt la manera de arte por donde es fundado. (451)

(This *desir* was made . . . when our king was born in Toro; it is well written, according to the art upon which it is based.)

Este desir fiso Don Mosse, çurgiano del rey Don Enrrique, quando nasçio el rrey nuestro sseñor en la çibdat de Toro. (453)

(This *desir* was made by Don Mosse, Don Enrique's surgeon, when our king was born in Toro.)

The unity of this text group is a pragmatic one: we have here five congratulatory poems on the birth of the future King Juan II. The relationship of the first two texts evokes the situation of the poetic game or the poets' competition, since the second text is introduced as a "response" to the first and is said to imitate it in places. The point of convergence of texts three through five is not the situation of the poetic competition, but the relationship of King Enrique III, the child's father, to the authors.

A reading of the five texts confirms what every literary historian will immediately suspect: this text group from the *Cancionero de Baena* is in its recurrent semantic structure sufficiently unspecific that it could be used not only each year at the celebration of the birthday of Juan II, but also at every celebration occasioned by a birth or a birthday at the court. This single finding can be generalized into the following (for the time being still unproved) thesis: the textual configurations of the *Cancionero de Baena* are neither universally applicable nor related to specific and unique events; rather, they can be adapted at any given time to certain *types of situations at the court* and can *define the structure of the interactions* constituting such situational types.

Indeed, the *desir* of Françisco Ynperial for the birthday of Juan II begins with a very specific reference to past reality: the screams of the mother giving birth are inserted into the text in English, because the mother of the king, Katilina of Lancaster, was an Englishwoman ("Mod hed god hep"). However, the allegorical dream narrative that follows (and is taken up again by Diego de Valençia), in which the planets of the astrological constellation of the year 1404 step forth to promise the newborn child a great future, offers every courtier at every birthday celebration a situationally typical role, which can naturally be varied and made specific for each individual event.

Let's take our thesis of the relationship of the text groups of the *Cancionero de Baena* to courtly situation types a step further. Juan II went down in Spanish history above all for his subservience to the favorite Alvaro de Luna, an attitude that has again and again since the fifteenth century provoked, as it were, "psycho-pathological" attempts at explanation. With respect to our question, this means that the speeches of the "moon-planet" (= *luna*) opened up a horizon of ambivalent connotations on every occasion when this text group was actually presented in celebration of

the birthday of Juan II. Following are the relevant passages in the
desir of Françisco Ynperial and in that of Diego de Valençia:

"En salud buena biua, dixo Luna,
e muy ygualada la su conplision,
en todos sus tiempos jamas en ninguna
tenpestat venga e nin corrupçion;
el ayre en su tiempo muy con sazon
venga, e derechos los tenporales,
panes e viñas, yeruas e frutales,
ayan abundaçias quantas en mi son.

"Gosen symientes e todas las flores,
peses e aves e todo ganado
sean perfetas en todos sabores;
el su tiempo ssea de aquesto abastado
e avn porque biua en mas gasajado,
de todas las aues ssea caçador,
muy grant montero e grant venador,
e dole mis flechas e arco en donado.

"E mando que sean los vientos suaues,
e sea abonança en toda la mar;
todas sus flotas, galeas e naos
puedan en popa ssienpre marear;
e por lo mas avn consolar
fijos e fijas en salud le biuan,
nietos e nietas otrosy le syruan
e le obedescan todo su mandar."

(427f.)

La Luna sentençie en aquesta pugna,
e judgue el Infante por su condiçion,
dizfaganle cama e muy rreal cuna,
e denle nutriçes de grant perfeçion;
e otrosy plazeres e consolaçion,
canten feçeninas e cantos rreales;
que cresca el niño con plazeres tales
a vista de ojo, syn rretardaçion.

Cantenle camenas de dulçes amores,
e faganle sienpre plazer señalado,
que siempre floresca a modo de flores
que nunca decaen en muy verde prado.
Si d'esta fygura el fuerte cryado

fara segunt fase el buen caçador,
la ave que cria e buela mejor
aquella mantiene en onrra e estado.

(444f.)

("Live in good health," said the Moon,
"and very fulfilled,
in all your days may you never encounter any
storms or decay;
may the wind come in timely fashion
and the seasons too,
and may the breads, vines, grains and fruits
in my domain be abundant.

May the seeds, flowers,
fish, fowl and flocks
be perfect in taste;
may his time be occupied in such pursuits,
and so that he live more pleasurably,
may the great hunter
hunt all kinds of foul,
and I give him my bows and arrow.

And I decree that the winds be mild,
and that there be an abundance at sea;
that all his ships
sail from the poop;
and that he be most consoled
by healthy sons and daughters,
grandsons and granddaughters to serve him
and obey him in every way.")

(May the Moon decide
and judge the Infante by his condition,
take away the royal crib,
and give him food of great perfection;
and pleasures and comforts,
and sing songs befitting royalty;
so that the child will grow quickly,
surrounded by such joys.

Have songs of sweet love sung to him,
and always provide him with great pleasure,
so that he will bloom as the flowers do
that never decay in the green field.

If in this way the strong servant
does as the good hunter,
the hunting bird that flies best
will be honored and esteemed.)

That which is, from a formalist perspective, no more than highly
conventional encomiastics, can, in a situation of paying birthday
respects to Juan II, turn into a sort of mockery, against which the
one being both congratulated and mocked cannot defend himself
without completely exposing his subservience through his own
actions. (Alvaro de) Luna sees to it—and so these passages may be
understood—that the king need not deny himself any pleasure,
but also therefore that it doesn't occur to him to fulfill his inherited role as the center and symbol of political power. (Alvaro de)
Luna puts the newborn child (the king) to bed in a "kingly cradle."

But shouldn't this ambivalence in the text be taken simply as a
symptom of poetic license in an exceptional situation, namely
the situation of courtly entertainment? This is how the compiler
Juan Alfonso de Baena presents it in the first of his two prologues.
Whoever likes anachronisms will accept the formulation that he
offers the king his *cancionero* as a medium of *compensation* for
a rigorous workday, as hobby, as "equalizing sport":[8]

> E avn otrosi con las muy agradables e graçiosas e muy singu-
> lares cosas que en el son escriptas e contenidas, la su muy
> redutable e real persona auera rreposo e descansso en los tra-
> bajos e afanes e enojos; e otrosi desechara e oluidara e apar-
> tara e tirara de sy todas tristesas e pesares e pensamientos e
> afliçiones del spiritu, que muchas de uezes atraen e causan e
> acarrean a los prinçipes los sus muchos e arduos negoçios
> rreales. (4f.)

> (And also with the pleasant and singular things that are con-
> tained within it, your highness will find relaxation and rest
> from your preoccupations; and likewise you will forget all sad-
> ness and afflictions of the spirit, that often beset princes in
> their many arduous affairs.)

It is precisely such attributions of function for court literature—
which are anything but original in the fifteenth century—that
have made it so easy for literary historians to identify "courtly literature" (supposedly without difficulty) with literature in the
sense of our own era. For this evaluation not to be completely mistaken, there has to have existed, along with the "play situation,"
a real workday from which play could serve as relief. Now as far as

Juan II and his son Enrique IV are concerned, the biographies composed by contemporary scribes cause us to doubt whether there really was another side to the "play at court," whether perhaps the entire sphere of interaction known as "the court" didn't consist of permanent games, beyond the framework of which the kings' favorites and their accomplices—but not the kings and their partners themselves—made use of the power never exercised by its legitimate representatives. The poetological erudition of specialists, the concern with good taste, the enthusiasm of the king for tournaments on the one hand, and on the other hand his utter abstinence from politics—all are so starkly highlighted by Fernán Pérez de Guzmán, one of the historiographers to whom we refer, that we can consider our question answered:

> E porque la condiçion suya fue estraña e marauillosa, es
> nesçesario de alargar la relaçion della, ca ansi fue que el era
> ome que fablaua cuerda e razonablemente e auia conosçimi-
> ento de los omes para entender cual fablaua mejor e mas aten-
> tado e más graçioso. Plaziale oyr los omes auisado se gra-
> çiosos e notaua mucho lo que dellos oya, sabia fablar [e]
> entender latin, leya muy bien, plazianle muchos libros e estor-
> ias, oya muy de grado los dizires rimados e conoçia los viçios
> dellos, auia grant plazer en oyr palabras alegres e bien apunta-
> das, e aun el mesmo las sabia bien dizir. Usaua mucho la caça
> e el monte e entendia bien toda la arte dello. Sabia del l'arte de
> la musica, cantaua e tañia bien, e aun en el justar e juegos de
> cañas se auia bien. Pero como quier que de todas estas graçias
> ouiese razonable parte, de aquellas que verdaderamente son
> virtudes e que a todo ome, e prinçipalmente a los reyes, son
> nesçesarias fue muy defetuoso. Ca la prinçipal virtud del rey,
> despues de la fee, es ser industrioso e diligente en la gouer-
> naçion e rigimiento de su reyno, e prueuase por aquel mas
> sabio de los reyes, Salamon, el cual, aviendo mandamiento de
> Dios que pidiese lo que quisiese, non demando saluo seso
> para rigir e hordenar el pueblo, la cual petiçion tanto fue agrad-
> able a neustro Señor, que le otorgo aquella e otras singulares
> graçias. De aquesta virtud fue ansi priuado e menguado este
> rey, que auiendo todas las gracias suso dichas, nunca una [ora]
> sola quiso entender nin trabajar en el regimiento del reino
> aunque en su tienpo fueron en Castilla tantas rebueltas e
> mouimientos e males e peligros cuantos non ouo en tienpo de
> reyes pasados por espaçio de dozientos años, de lo cual a su
> presona e fama venia asaz peligro.⁹

[And because his condition was so strange, it is necessary to describe it at greater length, for he was a man who spoke wisely and was a good judge of others. He enjoyed listening to wise and witty men and he could speak Latin. He was a good reader who enjoyed many kinds of books and stories, he enjoyed poetry and pleasant stories and knew how to recite them himself. He was an avid hunter. He knew about music as well as singing and playing instruments, in addition to jousting and games. But in spite of all these attributes, he was lacking in the most important princely virtues. For the most important virtue in a king, after faith, is diligence in the governance of his kingdom, as Solomon proved when God offered to fulfill any wish he had. Solomon asked that God give him wisdom to govern his people, a wish which God granted gladly, along with several other virtues. This king lacked wisdom for in spite of all the aforementioned qualities, he never spent any time governing his kingdom, although at that time Castile was more strife torn than in the preceding two hundred years. This irresponsible behavior endangered his reputation.]

Certainly what most amazed Pérez de Guzmán—who, to the extent that it is legitimate with regard to Spanish cultural history, can be called a "humanist"—was the observation that the exemplary content of the stories so avidly read by the king had no effect at all on his actions and behavior; it is this same observation that most substantially supports our social-historical thesis of the Castilian court as a "play world" devoid of any elements of that "other world" of political concerns:[10]

E como quier que en aquellas estorias que leya fallase los males e daños que vinieron a los reyes e a sus reynos por la nigligençia e remision de los reyes, e, ansimesmo, como quier que por muchos religiosos e caualleros le fue dicho que su presona e su reyno estauan en grant peligro por el non entender en el regimiento de su reyno, e que su fama era menguada por ello, e, lo que mas graue era, que su conçiençia era muy encargada e auia a Dios de dar muy estrecha cuenta del mal que a sus suditos venia por defeuto de su regimiento, pues le diera Dios discriçion e seso para entender en ello, con todo esto, aunque el mesmo veya la poca obidiençia que le era guardada e con cuan poca reuerençia era tratado e la poca mençion que de sus cartas e mandamientos se fazia, con todo esto, nunca un dia quiso boluer el rostro nin trabajar el spiritu en la ordenança de su casa nin en el regimiento de su reino, mas dexaua el cargo de todo ello al su condestable, del cual fizo tanta e tan singular fiança, que a los que lo non vieron pareçeria cosa increyble, e a los que lo vieron fue estraña e marauillosa obra . . .[11]

(Although in those stories that he read he saw depicted the harm that comes to kings and their kingdoms as a result of regal negligence, and despite the fact that many priests and knights told him that he and his kingdom were in great danger because he did not know how to rule, and that his reputation had declined as a result, and, worst of all, that he was guilty and would have to give an account to God of the hardship that had befallen his subjects because of his poor governance, in spite of all this, although he himself saw how little his subjects obeyed him and with what little respect he and his decrees were treated, he never devoted even one day to ordering of his household or his kingdom. Instead he left everything in the hands of his constable, in whom he put such total trust that it seemed incredible to those who did not see this situation with their own eyes, and even to those who did . . .)

If the court of Juan II (and, as we could prove, the court of Enrique IV) was a play world walled off from the workaday routine of the exercise of power, then we can not only imagine what kinds of situations were constituted by the use of the *cancioneros;* moreover, the notion presents itself to us that the codices of the *cancioneros,* in which the late-medieval book art of the Spanish kingdoms culminated, as "cult objects," metonymically represented this self-contained play world. A need may have existed for such representation in *one* object, because the (late-)medieval courts — not only in Castile — were heterogeneous spheres of interaction with regard to their personnel: here members of the various classes and of the most disparate groups gathered. The unity — or the self-containment — of the courts was constituted in the fact that all the members of a court stood, each according to his station, in various relationships to the king as the official center and legitimate representative of power. But where the court was void as a center of power, there, we suspect, the king in the role of the *maître de plaisir* gathered courtiers around himself; their roles in the play of the court were differentiated and graduated in the same manner as their relationships to power were elsewhere.

With this hypothesis we gain a new perspective from which to understand the final passage of the first prologue of the *Cancion-*

ero de Baena, which emphasizes that members of different social groups at the court could use the codex in different ways:

> E avn se agradara e folgara con este dicho libro el muy illu-strado e muy graçioso e muy generoso prinçipe don Enrrique, su fijo, a finalmente en general se agradaran con este dicho libro todos los grandes señores de sus reynos e señorios, asy los perlados, infantes, duques, condes, adelantados, almir-antes, como los maestres, pryores, mariscales, dottores, caual-leros e escuderos, e todos los otros fidalgos e gentiles ommes, sus donseles e cryados e ofiçiales de la su casa real, que lo ver e oyr a leer e entender bien quisieren. (5)

> (And the illustrious and generous prince, Don Enrique, would enjoy this book, as would all the great lords of his kingdom, and also the prelates, infantes, dukes, counts, governors, ad-mirals, masters, priors, military judges, doctors, knights and squires, as well as all other hidalgos and gentlemen, their pages and servants and officials of his royal house, who wanted to see and hear and read it.)

In spite of the surprising clarity that such formulations gain now, our reconstruction of the communication situation of the *Can-cionero de Baena* does not imply the assumption that the cour-tiers (and their contemporaries outside of the court) understood this situation and its social functions. In a brilliant essay on the historical specifics of intertextuality phenomena in the late Mid-dle Ages, Daniel Poirion has demonstrated that texts from the "autumn of the Middle Ages" constantly made references to a sup-posed extratextual "reality," which modern historical science can easily expose as fictional (play) worlds:

> A mes yeux l'intertextualité est la trace d'une culture dans l'écriture, que je vois être, au Moyen Age, une réécriture. Cul-ture latérale, définissant un code linguistique et des référ-ences à la vie, culture profonde, constituant la mémoire qui s'inscrit dans le grimoire des textes.[12]

> (In my opinion intertextuality is the written trace of a cul-ture. In the case of the Middle Ages, this constitutes a rewrit-ing. It is a lateral culture that defines a linguistic code with references to everyday life. It is a profound culture which con-stitutes the memory inscribed within the book of spells that is literature.)

Formulated from the "internal perspective of the court": if, by chance, Juan II and the courtiers who lived around him stepped out of the play world constituted by the *cancioneros*, then they might have fancied themselves in a "real world." However, this supposedly "real world" was—now formulated from the "external perspective of the court"—an *extratextual play world*. This extratextual play world seems thoroughly heterogeneous to us. For in it—as our analysis of the first individual texts and text groups from the *Cancionero de Baena* has already shown—the spheres of chivalry, of humanistic knowledge and humanistic text connoisseurship, and of theological intellectualism were interwoven. The mutual historical asynchronism and pragmatic distance between these spheres were suspended, as the second prologue to the *Cancionero de Baena* shows us, on the premise that the roles of the knight, of the humanistic literary specialist, of the intellectual, as a *complex role horizon*, constituted the social distinction of the king and his court. It would make little sense to ask whether the king and his courtiers "identified" with such roles. For as little as there existed for them a workaday routine *beyond* courtly play, just as little will they have had—as it were, "this side of the roles"—command of a subjectivity to which individual roles would have been able to stand in near or far relation. Life moved between various roles, but all these different roles were parts of one play.

The second prologue to the *Cancionero de Baena* begins with a text that, in a strictly philological sense, is taken verbatim from the prologue to the *Crónica general* of Alfons the Wise of Castile, which originated 200 years earlier. As soon as this "quotation" is carried further in the language and with the arguments of the fifteenth century, the theoretically oriented literary historian posits an "intertextuality phenomenon." From a "formalist" point of view, he is certainly justified in doing so; but from a literary-historical point of view, it is especially important to understand that for the users of the *Cancionero de Baena* no gaps in textual consistency and no "leap" into another world were perceivable here.

In referring to the *Crónica del Halconero de Juan II*, Francisco Rico[13] depicts a court festival that took place in Valladolid in the spring of 1428: there the infantes of Aragón and Castile met. We believe that it would not be appropriate with respect to the subjective experience of this festival to speak of "symbolic overstatement" or "sublimation" of political rivalries. Frivolous display of splendor was itself an exercise in politics:

El lunes, 24 de mayo, quien mantuvo fue el infante don
Juan, con otros cinco caballeros. «E traýa el señor rrey de
Nabarra treze pajes, todos con sus gorjales de argentería labra-
dos e sus caperuças de grana», en tanto el de Castilla llevaba
un venablo al hombro y una corneta a la espalda, y sus diez
caballeros, «todos con sus paramientos de azeytuný pardillo e
sus gentiles penachos», portaban lanzas de monte y bocinas:
atavío muy propio, por cuanto abrían la comitiva un león y un
oso, «con muchos monteros, e canes que yvan ladrando». Don
Enrique justó dos veces, y la segunda salió «solo en su cavallo
e syn tronpeta nenguna, con unos paramientos muy rricos,
vordados de oro; la qual vordadura eran esperas, e unos rrótu-
los con unas letras en que dezía: *Non es*». El rey de Navarra
ofreció una cena en una sala suntuosamente ornada; luego,
mientras se danzaba, «entraron dos alvardanes, con sendos tal-
egones de rreales a cuestas, dando bozes y diziendo: "¡Esto nos
fizo prender por fuerça el señor rrey de Navarra!"» (pág. 63),
por «hacer largueza» (pág. 447 *a*). Acabada la fiesta, todos se
retiraron a dormir «en ciertas cámaras que el rrey de Navarra
les avía mandado aparejar cerca de aquella sala donde avían
cenado y dançado» (pág. 63).

También para honrar a su prima, don Juan II organizó «una
justa en arnés rreal», el domingo 6 de junio. En la Plaza Mayor
mandó disponer un alfaneque o tienda de campaña «con diez
y ocho gradas de vien rricos paños de oro, e puso una tela de
paño de cestre ['Chester'] colorado, e a la otra parte de la tela
un cadahalso cercado de paños franceses». El rey de Castilla
venía «como Dios Padre, y luego doze cavalleros como los
doze apóstoles» (pág. 63), con diademas y rótulos donde se indi-
caba el nombre y el martirio del apóstol que contrahacía cada
uno: «e todas sus cubiertas de los cavallos de grana, e dárages
['adargas'] bordadas, e unos rrétolos que dezían: *lardón*. Así
que [fue] bien entendida la invención». Pues a tan santa cuad-
rilla se opuso el infante don Enrique, «con doze cavalleros,
todos por orden uno delante otro, los seys sus sobrevistas de
llamas de fuego e los otros seys todos cuviertos de fojas de
moral»; y aún tornó más tarde a la tela, «desconocido», con
sobrevistas de carmesí aterciopelado y brocado de oro y un
codo de guarnición de armiños, sin más séquito que tres pajes
enmascarados, «con cortapisas de martas»: hizo tres carreras,
«delibráronlo, e volvióse». Más admiración seguramente de-
bió de despertar el rey de Navarra, presentándose «en una rroca
metido, encima un cavallo, e encima de la rroca un ome con

un estendarte, e cinquenta cavalleros, todos armados en arnés de guerra . . . , que yban guardando la rrocca, los veynte y cinco delante e los otros detrás, e otros lançando truenos, a pie, de fuera de la rroca»: así dieron dos vueltas por el campo. La justa duró hasta que hubo estrellas en el cielo.

(On Monday, May 24, the infante and five other knights were present. "And the king of Navarre had with him thirteen pages, all wearing ornate metal neckplates and hoods," while the one from Castile bore a javelin on his shoulder, and his ten knights "each with his olive colored trappings," carrying hunting lances and trumpets: excellent finery on which the entourage bore a lion and a bear, "with many hunters and barking dogs." Don Enrique jousted twice, and the second time he appeared "alone on his horse, without any trumpet, richly attired with gold embroidery which bore the words *Non es*." The king of Navarre hosted a dinner in a sumptuous chamber; afterwards, while people danced, "there entered two jesters carrying bags of *reales* on their backs, crying: 'The lord of Navarre forced us to do this!'" (p. 63) to demonstrate "his generosity" (p. 447 a). Once the banquet was concluded everyone retired to sleep "in certain rooms that the king of Navarre had offered near the room where the banquet had taken place" (p. 63).

In addition, in order to honor his cousin, don Juan II organized "a joust in royal armor" on Sunday, the sixth day of June. In the main square of the city he ordered erected a tent "of eighteen different colors of "Chester" colored cloth including French cloth. The king of Castile came in the figure of "God the Father, with twelve knights clad as the twelve apostles" (p. 63), with crowns and signs indicating the name and specific martyrdom undergone by each: "and all the knights clad in red with embroidered shields and an inscription that read: *lardón*. Thus the artifice was clear to all." Don Enrique confronted this saintly group "with twelve knights, all in a line, six bearing coats with flames and six with mulberry leaves"; and there entered also an "unknown" figure wearing a crimson coat with gold brocade and ermine on one elbow. He came with only three masked pages "wearing the trappings of convent women": he made three paths, "they presented him and he returned." The king of Navarre was even more astonishing when he presented himself "on top of a rock, astride a horse along with a man bearing a flag and fifty knights, all wearing battle gear . . . They were guarding the rock, twenty-five in front and twenty-five behind, with still others shooting firearms on foot, from beyond the rock": thus they circled the field twice. The joust lasted until the stars appeared in the sky.)

The *Cancionero de Baena* is one means — among others — of establishing the existence of a play world at the court. The configurations of individual texts to text groups and the relationships between consecutive text groups — that is to say, both of those structural levels that constitute the distinctiveness of this corpus as an intertextuality phenomenon — can be explained by the intended reference to situational types (and not to specific situations), as well as by the suspicion that the play world of the court was a sphere closed off from the outside world but in itself heterogeneous. We suggest that this reconstruction of relationships between the play world of the court and a unique form of intertextuality has to do with a situation that is paradigmatic for the culture in the "autumn of the Middle Ages."

Can the spheres of chivalry and courtly love within the enclave of a complex play world be seen as late-medieval, or does it make more sense to see this play world as the beginning of the modern history of reception of medieval literature?

The Book, Reading, and Subjectivity

The *Cancionero de Llavia*[14] appeared in Zaragoza between 1486 and 1489. Despite the scant attention given it so far by literary historians, it is nevertheless of great cultural-historical significance as one of the first printed books on the Iberian peninsula — one which, by the way, also provides the most outstanding example of early Spanish printing. In a short prologue, Ramón de Llavia, the publisher and editor, addresses the wife of the regent (descended from a Jewish family) of the kingdom of Aragón:

No es cosa nueva, muy magnífica e virtuosa señora, si bien como los trasladadores fazen su prohemio en lo que trasladan, no embargante que el inventor mismo haya fecho otro, assí los que ni han trasladado ni de nuevo inventado, siquiera por haver sacado a luz alguna scriptura scondida, ponen de suyo algún dezir breve en el comienço del libro. Esto digo porque, puesto que ninguna obra de las contenidas asquí sea mía, empero porque desseando yo senyaladamente servir a vuestra merced e aprovechar a muchos a costa mía he divulgado por muchos volúmenes la presente obra, pareció conviniente cosa por un brevezito prólogo fazer de ello minción. Ca honesto e buen desseo parece que yo quiera que sepan los que leerán este libro mi diligencia en haver escogido de muchas obras cathólicas puestas por coplas, las más esmeradas e perfectas, e haun la mayor gloria que yo de ello spero recebir será que por haver escogido una persona que tanto abulta en este reino, para que auctorizasse e diesse ressollo a la presente obra, siendo vuestra merced tan cumplida en todas las virtudes que a mujeres convienen, seré tovido a lo menos por hombre de buen juhizio, e quedo besando las manos de vuestra merced. (1)

(It is nothing new, most virtuous lady, if translators offer a preface to have the author himself include yet another, as do even those who have neither composed or invented a work, but instead who have found a previously lost text. I say this because I have not composed any of the works contained herein, but wishing to serve you and please others as well, at great personal cost, I mention this fact in a brief prologue. I have wanted to provide honest pleasure to those who read my book, so I have chosen the finest examples of poetry, knowing that the greatest recompense for my labors is to have chosen you as the patroness of my book, given that you are the paragon of feminine virtues. Since I have chosen you as my patroness I will be esteemed as a man of good judgment. Thus I kiss your hands.)

With all due respect for the elocutionary merit of "modesty topoi," the first thing that catches the eye here in comparison to the prologue of Alfonso de Baena, who never tired of detailing the competence with which he approached the task of compiling his *cancionero*, is the little prestige that Ramón de Llavia attaches to his role as editor and compiler. He derives his justification for composing a prologue primarily from the economic risk he ran with the first edition of his printed *cancionero*, rather than from the work of selecting and compiling individual texts. It can be seen, nevertheless, that his selection of texts, no matter how much he made it dependent on the achievement of the authors, led (though differently than in the case of Juan Alfonso de Baena) to a thematic isotopy of the *cancionero*.

Ca honesto e buen desseo parece que yo quiera que sepan los que leerán este libro mi diligencia en haver escogido de muchas obras cathólicas puestas por coplas, las más esmeradas e perfectas. (1)

(I have wanted to provide honest pleasure to those who read my book, so I have chosen the finest examples of poetry.)

If one recalls Jacques Derrida, one might assert that in the decades between the *Cancionero de Baena* and the *Cancionero de Llavia* (and not only in the case of Plato!) begins that tradition of suppression of *écriture* which continues unbroken to the present day.[15] For the publisher-compiler withdraws from the textual structure for which he is responsible and thus contributes to the illusion of a "direct communication" between the individual authors and the (also probably) individual readers, because he suspects that these readers are interested in a lesson in faith—that is, in a model for the moral structuring of life. The role of the wife of the regent of Aragón, whom he addresses, stands in a metonymic relationship to the intended readership, and it is certainly no longer the role of a participant in the courtly play with texts.

The *Tabla del presente libro* that follows the prologue of the *Cancionero de Llavia* shows two significant differences in comparison with the *Cancionero de Baena*. In the first place, it is not possible here to form text groups of individual texts (the only structuring principle—and one that is not even consistently followed—is to be found in the arrangement together of the texts of each of the authors, none of whom, significantly, had been born in an earlier century). In the second place, the heading commentaries are devoted strictly to content—there is no talk of the elegance of the language or of the observance and variation of metrical schemes; the texts are usually characterized with such common terms as *obra* or as discourses (*confessión, regimiento de principe*, etc.) and once, with regard to their form, even as *coplas*. The religious contents with which the *Tabla* is concerned (instead of the forms) always refer to the conduct and behavior of specific *groups* of people. A strikingly large number of texts is directed at "virtuous ladies" and evokes the life, the sufferings, and the virtues of the Mother of God; in addition to texts of the type *regimiento de principe* and a version of the very popular dialogue type between "monk and knight," there are several catalogues of "cardinal virtues" and "mortal sins." One gets the impression that in spite of—or even because of—such concern with things of this world, the *contemptus mundi* is the unifying horizon of meaning of the *Cancionero de Llavia*.

The pragmatic framework of this corpus is formed by the ambiguity—characteristic, from the perspective of intellectual history, of the fifteenth century—of the subjective appropriation and realization of abstract religious guidelines of behavior. But we can go one step farther in our specification and our attempt (certainly clear by now) to expose the subjectivity of reading as the intended mode of reception of the *Cancionero de Llavia.* The fourth text (Fernán Pérez de Guzmán, the author of the biography cited above, wrote it!) places this horizon-problem of religious practice, the problem of just reward, in the thematic center:

> contra los que dizen que Dios en este mundo nin da bien por bien nin mal por mal. (207)

> (against those who say that God neither rewards good with good nor evil with evil.)

Fernán Pérez de Guzmán, let us say as an aside, strives to "save" this theologem. The observation weighs rather heavily that the same ambiguity is also treated in various texts (not mentioned in the present discussion) of the *Cancionero de Baena.* Nevertheless, if the different structures of compilation in the two *cancioneros* analyzed here are considered, then a clear picture emerges of that which cannot be grasped by the analysis, common in the field of Hispanic studies, of individual texts: identical semantic structures take on different functions in different pragmatic and structural contexts.

The discussion of "just reward" constitutes in the *Cancionero de Baena* the *role* of the theologically schooled intellectual, which the participants in the courtly play can fill; in the *Cancionero de Llavia* it seeks to move the readers to a *reflection* on their own actions (and therefore addresses these readers as behavioral agents). In one such context Ramón de Llavia has—one might almost say "naturally"—embedded the famous *Coplas por la muerte de su padre* of Jorge Manrique. We consider this text to be *modern* in a precise intellectual-historical sense not only because it shows the resistance of the "dying father" to his "divinely ordained death" evolve into resignation to God's will and the trust that he will attain forgiveness (not "of his own merit, but by the power of divine mercy alone"); modern also is the role of the reader written into the *coplas.* Here the "son" (the first-person narrator and the author are identical in this text) tells how he suffered *with* his father in the father's dying hour, and how the resignation to God's will of his dying father also became a consolation *for him.* The reflections at the beginning of the text over the vanity of human self-consciousness (which are filled with specific references to current events) can thus be seen as the result of a *process of discovery*, which the subjective narrator, identifying with the dying man, underwent at his father's death-bed, and which the reader is also invited to experience in iden-tification with the "I" of the text.

Literary-historical theses concerning functional-historical change and pragmatic differences of genres and individual texts—such is our thesis regarding the different reception forms presupposed on the one hand by the *Cancionero de Baena* and on the other hand by the *Cancionero de Llavia*—require not implicitly for their val-idation corroboration through sources indicating that these differ-ences were already perceived by contemporaries as decisive changes. Yet it is interesting that the Marqués de Santillana, one of the most famous "humanists" of the fifteenth century in Cas-tile, nephew of Fernán Pérez de Guzmán and addressee of one of his uncle's texts in the *Cancionero de Llavia*, confirms in his famous poetological and "literary-historical" treatise (*Carta al Condestable de Portugal*) a break in "literary evolution" and illus-trates this by means of two authors who are both represented in the *Cancionero de Baena:*

> E así por esto, commo por ser tanto conoscidas e esparzidas a todas partes sus obras, passaremos a micer Francisco Inperial, al qual yo no llamaría dezidor o trobador, mas poeta, commo sea cierto que sy alguno en estas partes del occaso meresció premio de aquella triunphal e laurea guirlanda, loando a todos los otros, este fué.[16]

> (Thus, since his works are so well known and disseminated, we will pass on to micer Francisco Imperial, whom I would not call a *dezidor* or *trobador*, but rather a *poeta*, for if any writer in the West deserves that triumphal garland, it is he.)

One could object that no textual finding speaks against the assumption that the compiler and the users of the *Cancionero de Baena* would also have known the distinction between *deçidor o trovador* on the one hand and *poeta* on the other, and would have considered themselves to be *poetas*. In defense of our thesis of the difference in the communicative roles presupposed by the two *cancioneros*, another passage of the *Carta* of the Marqués de San-tillana can be cited, in which the concept of *poesia* is tied to the claim to ethical instruction:

> ¿E qué cosa es la poesía, que en nuestro vulgar gaya sciencia llamamos, syno un fingimiento de cosas útyles, cubiertas o veladas con muy fermosa cobertura, conpuestas, distinguidas

y scandidas por cierto cuento, peso e medida? E ciertamente, muy virtuoso señor, yerran aquellos que pensar quieren o dezir que solamente las tales cosas consistan e tiendan a cosas vanas e lasciuas: que bien commo los fructíferos huertos habundan e dan conuenientes fructos para todos los tiempos del año, assy los onbres bien nascidos e doctos, a quien estas sciencias de ariba son infusas, usan de aquellas e del tal exercicio, segund las hedades. (210–11)

(And what is the nature of poetry which we call *gaya sciencia*, if not a fictional presentation of educational matter, covered with the most pleasing adornments? Certainly, virtuous lord, those people who claim that poetry is synonymous with vanity and lasciviousness are wrong; for just as gardens of fruit trees bear fruit throughout the year, so too wise men who are well educated use literature wisely.)

If Fernando del Pulgar, next to Fernán Pérez de Guzmán the second great historiographer in fifteenth-century Castile, may be trusted, then the insistence of the Marqués de Santillana on the *prodesse* of poetry is more than the appeal to a classical topos. For the admiration shown by Fernando del Pulgar in confirming how closely the everyday conduct of the Marqués de Santillana corresponded to the ethical intentions of his work is as great as the amazement of Peréz de Guzmán over the opposite case, namely Juan II, whom even the greatest amount of reading had not been able to lead to an awareness of his duties as king:

Fizo asimismo otros tratados en metros e en prosa muy dotrinables para prouocar a virtudes, a refrenar vicios: e en estas cosas pasó lo más del tiempo de su retraimiento.

Tenía grand fama e claro renonbre en muchos reinos fuera de España, pero reputaua mucho más la estimación entre los sabios, que la fama entre los muchos. E porque muchas vezes veemos responder la condición de los ommes a su complisión e tener sinistras inclinaciones aquellos que no tienen buenas complisiones, podemos sin dubda creer que este cauallero fué en grand cargo a Dios por le auer compuesto la natura de tan igual complisión, que fué abile para recebir todo uso de virtud, e refrenar sin grand pena cualquier tentación de pecado.[17]

(He also wrote other compositions in verse and prose, works that teach virtue rather than vice; and he spent most of his time on these texts.

He had a fine reputation in many lands beyond Spain, but

his reputation lay more among the wise men than among society at large. And because we often see men reflecting their temperament, men of bad temperament exhibiting evil inclinations, we can believe that this knight was well endowed by God with a fine temperament, virtuous in every way and able to refrain from the strongest temptation.]

We have to keep in mind that the form in which the contents of the *Cancionero de Llavia* are presented, and on the basis of which we have developed our hypothesis concerning the transformation of the reception form typical to the genre of *cancioneros*, is an exceptional case. Most *cancioneros* of the late fifteenth and early sixteenth centuries—foremost among them the *Cancionero General* of Hernando de Castillo, which appeared in Valencia in 1511 and was reprinted in 1517, 1520, 1527, and 1555—did indeed have book form, but presented distinct text groups, each with different subject matter; in this they are more similar to the *Cancionero de Baena* than to the *Cancionero de Llavia*. This fact has hindered literary-historical inquiry (based on observations regarding the compilation structure) into the functional transformation of the genre. We suspect, however, that the diversity with regard to contents of a *Cancionero General* is not, as in the case of the *Cancionero de Baena*, conditional upon reference to situational types in a closed play world. In complete contrast to the court scribe Juan Alfonso de Baena, Hernando de Castillo and his publisher must have been concerned with appealing to as many potential recipients and buyers as possible. If this aim could be satisfied most easily (and with success, as indicated by the series of subsequent editions) by way of thematic diversity, it is nevertheless by no means to be precluded that the individual texts of the late *cancioneros* were received by individual readers in the attitude of conscious subjectivity, in affective identification with roles of amorous play, in concern for the salvation of the soul, with the question of how one could attain a new "immortality in this world" through the renown of his actions.

Intertextuality and Forms of Reception on the Threshold of the Modern Era

There is a type of intertextuality, as demonstrated by our analysis of the *Cancionero de Baena*, that manifests itself in the configuration of individual texts into text groups of relatively little precision and in the linkage of consecutive text groups by

means of various equivalency phenomena. For this specific intertextuality structure the modern reader has no suitable form of reception readily at hand: it is—we repeat—more rigidly (and above
all, differently) determined than, for example, the structure of a
poetry anthology in the twentieth century (which, to be sure,
more closely resembles in all respects the structure of the *Cancionero de Llavia*) and more weakly determined than, for example, the structure of realistic novels of the nineteenth century,
which—like *cancioneros*—various areas of knowledge, various
genres, and various reader roles can enter into without the "common denominator" of textually immanent isotopy levels.

If the surrealistic texts of the early twentieth century had ever,
in a pragmatic sense, satisfied the programs and manifestos of
their authors, then it would probably be legitimate to call upon
the reception form that was to be applied by them in order to illustrate the practical application of early *cancioneros*. The texts of
the surrealists were not intended to be a medium for the convey-
ance of a "statement" of the authors to their readers, and it was certainly not intended that their form be overshadowed by this function. As in the case of the *Cancionero de Baena*, surrealistic texts
were intended to stimulate in their readers a productive play with
the language. While certainly the highest ambition of surrealist
programs lay in the problematization of concretized structures of
meaning common to everyday experience, the early *cancioneros*
seem at the courts actually to have furthered the concretization
of a courtly play world into a "play world without a beyond," and
at the same time to have systematically blocked the relativization
of the play world from the perspective of the everyday world
beyond court and text.

In one respect it certainly makes sense now to consider the presence of "typically medieval" motifs and text structures in the *cancioneros* of the early fifteenth century as a *form of reception* of
"medieval literature": the function that they assume here depends
on the quality of their distance from the everyday life of the
fifteenth century. Nevertheless, it seems more profitable in a
literary-historical sense to elucidate such a presence of the Middle
Ages in the fifteenth century as a phenomenon of the "synchron-
ism of the asynchronous." As part of the play world without a
beyond, around which the courts constituted themselves, "literary forms and contents" of the Middle Ages and typically medieval reception forms evoked by them contributed to the depletion
of these centers of power rooted in medieval traditions, and thus
became a prerequisite for that thoroughly *modern* relationship to

power that would only a few decades later characterize the rule of the Catholic kings.

Only if the printed *cancioneros* of the late fifteenth and early sixteenth centuries had appropriated subject matters and forms typical of the Middle Ages (which, however, does not seem to have been the case) could one speak of a "modern reception of medieval literature" in the full sense of the concept. This statement implies the proposal to pick up a transference—at any given time configured differently, but yet not to be ignored any more— between texts and reception tendencies as the red thread of a pragmatics of modern reception of medieval literature.[18]

NOTES

1. Paul Zumthor, *Le masque et la lumière* (Paris: Seuil, 1978).
2. Johan Huizinga, *Herbst des Mittelalters* (Stuttgart, 1941).
3. *Cancionero de Baena*, ed. José María Azáceta, Clásicos Hispánicos, vol. 10 (Madrid: Consejo Superior de Investigaciones Cientiticas, 1966). All citations are to this edition. References in text are page numbers.
4. Hans Ulrich Gumbrecht, "Literärische Gegenwelten, Karnevals Kultur und die Epochenschwelle vom Spätmittelalter zur Renaissance," in *Literatur in der Gesellschaft des Spätmittelalters* (Heidelberg: Winter, 1980), 95–144.
5. Ibid., 131–34.
6. Alberto Blecua, "'Perdióse un quaderno . . . ': Sobre los *Cancioneros de Baena*," *Anuario de Estudios Medievales* 9 (1974–79): 229–66.
7. Hugo Kuhn, "Aspekte des 13. Jahrhunderts," in *Entwürfe zu einer Literatursystematik des Spätmittelalters* (Tübingen: Niemeyer, 1980), 1–18. Translator's note: "Gebrauchssitutation" is the term used by Kuhn and cited here by the author.
8. Translator's note: "Ausgleichssport," the term used by the author, denotes sport chosen to exercise muscles that are not ordinarily exercised.
9. Fernán Pérez de Guzmán, *Generaciones y semblanzaz*, ed. J. Domínguez Bordana (Madrid: Ediciones de "La Lectura," 1924), 122–24.
10. Translator's note: The phrase employed by the author is "Spielwelt ohne Jenseits."
11. Pérez de Guzmán, *Generaciones y semblanzaz*, 124–25.
12. Daniel Poirion, "Écriture et ré-écriture au Moyen Age," *Littérature* 41 (1981): 117.
13. Francisco Rico, "Unas coplas de Jorge Manrique y las Fiestas de Valladolid en 1428," *Anuario de Estudios Medievales* 2 (1965): 519ff.
14. *Cancionero de Llavia*, ed. R. Benitez Claros. In Sociedad de Bibliófilos Españoles, Segunda Epoca, vol. 16 (Madrid: Oficina tipográfica Aldus, 1945). Translation by Marina S. Brownlee.
15. Jacques Derrida, "Freud et la scène de l'écriture," in his *L'écriture et la différence* (Paris: Seuil, 1967), 293–341.
16. Marqués de Santillana, *Carta al Condestable de Portugal, Poesías*

completas, vol. 2, ed. Manuel Durán (Madrid: Castalia, 1980), 221.

17. Fernando del Pulgar, *Carlos Varones de Castilla,* ed. J. Domínguez Bordana, Clásicos Castellanos, vol. 49 (Madrid: Ediciones de "La Lectura," 1924), 48f.

18. The preceding sketch of the problem draws on results of an advanced Hispanics seminar that I held at the Ruhr University in Bochum in the winter semester 1981–82. This sketch profited further from discussions with Claudia Krülls and Gisela Smolka-Koerdt of pertinent dissertation topics and from conversations concerning the presentation of Spanish "lyric poetry" of the late Middle Ages in *Grundriss der Romanischen Literaturen des Mittelalters,* vol. 9, ed. Walter Mettman (Heidelberg: Winter Universitätverlag, 1983–   ).